Measuring Utility

Oxford Studies in the History of Economics

Series Editor: Steven G. Medema, PhD,
University Distinguished Professor of Economics,
University of Colorado Denver

This series publishes leading-edge scholarship by historians of economics and social science, drawing upon approaches from intellectual history, the history of ideas, and the history of the natural and social sciences. It embraces the history of economic thinking from ancient times to the present, the evolution of the discipline itself, the relationship of economics to other fields of inquiry, and the diffusion of economic ideas within the discipline and to the policy realm and broader publics. This enlarged scope affords the possibility of looking anew at the intellectual, social, and professional forces that have surrounded and conditioned economics' continued development.

Measuring Utility

From the Marginal Revolution to Behavioral Economics

Ivan Moscati

OXFORD
UNIVERSITY PRESS

OXFORD
UNIVERSITY PRESS

Oxford University Press is a department of the University of Oxford. It furthers the University's objective of excellence in research, scholarship, and education by publishing worldwide. Oxford is a registered trade mark of Oxford University Press in the UK and certain other countries.

Published in the United States of America by Oxford University Press
198 Madison Avenue, New York, NY 10016, United States of America.

CIP data is on file at the Library of Congress
ISBN 978–0–19–937276–8 (hbk.)
ISBN 978–0–19–937277–5 (pbk.)

For Mila, Elia, Anita and, in memory, for my dad

CONTENTS

FIGURES AND TABLES

FIGURES

TABLES

Measuring Utility

Prologue

Since the origins of economic thought, economists have attempted to explain what determines the exchange value of commodities, that is, the ratio at which one commodity exchanges with other commodities or, in modern terms, its relative price. According to economists such as Adam Smith, David Ricardo, John Stuart Mill, and Karl Marx, the exchange value of a commodity ultimately depends on the quantity of labor needed to produce it. This theory, called the labor theory of value, dominated economic thought from around 1770 to 1870.

From 1871 to 1874, William Stanley Jevons in England, Carl Menger in Austria, and Léon Walras, a Frenchman based at the University of Lausanne in Switzerland, independently put forward a different explanation of exchange value. They argued that the exchange value of a commodity depends on the utility that it has for the individuals in the economy and more precisely on the marginal utility of the commodity. This latter notion is the additional utility associated with an individual's consumption of an additional unit of the commodity. Based on the notion of marginal utility and the assumption that the marginal utility of each commodity diminishes as an individual consumes a larger quantity of it, Jevons, Menger, and Walras were able to construct comprehensive theories of price, exchange, and markets that quickly rose to prominence among economists. This major change in the history of political economy is called the marginal revolution.

Although the notion of utility had played some role in economic thought even before 1870, it was only with the marginal revolution that utility took center stage in economic analysis. Between 1870 and the 1920s, in the works of Jevons, Menger, Walras, and the other economists who embraced and developed the marginal approach, utility became the basic factor explaining prices, consumer behavior, the demand for commodities, market equilibria, bilateral exchanges, and it also became a key variable in the evaluation of the efficiency of the economic allocation of goods. Over the course of the twentieth century, the concept of utility further expanded its reach and became the basis of attempts to analyze the economic decisions of individuals under uncertainty, in strategic situations, and when time, that is, present and future, is at issue.

During the first two decades of the twenty-first century, utility has maintained its prominent role in mainstream economic analysis, and even approaches critical of the mainstream, such as behavioral economics, have often made use of the utility notion. Thus, while behavioral economists have criticized certain mainstream models based on utility, such as expected utility theory, and have put forward alternative models, such as prospect theory, these behavioral models are often based on some modified version of the utility notion, such as the notion of "subjective value" or "experienced utility."

There is, however, a problem at the heart of the scientific story of the utility concept: utility cannot be observed and measured in a straightforward way. Since the marginal revolution, this circumstance has generated a number of discussions and developments in economics, not least because critics often pointed to the apparent unmeasurability of utility as a crucial flaw in the theory. Over the course of time, utility theorists have offered a variety of possible solutions to the issue of the measurability of utility: from the idea that utility can be measured directly by introspection, through the idea that, although not directly measurable, utility can be measured indirectly from willingness to pay, market data, or choice behavior, to the idea that utility theory is in fact independent of the measurability of utility. Some economists have argued that since utility is not observable, it should be ruled out from economic analysis, while others have devised econometric or experimental methods to measure utility.

In this book, I reconstruct the history of utility measurement in economics, from the marginal revolution of the 1870s to the beginning of behavioral economics in the mid-1980s, with four goals in mind.

I.1. FOUR GOALS

I.1.1. History of Utility Measurement and History of Utility Theory

The first goal is historical in nature and is met by reconstructing in detail economists' ideas and discussions about utility measurement and investigating how these ideas and discussions influenced the development of utility theory. I also study the economists' attempts to measure utility empirically and focus in particular on the experimental measurements of utility that began as early as 1930.

My historical reconstruction is based not only on economists' published works but also on their letters and personal recollections, as well as other archival materials. Since ideas about utility measurement, like all other ideas, walk with men's legs, I also pay attention to the personal connections and institutional contexts that explain why and how certain economists engaged in the theory or practice of utility measurement. Although bits and pieces of the history of utility measurement can be found in several works devoted to the history of utility analysis,[1] to the best of my knowledge, this book offers the first comprehensive, integrated, and historically rich account of the history of utility measurement from the 1870s to the mid-1980s.

1. See in particular Stigler 1950; Schumpeter 1954; Majumdar 1958; Howey 1960; Chipman 1976; Farquhar 1984; Fishburn 1989; Ingrao and Israel 1990; Mandler 1999; Guala 2000; Giocoli 2003b; Montesano 2006; Dardi 2008; Hands 2010; Heukelom 2014; Baccelli and Mongin 2016.

The narrative ends in 1985, the year in which John Hershey and Paul Schoemaker, two early behavioral economists, published an article that made it definitely clear that the experimental measurement of utility based on expected utility theory was plagued by a variety of biases. After 1985, several new research programs related to utility measurement began, such as the experimental measurement of utility conducted within nonexpected-utility frameworks, attempts to measure utility-related concepts such as experienced utility or remembered utility, or, more recently, the measurement of the activity of a specific population of neurons in the human brain, which is interpreted as the measurement of utility. Dealing appropriately with the post-1985 developments in the history of utility measurement would probably require another book. Moreover, these research programs are still ongoing and therefore do not yet lend themselves to proper historiographical study. For these reasons, 1985 is a suitable terminus for the narrative.

I.1.2. The Interplay between Utility Analysis and the Understanding of Measurement

There is a complication in the otherwise already intricate and multifaceted history of utility measurement: between 1870 and 1985, economists' understanding of the very notion of measurement changed; they came to understand what it means to measure a thing differently. Thus, while early utility theorists univocally associated the measurability of utility with the possibility of identifying a unit of utility that could be used to assess utility ratios, in the mid-1930s, economists such as Oskar Lange and Roy Allen began advocating a broader view of measurement, according to which utility is measurable even if no utility unit is available. In the early 1950s, Milton Friedman and other economists elaborated an even broader view of utility measurement as consisting of the conventional and prediction-oriented assignment of numbers to objects.

The second main goal of this book is to bring into focus the interplay among the evolution of utility analysis, economists' ideas about utility measurement, and their conception of what measurement in general means. Some of my fellow historians of economics, most notably Marcel Boumans (2005; 2007; 2015) and Mary Morgan (2001; 2007; Klein and Morgan 2001), have adopted a measurement viewpoint to analyze some important episodes in the history of economics, such as discussions concerning the construction of price index numbers or the measures of the velocity of money. However, such studies have not addressed the history of utility theory.

My focus on the interplay between economists' understanding of measurement and their utility analyses leads me to revise in many important aspects the canonical history of utility analysis. Among other things, I argue that the traditional dichotomy between cardinal utility and ordinal utility is conceptually too threadbare and barren to clothe an accurate narrative of the history of utility theory, that a third form of utility consistent with the unit-based conception of measurement, namely ratio-scale utility, should be added to the traditional dichotomy, and that the utility theories of Jevons and the other early utility theorists belong in the ratio-scale utility camp rather than the cardinal utility camp.

I.1.3. Utility Measurement, Psychological Measurement, Measurement Theory

The third goal of the book is interdisciplinary in nature and is to explore the relationships among the history of utility measurement in economics, the history of the measurement of sensations and intellectual abilities in psychology, and the history of measurement theory in general.

The initial idea for this book derived from reading Joel Michell's *Measurement in Psychology: A Critical History of a Methodological Concept* (1999). Although Michell does not discuss utility theory, his work points to important similarities between the history of sensation measurement in psychology and the history of utility measurement in economics. Michell's book convinced me that comparing these two histories might contribute to a better understanding of the history of utility measurement. Following this conviction, I explore here the relations between the history of empirical psychology and the history of utility theory and show that although the two histories have proceeded in a largely independent way, some significant intersections and similarities between them exist.

With respect to the relationship between the history of utility measurement and the history of measurement theory in general, I argue, among other things, that the "representational theory of measurement," which was elaborated by philosopher Patrick Suppes and his coauthors between 1958 and 1971 and quickly rose to prominence in measurement theory, originated in the research in utility theory that Suppes conducted in the early and mid-1950s.

I.1.4. The Epistemological Dimension of Utility Measurement

In *Inventing Temperature*, his book on the history of thermometry, Hasok Chang (2004, 6) remarks that measurement is "a locus where the problems of foundationalism are revealed with stark clarity." This is certainly true for the specific case of the measurement of utility. My fourth goal in this book is to discuss some primarily foundational, that is, epistemological, problems related to utility measurement. I do this in each of the sections that close the four parts of the book.

The first epistemological issue has been already mentioned and concerns the very understanding of measurement. Which forms of quantitative assessment of utility did the utility theorists of the period 1870–1985 consider to be actual utility measurement? And how has their understanding of measurement influenced their utility theories?

The second epistemological issue concerns the scope of the utility concept. How broadly has the utility concept been defined in the history of utility? And how has the scope of the utility concept affected the approach to utility measurement? In this respect, the general trend was toward the broadening of the notion of utility, which quickly lost its initial, narrow identification with the notions of pleasure (Jevons) or need (Menger) to become an all-encompassing concept capable of capturing any possible motivation to human action. The transformation of the utility notion into an all-encompassing black box made it difficult to identify a clear psychological correlate for it. This difficulty, in turn, undermined psychological introspection as a plausible device to measure utility directly and paved the way to the idea that utility can be measured only indirectly through its effects on some observable variable, such as willingness to pay or choice behavior.

The third issue regards the epistemological status of utility and its measures. I contrast two main views of this status, the "mentalist view" and the "instrumentalist view." According to the mentalist view, the concept of utility refers to some existing mental entity. The mental correlate of utility may vary from one economist to another—it was pleasure for Jevons, need for Menger, desire for Irving Fisher, and preference for Vilfredo Pareto. Nevertheless, somewhere in the individual's mind, this entity exists, and the magnitude of this mental entity is the actual "measurand," that is, the magnitude that the utility measure should express numerically. According to the instrumentalist view, by contrast, utility is only a parameter or a variable that appears in a model that has proven useful for describing or predicting some relevant class of economic phenomena. This parameter does not necessarily have any correlate in the individual's mind, and measuring utility amounts to "calibrating the model." That is, the numerical value assigned to the utility parameter is the value that, when inserted into the model, allows the model to best describe or predict the class of economic phenomena it refers to. Among those who advocated an instrumentalist view of utility and its measures were Walras and Friedman.

The fourth epistemological issue concerns the kind of data that legitimately can be used to measure utility. Generally speaking, we can say that the early utility theorists typically relied on psychological data obtained by introspection, while after 1900, psychological data lost importance in favor of choice data that, in principle, can be retrieved by experimental or statistical observations. However, at least until the rise of the experimental approach to utility measurement in the 1950s, distinctions between introspection and observation, preference and choice, and mind and behavior remained very much abstract and pertained more to the rhetoric of utility measurement than to its practice.

Like other parts of economic theory, utility theory has multiple scientific aims, which are usually grouped into the broad categories of "descriptive" and "normative." The fifth epistemological issue concerns the relationship between utility measurement and the specific aim for which the utility measures are used. For instance, utility measures obtained by "calibrating the model" can be legitimately used for prediction, but it is more difficult to use them for explanation without ending up in a circular argument.

Having explained the four main goals that have oriented my reconstruction of the history of utility measurement from 1870 to 1985, I now provide an overview of the story told in the book.

I.2. THE STORY

I.2.1. Utility Measurement in Early Utility Theories, 1870–1910

The book is divided into four parts. Part I covers the period 1870–1910 and discusses the issue of utility measurement in the theories of Jevons, Menger, Walras, and other early utility theorists. In order to illustrate the broad intellectual context within which the early discussions on utility measurement took place, chapter 1 reviews the history of the understanding of measurement in philosophy, physics, psychology, mathematics, and areas of economics before and beyond marginal utility theory. This review shows that between 1870 and 1910, all these disciplines were dominated by what I have called the unit-based or, equivalently, ratio-scale conception of measurement. According to this conception, measuring the property of an object consists of comparing it with some other object that is taken as a unit and then assessing the numerical ratio between the unit and the object to be measured. Chapter 1 also shows that late-nineteenth-century discussions of measurement in mathematics established the cardinal–ordinal terminology that later passed into economics. However, the mathematical concept of cardinal number is different from the economic concept of cardinal utility, which entered the scene only in the 1930s.

Chapter 2 discusses how Jevons, Menger, and Walras addressed the issue of the measurability of utility. The three founders of marginal utility theory identified measurement with unit-based measurement and, accordingly, searched for a unit of utility that could be used to assess utility ratios. The outcomes of this search were diverse and ranged from Jevons's idea that a unit to measure utility, although not available at present, may become so in the future, to Walras's assertion that although utility cannot be measured, constructing economic theory as if it were measurable is a scientifically legitimate procedure. In the final section of chapter 2, I argue that the current notion of cardinal utility is inadequate to understand the utility theories of Jevons, Menger, and Walras and accordingly contend that the three founders of marginal utility theory were not cardinalists in the modern sense of the term.

Chapter 3 moves to the second generation of marginalists and examines how Friedrich von Wieser, Eugen von Böhm-Bawerk, Francis Ysidro Edgeworth, Irving Fisher, and Alfred Marshall conceived of measurement and how, based on this conception, they addressed the issue of the measurability of utility. Their respective approaches to utility measurement were highly diverse. Wieser summed the utilities of goods as if they were measurable in terms of some unit. Böhm-Bawerk claimed that individuals can assess utility ratios. Edgeworth suggested the just-perceivable increment of pleasure as a unit to measure utility on the basis of introspection. Fisher proposed adopting a utility unit that could be derived from observable relations between commodities. Marshall took willingness to pay as an indirect measure of utility. Despite the diversity of their approaches, all these economists identified measurement with unit-based measurement. Therefore, just like Jevons, Menger, and Walras, so Wieser, Böhm-Bawerk, Edgeworth, Fisher, and Marshall were also not cardinalists in the current sense of the term.

I.2.2. Ordinal and Cardinal Utility and Early Empirical Measurements of Utility, 1900–1945

Part II deals with the emergence of the notions of ordinal and cardinal utility during the period 1900–1945 and discusses two early attempts to give an empirical content to the notion of utility. As chapter 1 does, chapter 4 broadens the narrative beyond utility measurement and reconstructs the discussions of measurement that took place in physics, philosophy, and psychology between 1910 and 1940. In physics and philosophy, the most influential discussion on measurement was that presented by Cambridge physicist Norman Robert

Campbell. Campbell articulated a theory of fundamental and derived measurement that ultimately maintained the identification of measurement with unit-based measurement. In the 1920s, psychologists such as William Brown and Godfrey Thomson in England and Louis Leon Thurstone in the United States argued that some of their quantification techniques were capable of delivering unit-based measurement of sensations. Physicists denied this, and the resulting clash of views generated a controversy that engaged British physicists and psychologists from 1932 to 1940. The controversy ended in deadlock, with physicists and psychologists unable to find agreement on the definition of measurement.

Chapter 5 deals with the ordinal revolution in utility analysis inaugurated by Vilfredo Pareto around 1900. The fundamental notion of Pareto's analysis was that of preference, and he conceived of utility as a numerical index expressing the preference relations between commodities. While Pareto's ordinal approach to utility analysis was highly innovative, his understanding of measurement remained the unit-based one. The second part of the chapter reconstructs an important debate on the measurability of utility that took place in Austria in the late 1900s and early 1910s. Franz Čuhel and Ludwig von Mises rejected Böhm-Bawerk's idea that individuals can assess utility ratios, and, independently of Pareto, both advocated an ordinal approach to utility. Especially through Mises's influence, the ordinal approach to utility rose to prominence among Austrian economists after World War I. In the final part of chapter 5, I review the differences between the Austrian and the Paretian approaches to ordinal utility.

Chapter 6 reconstructs the progressive definition and stabilization of the current notion of cardinal utility as utility unique up to positive linear transformations. This notion was the eventual outcome of a long-lasting discussion, inaugurated by Pareto himself, regarding an individual's capacity to rank transitions among different combinations of goods. This discussion continued through the 1920s and early 1930s and underwent a decisive acceleration from 1934 to 1938, that is, during the conclusive phase of the ordinal revolution. In this latter period, the main protagonists of the debate were Oskar Lange, Henry Phelps Brown, Roy Allen, Franz Alt, and Paul Samuelson. In the discussions that led to the definition of cardinal utility, some of these utility theorists began to envisage a broader notion of measurement according to which utility can be measurable even if no utility unit is available. Until the mid-1940s, however, cardinal utility remained peripheral in utility analysis.

Chapter 7 discusses two early attempts to measure utility empirically. In 1926, Ragnar Frisch of Norway applied an econometric approach to measure the marginal utility of money. In 1930, Thurstone, the American psychologist whose methods for measuring sensations are discussed in chapter 4, conducted a laboratory experiment to elicit the indifference curves of an individual. The idea of applying the experimental methods of psychology to economics was suggested to Thurstone by Henry Schultz, his economist colleague at the University of Chicago. Notably, both Frisch and Thurstone intended measurement in the unit-based sense. Most commentators of the 1930s and early 1940s judged the assumptions underlying both Frisch's and Thurstone's utility measurements to be highly problematic and therefore remained skeptical about the significance of their respective measurements. Among the most vocal critics of Thurstone's experiment were Allen Wallis and Friedman, then two young economists and statisticians who had studied at the University of Chicago under Schultz. The limited impact of Frisch's and Thurstone's pioneering studies notwithstanding, they nevertheless represent significant episodes in the history of the empirical measurement of utility

I.2.3. From Debating Expected Utility Theory to Redefining Utility Measurement, 1945–1955

While discussions of the measurability of utility before 1944 focused on the utility used to analyze decision-making between risk-free alternatives, after that year, discussions centered on the utility used to analyze decision-making between risky alternatives. The changing factor was the publication in 1944 of John von Neumann and Oskar Morgenstern's *Theory of Games and Economic Behavior*. In this book, von Neumann and Morgenstern put forward an axiomatic version of expected utility theory (EUT), a theory of decision-making under risk originally advanced by Daniel Bernoulli in the eighteenth century. Part III focuses on the 1945–1955 debate on utility measurement that was originated by von Neumann and Morgenstern's EUT.

As chapters 1 and 4 did, chapter 8 broadens the narrative beyond utility measurement and discusses an important outcome of the British controversy over psychological measurement of the 1930s, namely the operational definition of measurement put forward by American psychologist Stanley Smith Stevens in 1946. For Stevens, measurement consists of the assignment of numbers to objects according to certain rules. Since there are various rules for assigning numbers to objects, there are various forms, or scales, of measurement. From this operational viewpoint, unit-based measurement is just a particular, and quite restrictive, form of measurement. Stevens's definition of measurement was broad enough to include the psychologists' quantification practices as measurement and quickly became canonical in psychology. In the final section of chapter 8, I point out some drawbacks of Stevens's operational theory of measurement.

Chapter 9 discusses von Neumann and Morgenstern's axiomatic version of EUT and its differences from Bernoulli's nonaxiomatic EUT. In *Theory of Games*, the nature of the cardinal utility function u featured in von Neumann and Morgenstern's EUT and its relationship with the riskless utility function U of previous utility analysis remained ambiguous. In their book, von Neumann and Morgenstern also put forward an axiomatic theory of measurement, which presents some similarities to Stevens's measurement theory but had no immediate impact on utility analysis.

Chapter 10 reconstructs the debate on EUT from 1947, when the second edition of *Theory of Games* was published, to April 1950. In this period, a number of eminent American economists, including Friedman, Leonard Jimmie Savage, Jacob Marschak, Samuelson, and William Baumol, wrote papers in which they took stances on the validity of EUT and the nature of the cardinal utility function u featured in it. Friedman, Savage, and Marschak supported EUT, although for different reasons, while Samuelson and Baumol rejected it. Regarding the nature of the utility function u, however, they all shared the view that it is interchangeable with the utility function U that the earlier utility theorists had used to analyze choices between riskless alternatives.

Chapter 11 studies the second phase of the debate on EUT, starting in May 1950, when Samuelson, Savage, Marschak, Friedman, and Baumol began an intense exchange of letters. In their correspondence, these economists addressed several fundamental issues concerning EUT: they argued about the exact assumptions underlying EUT, quarreled over whether these assumptions should be considered compelling requisites for rational behavior under risk, discussed the descriptive validity and simplicity of EUT, and, finally, debated the nature of the von Neumann–Morgenstern utility function u featured in EUT. This correspondence modified the views of all five economists involved and, notably, transformed Samuelson into a supporter of EUT. From the perspective of our narrative, the most important single exchange is probably that between Friedman and Baumol; over the course of it, Friedman came to argue that the utility functions u and U are not linear transformations of each other, and accordingly, the expected value of U, even if available, cannot be used to make predictions about choice behavior under risk. Friedman's interpretation was quickly adopted by Baumol and Samuelson and later became standard in economics. After this epistolary exchange of 1950–1951, the American advocates of EUT went public. Their first major opportunity to do so was a prominent conference that took place in Paris in May 1952, where Friedman, Savage, Marschak, and Samuelson advocated EUT in the face of attacks from French economist Maurice Allais and other opponents of the theory. Later in the year, in October 1952, a symposium on EUT featuring contributions by Samuelson and Savage in support of the theory was published in *Econometrica*. The Paris conference and the *Econometrica* symposium saw the emergence of EUT as the mainstream economic model of decision-making under risk.

Chapter 12 analyzes the third phase of the EUT debate, which ranges from the end of 1952 to 1955. The issues concerning utility measurement gained an autonomous status in this phase, and discussion shifted from the question "What does the utility function u featured in EUT measure?" to the question "What does it mean, in general, to measure utility?" Friedman and Savage, along with three other utility theorists, Robert Strotz, Armen Alchian, and Daniel Ellsberg, came to elaborate a novel conception of utility measurement similar to Stevens's concept of measurement. With this step, they definitively liberated utility measurement from its remaining ties with units and ratios. According to these five economists, measuring utility consists of assigning numbers to objects by following a definite set of operations. While the particular way of assigning utility numbers to objects is largely arbitrary and conventional, the assigned numbers should allow the economist to predict the choice behavior of individuals. The novel notion of measurement advocated by Friedman, Savage, Strotz, Alchian, and Ellsberg became standard among mainstream utility theorists, and its success goes far toward explaining the peaceful cohabitation of cardinal and ordinal utility within utility analysis that began in the mid-1950 and has continued to the present day.

I.2.4. Expected Utility Theory and Experimental Utility Measurement, 1950–1985

EUT suggests a handy way to measure the von Neumann–Morgenstern cardinal utility function u of an individual on the basis of his choices between risky options. Beginning in 1950, a number of researchers attempted to implement this suggestion in controlled laboratory experiments. In particular, these researchers focused on lotteries and other gambles with monetary payoffs, and from their experimental subjects' choices regarding these monetary risky options, they inferred the utility function u, which they typically interpreted as the utility of riskless money. Part IV reconstructs the experimental attempts to measure the utility of money between 1950 and 1985 within the framework provided by EUT and shows that this history displays a definite trajectory: from a confidence in EUT and the EUT-based measurement of utility in the 1950s to a skepticism that from the mid-1970s haunted the validity of EUT as well as the significance of the utility measures obtained through it.

Chapter 13 discusses the EUT-based experimental measurements of the utility of money that were conducted in the 1950s at Harvard and Stanford by three groups of scholars: statistician Frederick Mosteller and psychologist Philip Nogee (1951), philosophers Donald Davidson and Suppes with the collaboration of psychologist Sidney Siegel (1957), and Suppes and his student Karol Valpreda Walsh (1959). These three groups of scholars were confident about both EUT and the possibility of measuring utility through it. They designed their experiments so as to neutralize some psychological factors that could jeopardize the validity of the theory and spoil the significance of the experimental measurements of utility and concluded that their experimental findings supported both the experimental measurability of utility based on EUT and the descriptive validity of the theory.

Chapter 14 continues the history of the EUT-based experimental measurement of the utility of money by discussing two further laboratory experiments performed at Yale University in the early 1960s, one by economist Trenery Dolbear (1963), the other by psychologist Gordon Becker and statistician Morris DeGroot in association with Marschak (1964). There are some differences in the design of the experiments of the 1950s and those of the 1960s, but, like Mosteller, Suppes, and their coauthors, Dolbear, Marschak, Becker, and DeGroot also assessed their experimental findings as validating EUT: the theory was not 100 percent correct, but in an approximate sense, it appeared to be an acceptable descriptive theory of decision-making under risk.

Chapter 15 offers a conclusion to the history of measurement theory begun in chapter 1 and continued through chapters 4, 8, 9, and 12 by reconstructing the origins of the "representational theory of measurement" in the early work of Suppes. In particular, chapter 15 shows that Suppes's superseding of the unit-based understanding of measurement that he had embraced in the early 1950s, his endorsement of a liberal definition of measurement à la Stevens in the mid-1950s, his conceiving the project of an axiomatic underpinning of this notion of measurement in the late 1950s, and the realization of this project during the 1960s all have their origins in the utility analysis research he conducted from 1953 to 1957 within the Stanford Value Theory Project. The representational theory of measurement found its full-fledged expression in *Foundations of Measurement* (1971), a book coauthored by David Krantz, Duncan Luce, Suppes, and Amos Tversky, and quickly became the dominant theory of measurement.

Between the mid-1960s and the mid-1970s, apparently, no further EUT-based experimental study on utility measurement was published. The first part of chapter 16 shows how the validity of EUT was increasingly called into question in this period, independently of any measurement issues. The choice patterns violating EUT originally conceived by Allais and Ellsberg were confirmed in actual laboratory experiments. Between the late 1960s and the early 1970s, other decision patterns violating EUT were highlighted by a group of young psychologists based at the University of Michigan: Sarah Lichtenstein, Paul Slovic, and Tversky, who, as discussed in chapter 15, was also working in those years on the representational theory of measurement. The experimental findings of Lichtenstein, Slovic, and Tversky were published in a series of works that are considered seminal in the field that from the late 1980s began to be called behavioral economics. The new experimenters who engaged with the EUT-based measurement of utility from the mid-1970s, namely Uday S. Karmarkar

(1974), Mark McCord and Richard de Neufville (1983), and Hershey, Howard Kunreuther, and Schoemaker (1982), were skeptical about the theory and aimed to falsify it. In contrast to Mosteller, Suppes, and the other experimenters of the 1950s and 1960s, they used their psychological insights to show that different elicitation methods to measure utility, which according to EUT should produce the same outcome, in fact generate different measures. These experimental findings undermined the earlier confidence that EUT makes it possible to measure utility. More generally, these findings contributed to destabilizing EUT as the dominant economic model of decision-making under risk and helped foster the blossoming of non-EUT models that began in the mid-1970s and has continued to the present. The history recounted in this book ends in 1985, when Hershey and Schoemaker published another article that definitively put the problem of the inconsistency between different EUT-based utility measures on the map of decision theorists.

1.3. NOT DISCUSSED HERE

Although this book provides a fairly comprehensive history of utility measurement from 1870 to 1985, some parts of that history are not discussed here.

First, the book focuses on the measurement of individual utility rather than social welfare. In economic theory, social welfare is typically conceived as a function of individual utility, and the measurability of social welfare depends on assumptions concerning the measurability of individual utility and the possibility of comparing the utilities of different individuals. Here I concentrate on issues concerning the measurement of individual utility and deal with the measurement of social welfare only insofar as the latter issue is relevant to the former, as it is in the case of Marshall's utility analysis.

Second, although the book discusses Frisch's 1926 pioneering attempt to measure utility using econometric methods, it does not cover subsequent developments in the econometric analysis of demand and choice behavior. In particular, it does not deal with the econometric approach to demand analysis developed by Richard Stone (1954), Henri Theil (1965), Angus Deaton (Deaton and Muellbauer 1980), and others, or with the analysis of discrete choices initiated by Daniel McFadden (1974).[2] Both latter research programs focus, in fact, on the empirical applications of utility theory—for example, the specification of the demand functions for various commodities, the estimation of demand elasticities, or the analysis and prediction of choices concerning transportation, occupation, or education—while utility measurement plays only a peripheral role in them. Moreover, when the two programs do deal with utility measurement, they rely on several auxiliary assumptions that concern the parametric form of the utility function to be estimated, the possibility of using aggregate data to estimate individual utility, or the statistical properties of the data employed to estimate the utility functions. In my opinion, the presence of these auxiliary assumptions obscures the specificity of the problems connected to utility measurement. I have therefore preferred to focus on the history of the experimental measurement of utility, which allows the problems of utility measurement to emerge with much more clarity.

2. For reviews, see Brown and Deaton 1972; Deaton 1986; Manski 2001; McFadden 2014.

Third, the book does not deal with revealed preference theory. This theory was originally introduced by Samuelson (1938b) as an approach to consumption analysis independent of the notion of utility. Hendrik Houthakker (1950) showed that the revealed preference approach and the utility-based approach are, in fact, equivalent. More precisely, Houthakker proved that a consistency assumption on consumption choices, later called the Strong Axiom of Revealed Preference, provides an exact characterization of utility theory in terms of choice behavior. Economists contributing to the revealed preference research program in the 1950s, 1960s, and 1970s worked out different systems of revealed preference axioms and applied these axioms to areas of economics beyond consumption analysis, such as social choice theory. However, they did not use revealed preference theory to measure utility. In a paper published in the late 1960s, Sidney Afriat (1967) advocated a more applied approach to revealed preferences and put forward a nonparametric method to construct utility functions rationalizing observed choices. However, not even Afriat applied his method to actual choice data. Concrete attempts to construct, and in this sense measure, utility functions by using nonparametric methods à la Afriat began only in the 1990s, that is, after the 1985 terminus chosen for the narrative.[3]

Finally, this book is not a methodological appraisal of the history of utility measurement informed by some normative philosophy of science. My goal is not to argue that someone did utility measurement scientifically right and someone else did it wrong. Rather, the book provides historical understanding and clarification of the epistemological issues that economists dealing with utility measurement have faced and of the diverse ways in which they have attempted to address these issues.

I.4. READERSHIP AND STYLE

This book is intended for three audiences: historians of economics and other behavioral sciences, especially psychology; economists, in particular mainstream choice theorists and behavioral economists; and philosophers of science, especially those working on the methodology of economics. The book is written at a level suitable for all three audiences, and mathematical and other technical components of the narrative are presented accordingly.

For those who do not read the story from beginning to end, each chapter begins with a brief introduction that should help the selective reader to understand at which point of the narrative he or she has landed. Moreover, numerous wrapping-up points are distributed over the course of the book and should assist any readers who have gotten lost in the vast land of utility measurement to find their way home.

3. On the history of revealed preference theory, see Hands 2013a; Hands 2014; Hands 2017. On the post-1985 developments of the theory, see also Cherchye et al. 2009; Moscati and Tubaro 2011; Chambers and Echenique 2016.

PART ONE

Utility Measurement in Early Utility Theories, 1870–1910

CHAPTER 1

When Unit-Based Measurement Ruled the World

An Interdisciplinary Overview, 1870–1910

Issues concerning the possibility of measuring different types of objects, the practical ways of measuring these objects, and the very meaning of measurement have been discussed since ancient times and within several different fields of inquiry. In order to illustrate the broad intellectual context within which the early discussions of utility measurement took place, this chapter reviews the understanding of measurement in philosophy, physics, psychology, mathematics, and areas of economics before and beyond the emergence of marginal utility theory. The review focuses on the period between 1870 and 1910, that is, the period of the rise and stabilization of marginal utility theory.

This review shows that in the period under consideration, a specific notion of measurement dominated all these disciplines. Some historians of measurement theory, such as Joel Michell (1999) and myself in previous works (e.g., Moscati 2013b), have called this notion the "classical view of measurement." I have come to believe, however, that it is preferable to call it "unit-based measurement" or, equivalently, "ratio-scale measurement," because these expressions make the key measurement-theoretic feature of the notion at issue more explicit.

According to the unit-based view of measurement, measuring the property of an object (e.g., the length of a table) consists of comparing it with some other object that displays the same property and is taken as a unit (e.g., a meter-long ruler) and then assessing the numerical ratio between the unit and the object to be measured (if the ratio is three to one, the table of our example is three meters long). The unit of measurement is arbitrary (the meter can be replaced by the yard), while the zero point is not (a zero length is the same in terms of both meters and yards).

As we see in parts II and III of this book, beginning in the 1930s, other forms of measurement besides unit-based measurement were accepted, and different measurement forms were characterized in terms of the mathematical transformations the numerical measures could be subjected to. From this new perspective, unit-based measurement is characterized by proportional transformations $F(x)$ of the form $F(x) = \alpha x$, where α is an arbitrary positive constant. The arbitrariness of α expresses mathematically the arbitrariness of the unit of measurement. In the case of meters and yards, since a yard is equal to 0.9144 meter, $\alpha = 0.9144$. Proportional transformations do not modify the ratio between numerical measures, and this explains the name "ratio-scale measurement." For instance, if x and y are the lengths of two tables measured in yards and the ratio between these measures is four, that is, $x/y = 4$, this ratio does not change if the two lengths are measured in meters, since $x/y = \alpha x/\alpha y = 4$.

In the late nineteenth century, mathematicians identified the key condition warranting ratio-scale measurement in the possibility of adding objects in a sense analogous to that in which numbers are summed (two tables can be "added" by placing them end to end, and the length of the resulting surface is equal to the sum of the lengths of the two single tables). Late-nineteenth-century discussions of measurement in mathematics are relevant for our narrative also because they established the cardinal–ordinal terminology that later passed into economics. However, the mathematical concept of cardinal number is significantly different from the current economic concept of cardinal utility, which in effect entered the scene only in the 1930s.

1.1. MEASUREMENT IN PHILOSOPHY

The unit-based understanding of measurement dates back to Aristotle. He strictly separated the notions of quality and quantity and associated the notion of measurement with those of quantity, unit, and number. Aristotle argued that a number is either one unit or a plurality of units (*Metaphysics*, bk. X, chap. 1) and defined *quantity* as that which is divisible into two or more constituent parts of which each is by nature a unit (V, 13). Measuring, in this philosophy, means assessing the number of units constituting a quantity, and measurement is in fact the specific way in which a quantity qua quantity is known (X, 1). Similar ideas can be found in Euclid, who defined measurement as a sort of relationship in respect of size between two magnitudes of the same kind (*Elements*, bk. V, definition 3), in which the lesser magnitude measures the greater, while the greater is said to be a multiple of the lesser.

Ancient and medieval scholars recognized that some qualities, although not measurable in the unit-based sense, admit of predication by the qualifiers *more* and *less*. Aristotle himself observed that a thing may be whiter, more beautiful, or warmer than another and that the same thing may exhibit a quality in different degrees at different moments (*Categories*, chap. 5), but he did not investigate measurement issues with respect to these kinds of qualities. In the Middle Ages, these issues were taken up in the context of theological discussions (e.g., can the virtue of charity increase or decrease?), but these medieval debates did not lead to any modification of the unit-based understanding of measurement. Thus, in his *Rules for the Direction of the Mind*, René Descartes ([1628] 1999, 64) continued to contrast ordering with measuring: "All the relations which may possibly obtain between entities of the same kind should be placed under one or other of two categories, *viz.* order or measure."[1]

1. Since this is the first quotation in the book from a text not written in English, it is useful to explain here how I deal with such texts and their English translations. Here and in other quotations from non-English texts, the reference is to their English translations, when available. However, the available English translations have been modified when this seemed appropriate. When no English translation was available, the translation is mine.

The distinction between properly measurable quantities and entities only admitting predication by the qualifiers *more* and *less* is also found in the distinction between extensive and intensive magnitudes introduced by Immanuel Kant in his *Critique of Pure Reason* ([1787] 1997, 288–292). For Kant, extensive magnitudes refer to spatial and temporal dimensions, are made of homogeneous parts, and thus can be measured in units. Intensive magnitudes, by contrast, are related to perception, cannot be conceived as composed of parts, and have only degrees; that is, one intensive magnitude can be larger or smaller than another. As instances of intensive magnitudes, Kant mentioned the same entities Aristotle referred to as qualities admitting predication by the qualifiers *more* and *less*, namely, color and warmth (292). Kant's distinction between extensive and intensive magnitudes lived on in philosophy well into the twentieth century, whereby extensive magnitude generally meant a magnitude measurable in the unit-based sense, while intensive magnitudes were conceived of as things that could be ranked but not measured.

1.2. MEASUREMENT IN PHYSICS

Although the quantitative natural philosophy that arose during the scientific revolution was in many ways opposed to Aristotle's qualitative physics, Galileo Galilei, Isaac Newton, and the other important natural philosophers of the period endorsed Aristotle's view of measurement. For example, in his *Arithmetica Universalis* (1707), Newton defined number as "the abstracted Ratio of any Quantity to another Quantity of the same kind, which we take for Unity" (quoted in Michell 2007, 20). More than 150 years later, at the very beginning of his *Treatise on Electricity and Magnetism*, the eminent Scottish physicist James Clerk Maxwell (1873, 1) expressed the same view: "Every expression of a Quantity consists of two . . . components. One of these is . . . a certain known quantity . . ., which is taken as a standard of reference. The other component is the number of times the standard is to be taken in order to make up the required quantity."

Between 1870 and 1910, the unit-based understanding of measurement remained fundamentally undisputed in physics, probably because most of the entities physicists dealt with in the period were measurable according to a ratio scale. Rather than questioning what measurement means, physicists focused on practical issues, such as how to attain precision and reproducibility in measurement tasks (Darrigol 2003).

An important physical magnitude that had long eluded unit-based measurement was heat. We saw that Aristotle considered the heat of a body as a quality admitting of more and less, and this view remained the standard one for centuries. From the seventeenth century, a gradual move toward the quantification of heat commenced: beginning with Galileo, several types of thermometers were introduced and continuously improved; different temperature scales were proposed, such as the Fahrenheit (in 1724) and the Celsius (in 1742) scales; various thermal units were put forward, such as Clemént's calorie (in 1824), which is the quantity of heat required to raise the temperature of a kilogram of water by one degree. This move toward quantification notwithstanding, Kant at the end of the eighteenth century still considered heat an intensive magnitude that could not be measured in the unit-based sense. Around 1850, however, William Thomson (Lord Kelvin) and James Prescott Joule showed how the thermodynamic properties of gases could be used to measure temperature in an absolute way, that is, on a ratio scale (Chang 2004).

1.3. MEASUREMENT IN PSYCHOLOGY

During the period 1870–1910, an important discussion about measurement took place in psychology in the context of the emergence of psychophysics, which is generally considered the parent of twentieth-century quantitative and experimental psychology. As we will see, both advocates and critics of psychological measurement consistently adhered to the unit-based understanding of measurement.

1.3.1. Fechner's Psychophysics

Gustav Fechner was a German philosopher and scientist who attempted to overcome the dualism between mental and physical phenomena by constructing an exact science of the relations between body and mind, which he called "psychophysics" (Fechner [1860] 1966, xxvii). For this purpose, Fechner sought to measure sensations, a goal he understood in terms of unit-based measurement: "Generally the measurement of a magnitude consists of assessing how many times another magnitude of the same kind taken as a unit is contained in the former" (38). As the unit of sensation, he took the "just-perceivable difference" of sensation, that is, the minimal discernible difference of sensation generated by a change in a physical stimulus. Fechner acknowledged that the change of physical stimulus necessary to produce a just-perceivable difference of sensation varies with the magnitude of the stimulus. Thus, if a subject carries an object weighing forty grams, an increment of one gram may be sufficient to produce the just-perceivable sensation of a heavier object, while if the object weighs eighty grams, it might be necessary to add two grams to produce the just-perceivable sensation of a heavier object. However, Fechner assumed that all just-perceivable increments of sensation are equal, that is, that they are independent of the magnitude of the generating stimulus. Based on this assumption, he argued that a given sensation can be divided into equal, just-perceivable increments and is measured—"as if by the bits of a yardstick" (50)—by the number of increments necessary to generate that sensation starting from the point where no sensation is perceived. Thus, if the sensation corresponding to carrying an object of 130 grams can be reached from the zero point of sensation through ten just-perceivable increments of sensation, the measure of the sensation associated with 130 grams is ten. If the sensation corresponding to carrying another object can be reached through twenty just-perceivable increments of sensation, the latter sensation is twice the former. More generally, Fechner arrived at a logarithmic formula connecting a physical stimulus x to the corresponding sensation y, according to which $y = \alpha \log(x)$, where α is a positive constant. This formula, which will appear again at various points in the next chapters, came to be known as the Weber-Fechner law.

1.3.2. The Debate on Psychophysical Measurement

Psychophysics was subsequently developed by, among others, Wilhelm Wundt (1873–1874) and Joseph Delboeuf (1873). In the 1870s and 1880s, however, Fechner's basic claim that sensations can be measured was attacked from many quarters, a few of which we now consider.[2]

French mathematician Jules Tannery argued that the only measurable magnitudes are those for which we can conceive addition and difference, which is not the case for sensations: "I can conceive neither the sum of two sensations nor their difference: when a sensation increases, it becomes another" (Tannery 1875, 1020). Therefore, he reasoned, sensations cannot be treated with mathematical tools such as differentiation and integration that presuppose the measurability of the objects to which they apply: "Since we do not know at all what the difference between two sensations means, how can we speak of the differential of a sensation? . . . Since we do not know what the sum . . . of two sensations is, what does integration, i.e. the sum of differentials of sensation, mean?" (877). Based on these considerations, Tannery attacked the supposed differentiation and integration of sensations that Fechner had employed to arrive at his logarithmic formula.

German physiologist Johannes von Kries ([1882] 1995) criticized Fechner's assumption that all just-perceivable differences of sensation are equal. For Kries, the increments of sensations occurring at different levels of stimuli are not comparable, and thus the claim that they are equal is meaningless: "If a location on the skin is subjected first to a two-pound and then to a three-pound load, and subsequently to a ten-pound and then a fifteen-pound load, . . . the one increment is something quite different from the other; at first they admit of no comparison. The claim that they may be equal makes absolutely no sense" (291). Kries went on to criticize Fechner's claim that a sensation can be divided into equal, just-perceivable differences of sensation: "A loud tone does not conceal within itself this or that many faint tones, in the same sense that a foot contains twelve inches or a minute sixty seconds" (292).

Echoing some of Tannery's arguments, French philosopher Henri Bergson ([1889] 1960) argued that sensations are not even intensive magnitudes admitting the more and the less. Different sensations are qualitatively different, and the interpretation of the transition from sensation S to sensation S' as an increase or a decrease is a symbolic but arbitrary "interpretation of quality as quantity" (69). For Bergson, because sensations are qualities, they are unmeasurable.

Fechner replied to some of these criticisms but did not modify his basic stance. By contrast, in their efforts to defend Fechner and psychophysics from these and other attacks, Delboeuf (1875; 1878; 1883), Wundt (1880), and other psychologists began to argue that psychophysics does not measure the absolute magnitude of sensations, as in Fechner's theory, but rather the magnitude of difference between sensations. Significantly, however, their revised measurement of sensation differences was still of the unit-based kind, as the unit by which these differences were to be measured was still the equal, just-perceivable

2. For more on the debate over the measurability of sensations, see Titchener 1905 and Heidelberger 2004.

increment of sensation. This modified solution left many problems open and failed to satisfy critics of psychophysics such as Tannery (1884; 1888).

1.3.3. Mental Measurement in the 1900s

From the end of the nineteenth century, quantitative psychologists began to extend their mental measurements from sensations to intellectual abilities. For our purposes, the important point is that while the object of attempted measurement may have changed, the understanding of measurement remained that based on units and ratios. For instance, in his entry on measurement for the *Dictionary of Philosophy and Psychology*, American James Cattell (1902, 57), one of the pioneers of mental measurement, asserted that measurement "is the determination of a magnitude in terms of a standard unit. . . . A ratio is the basis of all measurement."[3]

1.3.4. Measurement in Psychology: Summing Up

In the period 1870–1910, the emergence of psychophysics stimulated a discussion about measurement in psychology. Nevertheless, both advocates and critics of psychological measurement consistently referred to the unit-based understanding of measurement.

The entire debate on psychological measurement, however, may be viewed as originating from a conflict between the psychologists' unit-based understanding of measurement and the fact that their scientific practices did not square with it. On the one hand, psychologists pursued the scientific goal of making sensations and other mental variables measurable and elaborated different measurement practices to achieve this goal. But on the other hand, they consistently adhered to the unit-based understanding of measurement, with the consequence that these practices did not deliver true measurements. As I argue in chapter 2, the conflict faced by psychologists was very similar to that faced by Jevons, Menger, and Walras with their utility theories.

A possible resolution of that conflict in psychology would have involved the superseding of the unit-based understanding of measurement and the elaboration of a novel definition of measurement, broad enough to harbor the psychologists' quantification practices. However, in the period 1870–1910, such a reconceptualization of measurement did not occur. As discussed in chapter 8, it was worked out only much later, by Stanley Smith Stevens in the early 1940s.

1.4. MEASUREMENT IN MATHEMATICS

The 1870–1910 period witnessed major developments in mathematics, with mathematicians addressing explicitly the question of what conditions make a magnitude measurable in a

3. For more on the early history of the measurement of intellectual abilities, see Boring 1929; Michell 1999.

unit-based sense. The key condition came to be identified with the possibility of adding the objects to be measured in a sense analogous to that in which numbers are summed.

1.4.1. Additivity as a Condition for Measurability

In 1882, and in the context of the debate on psychophysics and the measurability of sensations, German mathematician Paul Du Bois-Reymond attempted to define the properties that make a magnitude measurable. By measurement, Du Bois-Reymond (1882, 23–48) meant the assessment of the ratio between the magnitude and a unit. He took length as the archetypal form of a measurable magnitude, labeled "linear magnitudes" those magnitudes analogous to length, and proceeded to indicate six formal properties that characterized them (23–47). Among other characteristics, he argued, any linear magnitude can be obtained from the sum of smaller linear magnitudes and can also be divided arbitrarily with the result always a linear magnitude.

In 1887, German physicist, physiologist, and philosopher Hermann von Helmholtz ([1887] 1999, 740–741) developed some of Du Bois-Reymond's ideas and defined a magnitude as measurable if it can be expressed as the sum of some kind of unit. Helmholtz then put forward a set of features identifying measurable magnitudes, but in contrast to Du Bois-Reymond, he conceived of these features as empirical conditions to be verified experimentally, rather than as formal properties. In particular, for Helmholtz there must be some practical procedure to compare two magnitudes and ascertain whether they are alike and a further procedure analogous to mathematical addition to connect them. For instance, physical magnitudes such as the weights of two bodies are compared by placing the bodies on the two pans of a balance, and they are connected by putting the two bodies in the same pan. However, Helmholtz provided no formal proof that the procedures he indicated were actually sufficient to make magnitudes measurable on a ratio scale.

The notion of measurement was also discussed by Henri Poincaré, a prominent French mathematician, physicist, and philosopher of science. In an article on the mathematical continuum, Poincaré (1893, 26–27) pointed out that order alone is insufficient to make continuum magnitudes measurable. A first condition of attaining measurability is the transitivity of the equality relation between magnitudes, which means that if magnitude A equals magnitude B, and magnitude B equals magnitude C, then magnitude A must equal magnitude C. Poincaré argued that sensations do not satisfy this transitivity condition and thus are not measurable (29). As a second condition for the measurability of magnitudes, Poincaré mentioned their divisibility into *n* equal parts. He did not elaborate, however, but simply referred approvingly to Helmholtz's 1887 article for a thorough treatment of the conditions required for the measurability of magnitudes. His reference to Helmholtz indicates that, like the German scientist, Poincaré understood measurement in the unit-based sense. Like Helmholtz, Poincaré did not provide any formal proof that his or Helmholtz's conditions were sufficient to make a magnitude measurable on a ratio scale.

A formal demonstration that a certain set of conditions makes magnitudes measurable on a ratio scale was given in 1901 by German mathematician Otto Hölder, who applied to measurement theory the axiomatic approach to geometry launched two years earlier by David Hilbert (1899). Hölder ([1901] 1996) laid down seven axioms on magnitudes and proved that if magnitudes satisfy them, the ratio between any two magnitudes is well defined, and one magnitude can be taken as a unit to measure the others. In particular, Hölder's Axioms III and VI postulate the existence of an associative additive operation between magnitudes.[4] Despite its importance for the theory of measurement, Hölder's article and his axiomatization of the concept of measurable magnitude passed unnoticed before the 1930s (see chapter 4).

1.4.2. Cardinal and Ordinal Numbers

The distinction between cardinal and ordinal numbers appears to have been introduced by German mathematician Ernst Schröder in 1873. Schröder's cardinal numbers match the unit-based understanding of number and measurement as stated by Aristotle: cardinal numbers express the total number of units constituting a given quantity, for example, five, and thus are the relevant ones for its measurement. Ordinal numbers, by contrast, come to the fore in the process of counting the units belonging to a quantity and express the position of a specific unit of the quantity, for example, the fifth unit (Schröder 1873, 13–14).

Helmholtz ([1887] 1999, 729) referred approvingly to Schröder's discussion of cardinal and ordinal numbers; but while Schröder treated cardinals and ordinals as associated with two different but equally original functions of number, Helmholtz suggested that ordinals are more fundamental than cardinals. For Helmholtz, numbers derive from our psychological capacity of "retaining, in our memory, the sequence in which acts of consciousness successively occurred in time" (730) and thus are originally ordinal in nature. Cardinal numbers come into play only when we apply the numbers generated by the internal intuition of time to external experience, typically in the attempt to determine the amount of objects belonging to a given set.

Although on different theoretical grounds, two other eminent German mathematicians, Leopold Kronecker ([1887] 1999) and Richard Dedekind ([1888] 1999), also argued that ordinals are more fundamental than cardinals.[5]

1.4.3. Cardinals and Ordinals from Mathematics to Economics

In an article published in 1893 in the political-economy journal *Zeitschrift für die Gesamte Staatswissenschaft*, German mathematician and economist Andreas Voigt made cursory

4. Hölder's axioms are as follows. Axiom I: if a and b are two magnitudes, either $a > b$, or $b > a$, or $a = b$. Axiom II: for any magnitude a, there exists another magnitude b such that $a > b$. Axiom III: for any two magnitudes a and b, there exists a magnitude c such that $a + b = c$. Axiom IV: $a + b > a$ and $a + b > b$. Axiom V: if $a > b$, there exists a magnitude x, such that $b + x = a$. Axiom VI (associativity): $(a + b) + c = a + (b + c)$. Axiom VII fundamentally requires that the order relationship $>$ is preserved under limits. For an extended discussion of Hölder's axioms, see Michell 1999, 47–59.

5. Georg Cantor ([1887] 1932), another important German mathematician, disagreed. His stance was related to the specific meanings he attributed to the terms *cardinal number* and *ordinal number* in his theory of transfinite sets. Although in mathematics these terms have generally been used according to Cantor's sense, in economics his terminology has had no significant influence.

mention of the distinction between ordinal and cardinal numbers as presented by Helmholtz, Kronecker, and Dedekind. He also endorsed their view that ordinals come first: "In accordance with the fundamental conceptions of the nature of numbers which mathematics has developed in recent times, we see the primary form of the number concept in the ordinal number and not in the cardinal number" (Voigt [1893] 2008, 502). As Torsten Schmidt and Christian Weber (2008, 498) have noted, this passage seems to mark the first appearance of the terms *ordinal* and *cardinal* in an economics paper. His reference to ordinal numbers notwithstanding, Voigt thought of measurement in the unit-based sense (Voigt [1893] 2008, 503–504). Moreover, Voigt's notion of cardinal was not the notion attached to cardinal utility in modern microeconomic theory. As explained in chapter 2, cardinal utility is currently associated with interval-scale measurement and the ranking of utility differences, while Voigt's notion of cardinal was the mathematical notion expressing the total number of units constituting a given quantity and, as such, was unrelated to intervals and differences (Voigt 1893, 606).

Among the early marginalists, only Francis Ysidro Edgeworth seems to have noticed Voigt's paper. As pointed out in chapter 3, in three *Economic Journal* articles, Edgeworth (1894; 1900; 1907) referred to Voigt and his distinction between cardinal and ordinal numbers, although always in a cursory way. The point to be stressed here is that, like Voigt, Edgeworth associated cardinal numbers with the availability of a unit and hence with unit-based measurement.

1.5. MEASUREMENT IN ECONOMICS, BEFORE AND BEYOND MARGINAL UTILITY THEORY

At least since William Petty's *Political Arithmetick* (1690), economists have attempted to measure many things aside from utility, such as the national income, the general price level, and the quantity and velocity of money. Like utility theorists, economists working in other areas of economics have also faced a number of theoretical and practical problems in their measurement attempts.[6]

An area of economics in which measurement issues were discussed thoroughly, even before 1870, was the theory of exchange value. Classical economists such as David Ricardo, as well as later marginalists, attempted to measure the exchange value of commodities. By measurement, all these authors meant the assessment of the ratio, which in this case was an exchange ratio, between a given commodity and another commodity, be it money or some other commodity, taken as a unit. Generally speaking, the problem they faced was that the unit available to measure exchange value was not fixed and invariable, as are the units used to measure physical magnitudes.

Even scholars who addressed the issue of the measurability of pleasure or utility prior to the emergence of marginal utility theory understood the measurement of these feelings in the unit-based sense. As explained more extensively in chapter 9, Daniel Bernoulli ([1738]

6. On economic measurement beyond utility theory, see Porter 1994; Rima 1995; Klein and Morgan 2001; Boumans 2005; Boumans 2007; Boumans 2015.

1954) argued that the value of a risky proposition for an individual depends on the average utility (*emolumentum medium*) that the proposition's outcomes give to him. However, Bernoulli did not discuss the theoretical issues related to the measuring and averaging of utilities, and he identified without further ado the utility of outcomes with that archetypal ratio-scale measurable magnitude, the length of segments (26). Moreover, Bernoulli talked of a utility that is "twice as much" (*duplum emolumentorum*) as another utility (25) and so implicitly took for granted the possibility of assessing utility ratios.

In the late eighteenth century, Jeremy Bentham claimed that pleasures can be measured directly by taking as a unit "that pleasure which is the faintest of any that can be distinguished to be pleasure" (quoted in Halevy 1901, 398). Bentham's faintest pleasure evidently resembles the just-perceivable sensation of later psychophysics. The founder of utilitarianism also suggested an indirect way to measure a pleasure, namely, by the quantity of money paid to obtain it (410). The soundness of his arguments aside, the point to note here is that both of Bentham's measures of pleasure in principle allow for the measurement of utility in the unit-based sense: in both cases, there is a unit, that is, the "faintest pleasure" or the monetary unit, which makes the assessment of utility ratios possible.

French engineer Jules Dupuit ([1844] 1952) took, as an indirect measure of the utility of an object, the maximum price a consumer is willing to pay for it. Although willingness to pay as a measure of utility presents a number of severe limitations (see chapters 2 and 3), in principle it allows for a ratio-scale measurement of utility: there is a definite unit, that is, the monetary unit, and utility ratios between commodities can be easily assessed by comparing the maximum prices the consumer is willing to pay for them.[7]

1.6. SUMMING UP

This concludes our review of the notion of measurement in various disciplines—philosophy, physics, psychology, mathematics, and economics—before and beyond marginal utility theory. The review has framed a picture of the broad intellectual context within which the early discussions of utility measurement took place and has shown that the unit-based understanding of measurement reigned unrivaled within all these fields of inquiry from their earliest origins. Given this background, the fact that Jevons, Menger, and Walras identified measurement with unit-based measurement is hardly surprising.

7. Heinrich Gossen ([1854] 1983) also argued that pleasures are measurable in the unit-based sense. On Gossen's understanding of utility measurement, see Stigler 1950.

CHAPTER 2

Is There a Unit of Utility?

Jevons, Menger, and Walras on the Measurability of Utility, 1870–1910

As explained in chapter 1, the notion of utility had been used in economic analysis well before 1870 by scholars such as Daniel Bernoulli and Jules Dupuit. However, it was only in the 1870s that the utility notion began playing the central role in economic theory that it has maintained—albeit through a number of transformations—until today. As discussed in the prologue, from 1871 to 1874, William Stanley Jevons, Carl Menger, and Léon Walras independently advanced an explanation of the exchange value of commodities (i.e., basically, of their price) that contrasted with the then-dominant labor theory of value. An outline of the evolution of this theory until around 1870 helps to clarify the background from which the utility theories of Jevons, Menger, and Walras emerged.

The labor theory of value was put forward by Adam Smith ([1776] 1976, 44–45), who ruled out utility as the determinant of exchange value by using an argument later called the water–diamond paradox. According to Smith, things such as water have great utility but often little exchange value; by contrast, things such as diamonds have great exchange value but frequently little utility. For Smith, this shows that utility does not explain exchange value. As an alternative explanatory factor, he pinpointed labor. More specifically, Smith argued that in the primitive state of society that precedes the existence of rents on land and profits on capital, the exchange ratio between two commodities is directly proportional to the quantity of labor needed to produce them: "If among a nation of hunters," he famously claimed, "it usually costs twice the labour to kill a beaver which it does to kill a deer, one beaver should naturally exchange for or be worth two deer" (65).

David Ricardo ([1821] 1951) advanced Smith's labor theory in many respects. In particular, he contended that the theory explains exchange value in any state of society, that is, even when rents and profits exist. Moreover, Ricardo stressed that the exchange value of a commodity depends not only on the quantity of direct labor, that is, the labor directly used to produce it, but also on the quantity of indirect labor, that is, the labor necessary to produce the capital employed in the production of the commodity. Restating Smith's beaver-and-deer example, Ricardo remarked: "Suppose the weapon necessary to kill the beaver, was constructed with much more labour than that necessary to kill the deer . . .; [then] one beaver would naturally be of more value than two deer" (23). Finally, Ricardo showed that if two commodities contain different proportions of direct and indirect labor, their exchange ratio depends not only on the quantity of labor necessary to produce them but also on the profit rate prevailing in the economy. Ricardo minimized this problem by claiming that the effects of the profit rate on exchange value are negligible.

John Stuart Mill (1848; 1871) attempted to systematize Ricardo's labor theory by distinguishing three classes of commodities. The first includes ancient sculptures and other commodities whose supply cannot be increased. The exchange value of these commodities depends not on the quantity of labor that was necessary to produce them but exclusively on their demand. Mill's second class refers to commodities whose supply can be increased by using the same quantity of labor. For Mill, the exchange value of these commodities can be wholly explained by the quantity of direct and indirect labor embodied in them. The third class includes commodities such as corn, whose supply can be increased only by employing increasing quantities of labor. The exchange value of these commodities depends partly on the quantity of labor necessary to produce them and partly on their demand. Mill's classification made evident that the exchange value of several commodities cannot be explained by the labor theory alone. Moreover, Mill did not address the problem indicated by Ricardo, namely that if two commodities contain different proportions of direct and indirect labor, their exchange ratio depends not only on labor but also on the profit rate of the economy. This is the case even if the two commodities belong to Mill's second class.[1]

Jevons, Menger, and Walras were unsatisfied with the labor theory of value, and in opposition to it put forward a novel theory according to which the exchange value of a commodity is determined by its marginal utility. This is the additional utility associated with an individual's consumption of an additional unit of the commodity. In particular, Jevons, Menger, and Walras assumed that the marginal utility of each commodity diminishes as the individual consumes a larger quantity of it. Based on the idea of diminishing marginal utility, they solved the water–diamond paradox: since water is usually abundant, its marginal utility is small, and therefore its exchange value is also small. In contrast, diamonds are typically scarce, so their marginal utility and therefore their exchange value are typically high. When water becomes scarce, as in a dry desert, its marginal utility increases, and in situations of extreme thirst, a glass of water may be worth more than a diamond (see, e.g., Menger [1871] 1981, 140; Jevons 1879, 86). More important than solving the water–diamond paradox was the fact that based on the idea of diminishing marginal utility, Jevons, Menger, and Walras constructed a unified theory of value that held for all commodities, independently of the Millian class they belong to, independently of whether they are material or, like

1. In this outline of the evolution of the labor theory of value, I have skipped Karl Marx's version of the theory (1867), because Jevons, Menger, and Walras did not discuss it. Only in the mid-1880s, when Marx's ideas became central to the European socialist movement, did marginal utility theorists such as Philip Wicksteed and Eugen von Böhm-Bawerk begin dealing with Marx's labor theory and the theory of exploitation associated with it. See more on the reception of Marx's economic thought among early marginalists in Marchionatti 1998.

services, immaterial, and independently of whether they are consumption goods or productive factors. Finally, building on their marginal-utility theories of value, Jevons, Menger, and Walras were able to construct comprehensive theories of price and markets. The change in economic analysis associated with their names is called the marginal revolution.

There was one major problem with the new theory, namely that utility and marginal utility cannot be observed and measured in a straightforward way. Jevons and Walras explicitly discussed this problem, not least because their critics often pointed to the apparent unmeasurability of utility as a crucial flaw in the new theory. Although Menger did not address the issue of the measurability of utility in an explicit way, he did take a tacit stance on it. But how did Jevons, Menger, and Walras conceive of measurement? According to what conception of measurement did they judge whether utility was measurable or not?

I argue in this chapter that the three founders of marginal utility theory identified measurement with unit-based measurement and that, accordingly, they searched for a unit of utility that could be used to assess utility ratios. The outcomes of this search were diverse and ranged from the idea that a unit to measure utility directly, although not available at present, may become so in the future, through the claim that marginal utility is indirectly measured by willingness to pay, to the assertion that although utility cannot be measured, constructing economic theory as if it were measurable is a scientifically legitimate procedure. In particular, I reconstruct in detail how Jevons, Menger, and Walras addressed the issue of the measurability of utility on the basis of their unit-based understanding of measurement. The period covered is from 1871, when Jevons and Menger published their seminal works, to 1909, when Walras published his last economic writing.

In most histories of utility theory, discussions of the measurability of utility in the period 1870–1910 are typically presented in terms of the notion of cardinal utility, and the stance on utility measurement of Jevons, Menger, and Walras is usually summarized by the statement that they were cardinalists. In the final section of this chapter, I explain why the notion of cardinal utility is inadequate for understanding the utility theories of the three founders of marginalism and contend that Jevons, Menger, Walras were not cardinalists.

2.1. JEVONS

One of the main motivations that led Jevons (1835–1882) to write his *Theory of Political Economy* (first edition 1871, second edition 1879) was his conviction that exchange value depends on utility, and more precisely on the law of diminishing marginal utility, rather than, as argued by classical economists, on labor. He writes in his introduction:

> Repeated reflection and inquiry have led me to the somewhat novel opinion, that *value depends entirely upon utility*. Prevailing opinions make labour rather than utility the origin of value; . . . I show, on the contrary, that we have only to trace out carefully the natural laws of the variation of utility [i.e., the law of diminishing marginal utility] . . ., in order to arrive at a satisfactory theory of exchange, of which the ordinary laws of supply and demand are a necessary consequence. (1871, 2)

In this section, I argue that Jevons adhered to the unit-based understanding of measurement and that he therefore faced a contradiction between the importance he assigned to measurement, his unit-based conception of it, and the apparent lack of an appropriate unit to measure utility.

Jevons contributed not only to utility analysis but also to other parts of economic theory, as well as to noneconomic disciplines as diverse as formal logic, meteorology, statistics, and the philosophy of scientific method. Before analyzing his utility theory, it is useful to consider Jevons's stance on measurement as it emerges from his works that do not concern utility analysis.

2.1.1. Jevons on Measurement beyond Utility Analysis

In *The Principles of Science*, his main work as a philosopher of science, Jevons (1874) assigned great importance to the measurement of phenomena, which he discussed at length in chapters 13 and 14, "The Exact Measurement of Phenomena" and "Units and Standards of Measurements" (313–386). Here Jevons associated the advance of scientific knowledge with "the invention of suitable instruments of measurement" (313). By measurement, he meant unit-based measurement: "The result of every measurement is to make known the purely numerical ratio existing between the magnitude to be measured, and a certain other magnitude, which should, when possible, be a fixed unit or standard magnitude" (331).

In his work as a scientist, Jevons also assigned great importance to measurement and engaged in numerous enterprises in empirical measurement. In the 1860s, for example, he attempted to measure the wear rate of gold coins in the United Kingdom, the variation in the value of domestic gold as a consequence of the influx of gold from Australia and the United States, and the annual growth rate of coal consumption in the country. In the 1870s, he turned to the measurement of business cycles and their supposed relationships to solar activity cycles. In these enterprises in empirical measurement, some unit of measure was readily available or could be constructed—be it a weight unit, a temporal unit, or a monetary unit—and thus Jevons's scientific efforts fit smoothly into the unit-based view of measurement.[2]

2.1.2. Pleasure, Economic Calculus, and Utility Measurement

Unlike Menger and Walras, Jevons was strongly influenced by the utilitarian philosophy of Jeremy Bentham, according to which human action is governed by the search for pleasure and the avoidance of pain. Echoing Bentham, Jevons (1871, vii) famously defined economics as "a Calculus of Pleasure and Pain." He was, however, well aware that if the notions of pleasure and pain are employed with a sufficiently broad meaning, the utilitarian theory of action becomes tautological: "Call any motive which attracts to a certain action pleasure,

2. For more on Jevons's empirical measurements, see Peart 1996; Peart 2001; Maas 2005.

and that which deters pain, and it becomes impossible to deny that all actions are prompted by pleasure or by pain" (31).

To avoid this problem and better delimit the scope of the economic calculus, Jevons advanced the idea that there is a hierarchy of pleasures and pains. At the lowest level of this hierarchy is the "mere physical pleasure or pain" of a man that arises "from his bodily wants and susceptibilities" (29). At a higher level, we find "mental and moral feelings" (29), which in themselves may be distinguished by various degrees of elevation. At the highest level of the hierarchy are pleasures and pains such as uprightness, honor, or public shame. For Jevons, the economic calculus deals only with the lowest level of the hierarchy:[3] "It is the lowest rank of feelings which we here treat. The calculus of utility aims at supplying the ordinary wants of man at the least cost of labour. Each labourer, in the absence of other motives, is supposed to devote his energy to the accumulation of wealth" (32).

The economic calculus is possible, Jevons argued, because pleasure and pain are "quantities," where by quantity he meant that which is "capable of being *more or less* in magnitude" (4). However, being a quantity in this sense does not warrant its measurability, and Jevons frankly acknowledged that pleasure and pain cannot be measured in the unit-based sense: "We have no means of defining and measuring quantities of feeling, like we can measure a mile, or a right angle, or any other physical quantity. . . . We can hardly form the conception of a unit of pleasure or pain, so that the numerical expression of quantities of feeling seems to be out of the question" (19).

Jevons's problem was that at least some parts of his economic calculus, such as the sum and integration of utility increments in order to obtain total utility (54–56) or the differentiation of total utility to derive the final degree of utility, that is, marginal utility (59–60), appeared to depend on "the numerical expression of quantities of feeling." Jevons therefore felt obliged to defend the soundness of his utility analysis, which he did with four main arguments.

2.1.3. Four Arguments in Defense of Utility Analysis

First, Jevons (9–11) speculated that although pleasure and pain could not then be measured directly, they might become measurable in some near future. In the history of science, he noted, there were several entities, such as probability, electricity, and heat, that had long appeared unmeasurable but had recently become amenable to exact measurement: "We cannot weigh, or gauge, or test the feelings of the mind; there is no unit of . . . suffering, or enjoyment. . . . If we trace the history of other sciences, we gather no lessons of discouragement. In the case of almost everything which is now exactly measured, we can go back to the time when the vaguest notions prevailed" (8–9). Here we observe only that Jevons's hope that utility would soon become directly measurable was overly optimistic and take note also of his insistence on an inextricable connection between the possibility of measurement and the availability of a unit.

3. On this aspect of Jevons's approach, see Mandler 1999, chap. 4.

Second, Jevons claimed that his theory was largely independent of the measurability of utility because it mainly relied on the direct comparison of different pleasures in order to determine which is the greater, and it "seldom or never affirm[s] that one pleasure is a multiple of another in quantity" (20). For Jevons, the mind of an individual is able to directly compare different pleasures just as the balance compares different weights, and insofar as this mental comparison is feasible, units to measure pleasures are unnecessary: "We only employ units of measurement . . . to facilitate the comparison of quantities; and if we can compare the quantities directly, we do not need the units. Now the mind of an individual is the balance which makes its own comparisons" (19). In this second argument, one may detect the seeds of an ordinal approach to utility (see chapter 5), which, however, Jevons did not develop. Moreover, the argument confirms by negation Jevons's understanding of measurement: if true measurement were possible, it would employ units and consist of assessing how many times a pleasure is a multiple of another; luckily, the economic calculus seldom relies on true measurement, for the mere ranking of pleasures usually suffices.

Third, Jevons argued that although not directly measurable, pleasure and pain can be measured through their indirect but observable market effects, notably through prices. In this respect, he claimed, feelings are analogous to gravity, for both are unobservable but both can be measured through their effects on, respectively, market prices and physical bodies: "We can no more . . . measure gravity in its own nature than we can measure a feeling, but just as we measure gravity by its effects in the motion of a pendulum, so we may estimate . . . feelings by the varying decisions of the human mind. The will is our pendulum, and its oscillations are minutely registered in all the price lists of the market" (14). Here Jevons again refers to measurement in relation to a physical force, namely gravity, which is measurable in the classical sense.

Although in 1871 he did not know Dupuit's 1844 article, in his fourth argument, Jevons put forward an idea similar to that proposed by the French engineer.[4] Jevons suggested that the final degree of utility that a commodity gives to an individual can be measured indirectly by the money he or she is willing to pay to purchase an additional unit. As observed in chapter 1, money is appealing as a measuring rod since it allows for classical measurement. Jevons, however, specified that money measures utility only if "the general utility of a person's income is not affected by the changes of the price of the commodity" (140). However, this condition is violated for commodities that absorb a significant fraction of a person's income, as in the case of bread for the nineteenth-century poor: "When the price of bread rises much, the resources of poor persons are strained, money becomes scarcer . . ., and . . . the utility of money, rises" (142). As a consequence, willingness to purchase an additional unit of bread and possibly other commodities decreases, although the final degree of utility of that unit may not have changed.

Two general remarks on Jevons's discussion of the measurability of utility are in order.

4. On Dupuit's 1844 article, see chapter 1, section 1.5. For more on Jevons and Dupuit's article, see section 2.3.2 in this chapter.

2.1.4. Measuring Marginal Utility, Not Total Utility

First, as with the other early marginalists, for Jevons, marginal utility rather than total utility was the key notion "upon which the whole Theory of Economy will be found to turn" (61–62). Marginal utility, and more specifically the principle of diminishing marginal utility, determines how commodities are distributed among different uses, the laws of exchange between them, and the offer of labor. Total utility is of secondary importance and, generally, also more difficult to assess than marginal utility (61). Accordingly, Jevons's discussion of the measurability of utility refers primarily to marginal utility, not total utility. It is marginal utility that is (at present) indirectly measured by prices (third argument) or by willingness to pay, at least in some special cases (fourth argument). It is marginal utility that in the future might even be measured in a direct way (first argument) and whose measurement, in the end, is seldom employed in the theory of political economy (second argument).

2.1.5. Direct and Indirect Measurement

The second remark concerns the idea of measuring (marginal) utility indirectly by willingness to pay. Indirect measurement will also be discussed in various other places in this book, but since it enters our main narrative with Jevons, this seems an appropriate place to discuss some general methodological problems associated with it.[5]

In indirect measurement, the magnitude of the object x to be measured, which in measurement theory is called the measurand, is inferred from the magnitude of another object y. We typically recur to indirect measurement when the measurand x is not directly observable—as is the case when the measurand is utility—while y is directly observable and measurable, as is the price of a commodity or the willingness to pay for it (the question of what extent willingness to pay is actually observable is not relevant for the present discussion).

We infer the magnitude of x from the magnitude of y because we assume that there is some functional relationship F between the two magnitudes: $y = F(x)$. The functional relationship F should be monotonic; otherwise, a single value of y would correspond to multiple values of x. In the case of utility (x) and willingness to pay (y), we assume that there is a causal relationship between the two: an individual is willing to pay a certain amount of money for an object because the object is somehow useful to him or her.

There are two main problems with indirect measurement: first, we may be uncertain about the exact functional form of the relationship F between x and y; second, y may be affected by other factors k, w, . . . besides x. Economists such as Alfred Marshall (see chapter 3), who advocated willingness to pay as an indirect measure of utility, typically ignored the first problem by taking for granted that the two magnitudes are linked by a proportional relationship $y = \alpha x$. The second problem is the one Jevons referred to in his discussion of willingness to pay. He noted that an individual's willingness to pay (y) for a commodity depends not

5. For a more philosophical discussion of the problems associated with indirect measurement, see Chang 1995 and van Fraassen 2008, chap. 5.

only on the utility of the commodity (x) but also on another factor, namely the individual's income. If this is the case, taking the direct measure of y as an indirect measure of x becomes questionable.

There are different ways out of the second problem. For instance, it could be argued that for some reason or under certain assumptions, the "disturbing" factors k, w, . . . are not operating. Alternatively, it could be claimed that k, w, . . . are indeed operating but that their effects on y are negligible. Or one may acknowledge that factors k, w, . . . are operating and that their effects are not negligible but contend that these effects offset each other, so that ultimately, y depends only on x. In chapter 3, we will see how Marshall justified willingness to pay as a reliable measure of utility by using some of these argumentative strategies. For the moment, however, let us return to Jevons.

2.1.6. Utility Measurement for Jevons's Critics

Anticipating the arguments of Fechner's critics (see chapter 1, section 1.3.2), several reviewers of *Theory of Political Economy* argued that Jevons's analysis relied on the assumption that utility is measurable but that he was unable to substantiate this assumption. As with Fechner's critics, when Jevons's critics wrote of measurability, they, too, meant unit-based measurability.

An anonymous reviewer in the *Saturday Review* argued that the mathematical treatment of utility, and specifically its differentiation, presupposed the measurability of utility in terms of a unit but that Jevons had not established his own presuppositions: "When a mathematician wishes to calculate the variations of a force, he begins by telling us distinctly what is the measure of force. . . . But what is the measure of utility? To this we can discover no answer in Mr. Jevons's book" ("Jevons on the Theory of Political Economy" [1871] 1981, 153). In the *Glasgow Daily Herald*, another anonymous reviewer criticized Jevons's assumption that utilities can be added or subtracted on the ground that this kind of manipulation would require the possession of "some unit of pleasure . . . by which [pleasures] might be measured" (quoted in Howey 1960, 62). For this reviewer, such a unit was simply not available.

Classical economist John Elliott Cairnes ([1872] 1981, 150) maintained that Jevons's argument that utility, while not directly measurable, may nevertheless be measured indirectly by prices is circular: "How are we to measure pleasure? . . . We may take exchange-value as the criterion of utility; and this is the test that Mr. Jevons ultimately adopts. . . . So that what we come to is this—exchange-value depends upon utility, and utility is measured and can only be known by exchange-value." In an 1872 letter to Cairnes, Jevons replied to this criticism by repeating a point he had already made, namely that the method of measuring utility is indirect but analogous to that used to measure gravity and that insofar as the latter is appropriate, so is the former (Black 1972–1981, 3: 246).

The opinions Jevons expressed in the second edition of the *The Theory of Political Economy* (1879) on the measurability of utility are almost identical to those presented in the first edition, and this suggests that the critical remarks of Cairnes and others did not change Jevons's ideas on utility measurement. In his writings from 1879 to 1882, the year he died, Jevons does not appear to have returned to the issue of the measurability of utility.

2.1.7. Conclusions on Jevons

Jevons adhered to the unit-based understanding of measurement and faced a contradiction between the acknowledged unmeasurability of utility in the unit-based sense and the fact that at least certain parts of his utility theory appeared to depend on the availability of a unit to measure utility. He put forward different arguments to avoid or at least soften this contradiction, though with only limited success.

A different way out of this contradiction could have been to abandon the unit-based notion of measurement and elaborate a novel definition of measurement, broad enough to harbor utility as a measurable concept. However, like the psychologists of the 1870–1910 period, Jevons did not take this route. Indeed, each of his arguments shows that he consistently stuck to the unit-based understanding of measurement. Another possible route would have been to show that the economically relevant outcomes of utility analysis are in effect independent of the unit-based measurability of utility. This is the solution reached during the ordinal revolution, which Jevons foreshadowed in his second argument but did not carry through.

2.2. MENGER

As with Jevons, Menger (1840–1921) was led to write his *Principles of Economics* ([1871] 1981) by the conviction that the labor theory of exchange value was inadequate and contrary to experience. He argued:

> There is no necessary and direct connection between the value of a good and whether, or in what quantities, labor and other goods . . . were applied to its production. . . . Goods on which much labor has been expended often have no value, while others, on which little or no labor was expended, have a very high value. . . . The quantities of labor . . . cannot, therefore, be the determining factor in the value of a good. (146–147)

For Menger, the determining factor in the value of a good is the importance of the need satisfied by the last unit of the good, that is, by what today we would call the marginal utility of that unit (132).

Despite the similarity of their marginal-utility explanations of exchange value, there are significant differences between the utility analyses of Menger and Jevons.[6] Here I mention only two. First, they associated the notion of utility with two distinct mental correlates. While Jevons was influenced by Bentham's utilitarianism and identified utility with pleasure (see section 2.1.2), Menger was not a Benthamite and related utility to need: "Utility [*Nützlichkeit*] is the capacity of a thing to serve for the satisfaction of human needs [*menschlicher Bedürfnisse*]" (119). In particular, for Menger, needs have a distinct biological

6. For more on the differences between Menger and Jevons, see Jaffé 1976.

and physiological characterization and are largely independent of human will.[7] In this sense, Menger's needs appear to be less subjective and arbitrary than Jevons's pleasures.

Second, unlike Jevons, Menger avoided taking an explicit stance on issues surrounding the measurability of utility. Therefore, in order to appraise his views on this subject, we need to take a roundabout path and start from his discussion of money as a possible measure of the exchange value of goods.

2.2.1. The Measurement of Exchange Value

In *Principles* ([1871] 1981, 272–280), as well in other works, Menger discussed whether money measures the exchange value of goods. His most thorough discussion of the issue can be found in a dictionary entry on money published in 1909. Here he asked whether "the valuation of goods in money [should] be regarded as measurement of their exchange value by the monetary unit" ([1909] 2002, 60). In answering, Menger first described measurement as "a procedure by which we determine the as yet unknown magnitude of an object by comparison with a known magnitude of the same kind taken as a unit" (60) and then argued that money does not measure the exchange value of goods. In fact, he concluded, the exchange ratios between money and goods, that is, prices, vary from time to time and from place to place, and it is not only absolute but also relative prices that vary. This variation may be due not only to modifications in the exchange value of goods but also to modifications in the exchange value of money: unlike the fixed and invariable units used in physical measurement, the monetary unit changes.

Menger's definition of measurement and his rejection of the idea that money measures the exchange value of goods show that his general understanding of measurement was the unit-based one. We turn now to the question of whether Menger applied this understanding to utility measurement.

2.2.2. Menger's Utility Numbers

As mentioned, for Menger, the value to an individual of a given quantity of a good is measured by the importance of the need satisfied by the last unit of the good, that is, by the marginal utility of that unit. Thus, in chapter 3 of *Principles* ([1871] 1981, 125–127), Menger considered the marginal utility of ten different goods, assumed that the marginal utility of each good was diminishing, and associated the diminishing marginal utilities with a decreasing series of numbers. For instance, he imagined that for a particular individual, the first unit of the first good, identified as food, has a marginal utility of 10, the second unit has a marginal utility of 9, the units following have a marginal utility of 8, 7, 6, and so on,

7. See the chapter on "The Theory of Needs" in the second edition of the *Principles*, posthumously published by Menger's son (Menger 1923, 1–9).

respectively, while the eleventh unit of this first good has zero marginal utility. The marginal utilities of the other nine goods display a similar trend.

Menger represented this situation with a numerical table, which is reproduced in table 2.1. In the table, each good corresponds to a column and a roman numeral (e.g., food is associated with the first column and the roman numeral I). Each row indicates which unit of the good is considered (the first unit, the second, etc.). The arabic numbers in the cells express the marginal utility of each unit of the good under consideration (e.g., the marginal utility of the sixth unit of good IV is 2).

During the heyday of the ordinal revolution (see chapter 5), Friedrich Hayek (1934) and George Stigler (1937) rushed to enroll Menger in the ordinal camp, claiming that his utility figures represented only the ranking of the importance of needs. As with Jevons, one may indeed find some ordinal insights in Menger, but an ordinalist interpretation clashes with the fact that in several passages of *Principles*, Menger treated the numbers in the table as if they directly measured marginal utilities in the unit-based sense of the term.

For example, he took for granted that there is a zero point of marginal utility ([1871] 1981, 126–127, 135, 183–186). In a purely ordinal approach, where the individual can only state whether a marginal utility is larger or smaller than another, the proper way to identify a zero point of utility is far from obvious. Moreover, on two occasions, Menger claimed that his utility figures expressed the ratio of marginal utilities. In a footnote in the chapter of *Principles* devoted to the theory of exchange, Menger in fact specifies: "When I designate the importance of two need-satisfactions with 40 and 20 for example, I am merely saying that the first of the two satisfactions has twice the importance of the second to the economizing individual concerned" (183). In another passage, Menger argued that if the marginal utility of a cow to an individual is 10 while the marginal utility of an additional horse is 30, then the horse has "three times the value of a cow" (184). All of this entails that Menger's utility numbers measure marginal utility in the unit-based sense in terms of some (unspecified) unit of satisfaction.

Table 2.1. MENGER'S UTILITY NUMBERS (ADAPTED FROM MENGER 1981 [1871], 127)

	I	II	III	IV	V	VI	VII	VIII	IX	X
1st unit	10	9	8	7	6	5	4	3	2	1
2nd	9	8	7	6	5	4	3	2	1	0
3rd	8	7	6	5	4	3	2	1	0	
4th	7	6	5	4	3	2	1	0		
5th	6	5	4	3	2	1	0			
6th	5	4	3	2	1	0				
7th	4	3	2	1	0					
8th	3	2	1	0						
9th	2	1	0							
10th	1	0								
11th	0									

2.2.3. Conclusions on Menger

His elusiveness notwithstanding, Menger clearly understood measurement in the unit-based sense and treated marginal utility as if it were directly measurable on a ratio scale. In contrast to Jevons, Menger never explicitly addressed the tension between his understanding of measurement and his utility analysis. One may speculate why this was the case. Perhaps Menger understood that the problem of utility measurement could undermine his economic theory and hence intentionally decided to avoid the issue. Alternatively, the absence of criticisms of the kind received by Jevons regarding the measurability of utility or Menger's fundamentally unmathematical approach to utility theory might have prevented the Austrian economist from properly appreciating this tension.[8]

We might have thought that some passage in his correspondence with Walras might help us better understand Menger's position.[9] Unfortunately, the Menger–Walras correspondence is disappointing in this respect, for the two economists never discussed the issue of utility measurement.

2.3. WALRAS

Walras (1834–1910) published his *Elements of Pure Economics* ([1874] 1954) three years after Jevons's *Theory* and Menger's *Principles*, but he elaborated his theories independently of them. Like Jevons and Menger, Walras also criticized the classical theory of value (201–203) and explained the exchange value of a commodity as determined by its marginal utility, which he called intensive utility or *rareté* (rarity).

Walras associated the notion of utility with both use and need: "Things are useful whenever they can be put to any use [*usage*] at all; whenever they answer any need [*besoin*] at all and permit its satisfaction" (65). Walras intended *useful* in a very broad sense, which includes not only what satisfies Menger's physiological needs and Jevons's low-level pleasures but also the moral pleasures that Jevons had excluded from the scope of the economic calculus. Walras argued:

> For present purposes, necessary, useful, agreeable and superfluous simply mean more or less useful. Furthermore, we need not concern ourselves with the morality or immorality of any desire which a useful thing answers or serves to satisfy. From other points of view the

8. Menger did face strong criticisms of his economic theory from the German Historical School, whose members advocated a fundamentally descriptive approach to economic analysis and criticized the methods of both classical political economy and marginal utility theory as too abstract. In the 1880s, Menger replied to these criticisms during the so-called *Methodenstreit*, a famous methodological dispute he had with Gustav Schmoller, leader of the German Historical School. The issue of the measurability of utility, however, was not among the topics Menger and Schmoller debated. On the *Methodenstreit*, see Bostaph 1978.

9. There exists no Menger–Jevons correspondence, for the English economist died in 1882, unaware of Menger and his work.

question of whether a drug is wanted by a doctor to cure a patient, or by a murderer to kill his family is a very serious matter, but from our point of view, it is totally irrelevant. (65)

Regarding the issue of utility measurement, in many respects, Walras's problem situation was very similar to that faced by Jevons. On the one hand, Walras always maintained an unequivocally unit-based understanding of measurement and, accordingly, had to acknowledge that utility was not directly measurable. On the other hand, Walras believed that his economic analysis depended on the measurability of utility. Again, as with Jevons, a number of commentators criticized Walras for relying on the false assumption that utility was measurable. Like Jevons, therefore, Walras put forward a number of arguments in order to reconcile his economic analysis with the apparent unmeasurability of utility.

2.3.1. Utility Measurement at the Académie and in the *Elements*

During two 1873 meetings of the Académie des Sciences Morales et Politiques of Paris, Walras read a paper titled "Principle of a Mathematical Theory of Exchange" (henceforth "Principle"), which outlined the theory of utility and exchange later expounded in *Elements of Pure Economics*. The paper was subsequently published in the *Journal des Économistes* (Walras [1874] 1987).

In this paper, Walras discussed how to derive the demand curves of commodities from their "intensive utility," that is, their marginal utility (273–277). In this context, he addressed the measurability of utility and took up the stance he was to maintain for the next forty years: although utility is not directly measurable, we can nevertheless derive demand curves from it and thus carry out a suitable analysis of demand by treating marginal utility as if it were measurable. It should be emphasized that Walras was concerned with the measurement of intensive or marginal utility, not of total utility. Moreover, he associated the measurability of marginal utility, however fictitious, with the availability of a unit: "Let us suppose, for a moment, that utility is directly measurable, and we shall find ourselves in a position to give an exact, mathematical account of the influence it exerts . . . on demand curves and hence on prices. I shall, therefore, assume the existence of a standard of measure [*étalon de mesure*] of intensive utility" (274). Walras briefly justified this as-if procedure by claiming that it is the same as that employed in physics and mechanics, where masses enter into scientific calculations despite the fact that they are not directly measurable (274). Although in 1873 he did not know Jevons's *Theory*, his justification is similar to Jevons's third argument, according to which the method of measuring utility through its effects on market prices is scientifically appropriate because it is analogous to the method used in physics to measure gravity through its effects on physical bodies (see section 2.1.3).

Walras's paper was not well received at the Académie, and one of the objections raised concerned the measurability of utility. Emile Levasseur, a professor of economic history, geography, and statistics at the Collège de France, argued that Walras's analysis was misleading because it relied on the false assumption that utility is measurable: "It would be very good if desire and need were measurable in an exact way . . . but it is not like that, quite the opposite. . . . [Walras's] data are, so to say, incommensurable; it follows that his [intensive utility] curves are without foundation; . . . they are false" (Levasseur [1874] 1987, 530). Levasseur denied that intensive utility is measurable, but he did not object to Walras's association of measurement with the availability of a unit.

Levasseur's objection did not modify Walras's stance on the measurability of utility. *Elements* repeats almost word for word the argument made in "Principle" the previous year: marginal utility is not measurable, but by assuming that it is, that is, by assuming the existence of a unit, we can analyze individual demand. Therefore, Walras now declared ([1874] 1954, 117), "I shall . . . assume the existence of a standard of measure of intensive utility." The main difference between the arguments of "Principle" and *Elements* is that in the latter, Walras did not attempt to justify his as-if approach by analogy with the methodology of physics and mechanics. Possibly, Levasseur's objections suggested to him that it would be safer to remove this claim.[10]

2.3.2. Walras on Willingness to Pay as a Measure of Utility

As we have seen in chapter 1 and in section 2.1.3 of this chapter, Dupuit and Jevons had independently suggested that the consumer's willingness to pay can be used as a measure of marginal utility. Walras's correspondence with Jevons illustrates his conviction that this idea was ill founded.

In 1874, Walras sent Jevons an article from the French journal *Le Temps*, which attributed the discovery of marginal utility theory to the two of them, together with a subsequent letter to the journal claiming that Dupuit had already arrived at the theory in 1844. In his letter to Jevons, Walras acknowledged that Dupuit "had in fact addressed the problem of the mathematical expression of utility" but argued that "he did not solve it at all" (Jaffé 1965, 1: 456). In 1877, Jevons wrote to Walras that he had finally read Dupuit's 1844 article and affirmed that Dupuit "had anticipated us as regards the fundamental ideas of utility" (533). Walras disagreed. In his reply, he insisted that Dupuit had confused the marginal utility and the demand functions and had failed to see that the maximum price an individual is willing to pay for a commodity depends not only on the utility of the commodity itself but "also, in part, on the utility of other commodities; and it depends also, in part, on the quantity of wealth . . . the consumer possesses" (535).

In the terms of the discussion of indirect measurement in section 2.1.5, Walras argued that y (the individual's willingness to pay for a commodity) depends not only on x (the utility of that commodity for the individual) but also on k (the utility of other commodities) and w (the individual's wealth). Therefore, y (willingness to pay) cannot be taken as a reliable indirect measure of x (utility).

10. The as-if-utility-were-measurable case presented in the first edition of *Elements* remained in identical form in the following editions of the book (Walras 1988, 105–107). The argument was also repeated in an article in the *Giornale degli Economisti* (Walras [1876] 1987), in an appendix to the third edition of *Elements* (Walras 1988, 694), in *Théorie de la monnaie* (Walras 1886), and in a number of letters (Jaffé 1965, letters 232, 268, 789). Walras's unit-based understanding of measurement is confirmed by his analysis of the measurement of exchange value in lesson 25 of *Elements* ([1874] 1954, 186–188).

In the second part of the first edition of *Elements*, which was published in September 1877, Walras (1988, 670–671) repeated almost word for word this criticism of Dupuit's utility measure. Jevons seems to have been unimpressed by Walras's argument. He wrote Walras that his "remarks upon the Memoirs of M. Dupuit, shall have my best attention" (Jaffé 1965, 1: 538) but made no specific comment on Walras's points, and in the second edition of his *Theory* (1879, xxx), Jevons credited Dupuit with "the earliest perfect comprehension of the theory of utility." Moreover, Jevons continued to argue that at least in some circumstances, marginal utility is measured by the individual's willingness to pay (158–160).

This exchange between Jevons and Walras reveals different argumentative strategies for addressing the problem of the apparent unmeasurability of utility. While Walras univocally insisted on his epistemological as-if-utility-were-measurable argument, Jevons put forward a wider and more diverse array of arguments. It is also notable that the discussion of willingness to pay as a measure of utility is the only part of the entire correspondence that touches on the issue of utility measurement. That two of the founders of marginal utility analysis did not exchange more ideas about this crucial issue corroborates the claim that they looked at it within a shared conceptual framework, namely the one offered by the unit-based conception of measurement.

2.3.3. Discussion with Laurent and Poincaré on Utility Measurement

In 1900, now sixty-six years old and having almost completed the fourth and (in the event) final edition of *Elements*, Walras was returned to the issue of the measurability of utility by criticisms leveled by Hermann Laurent, a distinguished French mathematician. In an exchange of letters in May 1900 (Jaffé 1965, letters 1452–1456) and in a communication at a 1900 meeting of the Institut des Actuaires Français, Laurent objected that Walras's analysis of demand and exchange was based on the assumption that utility is measurable, an assumption that Laurent denied: "How can one accept that satisfaction is capable of being measured? Never will a mathematician agree to that" (Jaffé 1965, 3: 113). In reply, Walras maintained his earlier stance that his analysis was in fact independent of any actual measurement of utility: "I skip completely the standard of utility and *rareté*" (119).

The issue cropped up again the following year in an exchange of letters between Walras and mathematician, physicist, and philosopher Henri Poincaré. As we saw in chapter 1, section 1.4.1, Poincaré (1893; [1902] 1905) stressed order as the basic property of continuum magnitudes, but he also argued that for magnitudes to be measurable, further conditions such as those indicated by Helmholtz ([1887] 1999) are necessary.

In September 1901, Walras sent to Poincaré, whom he did not know, a copy of the fourth edition of *Elements*. A brief correspondence followed, in the course of which Walras solicited Poincaré's opinion on his as-if treatment of utility measurement. Walras now brought back into play the analogy with the physical sciences advanced in "Principle": "I open Poinsot's *Statics* . . .; I see that he defines the mass of a body as 'the number of molecules composing it.' . . . I notice that, by so doing, he too regards as appreciable a magnitude which is not, given that no one has ever counted the molecules in a body" (Jaffé 1965, 3: 161).[11]

In his reply, Poincaré observed that satisfactions can be ordered but not measured. But he agreed with Walras that the immeasurability of satisfactions does not preclude their mathematical treatment:

> Can satisfaction be measured? I can say that one satisfaction is greater than another . . ., but I cannot say that the first satisfaction is two or three times greater than the other. . . . Satisfaction is therefore a magnitude but not a measurable magnitude. Now, is a non-measurable magnitude *ipso facto* excluded from all mathematical speculation? By no means. (162–163, translation in Jaffé 1977, 304)

Poincaré also pointed out that as satisfactions can only be ordered, the mathematical function expressing them is not unique, and in particular any increasing transformation of the function represents the same sensations equally well. Finally, Poincaré warned that the lack of uniqueness of the function representing satisfactions limits the significance of the results obtained by their mathematical treatment.

Two brief comments on Poincaré's reply are in order. First, his remark about the invariance of the utility function to any increasing transformation recalls the ordinal approach that Pareto ([1898] 1966; [1900] 2008) had recently put forward (see chapter 5). There is no evidence, however, that in September 1901 Poincaré was aware of Pareto's ordinal approach, and his remark appears rather to be related to the German debates about the conditions for measurement and to his own work on the mathematical continuum. More important, in order to argue that satisfactions are not susceptible to measurement, Poincaré claimed that it is impossible to identify their ratios ("I cannot say that the first satisfaction is two or three times greater than the other"). This argument confirms that, as already suggested in chapter 1, Poincaré maintained a unit-based understanding of measurement and thus was, at least in this respect, completely in accord with Walras.

In the final letter of the correspondence, Walras cursorily acknowledged the partial arbitrariness of the utility function but passed over Poincaré's warnings about the significance of the results obtained in an ordinal utility framework and self-servingly interpreted Poincaré's comments as an unreserved statement of support for his own as-if-measurable treatment of marginal utility (Jaffé 1965, 3: 167).

In conclusion, his exchanges with Laurent and Poincaré toward the end of his scientific career did not modify Walras's understanding of measurement or his stance on the measurability of marginal utility as expressed in "Principle" almost thirty years earlier.

2.3.4. Utility Measurement in "Economics and Mechanics"

In 1909, in his last economic article, "Economics and Mechanics," Walras returned to the issue of utility measurement. Walras here compared economics with mechanics and

11. Louis Poinsot was a French mathematician and physicist; Walras refers here to Poinsot 1842. On Poinsot's influence on Walras's thought, see Jaffé 1965, 3: 148–150.

claimed that both investigate quantitative facts using mathematics and arrive at equilibrium conditions that are formally identical. The nature of the facts investigated is, however, different: mechanics studies exterior or physical facts; economics deals with interior or psychological facts, such as need. The main dissimilarity between physical and psychological facts is, in turn, that units and instruments may be used to measure the former but not the latter: "There are meters and centimeters to establish the length of the arms of the steelyard balance, grams and kilograms to ascertain the weight supported by these arms. . . . There are no [instruments] to measure the intensities of need of traders" (Walras [1909] 1990, 212–213). Just as before, Walras claimed that the lack of instruments to measure psychological facts entails no difficulty for economics, but he now developed this argument along three new and different lines.

The first line echoes not only Jevons's idea of the mind balancing pleasures but also the point Poincaré had made in his 1901 letter (published as an appendix to "Economics and Mechanics") and Pareto's ordinal approach to utility.[12] Walras pointed out that at the subjective level, each trader compares the utility of different things and determines that which is greater for him or her. In this sense, although not measurable, utility is at least appreciable: "The *need* which we have for things, or their *utility* for us, is an internal quantitative fact, appreciation of which remains subjective and individual. So be it! Nonetheless it is a magnitude and, I would say, an appreciable magnitude" (207). As in Jevons's mind-as-a-balance argument (the second of the arguments illustrated in section 2.1.3), one may read here the flavor of ordinal utility theory. However, the seventy-five-year-old Walras did not venture into the ordinal approach, and his distinction between appreciable and measurable magnitudes demonstrates that he did not consider comparison to be measurement.

Second, Walras argued that the point of maximum satisfaction for the individual, as well as the point of general equilibrium for the market, is characterized by the equality of marginal utility ratios with price ratios. The circumstance that individuals maximize their utility and markets are in equilibrium would prove, according to Walras, that traders are capable not only of comparing utilities but also of assessing their ratios and therefore of measuring utility: "Each trader . . . decides by himself in his internal theatre if his last needs satisfied are proportional to the values of the commodities. The circumstance that the measure is . . . interior . . . does not prevent it from being a *measure*, that is, a comparison of *quantities and quantitative ratios*" (213). Scholars such as Levasseur and Laurent may well have objected that this argument begs the question, as the derivation of the conditions for utility maximization and market equilibrium seems to depend on the measurability of utility. The important point for us here, however, is simply that Walras's train of reasoning confirms once more that he associated measurement with the assessment of ratios.

The third of Walras's arguments suggests that even the measurement of physical magnitudes may be problematic. In making this point, Walras first quoted from Poinsot's definition of the mass of a body as "the number of molecules contained in it." He then appealed

12. Walras had become aware of Pareto's ordinal approach to utility theory by November 1901. Early in that month, Pareto sent to Walras the summary of three lessons in which he presented his new ordinal approach (Pareto [1901] 1966). Walras commented on Pareto's summary and noted, among other things, the similarity between Pareto's and Poincaré's ordinal insights. See Jaffé 1965, letters 1501, 1502.

once again to the authority of Poincaré, who had now published *Science and Hypothesis* ([1902] 1905), which advanced a conventionalist view of science. Walras noted approvingly Poincaré's conventionalist definition of masses as "co-efficients which it is found convenient to introduce into calculations" (Poincaré [1902] 1905, 103, quoted in Walras [1909] 1990, 213). Walras suggested that utility and *rareté* could be considered in an analogous way, that is, as hypothetical causes to be introduced into the calculations of economics in order to derive the empirical laws of demand, supply, and exchange in a convenient way: he wondered whether "all these concepts, those of *mass* and *force* as well those of *utility* and *rareté*, might not simply be names given to hypothetical causes which should be necessarily and justifiably introduced into the calculations with a view to linking them to their effects" (213). Although now presented in a more sophisticated epistemological dress, the underlying argument is here the same as in "Principle."

A final comment is in order. In the above quoted passage Walras delineates an indirect approach to utility measurement: utility and *rareté* are indirectly quantified through their observable effects on demand and supply. How can we accommodate Walras's indirect approach to measurement with his criticism of willingness to pay as an indirect measure of utility? In fact, there is no contradiction here. Walras did not criticize the indirect measurement of utility per se, as other economists such as Joseph Shield Nicholson (1893; 1894) actually did (see chapter 3). Rather, Walras criticized willingness to pay (y) as an *incorrect* indirect measure of utility (x), because willingness to pay also depends on the utility of other commodities (k) and the individual's wealth (w). Walras seems to suggest that in a correctly specified model, where all the other relevant variables are measurable, utility could indeed be measured indirectly.

2.3.5. Conclusions on Walras

From the first public presentation of his economic theories in 1873, Walras attempted to reconcile his utility analysis with the fact that from the perspective of the unit-based understanding of measurement he shared with his critics, marginal utility appeared unmeasurable. One possible way out of this difficulty would have been to abandon the unit-based notion of measurement. Yet Walras, like his contemporaries, consistently adhered to this notion of measurement. Another possible way out might have been the development of an ordinal approach to utility along the lines suggested by Poincaré and Pareto. However, Walras never explored this path. Walras's actual strategy was to deny the existence of a real conflict between his utility analysis and the unmeasurability of marginal utility by claiming that if one treats marginal utility as if it were measurable, one can derive the empirical laws of demand, supply, and exchange. He maintained this stance from 1873 to 1909.

2.4. WHY JEVONS, MENGER, AND WALRAS WERE NOT CARDINALISTS

In this section I argue that contrary to the canonical narrative of utility theory, Jevons, Menger, and Walras were not cardinalists in the current sense of the term. To make this point, I need a preliminary measurement-theoretic discussion of cardinal utility and other forms of utility.

2.4.1. Ordinal, Cardinal, and Ratio-Scale Utility

In current microeconomic theory, two main forms of utility are used: ordinal and cardinal utility. Both are typically characterized in terms of the mathematical transformations they can be subjected to.

A utility function representing the preferences of an individual is called ordinal if it is unique up to any monotonic increasing transformation. This means that if the utility function $U(x)$ represents the individual's preferences, another utility function $U^*(x) = F[U(x)]$, where F is any increasing function, also represents the individual's preferences.[13] If the function F is differentiable, its increasing pattern is expressed by the fact that F', the first derivative of F, is positive: $F' > 0$.

Using the terminology introduced by Stanley Smith Stevens in the 1940s, which has become standard in measurement theory (see chapter 8), ordinal utility is measurable according to the ordinal scale of measurement. Ordinal-scale measurement preserves the order between the numerical measures of objects. In the case of utility, this means that $U(x) \geq U(y)$ if and only if $F[U(x)] \geq F[U(y)]$, where F is increasing. A number of branches of current microeconomics, such as demand analysis and general equilibrium theory, are based on ordinal utility only.[14]

Cardinal utility is more demanding than ordinal utility. A utility function representing the preferences of an individual is called cardinal if it is unique only up to a subset of the monotonic increasing transformations, namely the linear increasing transformations, or, equivalently, the positive linear transformations.[15] This means that if the utility function $U(x)$ represents the individual's preferences, another utility function $U^*(x)$ obtained by multiplying $U(x)$ by a positive number α and then adding any number β, that is, a transformation $U^*(x) = \alpha U(x) + \beta$, with $\alpha > 0$, also represents the individual's preferences. The arbitrariness of α expresses mathematically the arbitrariness in the choice of the unit of measurement, while the arbitrariness of β corresponds to the arbitrariness of the zero point of measurement. The latter means that the zero-utility point could be either the point corresponding to $x = 0$, so that $U(0) = 0$, as well as the point corresponding to any other value of x, such as $U(100) = 0$.

13. More precisely, the transformation function F should be *strictly* increasing, that is, $F[U(x)] > F[U(y)]$ whenever $U(x) > U(y)$. This prevents the possibility that $U(x) > U(y)$ but $F[U(x)] = F[U(y)]$. For the sake of readability, and since the strictly-increasing requirement is not relevant for our discussion, in what follows I will simply talk of increasing, or monotonic increasing, functions and transformations.

14. See, e.g., Mas-Colell, Whinston, and Green 1995, chaps. 3, 4, 15, and 16.

15. In the economic literature, the positive linear transformations are sometimes called "affine positive transformations." In this book I prefer avoiding the technical term "affine," and stick to more intuitive term "linear."

In Stevens's terminology, cardinal utility is measurable according to an interval scale of measurement. Interval-scale measurement preserves not only the order between the numerical measures of objects but also the order between the differences, or intervals, between those measures. In the case of cardinal utility, this means that: (1) $U(x) \geq U(y)$ if and only if $U^*(x) \geq U^*(y)$; (2) $U(x) - U(y) \geq U(w) - U(z)$ if and only if $U^*(x) - U^*(y) \geq U^*(w) - U^*(z)$, whereby in both cases $U^*(x) = \alpha U(x) + \beta$.[16] It is easy to see that utility differences are not preserved under ordinal utility, that is, it can be the case that $U(x) - U(y) \geq U(w) - U(z)$, while if we only require that F is increasing, $F[U^*(x)] - F[U^*(y)] < F[U^*(w)] - F[U^*(z)]$.[17] Cardinal utility, however, does not preserve everything, and in particular, it does not preserve the value of utility ratios. In fact, $U(x)/U(y)$ is typically different from $[\alpha U(x) + \beta]/[\alpha U(y) + \beta]$. Cardinal utility plays a prominent role in a number of areas of current microeconomics, such as the theory of decisions under risk, game theory, the theory of intertemporal decisions, and welfare analysis.[18]

If ordinal utility is associated with ordinal-scale measurement and cardinal utility is associated with interval-scale measurement, one may conceive of a third form of utility that is associated with ratio-scale measurement, which, for lack of a better term, can be called ratio-scale utility. Ratio-scale utility is more demanding than cardinal utility, since it is unique only up to a subset of the positive linear transformations, namely the proportional transformations. These are the transformations of the form $U^*(x) = \alpha U(x)$, where α is an arbitrary positive scalar whose arbitrariness expresses the arbitrariness of the measurement unit. The parameter β, which in the linear transformations expresses the arbitrariness of the zero point of measurement, has disappeared. This means that in ratio-scale utility, the point of null utility is not arbitrary but is uniquely determined, for example, $U(0) = 0$. Proportional transformations of the utility function preserve the order of utilities, $U(x) \geq U(y)$ if and only if $\alpha U(x) \geq \alpha U(y)$, and the order of utility differences, $U(x) - U(y) \geq U(w) - U(z)$ if and only if $\alpha U(x) - \alpha U(y) \geq \alpha U(w) - \alpha U(z)$. In addition, and unlike the linear transformations, they do not modify the ratios of utilities: $U(x)/U(y) = \alpha U(x)/\alpha U(y)$.

The three different forms of utility and the associated forms of measurement are summarized in table 2.2.

One might think that ratio-scale utility has played no role at all in utility analysis. This is incorrect. For instance, in 1959, R. Duncan Luce advanced a model of choice, the "strict binary utility model," which enjoyed some popularity in economics and psychology in the 1960s and features a utility function unique to proportional transformations (Luce 1959; Luce and Suppes 1965). I contend here that the theories of Jevons, Menger, and

16. To be precise, the order between utility differences is preserved not only by cardinal (i.e., interval-scale) utility but also by a form of utility called ordered-metric utility (Coombs 1950, Siegel 1956). Ordered-metric utility is less restrictive than cardinal utility and more restrictive than ordinal utility, but its characterization in terms of the mathematical transformations is tricky (Krantz, Luce, Suppes, and Tversky 1971, 431). Partly for this reason, ordered-metric utility has played only a minor role in the history of utility theory and therefore can be neglected here.

17. For instance, imagine that $U(1) = 4$, $U(2) = 7$, $U(3) = 9$, $U(4) = 10$. In this case, $U(2) - U(1) = 3$, $U(4) - U(3) = 1$, and therefore $U(2) - U(1) > U(4) - U(3)$. Then take $F(x) = x^4$, which is increasing. Then $F[U(1)] = 256$, $F[U(2)] = 2{,}401$, $F[U(3)] = 6{,}561$, $F[U(4)] = 10{,}000$, and $F[U(1)] - F[U(2)] = 2{,}145 < 3{,}439 = F[U(4)] - F[U(3)]$.

18. See, e.g., Mas-Colell, Whinston, and Green 1995, chaps. 6, 8, 20, 22.

Table 2.2. FORMS OF UTILITY AND FORMS OF MEASUREMENT

Forms of utility	Corresponding forms of measurement	Admissible mathematical transformations	What is preserved
Ordinal utility	Ordinal measurement	Increasing transformations: $U^*(x) = F[U(x)]$, with F increasing	Order between utilities
Cardinal utility	Interval-scale measurement	Positive linear transformations: $U^*(x) = \alpha U(x) + \beta$, with $\alpha > 0$	Order between utilities Order between utility differences
Ratio-scale utility	Ratio-scale measurement	Proportional transformations: $U^*(x) = \alpha U(x)$, with $\alpha > 0$	Order between utilities Order between utility differences Utility ratios

Walras also belong in the ratio-scale utility camp rather than the cardinal utility camp and that recognizing this allows us to better understand the utility theories of the founders of marginalism.

2.4.2. Jevons, Menger, and Walras Belong in the Ratio-Scale Utility Camp

As explained in section 2.4.1, current microeconomic theory uses two main forms of utility: ordinal and cardinal. As chapters 5 and 6 show, this twofold approach is the result of a series of developments in utility analysis that took place in the first half of the twentieth century. However, historians of economic thought appear to have imported this twofold approach from current microeconomics and projected it back onto the history of utility theory, which they have reconstructed in terms of the contrast between ordinal and cardinal views of utility. As a result, the canonical history of utility theory posits a first phase, lasting roughly from 1870 to 1910, in which Jevons, Menger, Walras, and other early marginalists treated individual utility as cardinally measurable. In a second phase, inaugurated by Pareto ([1900] 2008) and virtually concluded by John Hicks's *Value and Capital* (1939b), utility theorists are said to have moved away from cardinalism and embraced an ordinal approach to utility.[19]

This standard story overlooks the fact that Jevons, Menger, and Walras adhered to a unit-based conception of measurement and applied it consistently to the measurement of utility. Accordingly, they focused on the possibility of ascertaining a unit of utility and assessing

19. See, e.g., Schumpeter 1954; Jaffé 1977; Niehans 1990; Ingrao and Israel 1990; Mandler 1999; Giocoli 2003b; and even Moscati 2007b.

utility ratios rather than on the ranking of utility differences as in a cardinal utility approach. Therefore, and contrary to the canonical narrative of the history of utility theory, they were not cardinalists in the current sense of the term.

To put it differently, I suggest that a third form of utility consistent with the unit-based conception of measurement, namely ratio-scale utility, should be added to the traditional dichotomy between cardinal utility and ordinal utility and that the utility theories of Jevons, Menger, and Walras belong in the ratio-scale utility camp rather than the cardinal utility camp.

At issue here is not merely a point of classification. The substantial point is that the traditional cardinal–ordinal dichotomy is conceptually too threadbare and barren to clothe an accurate narrative of the history of utility theory and, more specifically, to illuminate the problem situation that Jevons and Walras in particular were facing. As discussed in the previous sections, both of these economists clearly perceived that the measurability of utility would have made their economic theories scientifically sounder and more defensible against the attacks of their critics and, at the same time, believed that they knew what measurement was: unit-based measurement.

Because of their unit-based understanding of measurement and given the apparent impossibility of identifying a unit of utility and assessing utility ratios, Jevons and Walras believed that the utility featured in their theories was not measurable. Accordingly, their discussions of the measurability of utility and the extent to which their theories actually relied on such measurability largely originated from a tension between their unit-based understanding of measurement and the fact that their scientific practices did not square with it.

2.4.3. Objections and Replies

Let me anticipate and address some possible objections to my claim that Jevons, Menger, and Walras were not cardinalists. First, since the ratio-based measurability of utility entails its cardinal measurability, the approach to utility of the three founders of marginalism is consistent with cardinalism: they were "more than cardinalists" or "hyper-cardinalists"; so the standard narrative of the history of utility theory is fundamentally correct. But I maintain that this interpretation fails to appreciate the specific measurement-theoretic dimension of their utility theories and prevents us from properly understanding their search for utility units and ratios rather than utility differences. It also hinders our appreciation of the main problem they faced: reconciling a unit-based understanding of measurement with their scientific practices.

Second, the three founders of marginal utility theory assumed that the marginal utility of each commodity is diminishing. To modern eyes, this assumption entails that individuals are able to rank variations of their total utility and state that the increment of total utility obtained from the consumption of the nth unit of the good is larger than the increment obtained from the $(n + 1)$th unit; this ranking, however, is none other than the ranking of utility differences that delivers cardinal utility, and thus Jevons, Menger, and Walras were cardinalists. But the three marginalists did not associate diminishing marginal utility with the ranking of variations of total utility. In discussing the measurability of utility, they all referred to unit-based measurement, and they did so with respect to *both* marginal and total utility. Furthermore, and contrary to contemporary microeconomic analysis, for them, the key notion of utility theory was not total but marginal utility. Accordingly, they conceived of the challenge of utility measurement as related to the search for a unit to measure marginal utility, which is a search that goes well beyond current cardinal utility analysis.

Finally, one may claim that in the canonical narrative, the expression *cardinal utility* is used not in its current meaning as connected with rankings of utility differences but in a much vaguer sense that encompasses any form of utility stronger than ordinal utility and hence includes even classically measurable utility. But if in the canonical story, the term *cardinal utility* is used in this vague sense, the pursuit of historical fidelity and conceptual clarification calls for the introduction of a more appropriate conceptual framework, which distinguishes between cardinal utility and ratio-scale utility and upon which may be built a more accurate narrative of the history of utility theory.

In the next chapter, I examine how five spokesmen of the second generation of marginalism—Wieser, Böhm-Bawerk, Edgeworth, Fisher, and Marshall—conceived of utility measurement. Among other things, I argue that these economists also belong in the ratio-scale utility camp rather than the cardinal utility camp.

CHAPTER 3

Still on the Quest for a Unit

Utility Measurement in Wieser, Böhm-Bawerk, Edgeworth, Fisher, and Marshall, 1880–1910

The revolution in economics initiated by Jevons, Menger, and Walras was successful, and in the period 1880–1910, their marginal utility theories were refined and extended by a second generation of marginalists, which included Friedrich von Wieser and Eugen von Böhm-Bawerk in Austria, Francis Ysidro Edgeworth and Alfred Marshall in England, and Irving Fisher in the United States.

In this chapter, I examine, more cursorily than I did for Jevons, Menger, and Walras, how these five eminent economists conceived of measurement and how, based on this conception, they addressed the issue of the measurability of utility. Their respective approaches to utility measurement were highly diverse. Wieser declared that the marginal utilities of goods can only be ranked, but in fact he summed and multiplied these utilities as if they were directly measurable in terms of some unit. Böhm-Bawerk explicitly claimed that individuals can assess utility ratios. Connecting utility theory to psychophysics, Edgeworth suggested the just-perceivable increment of pleasure as a unit to measure utility on the basis of introspection. In explicit opposition to Edgeworth, Fisher proposed adopting a utility unit, which he named the util, that could be derived from observable relations between commodities rather than from unobservable sensations. Finally, Marshall took willingness to pay as an indirect measure of utility. Despite the diversity of their approaches, all these economists identified measurement with unit-based measurement and, accordingly, judged utility to be measurable or unmeasurable according to whether a unit of utility was available or not. Therefore, just like Jevons, Menger, and Walras, these five economists were also not cardinalists in the current sense of the term.

The theories of Wieser, Edgeworth, and especially Fisher present several ordinal insights. However, and again like Jevons, Menger, and Walras, these three marginalists did not develop their insights into a systematic ordinal utility approach like that advanced a few years later by Pareto (see chapter 5).

The time span covered in this chapter ranges from 1881, when Edgeworth published his *Mathematical Psychics*, to 1909, when Böhm-Bawerk began publishing the third edition of *Capital and Interest: The Positive Theory of Capital*. In the final section of the chapter, which is also the final section of part I, I appraise the debates on utility measurement over the entire 1870–1910 period, that is, from Jevons to Marshall, with respect to the five epistemological dimensions of the problem of utility measurement illustrated in the prologue, namely the understanding of measurement, the scope of the utility concept, the status of utility, the data for utility measurement, and the aims of utility theory.

3.1. WIESER AND BÖHM-BAWERK

For more than a decade after the publication of Menger's *Principles*, there was in Austria no public indication that the book had attracted attention.[1] But two fellow students at Vienna University read the work, were struck by the theories expounded in it, and became Menger's first disciples. The two students (who would become brothers-in-law) were Friedrich von Wieser (1851–1926) and Eugen von Böhm-Bawerk (1851–1914).

3.1.1. Wieser and the Sum of Marginal Utilities

In 1884, Wieser published the second important contribution to Austrian marginal utility theory after Menger's *Principles*, a treatise titled *Über den Ursprung und die Hauptgesetze des wirtschaftlichen Werthes* (On the Origin and Fundamental Laws of Economic Value). This work is usually remembered in the history of economics because Wieser here extended Menger's explanation of the value of production factors and introduced into German the term *Grenznutzen*, that is, marginal utility (1884, 128).

With respect to issues concerning the measurability of utility, in *Ursprung*, Wieser took a stance that is ordinal in character. He contrasted the unmeasurability of the psychological phenomena that are at the origin of economic value, such as wants, desires, and interests, with the measurability of economic value itself. By measurement, he understood unit-based measurement: "[Economic] value is not only evaluated, but also measured . . ., that is, value is not only ascribed a magnitude, but the ascribed magnitude is also reduced to a unit, a yardstick, and expressed as a multiple of it" (180). For Wieser, economic value is in practice measured by money.

Wieser argued that the psychological phenomena at the origin of economic value also have a magnitude and, more specifically, an intensity. However, this intensity cannot be directly measured. We can compare the intensities of psychological phenomena, such as interest in goods, possibly even compare the difference between these intensities, but we are not able to measure an intensity, that is, to express it as a multiple of a unit: "We are able to state that the intensities of certain interests are of equal or different magnitude; we can even state whether the difference between the perceived intensity levels is larger or smaller. . . . But

1. On the reception of Menger's work and the rise of the Austrian School, see Howey 1960.

we are not capable of . . . reducing them to a unit; we are not even able to specify how many times one level of interest is stronger than, i.e. a multiple of, another level" (180). In this passage, Wieser talks of "interest" rather than "utility," but from the context of his discussion, it is clear that for him, the intensity of the interest in a good coincides with the marginal utility of the good. Thus, if we pass over for the moment the cursory reference to the comparison of intensity differences (chapters 5 and 6 discuss this type of comparison at length), the passage suggests that Wieser adopted a fundamentally ordinal conception of marginal utility.

However, the solution Wieser gave to the problem of reconciling the unmeasurability of marginal utility with the measurability of economic value shows that, in effect, his ordinal conception was far from consistent. He argued that the economic value W (W stands for *Werth*, i.e., value) of n items of a given good is equal to the number of items, n, multiplied by the marginal utility of the least useful item, indicated as I_1 (I stands for *Intensität*, i.e., intensity). Wieser even expressed this idea in a mathematical formula: "$W = n \times I_1$ or $= I_1 + I_1 + I_1 + I_1 + \ldots$ n times" (196).

Wieser's formula is questionable on several counts and became the subject of an intense discussion among Austrian economists. With regard to the specific issue of utility measurement, the formula is problematic because it requires that the I figures associated with marginal utilities have more than ordinal meaning. For if they were purely ordinal, the economic value of a given quantity of a good could be larger or smaller than the economic value of another quantity, depending on the ordinal magnitude chosen for the I figures.[2] More generally, and as would become clear only much later in the Austrian debates on the measurability of utility, if figures have only an ordinal meaning, their summation and multiplication are meaningless (see chapter 5).

In his subsequent works, notably in *Natural Value* ([1889] 1893, 10–11, 27–32) and *Social Economics* ([1914] 1927, 124–126), Wieser maintained this puzzling approach to issues concerning the measurability of utility. On the one hand, he declared that the marginal utilities of goods can be compared but not measured, and his stance on this point was more explicit than Menger's. On the other hand, he treated marginal utilities just as Menger did: he associated them with numbers and then summed and multiplied these numbers as if they measured utilities directly in terms of some unit of satisfaction.[3]

3.1.2. Böhm-Bawerk's Case for the Measurability of Utility

The other early disciple of Menger was Böhm-Bawerk. In his first two books, Böhm-Bawerk ([1881] 1962; [1884] 1890) dealt only tangentially with marginal utility theory and did not

2. For instance, if the two quantities consist of nine and ten units, and the marginal utilities of the ninth and tenth units are associated, respectively, with figures 6 and 5, then the economic value of nine units ($9 \times 6 = 54$) is larger than the economic values of ten units ($10 \times 5 = 50$). But if the marginal utility numbers are ordinal in nature, the marginal utilities of the ninth and tenth units could also be associated, respectively, with figures 12 and 11. In this case, however, nine units have a smaller economic value ($9 \times 12 = 108$) than ten units ($10 \times 11 = 110$).

3. For more on Wieser's handling of utility measurement in *Natural Value* and *Social Economics*, see Moscati 2015.

discuss issues related to utility measurement. His first important contribution to marginalism was a long two-part article titled "Grundzüge der Theorie des wirtschaftlichen Güterwerts" (Fundamental Elements of the Theory of the Economic Value of Goods), which was published in 1886 in the *Jahrbücher für Nationalökonomie und Statistik*, the leading German economic journal ([1886] 1932). In contrast to Wieser, Böhm-Bawerk explicitly argued in favor of the measurability of utility.

In the first two sections of the article, Böhm-Bawerk presented the theory of marginal utility very much along the lines of Menger and reproduced Menger's table of marginal utilities (25). Then, in the third section, he explicitly addressed the criticism raised by German economist Friedrich Julius Neumann against the claim of the measurability of sensations and desires.[4] Echoing the arguments of the early critics of psychophysics (see chapter 1, section 1.3.2), Neumann (1882) had argued: "It is impossible for me to say that this picture of my father . . . is worth to me 1¼ . . . times as much as the picture of my brother. . . . The totality of the sensations, desires, interests, etc. that are here in question cannot be at all reduced to units, and therefore is not subject to measurement" (quoted in Böhm-Bawerk [1886] 1932, 46).

To Neumann's criticisms, Böhm-Bawerk replied that in the first place, we are at least undoubtedly able to compare different sensations of pleasure and state whether one sensation is stronger or weaker than another. In a passing comment that echoed Wieser, he added that we are also able to compare differences of sensations and judge "whether one sensation of pleasure is considerably or only negligibly stronger than another" (48). Böhm-Bawerk then asked whether we can do even more, namely judge whether one sensation of pleasure is, for example, three times as large as another. His bold answer was: "I definitely believe we can do that" (48).

To make his case, Böhm-Bawerk argued that when we face the alternative between one great pleasure on the one hand and a multiplicity of lesser pleasures on the other, in order to make a decision, it is not sufficient to judge that the first kind of pleasure is greater than the second kind. Indeed, even judging that the first kind of pleasure is considerably greater than the second kind will not do. For Böhm-Bawerk, the decision between those two alternatives requires us to judge "how many times greater the one pleasure is than the other" (48). For example, if a boy has to choose between one apple and six plums, he must judge "whether the pleasure of eating an apple is *more or less six times greater* than the pleasure of eating a plum" (48). Böhm-Bawerk's line of thought has an obvious corollary: if the boy considers as equal the pleasure of eating an apple and the pleasure of eating six plums, then the pleasure of eating the apple is *exactly* six times greater than the pleasure of eating a plum (49–50, n. 2).

I postpone the full discussion of Böhm-Bawerk's argument to chapter 5, where I examine Franz Čuhel's (1907) critique of Böhm-Bawerk's case for the measurability of utility and Böhm-Bawerk's reply to Čuhel ([1909–1912] 1959). Here I mention only that large parts of the 1886 article passed with only minor modifications into Böhm-Bawerk's *Capital and Interest: The Positive Theory of Capital*, the first edition of which appeared in 1889 (English

4. Neumann was an important member of the German Historical School (see chapter 2, footnote 8). Böhm-Bawerk's response to Neumann's criticism can be seen as a minor episode of the *Methodenstreit* slugged out between the rising Austrian School led by Menger and the Historical School led by Schmoller.

translation 1891). The second, unaltered edition of *The Positive Theory* was published in 1902, while the third, two-volume edition, came out from 1909 to 1912 (as we will see in chapter 5, these dates of publication play some role in our narrative). It was especially through *The Positive Theory* that Böhm-Bawerk's confident stance on the measurability of utility came to be known.

3.2. EDGEWORTH'S RELUCTANT HEDONIMETRY

Outside Austria, one important consolidator of marginal utility theory was Francis Ysidro Edgeworth (1845–1926). Edgeworth became interested in economics through his personal acquaintance with Jevons, with whom he used to take long walks on Hampstead Heath in London. Building on Jevons's ideas, in 1881, he published a slender volume titled *Mathematical Psychics: An Essay on the Application of Mathematics to the Moral Sciences.* As the title suggests, Edgeworth followed Jevons in conceiving of economic theory as a calculus of "hedonic forces," that is, pleasure and pain, which investigates the conditions under which pleasure is maximized: "The Economical Calculus investigates the equilibrium of a system of hedonic forces each tending to maximum individual utility" (1881, 15).

3.2.1. Hedonimetry

Among the early utility theorists, Edgeworth was the only one who was influenced by Fechner's psychophysics and the related continental discussion of psychophysical measurement.[5] From a psychophysical point of view, utility can be considered as one sensation among others, namely the sensation of pleasure. As such, Edgeworth suggested, utility could be measured directly just as heaviness, loudness, and other sensations are measured, that is, by using the just-perceivable increment of the sensation of pleasure as a measurement unit: "There remains the objection that in Physical Calculus there is always . . . an expectation, of measurement; while Psychics want the first condition of calculation, *a unit.* The following brief answer is diffidently offered. . . . The unit [of pleasure] is the just perceivable increment" (7; see also 59–60). In particular, for Edgeworth, a pleasure could be measured by the number of just-perceivable increments necessary to obtain it from a zero-level situation with no stimulus (100–101).

Edgeworth labeled the science concerned with the measurement of pleasure "hedonimetry" and for the sake of argument imagined the possibility of constructing a "hedonimeter," an instrument capable of measuring the pleasure of an individual just as physical instruments measure physical magnitudes such as energy: "To precise the ideas, let there be granted to the science of pleasure what is granted to the science of energy; to

5. Some popular histories of economic thought, such as those by Blaug (1997) or Ekelund and Hébert (1990), have claimed that other early marginalists, most notably Jevons, were also influenced by psychophysics. However, this claim is unsubstantiated; see White 1994; Maas 2005; Moscati 2013b. On Edgeworth's approach to utility measurement, see in particular Colander 2007.

imagine an ideally perfect instrument, a psychophysical machine, continually registering the height of pleasure experienced by an individual" (101).

Edgeworth was well aware, however, that the hedonimeter, if conceivable, did not exist and that as a matter fact, "*atoms of pleasure* are not easy to distinguish and discern" (8). He attempted to avoid this difficulty by using the ordinal utility argument already employed by Jevons and other early marginalists, namely that the unit-based measurement of pleasure is in practice superfluous for the economics calculus since it depends on the ranking of pleasures only: "We cannot *count* the golden sands of life; we cannot *number* the 'innumerable smile' of seas of love; but we seem to be capable of observing that there is here a *greater*, there a *less*, multitude of pleasure-units, mass of happiness; and that is enough" (9). However, like Jevons and the other early marginalists, Edgeworth did not develop these ordinal insights into a systematic theory.

3.2.2. From Hedonimetry to Ordinal Numbers

In later writings of the 1880s, Edgeworth (1884; 1887) touched again on utility measurement but without modifying the views on the subject expressed in *Mathematical Psychics.* In his writings of the 1890s, Edgeworth no longer insisted on hedonimetry. In an article published in 1894, he defended Marshall's claim that utility can be measured by money against the criticisms raised by Joseph Shield Nicholson (see section 3.4.3 here). In a footnote in this article (1894, 155 n. 1), Edgeworth referred for the first time to Andreas Voigt's ([1893] 2008) distinction between cardinal and ordinal numbers (see chapter 1, section 1.4.3). In the 1900s, Edgeworth (1900; 1907) mentioned Voigt's distinction two further times to support the idea that the economic calculus depends only on the ranking of utilities and not on their unit-based measurement. For instance, he wrote: "With what unit are they [utilities] measured? . . . Perhaps it is better to say, with Professor A. Voigt, that no unit is required: quantities like utility are to be measured only by *ordinal* numbers" (1907, 222; emphasis added). But again, Edgeworth did not venture into an exploration of the ordinal approach and refrained from investigating whether his "perhaps" could be transformed into an "indeed."

3.3. FISHER AND THE UTIL

The economist before Pareto who advanced most into ordinal territory was American Irving Fisher (1867–1947). Fisher studied at Yale, where he received an interdisciplinary formation in mathematics, physics, and the social sciences. At Yale, his mentors were mathematical physicist Willard Gibbs and political economist and sociologist William Graham Sumner. Following a suggestion by Sumner, Fisher wrote his doctoral dissertation on a topic that was arcane at the time, especially in American universities: mathematical economics. The dissertation was published in 1892 under the title *Mathematical Investigations in the Theory of Value and Prices.*[6]

6. See more on Fisher and his formative years at Yale in Allen 1993; Barber 2005.

In *Mathematical Investigations*, Fisher advanced a number of explicitly ordinal ideas about utility. However, and in contrast to Pareto and other later full-fledged ordinalists, Fisher believed that certain important results of utility analysis depend on the unit-based measurability of utility, and accordingly, he searched for a unit to measure utility.

3.3.1. Economics, Psychology, and Desire

Influenced by his background in mathematics and physics, Fisher conceived of economics as a discipline that aimed to explain "*economic* facts," that is, "the facts of human preference or decision as observed in producing, consuming and exchanging goods and services" (1892, 11). In his view, it is not the economist's province to build a detailed psychological theory; rather, the economist should deal with psychology only insofar as it is useful to explain economic facts. Accordingly, Fisher criticized Edgeworth and Jevons for their psychological definition of economics as a calculus of pleasure and pain: "This foisting of Psychology on Economics seems to me inappropriate and vicious" (vii).

For Fisher, the point of contact between psychology and economics is not the notion of "pleasure" but that of "desire" or, equivalently, "preference." He saw the desire or preference for an object as the direct psychological determinant of economic action. In turn, desire can be generated by different second-level psychological factors, such as pleasure, duty, or fear. But the economist should stop at the first level, that of desire, and leave the investigation of the determinants of desire to the psychologist: "No one ever denied that economic acts have the invariable antecedent, desire. Whether the necessary antecedent of desire is 'pleasure' or whether independently of pleasure it may sometimes be 'duty' or 'fear' concerns a phenomenon in the second remove from the economic act of choice and is completely within the realm of psychology" (11).

3.3.2. Desire and Utility

Fisher reasoned that because of its hereditary connections with Bentham's theory of pleasure and pain, the term *utility* is not the most suitable to denote the key concept of marginal analysis. He argued that the term *desirability* would be "less misleading" (23) but ultimately bowed to established convention and maintained the utilitarian terminology adopted by Jevons and the other marginalists. Nevertheless, Fisher attempted to strip the term *utility* of its hedonic, physiological, and even ethical connotations by defining it in terms of desire.[7]

For Fisher, utility is defined by two main properties: (1) the utility of alternative A exceeds the utility of alternative B if "the individual prefers (has a *desire* for) A to the exclusion of B rather than for B to the exclusion of A" (12); (2) the utility of the two alternatives is equal "if the individual has *no desire* for the one to the exclusion of the other" (12). Properties (1) and

7. In a later article, Fisher (1918) claimed that even the term *desirability* is imprecise because it carries with it a still too strong ethical connotation, and he proposed to replace it with the term *wantability*.

(2), however, only allow us to rank utilities; they do not suffice to make utility a quantity measurable on a ratio scale like physical quantities. In order to arrive at this further level of exactitude, Fisher claimed, we need to identify a unit of utility that enables us to assess utility ratios.

Fisher first argued that this unit cannot be the just-perceivable increment of pleasure suggested by Edgeworth. For Fisher, the unit of utility should be defined in terms of observable relations between commodities rather than unobservable psychological entities:

> Mathematical economists have been taunted with the riddle: What is a unit of pleasure or utility? Edgeworth, following the Physiological Psychologist Fechner, answers: "Just perceivable increments of pleasure are equitable." I have always felt that utility must be capable of a definition which shall connect it with its positive or objective commodity relations. (vii; quotation from Edgeworth 1881, 99)

3.3.3. The Util

Fisher stressed that his method of identifying a unit of utility and, more precisely, a unit of marginal utility works only in the special case where the marginal utility of each commodity does not depend on the quantities of other commodities, that is, in current economic terminology, when the utility function is additively separable or, more concisely, additive.[8] Jevons, Menger, and Walras had more or less explicitly adopted the additive-utility assumption, but Edgeworth (1881) had already argued that such an assumption is problematic because it rules out the interdependence of the utility of goods. Fisher (1892, 64–66) was well aware of the problem and even referred to the definition of complementary and substitute goods recently advanced by Austrian businessmen and economists Rudolf Auspitz and Richard Lieben (1889), which was based on how the marginal utility of one good varies when the quantity of another varies.[9] However, Fisher considered the additivity of the utility function a "necessary first approximation" (1892, 64) and adopted it in part I of *Mathematical Investigations*.[10]

8. This means that the utility U of commodity bundle $(x_1, \ldots, x_n)$ can be expressed as $U(x_1, \ldots, x_n) = \sum_{i=1}^{n} U^i(x_i)$, where U^i is the utility function relative to commodity i. In this case, the marginal utility of commodity i is given by $\partial U / \partial x_i$, which is independent of x_j, for $j \neq i$. This may also be expressed by saying that $\partial^2 U / \partial x_i \partial x_j$, the cross partial derivative of the utility function U, is equal to zero for $j \neq i$.

9. According to Auspitz and Lieben (1889, 482), two goods i and j are complementary if the cross partial derivative of the utility function U is positive, that is, if $\partial^2 U / \partial x_i \partial x_j > 0$, and substitute if $\partial^2 U / \partial x_i \partial x_j < 0$. As discussed in chapters 5 and 6, the Auspitz–Lieben definition of complementarity and substitutability is inconsistent with the ordinal approach to utility analysis, and this circumstance eventually led to its replacement with a different definition in terms of cross demand effects of price changes. On the early history of the definition of complementarity and substitutability, see Stigler 1950.

10. For more on the additive-utility assumption in early utility analysis, see Moscati 2007b.

Fisher contended that under this assumption, the individual's utility can be measured as follows. He imagined an individual who consumes 100 loaves of bread and B gallons of oil per year and assumed that for this individual, the marginal utility of the 100th loaf is equal to the marginal utility of an increment of β gallons over B. In Fisher's notation, U(100th loaf) = U(β). Moreover, Fisher also hypothesized that for the individual, the marginal utility of the 150th loaf equals the marginal utility of an increment of $\beta/2$ gallons over B: U(150th loaf) = U($\beta/2$). Based on the additional but tacit assumption that the marginal utility of $\beta/2$ is half the marginal utility of β, that is, the assumption that U($\beta/2$) = U(β)/2, Fisher concluded that "the utility of the 150th loaf is said to be half the utility of the 100th" (15).[11] In particular, U($\beta/2$) could be taken as the unit of marginal utility, and in this case, U(150th loaf) = 1 and U(100th loaf) = 2.

Fisher also showed that the ratio between U(100th loaf) and U(150th loaf) is independent of the particular commodity employed for the comparison, oil, as well as of the initial quantity of that commodity, B gallons. He therefore concluded that "*the marginal utility of any arbitrarily chosen commodity on the margin of some arbitrarily chosen quantity of that commodity may serve as the unit of utility*. . . . This unit may be named *util*" (18).

3.3.4. When No Util Is Available

In part II of *Mathematical Investigations*, Fisher removed the assumption that the marginal utility of each commodity is independent of the quantities of other commodities. In this more general case, he stressed, his method of measuring utility breaks down. In fact, if the marginal utility of $\beta/2$ gallons of oil changes when the quantity of bread increases from 100 loaves to 150 loaves, then the unit of utility U($\beta/2$) is no longer fixed and can no longer be used to measure the marginal utility of bread. Moreover, if instead of oil, we use another commodity to measure the marginal utility of bread, say milk, and the marginal utility of milk changes differently from the marginal utility of oil when the quantity of bread increases from 100 loaves to 150 loaves, then the ratio U(100th loaf)/U(150th loaf) assumes different numerical values according to whether it is assessed using milk or oil.

When the assumption of additive utility is removed, utilities cease being quantities measurable on a ratio scale and return to being magnitudes that can be ranked only according to properties (1) and (2). Fisher devoted part II of *Mathematical Investigations* to exploring which of the results obtained in part I under the additive-utility assumption hold also when that assumption is removed. In so doing, he anticipated many of the results later obtained by Pareto and other ordinalists (see chapter 5).

In the early 1900s, a number of economists, including Arthur Cecil Pigou (1903) in Cambridge and Joseph Schumpeter (1908) in Vienna, endorsed Fisher's method of measuring utility and argued that it solved the problem of utility measurement. However, in 1912, Ludwig von Mises, another Austrian economist, argued that Fisher's method does not work even if one assumes that utility is additively separable. I discuss Mises's criticism of Fisher in

11. In fact, U(150th loaf) = U($\beta/2$) = U(β)/2, and since U(β) = U(100th loaf), then U(150th loaf) = U(100th loaf)/2.

chapter 5. In the 1920s, Fisher attempted to implement his method of measuring utility by using actual statistical data. However, as we will see in chapter 7, his attempt was not very successful.

3.4. MARSHALL AND WILLINGNESS TO PAY AS A MEASURE OF UTILITY

The last economist considered in this chapter is Alfred Marshall (1842–1924), the founder of the so-called Cambridge School of economics. Among the early utility theorists, Marshall is eccentric in at least two important respects. First, he developed some of his core ideas about the theory of value and markets in the late 1860s and early 1870s, being influenced more by classical economist John Stuart Mill (1848) and French mathematician, philosopher, and economist Antoine Augustin Cournot ([1838] 1897) than by Jevons. In this early phase, Marshall analyzed economic transactions directly in terms of monetary transfers, and the Jevonian utilitarian approach began playing an important role in his theory only from the late 1870s. Second, for Marshall, the study of how market conditions affect the collective welfare of economic agents, what today we call social welfare analysis, was much more important than it was for other early utility theorists. Both these distinctive features of Marshall's economic thought provide important contexts for the approach to utility measurement that he expounded in his magnum opus, *Principles of Economics*, the first edition of which was published in 1890.[12]

3.4.1. Willingness to Pay Measures Utility

Measurement issues enter the economic theory of Marshall's *Principles* from the beginning, for he early defines economics as a science that "deals mainly with just that class of motives which are measurable" (Marshall 1890, 78). The measurability of economic motives makes them amenable to scientific treatment and is said to be the chief reason "economics has been able to get in advance of every other branch of social science" (78). Marshall stressed that the motives behind human actions, including economic actions, are extremely varied: they can be selfish or altruistic, noble or ignoble, material or spiritual, based on wise judgment or on ignorant prejudice. Yet all these diverse motives are measurable if there exists a method capable of "reducing to a common measure the things that must be given to people to induce them to perform or abstain from performing certain actions" (79 n. 1). In modern society, where nearly all transactions are settled by money transfers, the purchasing power represented by money is the best available measure of the force of the diverse motives of human action:

12. On the evolution of Marshall's ideas on utility theory and utility measurement from the early writings to *Principles*, see Aldrich 1996. On Marshall's thought in relation to utility measurement, see Dardi 2008.

> Nearly all actions of life are governed, at least in part, by desires the force of which can be measured by the sacrifice which people are willing to make in order to secure their gratification. . . . In our world [this sacrifice] has nearly always consisted of the transfer of some definite material thing which has been agreed upon as the common medium of exchange, and is called "money." (151)

Adopting a utilitarian terminology, Marshall called the "utility" of a thing to a person the resultant of the various motives for which the person desires the thing (except its price) and argued that the marginal utility of a thing can be indirectly measured by the monetary price the person is willing to pay for an additional unit of the thing: "The desirability or utility of a thing to a person is commonly measured by the money price that he will pay for it" (151). The total utility of a group of things can be calculated by summing the prices the person is just willing to pay for each successive unit of the thing. For instance, if an individual is willing to pay just £10 and no more for a first ton of coal, £7 for the second ton of coal, and £5 for the third ton of coal, the total utility of the first three tons of coal would be measurable by £10 + £7 + £5 = £22 (176).

It is important, as noted already in chapter 2, section 2.1.5, that Marshall implicitly assumes that the relationship between the measurand, that is, utility, and its indirect measure, that is, willingness to pay, is a proportional one, so that the ratio between the amounts of money a person is willing to pay for two things mirrors the ratio between the utilities those things have to the person: "If at any time [a person] is willing to pay a shilling, but no more, to obtain one gratification; and sixpence, but no more, to obtain another; then the utility of the first to him is measured by a shilling, that of the second by sixpence; and the utility of the first is exactly double that of the second" (151). Thus, willingness to pay as a utility measure makes utility measurable in the ratio-scale sense.

Chapter 2 discussed at some length the general problems associated with indirect measurement as well as the specific problems involved in the use of willingness to pay as an indirect measure of utility. In particular, Walras argued that the maximum price y that an individual is willing to pay for a commodity is determined not only by the utility x of the commodity but also by the utility of other commodities available to the individual, as well as by the individual's wealth.

Marshall (55–60) was aware of the problem. But he made two assumptions that neutralize the effects of these disturbing factors: (1) the utility function is additively separable, so that the utility of a commodity does not depend on the availability of other commodities; (2) the marginal utility of money is constant, that is, the marginal utility a person can obtain by spending an additional unit of money, say, an additional shilling, does not depend on the person's wealth. These are strong assumptions, and as we will see in section 3.4.3 and in chapter 5, many of Marshall's contemporaries were not prepared to accept them.

3.4.2. Measuring Social Welfare

Marshall stressed that in order to be truly relevant for economics, the method of measuring economic motives should be applicable not only to the single individual but also to a group of individuals: "We look at the individual, not as a 'psychological atom' but as a member of a social group: and no method of measurement is of any avail which is not generally applicable to the whole of that group" (79 n. 1). For Marshall, the monetary measure does have this capacity. The monetary-based measure of social welfare he proposed is consumers' rent (or consumers' surplus).[13]

Marshall defined the rent of a single consumer as "the excess of price which he would be willing to pay [for a thing] rather than go without it, over that which he actually does pay" (175). In the coal example used above, if the market price of a ton of coal is £5, the cost of three tons of coal is £15. Since an individual is willing to pay £22 for three tons of coal rather than go without it, his consumer's rent is £22 – £15 = £7. Marshall was well aware that because of differences in wealth or sensibility, the same amount of money buys different utilities for different persons. However, he argued that at the aggregate level, these differences average out: "Such differences . . . may generally be neglected when we consider the average of large numbers of people" (152, marginal note). In this case, the rents of different consumers can be summed and the resulting aggregate consumers' rent adopted as an approximate measure of the consumers' happiness or welfare (176–177).

Rather than entering into the enormous debate generated by Marshall's proposal to use consumers' rent as a measure of social welfare, I discuss here some reactions to his idea of using willingness to pay as measure of individual utility.[14]

3.4.3. Nicholson and Edgeworth on Willingness to Pay

In the first volume of his *Principles of Political Economy* (1893) and then in an article published in the *Economic Journal* (1894), English economist Joseph Shield Nicholson attacked Marshall's idea of using willingness to pay as measure of utility on two grounds. In the first place, Nicholson criticized the very idea of measuring utility in an indirect way, that is, through its effects on something that is not utility. To make his case, Nicholson compared the measurement of utility by money to the measurement of warm sensations by the clinical thermometer: "Price is objective, utility is subjective. . . . A clinical thermometer will measure accurately the heat of the body, but it says nothing of the corresponding feeling. A patient may feel feverish with the temperature quite normal, and he may be in high fever and shiver" (1894, 344; see also 1893, 60 n. 1).

Second, Nicholson argued that Marshall's assumptions that the utility of a commodity is independent of the utility of other commodities and that the marginal utility of money is constant are untenable. Accordingly, he judged as misleading the scientific strategy of formulating those assumptions in order to make utility measurable by money: "Can we estimate utility in money without constructing hypotheses which make the problem unreal? . . . [This] seems to me illusory and misleading" (1894, 343; see also 1893, 59).

A rapid reply to Nicholson came from Edgeworth (1894) in another *Economic Journal* article. Concerning Nicholson's first criticism, Edgeworth noted that indirect measures also

13. The idea of consumers' rent can be found also in the works of Dupuit and other economists, but Marshall apparently arrived at it independently. On the history of consumers' rent, see Ekelund and Hébert 1985.

14. On the consumers' rent debate, see Dooley 1983; Ekelund and Hébert 1985.

can be useful. Building on Nicholson's analogy with the thermometer, Edgeworth ironically pointed out that although the thermometer does not measure warm sensations directly, it can be and in fact is frequently used to modify warm sensations: "In the reading-room of the British Museum the temperature is maintained at 65° [Fahrenheit]. . . . I am disposed to think that the comfort of the studious public would be increased if the temperature were reduced from 65° to 60°; judging from the emphatic complaints about the excessive heat which I have heard many readers express" (1894, 155). In an analogous way, Edgeworth continued, willingness to pay and consumers' rent are indirect measures of, respectively, individual utility and social welfare. Their indirect and rough character notwithstanding, they are practically useful, as, for example, in judging which form of taxation is preferable: "Suppose that a tax must be imposed, or a railway rate fixed by Government, and that the amount of Consumers' Rent lost by the tax . . . were estimated to be according to one proposed plan x, and, according to another, x/2; it would be advisable to adopt the latter rather than the former plan. This is a rough, but may be a useful, conclusion" (158).

As for the second of Nicholson's criticisms, Edgeworth basically argued that the assumptions Marshall formulates in order to make individual utility measurable by willingness to pay are acceptable approximations that do not alter the practical usefulness of the monetary measure.

3.4.4. Subsequent Editions of the Principles and Beyond

Marshall himself took some account of the criticisms of willingness to pay as a measure of utility advanced by Nicholson and other economists, such as Simon Nelson Patten (1893a; 1893b), and in the third edition of *Principles* (1895), he rewrote many of the passages devoted to utility measurement. Marshall now stated more carefully the assumptions under which utility is measured by money and expunged some of the more contentious passages of the first edition, such as the claim that if a person is willing to pay a shilling for a gratification and sixpence for another, then the utility of the first gratification is exactly double that of the second. Marshall replied directly to Nicholson only in footnotes (1895, 203 n. 1, 208 n. 1) and referred the reader to Edgeworth's 1894 paper and other articles (Barone 1894; Sanger 1895) for more extended discussions.

The 1895 restyling notwithstanding, it is fair to say that Marshall's substantial position about the possibility of measuring utility by willingness to pay remained that of the first edition of *Principles* and actually the one he had held since the late 1870s. Subsequent editions of *Principles* suggest no change of mind.[15] Thus, in the edition of 1920, the eighth and final edition of the book published in his lifetime, we still find passages such as the following: "Desires cannot be measured directly, but only indirectly by the outward phenomena to which they give rise: and that in those cases with which economics is chiefly concerned the measure is found in the price which a person is willing to pay for the fulfilment or satisfaction of his desire" ([1920] 1961, 92).

15. On the substantial stability of Marshall's ideas on utility measurement, see in particular Aldrich 1996.

For our purposes, the economic-theoretic question of whether Marshall was "right or wrong" is not relevant. What is important is rather to emphasize the following two points. First, the reconstruction of Marshall's approach to the measurability of utility shows that when he thought of measurement, he thought of unit-based measurement. Thus, despite Marshall's eccentricity with respect to the other utility theorists considered so far, his general understanding of measurement was exactly like theirs.

Second, Marshall's *Principles* was immensely influential in the English-speaking academic world at least until the 1930s. For the many economists who in Cambridge, Chicago, and elsewhere endorsed Marshall's money-based approach to utility measurement, the issue of the measurability of utility ceased to be an urgent problem. Nevertheless, other economists, such as Pareto in Lausanne and Mises in Vienna, rejected the thesis that willingness to pay provides an acceptable measure of utility. For them, the problem of the measurability of utility remained an open one, and, as discussed in chapter 5, the solution they eventually advanced involved the adoption of an ordinal conception of utility.

3.5. EPISTEMOLOGICAL ANALYSIS

This final section of part I reviews the debates of the period 1870–1910 with respect to the five epistemological dimensions of the problem of utility measurement illustrated in the prologue to the book.

3.5.1. The Understanding of Measurement

The first dimension concerns the forms of quantitative assessment of utility considered as actual measurement in the period 1870–1910. In chapter 2, we saw that Jevons, Menger, and Walras identified measurement with unit-based measurement and that, accordingly, they searched for a unit of utility that could be used to assess utility ratios. In this chapter, we saw that the same holds for Wieser, Böhm-Bawerk, Edgeworth, Fisher, and Marshall: they, too, judged utility measurable or unmeasurable according to whether a unit of utility was available or not, and, accordingly, they also embarked on a quest for a utility unit. Therefore, we may also conclude that, like Jevons, Menger, and Walras, Wieser, Böhm-Bawerk, Edgeworth, Fisher, and Marshall were also not cardinalists in the current sense of the term. They all belonged to what I have called the ratio-scale utility camp rather than, as usually assumed in histories of utility theory, the cardinal utility camp.

As in the case of the three founders of marginalism, at issue here is not merely a point of classification. The substantial point is that the category of cardinal utility, which is associated with interval-scale measurement rather than ratio-scale measurement, prevents us from properly understanding the fact that Wieser, Böhm-Bawerk, Edgeworth, Fisher, and Marshall looked for utility units rather than utility differences. It also hinders our appreciation of the main problem they faced: reconciling the difficulty of measuring utility in the unit-based sense with the conviction that at least part of their economic theories relied on the unit-based measurability of utility.

It would be possible to show that other utility theorists active in the period 1870–1910, such as Philip Wicksteed, Knut Wicksell, and Maffeo Pantaleoni, were also not cardinalists. However, I will not embark on this exercise, because it would add little to the picture we already have. Rather, I will confine my attention to showing, in chapter 6, just when cardinal utility did actually enter utility analysis, an event that occurred not in the last decades of the nineteenth century but in the 1930s.

3.5.2. The Scope of the Utility Concept

The second epistemological dimension of the utility-measurement problem is concerned with how broadly the concept of utility is defined and how the scope of the utility concept affects the approach to utility measurement. We saw that Jevons and Menger gave a relatively narrow definition of utility. Jevons identified it with low-level pleasures, while Menger associated utility with the capacity of a thing to satisfy some human need. Walras and, more explicitly, Fisher and Marshall gave a broader definition of utility, basically identifying it with whatever satisfies a desire, any desire, selfish or altruistic, material or spiritual, moral or immoral, healthy or unhealthy.

To a significant extent, this broadening of the notion of utility was a response to those who criticized economic analysis in general and utility analysis in particular for dealing with an idealized and potentially unrealistic "economic man"—the notorious *homo economicus*—who pays no heed to others and is not only selfish but focused purely on his material well-being at the expense of any social, ethical, or religious motivations. As one nineteenth-century critic put it, economics would deal "with imaginary men—'economic men' . . . conceived as simply 'money-making animals' " (Ingram 1888, 224).[16]

The strategy of broadening the notion of utility to avoid the criticism that it is too narrow to capture all possible motivations to human action is effective, but it comes at a cost. The price paid is that the notion of utility loses its intuitive psychological content and becomes a black box containing all possible motives to action. Adopting the terminology introduced by Daniel Hausman (2012), I call this all-encompassing utility notion "utility-all-things-considered."[17] Jevons's low-level pleasures and Menger's needs probably do not allow us to explain all human actions, but pleasures and needs are familiar concepts, and we understand what they refer to, at least on the level of common-sense psychology. When, in contrast, utility becomes utility-all-things-considered, it is difficult to identify a clear psychological correlate for it.

This cost affects the approach to utility measurement. If utility-all-things-considered does not have any clear psychological correlate, it becomes more problematic to invoke

16. John Kells Ingram (1823–1907) was a member of the English Historical School, which, like its German counterpart (see chapter 2, footnote 8), advocated an inductive approach to economic analysis and criticized the allegedly too abstract method of both classical political economy and marginal utility theory. For more on the history of *homo economicus* and its detractors, see Viner 1925; Persky 1995; Morgan 2006.

17. While I find Hausman's terminology effective, I find his philosophical analysis of the notion of preference problematic. For a critical discussion of the latter, see Moscati 2012; Lehtinen 2013.

psychological introspection to measure it in a direct way. For instance, even if we admit that an individual is capable of identifying introspectively just-perceivable increments of pleasure or need, it is much more difficult to imagine that he or she can also identify just-perceivable increments of utility-all-things-considered. As chapters 5 and 6 show, introspection might work even with an all-encompassing concept of utility. However, the kind of introspective judgments that appear plausible in this case are just ranking judgments, which are much simpler than those involving the identification of just-perceivable increments of utility.

3.5.3. The Status of Utility

The third issue regards the epistemological status of utility and its measures. For the purpose of our narrative, we can focus on two main views, which I call the mentalist view and the instrumentalist view of utility. According to the mentalist view, the concept of utility refers to some existing mental entity, which can be defined more or less broadly and can be located at different levels, such as the mind or, as in current neuroeconomics (see the epilogue), the brain. Jevons, Menger, Wieser, Böhm-Bawerk, Edgeworth, Fisher, and Marshall all adhered to a mentalist view of utility, this despite the fact that they associated utility with different mental entities, such as pleasure, need, and desire.

In the instrumentalist interpretation, utility is seen as a purely theoretical construct that has proven useful for describing or predicting some important economic phenomena but does not necessarily have any actual correlate in the mind. Among the early utility theorists, only Walras appears to have adopted the instrumentalist view. As illustrated in chapter 2, under the influence of Poincaré's philosophy of science, Walras ([1909] 1990, 213) advanced an instrumentalist interpretation of utility, according to which it is a "hypothetical cause" that is introduced into the calculations of economics in order to derive the empirical laws of demand, supply, and exchange in a convenient way.

The interpretation of the epistemological status of utility affects the approach to its measurement. In a mentalist perspective, utility can be measured either directly, as, for example, Edgeworth suggested, or indirectly, as Marshall proposed. In the instrumentalist view, by contrast, utility can be measured only indirectly, that is, as the numerical value that solves the equation or the model representing the economic phenomenon at issue. For instance, if the model states that the utility U of a commodity is linked with two observable variables, such as the commodity's price p and the individual's monetary income m, by a known functional relationship G, that is, $p = G(U, m)$, and if data about the values of p and m are available, then the measure of utility is the numerical value of U that solves the equation $p = G(U, m)$ given the values of p and m. As part III shows, in the 1950s, this instrumentalist interpretation of utility gained momentum among utility theorists.

3.5.4. The Data for Utility Measurement

The fourth dimension of the problem of utility measurement concerns which kind of data can be legitimately used to measure utility. The early marginalists tended to focus on introspective psychological data, but they also admitted market data. Psychological data can be used either as direct measures of utility, as in the case of Menger's marginal utilities or Edgeworth's just-perceivable increments of pleasure, or as a means to measure utility indirectly, as in Marshall's willingness to pay (unlike market price, willingness to pay is a psychological datum). In contrast, market data, such as Jevons's market prices or Walras's demand and supply data, only allow for an indirect measurement of utility.

As discussed in chapters 2 and 3, the indirect measurement of utility, independently of whether the data for it come from introspection or market records, raises a number of problems. Generally speaking, in indirect measurement, we want to infer the magnitude of object x, which is not directly observable, from the magnitude of another object y, which is observable and allegedly linked to x by some functional relationship F: $y = F(x)$. A first problem is that we may be uncertain about the exact functional form of the relationship F between x and y. Second, and more generally, we may be unsure whether y is influenced only by x or also by other factors k, z, . . . so that the actual functional relationship between y and x has the form $y = G(x, k, z, \ldots)$. The problem now is not only that we may be uncertain about the exact functional form of G but also that some of the variables k, z, . . . may be as unobservable as x. This is the case, for instance, if y, the willingness to pay for a certain commodity, depends not only on the utility x of that commodity but also on the utility k of some other commodity or on our subjective beliefs z about the likelihood that a certain event will occur.

3.5.5. The Aims of Utility Theory

Like most of economic theory, utility theory has multiple scientific aims, which can be sketched as follows.[18] A first aim is the explanation of observed economic phenomena, that is, answering why questions such as "Why is the price of diamonds typically higher than the price of water?" "Why does the demand for commodities typically, but not always, decrease when their prices increase?" or "Why do individuals of all income levels buy insurance?" A second aim is to provide a valid description of the observed economic phenomena, in the sense that the theory aims at fitting the available data. In principle, descriptive validity is independent of explanation, for a theory can describe well how things or individuals behave without explaining why they do so. A third aim is the prediction of phenomena not yet observed, such as the prediction of the consequences of an increase in the price of a commodity on the demand for that commodity. Following Milton Friedman's influential essay on "The Methodology of Positive Economics" (1953b), until some years ago, the explanatory, descriptive (in the fitting-the-data sense), and predictive aims of economic theory were usually collected under the label *positive economics*. This latter expression, however, has somehow fallen out of use, and in current parlance, these three goals are collectively labeled the *descriptive* aims of economics.

The descriptive aims of utility theory are usually contrasted with its *normative* aims, such as evaluation, advice, and intervention. With respect to evaluation, utility theory identifies the optimal conduct of an individual as the conduct that maximizes his or her utility. Accordingly, utility theorists evaluate a given conduct as optimal or, as they began to express

18. For a more sophisticated discussion, see Reiss 2013.

it in the 1950s, rational if it maximizes utility. Based on this idea, utility theory can also advise individuals on how they should behave, namely that they should act to maximize their utility. Finally, if a given economic situation, such as a given allocation of resources, does not maximize the utility of one or more individuals, then utility theory may suggest how to intervene and improve things.

The economists considered in part I focused on the explanation of economic phenomena, such as exchange value, price, demand, supply, and market equilibrium, while paying little attention to data fitting or prediction. Marshall was also interested in evaluation and to some extent policy intervention but at the level of social welfare rather than individual utility.

With respect to issues concerning utility measurement, there is a significant difference between description and prediction on the one side and explanation on the other. In fact, utility theory can be descriptively or predictively valid even if utility is measured only indirectly. Consider the simple case in which we assume that there exists a certain relationship F between the utility U, which is not directly measurable, and a measurable variable, say, price p: $p = F(U)$. Based on the available data on p, we can measure indirectly certain values of U and claim that the model $p = F(U)$ provides a fitting description of the phenomenon at issue. Using the indirect measures of U so obtained, we can then predict some still unobserved values of p, that is, some prices. If when prices are eventually observed, we find that the predictions of the model $p = F(U)$ are correct, we can claim that it is valid from a predictive viewpoint. This description-and-prediction exercise is sometimes called "the calibration of the model."[19] Notably, model calibration is independent of the interpretation of the epistemological status of utility. That is, the calibration exercise can be carried out independently of whether one is mentalist or instrumentalist about utility (see section 3.5.3).

For explanation, however, things are more complex. If we argue that utility explains price, we cannot measure utility only by price without ending up in a circular argument. That is, we cannot claim that the market price of diamonds is 100 *because* their utility is, say, 200 and pretend at the same time to gauge the utility of diamonds at 200 on the basis of the fact that their market price is 100. As seen in chapter 2, this was in fact the criticism of Jevons's utility theory advanced by John Elliott Cairnes ([1872] 1981, 150): "What we come to is this—exchange-value depends upon utility, and utility is measured and can only be known by exchange-value."

One way out of this circularity would consist of showing that a very simple, non-unit-based form of utility measurement is possible and that it is sufficient to explain prices. This is the kind of solution associated with the ordinal approach to utility analysis. As mentioned in chapters 2 and 3, many early utility theorists—Jevons, Menger, Walras, Wieser, Böhm-Bawerk, Edgeworth, and Fisher—adumbrated this approach, but none of them developed it in a systematic way. Part II shows that ordinal utility theory was worked out by Pareto in the 1900s and subsequently elaborated in the 1930s by a new generation of economists.

19. See, e.g., Rabin 2000; Safra and Segal 2008.

PART TWO

Ordinal and Cardinal Utility and Early Empirical Measurements of Utility, 1900–1945

CHAPTER 4

Fundamental Measurement, Sensation Differences, and the British Controversy on Psychological Measurement, 1910–1940

Like chapter 1, this chapter broadens the narrative beyond utility measurement. The chapter reconstructs the discussions of measurement that took place in physics, philosophy, and psychology between 1910 and 1940, that is, during the period that in utility analysis is associated with the ordinal revolution. In physics and philosophy, the most influential discussion of measurement was presented by Cambridge physicist and philosopher of science Norman Robert Campbell (1920). Campbell articulated a theory of fundamental and derived measurement that ultimately maintained the identification of measurement with a ratio-scale or, equivalently, unit-based measurement. But in this period, psychologists such as William Brown and Godfrey Thomson (1921) in England and Louis Leon Thurstone (1927a, 1927b) in the United States argued that some of their quantification techniques were capable of delivering unit-based measurement of sensations. Physicists denied this, and the resulting clash of views generated a controversy that engaged British physicists and psychologists from 1932 to 1940. The controversy ended in deadlock, with physicists and psychologists unable to find agreement on the meaning and the conditions of measurement.

4.1. MEASUREMENT IN PHILOSOPHY AND PHYSICS

In his treatise *Physics: The Elements*, Campbell (1880–1949) advanced a novel and broad definition of measurement according to which measurement is associated with the existence of a relationship between objects and numbers, rather than with the existence of a unit: "Measurement is the process of assigning numbers to represent properties"

(1920, 267).[1] However, for Campbell, this process is applicable to some properties (e.g., weight) but not to others (e.g., color). In order to be measurable, in fact, properties must possess certain features that characterize numbers.

4.1.1. Campbell's Fundamental Measurement

The first condition for measurement is the existence of a complete and transitive relation R that places the properties to be measured in an order relationship (1920, 270–274). Following Helmholtz's empiricist approach to measurement (see chapter 1, section 1.4.1), Campbell argued that the existence of the relation R should be verified by experiment. For instance, in the case of weight, the existence of the complete and transitive relation *heavier than* is experimentally verified by placing two bodies on the opposite pans of a beam balance and observing how the balance swings. In the case of the hardness of minerals, the experiment becomes the scratch test suggested by German geologist Friedrich Mohs: if one mineral scratches another, the former is harder than the latter. For density, the experiment is the floating test: body a is denser than body b if there is liquid in which b floats and a sinks. For temperature, the experiment is the expansion test: body a is warmer than body b if the mercury contained in a bulb expands more when the bulb is brought into contact with a than it does with b. For colors, however, there exists no complete ordering relation; relations such as *redder than* are transitive but incomplete, because some colors are neither redder nor less red than others (272–273).

However, the possession of order alone is not sufficient for measurement. For Campbell, measurement requires a second Helmholtzian condition, namely the existence of a physical process of connection of the properties to be measured analogous to numerical addition (282–290). In particular, the physical process of connection should be such that the sum is greater than the summands ($a + b > a$ and $a + b > b$), and it should satisfy the commutative law ($a + b = b + a$) as well as the associative law ($[a + b] + c = a + [b + c]$). Campbell called the properties satisfying the conditions of order and additivity "fundamentally measurable," because, he argued, these conditions make it possible to measure the properties directly, that is, independently of the measurement of other properties. As we will see, fundamental measurement is in fact only a particular form of direct measurement.

According to Campbell's notion of fundamental measurement, weight is fundamentally measurable, because two bodies can be physically added by putting them in the same pan of the balance, and this physical addition satisfies the commutative and associative laws as well as the sum-greater-than-summands requirement. In contrast, hardness, density, and temperature are not fundamentally measurable, at least at present, because currently there exists no physical process of addition satisfying the required conditions.

1. Bertrand Russell (1903, 158) had given an analogous definition of measurement but had done little with it. On Russell's measurement theory, see Michell 1999.

4.1.2. Back to Ratio-Scale Measurement

Campbell then showed that if a process of measuring a property in a fundamental way can be found, then the assignment of numbers to represent the property has only "one arbitrary element, namely the choice of the unit" (290). Therefore, and despite his initial broad definition of measurement as the process of assigning numbers to represent properties, Campbell eventually returned to the traditional conception of unit-based measurement. His fundamental measurement is a particular form of direct measurement, namely ratio-scale measurement.

4.1.3. Campbell's Derived Measurement

A final element of Campbell's theory of measurement worth noting is his theory of "derived measurement" (275–277). Some properties, such as the density of liquids mentioned above, are not fundamentally measurable, because there does not exist for them any physical process of addition satisfying the required conditions (sum greater than summands, commutative and associative laws). However, if these properties can be expressed in terms of other fundamentally measurable properties, they become measurable in a derived way.

For instance, the weight and volume of a liquid are both measurable in a fundamental sense, and the ratio of weight to volume of a liquid is experimentally found to be independent of the volume considered. In particular, this ratio is 0.79 for alcohol, 1.0 for water, and 13.6 for mercury. Moreover, the order of these ratios happens to be the same as the order of densities assessed through the floating test (alcohol floats on water, which in turns floats on mercury). The weight/volume ratio can be taken therefore as a derived measure of the density of liquids.

For Campbell, temperature had become measurable in a derived way in the nineteenth century. This happened when temperature was related to the fundamentally measurable thermodynamic properties of gases, as in the Kelvin scale. In contrast, the Celsius and Fahrenheit scales do not provide derived measurement of temperature and are, according to Campbell, "the relics of the arbitrary system of measuring temperature (a system as arbitrary as Mohs' scale of hardness) which prevailed before modern conceptions of temperature were developed" (397).

Campbell's distinction between fundamental and derived measurement is a particular case of the more general distinction between direct and indirect measurement discussed here in chapters 2 and 3. A fundamentally measurable magnitude is a magnitude that is (1) directly measurable and, moreover, (2) measurable in a ratio sense. A magnitude derivatively measurable in Campbell's sense is a magnitude that (1) is indirectly measurable, (2) has a well-defined functional relationship with one or more directly measurable magnitudes (density, for instance, is defined as the ratio between weight and volume), and (3) is measurable in a ratio sense.

In the 1920s, Campbell reiterated his theory of measurement in two books: *What Is Science?* (1921), a popular introduction to science, and *An Account of the Principles of*

Measurement and Calculation (1928), the authoritative text on the theory of measurement throughout the 1930s and 1940s.

4.1.4. Nagel and Cohen

In 1931, American philosopher Ernest Nagel published an article on "Measurement" in *Erkenntnis*, the journal of the rising logical-positivist movement in philosophy. The article was part of the dissertation on the logic of measurement that Nagel defended in 1931 to obtain his Ph.D. in philosophy from Columbia University.

Nagel's theory of measurement is based on Campbell's. Like Campbell, Nagel initially gave a broad definition of measurement as "the correlation with numbers of entities which are not numbers" (1931, 313) but then focused on fundamental, that is, ratio-scale, measurement. One notable aspect of Nagel's contribution is that he rediscovered the article in which, in 1901, German mathematician Otto Hölder had provided an axiomatic treatment of ratio-scale measurability (see chapter 1, section 1.4.1). In particular, Nagel framed Campbell's conditions for fundamental measurement in terms of a set of axioms that he derived, with some modifications, from Hölder's set of axioms (Nagel 1931, 315).

In 1934, Nagel and his philosophical mentor, Morris R. Cohen, published *An Introduction to Logic and Scientific Method*, a textbook containing an entire chapter on measurement in which Cohen and Nagel reframed Campbell's theory of fundamental measurement in terms of the Kantian distinction between intensive and extensive qualities (see chapter 1, section 1.1). The textbook became very influential in Anglo-American philosophy of science between the mid-1930s and the mid-1950s.

4.1.5. Measurement in Philosophy and Physics: Summing Up

To conclude this section, I remark once again that the conception of measurement developed by Campbell, Nagel, and Cohen in the 1920s and 1930s is substantially analogous to the traditional, unit-based view of measurement expounded by Helmholtz in 1887 and Hölder in 1901. More than these German mathematicians had done, however, Campbell, Nagel, and Cohen emphasized the connection between (fundamental) measurability and the possibility of adding magnitudes. Accordingly, in philosophy and physics, additivity came to be viewed as the hallmark of measurability.

4.2. MEASUREMENT IN PSYCHOLOGY

As mentioned in chapter 1, in the debate on psychophysical measurement, Delboeuf (1875; 1878; 1883), Wundt (1880), and other psychologists had backed the idea that their quantification practices could deliver some form of sensation measurement by bringing into play the differences of sensations. In particular, Delboeuf (1878) and other psychologists had found that when individuals are presented with two sensations, such as two shades of gray or two sounds, and are asked to identify a third sensation that lies halfway between the first two, they are able to respond, and their responses are consistent under a number of circumstances. Analogously, individuals often appear capable of judging whether the difference in brightness, loudness, or warmness between two objects is larger or smaller than the sensation difference generated by two other objects. However, in the period 1870–1910 considered in chapter 1, issues surrounding the measurability of sensation differences remained unsettled, which prompted further debate after 1910.

4.2.1. Brown and Measurement through Sensation Differences

An early important occasion for discussion was a symposium on the topic "Are the Intensity Differences of Sensations Quantitative?" at a meeting of the British Psychological Society held in London in 1913. Contributing to the symposium were philosopher G. Dawes Hicks and psychologists Charles S. Myers, Henry J. Watt, and William Brown, the last of whom had recently published a textbook on *The Essentials of Mental Measurement* (1911).

All contributors agreed that the intensities of sensations can be ranked but not measured in the unit-based sense, so that it is impossible to say that a sensation is two or three times more intense than another. The contributors also agreed that differences of sensations are not merely qualitative in nature, as claimed, for example, by Bergson (see chapter 1, section 1.3.2), but are magnitudes that can also be ranked.

Brown went a little further. He identified certain conditions for measurement and argued that if some of these conditions are not fulfilled, the attribute does not necessarily become unmeasurable, for "there may be different kinds of measurement, of different degrees of completeness" (1913, 185). In particular, for Brown, the assessment of sensation differences satisfies at least certain conditions for measurement, and therefore sensation differences are measurable, albeit only in an imperfect form.

In 1921, Brown coauthored a second edition of his textbook on mental measurement with psychologist Godfrey Thomson. The two authors now suggested that if we can rank all orders of sensation differences, that is, differences of sensations, differences of sensation differences, and so on indefinitely, then we reach something that is "almost indistinguishable from, if indeed it be not identical with, true measurement" (Brown and Thomson 1921, 11–12), where by "true measurement" they meant unit-based measurement. Brown and Thomson called this form of "almost-true" measurement "grading." While they acknowledged that the grading of sensations is difficult in practice, they argued that the very fact that grading is in principle possible, and that grading is as accurate as unit-based measurement, shows that there is no fundamental difference between the psychological measurement of sensations and physical measurement.

4.2.2. Thurstone's Method of Comparative Judgment

Thurstone (1887–1955) was a pivotal figure in experimental psychology in North America from the early 1920s through the mid-1950s. From 1924 to 1952, he was a professor at the University of Chicago, where in the early 1930s, he established the Psychometric Laboratory. He made important contributions to the development of psychometric techniques and the study of intelligence.[2] In particular, in 1927, he put forward a probabilistic method of measuring sensations known as the "method of comparative judgment."

In Thurstone's approach, a subject is confronted with pairs of stimuli, for example, pairs of lights, and asked to compare them with respect to some dimension, such as brightness. Because of judgment errors, distraction, and variation in sensibility, the subject's comparative judgment "is not fixed. It fluctuates" (1927a, 274). As a consequence, when confronted more than once with the same pair of stimuli *a* and *b*, sometimes the subject will rank *a* over *b* and sometimes *b* over *a*. Thurstone used the frequency of the comparative judgments to rank, in the first place, the stimuli: the light perceived as brighter more than 50 percent of the time is taken to be brighter. Second, he used the frequency of the comparative judgments to rank the differences between the stimuli: if 60 percent of the time light *a* is perceived as brighter than light *b*, while 80 percent of the time light *c* is perceived as brighter than light *d*, then the difference between *c* and *d* is taken to be larger than the difference between *a* and *b*.

Based on the frequency of comparative judgments on multiple pairs of stimuli, Thurstone claimed that it is possible to construct a well-defined scale for brightness and other sensations and even to identify a unit of measurement for the scale, which he called the "standard discriminal error" (1927b). Thurstone's claim, however, depends on a number of demanding statistical assumptions about the probabilistic process generating the comparative judgments. These assumptions notwithstanding, since the late 1920s, his method of comparative judgment has been extensively used in experimental psychology.

As we will see in chapter 13, in the 1950s, Thurstone's probabilistic approach to measurement was used in an important experiment to measure utility. In the 1930s, Thurstone also performed an experiment to elicit the indifference curves of an individual, which is discussed in chapter 7.

4.2.3. Measurement in Psychology: Summing Up

Brown, Thomson, and Thurstone were still driven by the unit-based understanding of measurement. They attempted to show that, at least in principle (in the case of grading) or under some additional assumptions (in the case of comparative judgments), their psychometric quantification techniques allowed the identification of a measurement unit or were as accurate as if such a unit had been identified.

However, the incompatibility between the unit-based conception of measurement and the psychologists' quantification practices became apparent in a controversy that engaged British physicists and British psychologists from 1932 to 1940.

2. See more on Thurstone's life and research in Jones 1998.

4.3. THE BRITISH CONTROVERSY OVER PSYCHOLOGICAL MEASUREMENT

At the meeting of the British Association for the Advancement of Science held in York in 1932, the Mathematical and Physical Sciences Section and the Psychology Section of the association organized a joint session on psychological measurement. Since the contributing physicists and psychologists were unable to reach agreement on the issue of whether sensations are measurable, a special committee of physicists and psychologists was appointed to address the question. The committee was chaired by physicist Allan Ferguson and included Norman Robert Campbell and psychologist William Brown. For eight years, the nineteen members of the Ferguson committee met and exchanged correspondence, but they were ultimately unable to reach consensus on the possibility of measuring sensations and, more generally, on the very meaning of the term *measurement*. The committee produced an interim report in 1938 and a final report in 1940, which we will examine shortly.

4.3.1. Campbell versus Richardson

From 1932 to 1938, the confrontation between British physicists and psychologists on the measurability of sensations was carried out also in other arenas. In a talk on vision held at Imperial College in London, Lewis Fry Richardson ([1932] 1993), a meteorologist, psychologist, and member of the Ferguson committee, illustrated different methods of measuring the sensations of hue and brightness. Richardson referred to Campbell's classification of measurable magnitudes into fundamentally measurable and derivatively measurable and acknowledged that sensations are not measurable in Campbell's fundamental sense because they cannot be added.

For Richardson, however, this did not mean that sensations are unmeasurable but only that they either are derivatively measurable or, as he believed, they belong "to some more primitive type of magnitude which has hitherto escaped classification" (Richardson [1932] 1993, 213). In other words, Richardson found Campbell's twofold classification of measurable magnitudes too restrictive to account for psychological measurement.

In an article published in 1933 in the *Proceedings of the Physical Society*, Campbell criticized the methods of measuring visual sensations illustrated by Richardson and rejected the latter's reservations about his own theory of measurement. For Campbell, Richardson's suggestion that there exists a third category of measurable magnitudes beyond those of fundamentally and derivatively measurable magnitudes was misleading: "Nothing but confusion and error can result from using 'measurement' in any but its accepted sense. I call nothing measurement that does not possess the distinctive features of the processes physicists accept as measurement" (Campbell 1933, 589).

Campbell acknowledged that the psychologists' methods of assessing sensations "give more than order" but denied "that they give enough more to constitute measurement" (589). He also discussed the possibility of measuring sensations by ranking all orders of sensation differences, that is, by the grading method suggested by Brown and Thomson (1921). Campbell agreed that if all orders of sensation differences could be ranked, sensations would be measurable. However, he believed that in practice, it is not possible to rank higher orders of sensation differences: "As a matter of fact, we can rarely, if ever, order any differences higher than the first or second" (571).

As we will see in chapter 6, from the 1900s, Vilfredo Pareto and other economists began to consider the possibility that individuals are able to rank differences of utility, and in the 1930s, the ranking of utility differences played an important role in the emergence of the modern notion of cardinal utility. However, before the 1950s, the debate on the ranking of utility differences in economics and the debate on the ranking of sensation differences in psychology did not intersect. In particular, the utility theorists of the 1930s do not mention Brown and Thomson's grading method or Campbell's critical appraisal of it.

4.3.2. The Ferguson Committee's Reports

As noted earlier, in 1938, the Ferguson committee published an interim report that basically gave an account of the disagreement between the physicists and the psychologists over the measurability of sensations. The most extended contribution to the interim report was written by physicist John Guild.

Referring explicitly to Campbell's theory of measurement, Guild argued that the intensity of sensations is neither fundamentally nor derivatively measurable and therefore is not measurable at all (Ferguson et al. 1938, 296–328). In his reply to Guild within the report, Richardson reiterated the point he had made in 1932, namely that although fundamentally and derivatively measurable magnitudes may be "the only sorts of magnitude which are respectable in practical physics" (329), this does not mean that in psychology and other nonphysical disciplines there exist no other types of measurable magnitudes.

For his part, Brown believed that Guild's argument did not touch on the measurability of sensation differences. He found "nothing in Mr. Guild's argument that would move me to withdraw anything that I have written on this matter in Chapter I of *The Essentials of Mental Measurement*"; in other words, he recanted nothing from his argument that the grading of sensation differences allows, at least in principle, the measurement of sensations as though by means of a unit (330). The interim report testifies that no progress had been made in the discussion.

Nevertheless, the Ferguson committee asked for a final extension of its term "to consider whether the views put forward are, or are not, irreconcilable" (Ferguson et al. 1940, 332). Attempting at least to locate some common ground for discussion, in its concluding report, the Ferguson committee chose to focus on a concrete example of sensory scale. This was the scale of loudness proposed by two Harvard scientists, physiologist Hallowell Davis and experimental psychologist Stanley Smith Stevens, in *Hearing: Its Psychology and Physiology* (1938). But the physicists and the psychologists were unable to agree on whether Davis and Stevens's scale succeeded in measuring loudness, and fundamentally, they remained at odds regarding what was even meant by measurement.

On the one hand, Kenneth J. W. Craik, Richardson, and other psychologists wanted to widen the physical definition of measurement so as to include the quantification practices of experimental psychology. For example, Craik claimed that we should find "a definition of measurement which fits its use in other sciences [such as psychophysics]. . . . It is important not to base the definition of measurement only on the most stringent instances, such as length" (Ferguson et al. 1940, 343). On the other hand, Campbell, Guild, and other physicists stuck to the physical definition of measurement based on the possibility of adding magnitudes and argued that any different use of the term *measurement* generates confusion and error. Thus, in his contribution to the final report of the Ferguson committee, Campbell expressed his condemnation of the psychologists' scientific practices in a way worth quoting at length:

> Having found that individual sensations have an order, they [some psychologists] assume that they are measurable. Having travestied physical measurement in order to justify that assumption, they assume that their sensation intensities will be related to stimuli by a numerical law. And having thus established these laws which, if they mean anything, are certainly false, they hope by the study of them to arrive at far-reaching theories. (347)

In introducing the committee's final report, Ferguson had to admit that the physicists and the psychologists had been unable to find a common viewpoint on the meaning of and conditions for measurement: "No practicable amount of discussion would enable [us] to express an agreed opinion concerning these views" (334).

In chapter 8, we will see how Stevens broke this impasse by advancing a theory of measurement that was based on Campbell's definition of measurement as the process of assigning numbers to objects yet was broad enough to include the psychologists' quantification practices as measurement.

We now return to the history of utility measurement, where the period 1910–1940 is characterized by the rise of the ordinal approach to utility. As we will see, the ordinal approach provided a solution to the problem of the measurability of utility that did not require any reconceptualization of measurement. The period 1910–1940 is also characterized by the emergence of the notion of cardinal utility, which, as mentioned earlier, was initially associated with the idea that utility differences can be ranked.

CHAPTER 5
Ordinal Utility
Pareto and the Austrians, 1900–1915

In the history of utility theory, the period from around 1900 to 1940 is associated with the so-called ordinal revolution, inaugurated by Vilfredo Pareto ([1900] 2008; [1906/1909] 2014) and virtually concluded by John Hicks's *Value and Capital* (1939b). As pointed out in chapters 2 and 3, the idea that utility theory may work even if we assume only that individuals are able to order combinations of goods had been suggested already by Jevons, Walras, and other early utility theorists. In *Mathematical Investigations* (1892), Irving Fisher advanced considerably into ordinal territory. Building on Fisher's work, in his *Manual of Political Economy* ([1906/1909] 2014), Pareto showed that the main results of demand and equilibrium analysis can be obtained also in an ordinal utility framework and are therefore independent of the measurability of utility. He was the first to do so.

While Pareto's utility analysis was highly innovative, his understanding of measurement remained the traditional one: he maintained the identification of measurement with unit-based measurement. Accordingly, for him, ordinal utility was not a form of utility measurable on a measurement scale weaker than the ratio scale but, more simply, unmeasurable utility. In section 5.1, I review Pareto's ordinal approach to utility with a focus on its measurement aspects.

Around the same time Pareto's *Manual* was published, an important debate on the measurability of utility was taking place in Austria between Franz Čuhel, a Czech scholar little known in the history of economics; Eugen von Böhm-Bawerk; and Ludwig von Mises. Čuhel (1907) and Mises ([1912] 1953) rejected Böhm-Bawerk's idea that it is possible to identify a unit to measure utility, and, independently of Pareto, they both advocated an ordinal approach to utility. Especially through Mises's influence, the ordinal approach to utility rose to prominence among Austrian economists after World War I. Sections 5.2 through 5.4 reconstruct the Austrian path to ordinal utility and discuss the differences between the Austrian and Paretian approaches.

As we will see, the fundamental notion of Pareto's ordinal theory is that of preference, not utility. Pareto conceived of utility as a numerical index that expresses the preexisting preference relations between commodities. From a Paretian viewpoint, therefore, the actual measurand is preference, while the utility number is only a measure of preference. In section 5.5, I explain why I deem it convenient to continue to use "utility measurement" (rather than "preference measurement") to refer to the general topic of this book.

5.1. PARETO BETWEEN MEASURABLE AND UNMEASURABLE UTILITY

Vilfredo Pareto (1848–1923) was an Italian engineer who, around 1890, became interested in economic theory through his acquaintance with marginalist economist Maffeo Pantaleoni and, in 1893, succeeded Walras at the University of Lausanne when the latter retired. Unlike Walras, but similar to Fisher, Pareto was basically a positivist who saw economics as an empirical science that aimed at explaining economic facts.[1]

5.1.1. The Measurability of Utility in Pareto's Early Writings

In his main works of the 1890s, Pareto extended and made mathematically precise several results of previous utility theory, but his general approach remained very much in line with that of the other early marginalists. Notably, like Walras, Jevons, and Edgeworth, Pareto also understood measurement in the unit-based sense. For instance, in his first important work, *Considerations on the Fundamental Principles of Pure Political Economy*, Pareto ([1892–1893] 2007, 56) wrote that one main difficulty in measuring marginal utility is "choosing the units" of measurement. He added, however, that this difficulty is not specific to utility measurement, for "one faces it every time one wants to measure economic goods."

In *Considerations* (58) and even more clearly in *Cours d'économie politique* (1896), his second major work, Pareto distinguished between the practical difficulty of measuring utility and the fact that as a quantity, utility is in principle measurable. Thus, Pareto argued: "the utility of a thing for a given man . . . has degrees; it is . . . a quantity. We should not confuse two quite distinct issues: the issue of the existence of a quantity, and the issue concerning the practical means to measure it" (1896, 8). To clarify this distinction, Pareto drew an analogy between utility and the distances of the stars from the earth. Astronomical distances are certainly quantities, but many of them, just like utility, have not been measured. As we will see, Pareto maintained this position about the measurability of utility—that utility is measurable in principle but not in practice—even in his later writings.

5.1.2. Eureka!

Given his unit-based understanding of measurement, Pareto in the 1890s faced a problem analogous to that faced by Jevons, Walras, and the other early marginalists some years earlier,

1. See more on Pareto's methodological views in Marchionatti and Gambino 1997; Bruni and Guala 2001; Bruni 2002.

namely how to reconcile the practical impossibility of measuring utility in a unit-based sense with the conviction that at least part of his theory relied on the measurability of utility. By late 1898, however, Pareto had begun exploring the possibility that the main results of demand and equilibrium analysis are in fact independent of utility measurement. More precisely, he worked out the hypothesis that these results draw from the single assumption that individuals are able to compare combinations of goods and state whether they prefer one combination to another or are indifferent between them.[2]

In 1900, Pareto published a first outline of his ordinal approach in a lengthy, two-part article in the *Giornale degli Economisti* titled "Summary of Some Chapters of a New Treatise on Pure Economics" ([1900] 2008). Concerning the issue of the measurability of utility, and with a clear reference to his theoretical approach before 1898, he wrote:

> When, in order to establish the fundamental equations of pure economics, we start from the notion of pleasure and of its measurement, we come up against an insurmountable difficulty right from the start: there is no practical means of measuring this pleasure directly. We have just seen that such measurement is superfluous for attaining our end, which is the determination of economic equilibrium. (477)

The new treatise announced in the title of "Summary" was published in Italian in 1906 as *Manual of Political Economy*. In 1909, Pareto published a French edition of the book, which included a significantly enlarged mathematical appendix ([1906/1909] 2014). Eventually, from around 1910 onward, the French edition of *Manual*, with its mathematical appendix, became the standard point of reference for the ordinal approach to utility analysis.[3]

5.1.3. Preferences Are Primary

The primary notions of Pareto's ordinal approach are those of preference and indifference rather than utility. As already mentioned, Pareto assumed that individuals are always able to compare two combinations of goods and state which they prefer or, alternatively, to state that they are indifferent between them.

In two ways, Pareto's preferences are analogous to Fisher's desires (see chapter 3, section 3.3.1). First, for Pareto, a given preference ranking can express any type of taste: selfish, altruistic, or even masochistic, healthy or unhealthy, material or spiritual. In this sense, Pareto observed, we can say that "an ascetic *prefers* ten strokes to the good dinner" ([1900] 2008, 457) or that an addict prefers morphine to the absence of morphine even though the drug is harmful to him ([1906/1909] 2014, 78).

2. See, in particular, Pareto [1898] 1966, the correspondence with French mathematician Hermann Laurent of January 1899 (Businо 1989, letters 224–227), and Pareto's famous letter to Pantaleoni of December 28, 1899 (De Rosa 1960, letter 438). For a reconstruction of the evolution of Pareto's thought from 1898 to 1900, see Bruni 2002.

3. Pareto's ordinal approach has been widely discussed in the literature. See, among others, Chipman 1976; Mandler 1999; Bruni and Montesano 2009; Hands 2010; and the editorial notes to Pareto [1906/1909] 2014.

Second, like Fisher, Pareto was uninterested in the many different psychological factors, such as pleasure, duty, and fear, that may determine preference. For him, only preference—the final outcome of a potentially quite complex psychological process of evaluation—is relevant for economic analysis. Thus, in "Summary," he wrote: "Here all psychological analysis is eliminated; the *reasons* for the preference or the indifference no longer interest us" ([1900] 2008, 454). In a similar vein, Pareto argued in his *Manual* that when the economist has a complete picture of an individual's preferences and indifferences, the individual himself, that is, the evaluations and psychological processes that determined his preferences, "may disappear" ([1906/1909] 2014, 84).

As Jean Baccelli (2016, chap. 1) rightly points out, this does not mean that Pareto was, in the terminology adopted in the present book, an instrumentalist about preferences. On the contrary, like Jevons and Fisher, Pareto was a mentalist about preferences and conceived of them as an existing psychological entity. Preferences are, for Pareto, ontologically similar to the astronomical distances between stars: preferences belong to the psychological realm, while astronomical distances belong to the physical realm, but they are both existing entities that cannot be practically measured on a unit-based scale, at least at present.

5.1.4. From Preferences to Utility Indices

Pareto took from Fisher also the idea that the concept of utility, or, as Pareto called it, ophelimity, is derived from the primitive concept of preference. Pareto defined utility as an index that represents the preference ranking of an individual and is introduced into economic analysis only for practical reasons, that is, because it makes it "much easier to set forth the theory of economic equilibrium" ([1906/1909] 2014, 79).

Notably, Pareto's utility index refers to total, not marginal, utility, where marginal utility is defined as the mathematical derivative of the total utility index. In Pareto's approach, in effect, the concept of marginal utility loses the centrality it had in early utility theories such as those of Jevons, Menger, and Walras. While in these earlier theories, marginal utility was the key notion "upon which the whole Theory of Economy will be found to turn" (Jevons 1871, 61), in Pareto's approach, it is a third-tier concept, in the sense that marginal utility is obtained from total utility, which, in turn, is obtained from preference.

Returning to the (total) utility index, for Pareto, it should satisfy only the two properties already suggested by Fisher: if the individual is indifferent between two combinations of goods, these must both be associated with the same utility index, and if the individual prefers one combination over another, a larger index should be attached to the former: "Let us attach to each of these combinations an index which must satisfy the following two conditions, and which is otherwise arbitrary: (1) two combinations with respect to which choice is indifferent must have the same index; (2) of two combinations, the one which is preferred to the other must have a larger index" ([1906/1909] 2014, 83).[4] Pareto's choice of "index [*indice*] of utility" rather than, say, "measure of utility" appears to depend on his

4. In fact, in order to obtain a unique and well-behaved solution to the equilibrium problem, Pareto assumed that preferences, and thus the utility indices representing them, have two further properties, namely convexity and nonsatiation. For a discussion of the problems associated with the

unit-based understanding of measurement. After his ordinal turn, Pareto in his *Manual* continued to identify measurement with unit-based measurement (see, e.g., [1906/1909] 2014, 78–79, 312–313). According to this conception, ordinal utility is unmeasurable, and therefore the numbers associated with preferences cannot be labeled as measures of utility but only as indices of utility. Correspondingly, in the special case where utility is measurable on a unit base (see section 5.1.6), Pareto talked of "measure of pleasure" rather than "index of pleasure" (313).

5.1.5. Indifferences Curves and Hills of Pleasure

Each utility index is associated with an indifference curve, which is a line connecting all the combinations of goods among which the individual is indifferent. Preferred combinations correspond to higher indifference curves, to which, in turn, are attached larger utility indices.

Pareto compared the indifference lines to the contour lines that in the topographical representation of a hill or a mountain indicate the common height above sea level of all points on the same curve. To make the topographical analogy more vivid, he referred to "the hill of pleasure or of ophelimity" ([1906/1909] 2014, 84). But there is a major difference between the utility numbers associated with indifference lines and the altitude numbers associated with topographical contour lines: while the altitude numbers are unique up to a proportional factor corresponding to the choice of the unit (e.g., meter or yard), the utility numbers must only preserve the order of the indifference lines (higher indifference curve, larger number) but for the rest are totally arbitrary.

Accordingly, in a metaphorical walk on the hill of pleasure, the hiker knows when the path ascends, descends, or maintains the same height (this happens, respectively, when the hiker moves from one combination of goods to a more preferred, less preferred, or indifferent combination). But the hiker does not know exactly how much he or she ascends or descends or, if the path is flat, what is its height. Pareto noticed that if utility could be measured as height is measured, we would have this type of information. Luckily, however, this information is not necessary to determine which is the highest point on a given path, that is, to determine which is the combination of goods the individual will choose.

In the mathematical appendix to *Manual*, Pareto (310) also gave a mathematical characterization of the arbitrariness of the utility indices: they are unique up to any monotonic increasing transformation F; if U is a set of utility indices representing the individual's preferences, also the set $U^* = F(U)$, with $F' > 0$, represents the individual's preferences.

5.1.6. Two Cases of Measurable Utility

As mentioned here in chapter 4, the Mohs scale orders the hardness of minerals according to their ability to scratch each other: if one mineral scratches another, the former is harder

assumptions of convexity and nonsatiation in Pareto's theory, see Ranchetti 1998; Moscati 2007b. On how convexity is relevant for measurement issues, see chapter 6, sections 6.2 and 6.7.

than the latter and is assigned a higher number in the scale. According to Pareto's view, preferences are measurable the way minerals are measurable in the Mohs scale, that is, only on an ordinal scale, at least given the current state of knowledge and technology.

In *Manual*, Pareto cursorily suggested, and quickly discarded, two special cases in which utility is measurable on a unit-based scale. In the first case, the utility of each commodity is independent of the quantities of other commodities. This is the additively-separable-utility case already considered by Fisher (see chapter 3, section 3.3.3). Pareto argued that in this situation, the marginal utility of any commodity can be taken as a unit, and the marginal utility of the other commodities can be expressed as a multiple number of that unit (78–79, 312–313).[5] He called such a number a "measure of pleasure," rather than an "index of pleasure" (313), confirming his steadfast unit-based understanding of measurement. Like Fisher, however, Pareto discarded the hypothesis of additively separable utilities as farfetched, and therefore rejected also the possibility of measuring utility by the method suggested by Fisher.

The second case of measurable utility is based on a suggestion similar to that advanced in the 1880s by Wieser and Böhm-Bawerk (see chapter 3, section 3.1), namely that individuals might be able to rank transitions among different combinations of goods. More precisely, Pareto (132–133) argued that utility is measurable when individuals (1) are able to rank combinations of goods, (2) are also capable of ranking transitions from one combination to another, and (3) are also capable of stating that a given transition is equally or twice as preferable to another.

For Pareto, assumption (2) is in accord with the idea of diminishing marginal utility and appeared plausible, at least for adjacent transitions. In particular, he claimed that this assumption restricts the arbitrariness of the utility index to those increasing transformations that display the following additional property: "If more pleasure is experienced in passing from [combination] I to [combination] II than in passing from II to III, the difference between the indices of I and II should be greater than the difference between the indices of II and III" (133). However, Pareto did not provide a mathematical characterization of how this property restricts the set of admissible transformations of utility indices. It should also be noted that in the passage just quoted, Pareto takes for granted that the ranking of transitions from one combination to another implies the ranking of the differences between the utility indices associated with the combinations. As became clear only much later (see chapter 6), this implicit supposition is unwarranted.

With respect to assumption (3), Pareto deemed it highly unrealistic, and so, in the end, for him, utility remained unmeasurable.

5.1.7. Diminishing Marginal Utility and Other Open Problems

To conclude our discussion of Pareto, we turn to some problems he left open. As subsequent utility theorists remarked, in his *Manual*, Pareto frequently referred to notions that are not invariant to increasing transformations of the utility index and are therefore inconsistent

5. For a more detailed discussion of Pareto's measurement procedure, see Montesano 2006.

with the ordinal approach to utility. The most important of these notions is the one at the core of early utility theories, namely that marginal utility is diminishing. To see why, consider the following example.

An individual prefers three apples to two apples and prefers two apples to one apple. The utility index U representing this preferences should then satisfy the following property: U(3 apples) > U(2 apples) > U(1 apple); for brevity, U(3) > U(2) > U(1). For instance, it could be that U(3) = 6, U(2) = 5, and U(1) = 3. In this case, the marginal utility of the apples is diminishing: the marginal utility of the first apple is 3 – 0 = 3, the marginal utility of the second apple is 5 – 3 = 2, and the marginal utility of the third apple is 6 – 5 = 1. But U is unique up to any monotonic increasing transformation, so that, for instance, also $U^* = U^4$ represents the individual's preferences regarding apples: U*(1) = 81, U*(2) = 625, and U*(3) = 1,296, and in fact U*(3) > U*(2) > U*(1). However, the marginal utility of the apples is now increasing: the marginal utility of the first apple is 81 – 0 = 81, the marginal utility of the second apple is 625 – 81 = 544, and the marginal utility of the third apple is 1,296 – 625 = 671.[6]

The notion of diminishing marginal utility is not the only one used by early utility theorists that is not invariant to increasing transformations of the utility index, and it is therefore inconsistent with the ordinal approach. In particular, the traditional definition of complementary and substitute goods, introduced by Auspitz and Lieben (1889), adopted by most early utility theorists, and based on how the marginal utility of one good varies when the quantity of another varies, also suffers from the same problem.[7]

Pareto was probably well aware of these restrictive implications of the ordinal approach. However, when he required diminishing marginal utility or the traditional definition of complementarity for considerations going beyond pure equilibrium analysis, he simply used these traditional notions. More generally, he did not address the problem of clarifying which notions of earlier utility theory had to be abandoned in passing to an ordinal framework or what could be put in their place.[8]

The Paretians of the 1920s and early 1930s attempted to save the notion of diminishing marginal utility and the traditional definition of complementarity in a more sophisticated way, namely by referring to the possibility that individuals can also rank transitions among different combinations of goods. I discuss these developments in chapter 6. For now, we move to Vienna, where, around the same time that Pareto's *Manual* was published, an important debate on the measurability of utility was taking place between Franz Čuhel, Eugen von Böhm-Bawerk, and Ludwig von Mises. This debate is important for our narrative because it

6. More formally, let $U(x_1, \ldots, x_n)$ be the utility function, and denote U_i the first-order partial derivative of U with respect to x_i and U_{ii} the second-order partial derivative of U with respect to x_i. The principle of diminishing marginal utility implies that $U_{ii} < 0$. Consider now an increasing transformation F(U) of U with $F' > 0$. The second-order partial derivative of F(U) is $F' \times U_{ii} + F'' \times (U_i)^2$. Now, even if $U_{ii} < 0$, if $F'' \times (U_i)^2$ is large enough, $F' \times U_{ii} + F'' \times (U_i)^2$ can be positive.

7. As discussed in chapter 3, section 3.3.3, according to the Auspitz–Lieben definition, two goods i and j are complementary if the cross-partial second-order derivative of the utility function U is positive, that is, if $U_{ij} > 0$, and substitute if $U_{ij} < 0$. If we consider an increasing transformation F(U) of U with $F' > 0$, the second-order cross-partial derivative of F(U) is $F' \times U_{ij} + F'' \times U_iU_j$, whose sign can be different from that of U_{ij}.

8. For a discussion of this aspect of Pareto's economic thought, see Bruni and Guala 2001.

paved the way to the ordinal approach in Austria, although, and as we shall see, the Austrian version of ordinalism was somewhat different from Pareto's.

5.2. ČUHEL: HOW DIMINISHING MARGINAL UTILITY PREVENTS UTILITY MEASUREMENT

As observed in chapter 3, section 3.1.2, Böhm-Bawerk ([1886] 1932; [1889] 1891) had claimed that it is possible to assess how many times one pleasure is greater than another. To make his point, he used the example of a boy who has to choose between one apple and six plums, and he argued that in order to make this choice, the boy must judge "whether the pleasure of eating an apple is *more or less six times greater* than the pleasure of eating a plum" ([1886] 1932, 48). By criticizing Böhm-Bawerk's stance on the measurability of utility, Čuhel, a Czech scholar little known in the history of economics, set in motion a discussion that paved the way to ordinalism in Austria.

5.2.1. Introducing Čuhel

Čuhel (1862–1914) studied law in Vienna and then Prague in the 1880s and after graduation became a clerk in the Prague Chamber of Commerce.[9] In 1903, he retired and devoted himself to research. He moved back to Vienna and participated in the famous economics seminar that Böhm-Bawerk began running at Vienna University in 1905.[10] In 1907, Čuhel published *Zur Lehre von den Bedürfnissen* (On the Theory of Needs), his only book. In his introduction, Čuhel thanked Böhm-Bawerk for having supported the publication of the volume and Menger for helpful suggestions. Unfortunately, the book was not sufficient to secure Čuhel an academic position, and in 1908, he returned to administrative work in Vienna.

In *Zur Lehre*, Čuhel undertook a painstaking analysis of the concept of need, which he deemed fundamental to economics in general and to marginal utility theory in particular. He distinguished no fewer than twenty-nine different types of need, and introduced a rich new terminology to name them. He also proposed that *utility* be replaced by the allegedly more precise technical term *egence* (*Egenz*). As Čuhel himself acknowledged, his fundamental investigations were conducted in the region of psychology and belonged to economics only to a minor degree. For our purposes here, the relevant part of Čuhel's *Zur Lehre* is its sixth chapter, in which he addressed the issue of the measurability of egences, that is, utilities.[11]

9. See more on Čuhel's biography in Hudik 2007. Note that prior to World War I, the Czech territories were part of the Austro-Hungarian Empire.

10. On the importance of Böhm-Bawerk's seminar in the history of the Austrian School of economics, see Mises [1978] 2009.

11. For an overview of Čuhel's book, see Mussey 1909 and the summary written by Čuhel [1907] 2007. Only chapter 6 of *Zur Lehre* has been translated into English; see Čuhel [1907] 1994.

5.2.2. The Distortion Effects of Diminishing Marginal Utility

In the first place, Čuhel distinguished between "comparing" and "measuring" magnitudes. In comparing two magnitudes, he argued, it is sufficient to state which of them is larger, "but the amount by which it is larger is not ascertained in the comparison" ([1907] 1994, 313). For measuring, more is required, namely finding "a number which indicates how many times a magnitude accepted as a unit is contained in the magnitude to be measured" (313). Thus, Čuhel also adhered to the unit-based conception of measurement.

Having made this preliminary distinction, Čuhel moved to the question of whether the utilities of goods can be not only compared, which he took as self-evident, but also measured. He answered that in principle, an ideal unit of utility could be conceived of and that utilities therefore could be expressed as multiples of this ideal unit. In practice, however, the measurement of utility is impossible because of the distortion effects induced by the law of diminishing marginal utility, which, especially for the Austrian marginalists, was the fundamental law of marginal analysis.

To illustrate the issue, Čuhel considered Böhm-Bawerk's example involving apples and plums and imagined that for a particular individual, the utility of one apple is equal to the utility of six plums. If the utilities of all plums were identical, one could take the utility of any plum as a unit and state that the utility of one apple is six times the utility of a plum. But because of the law of diminishing marginal utility, the utilities of the six plums are *not* identical but are precisely diminishing: U(1st plum) > U(2nd plum) > . . . > U(6th plum). Moreover, we have no idea about how much larger the utility of each plum is compared with the utility of the following plum in the series. Therefore, according to Čuhel, the only thing we can state is that the utility of one apple is equal to the *sum* of the utility of the first plum, the utility of the second plum, and so on: U(1 apple) = U(1st plum) + . . . + U(6th plum). By this, however, we are not expressing the utility of the apple as a multiple of some unit; that is, we are not measuring the apple's utility (315–316).[12]

5.2.3. Against Böhm-Bawerk

Given Čuhel's views on the measurability of utility, it is clear why he criticized Böhm-Bawerk's stance on the subject. Böhm-Bawerk had argued that in order to decide between one apple and six plums, an individual would need to judge how many times greater the pleasure of eating the apple is than the pleasure of eating one plum. Čuhel replied that the

12. One may imagine avoiding the distortion effects of diminishing marginal utility by taking as a yardstick for measurement the utility of single units of different goods. With single units, in fact, diminishing marginal utility does not enter the picture. Thus, if we find that the utility of one apple is equal to the utility of a combination of other goods, say, one plum, one orange, and one cup of tea, it might appear, Čuhel argued, that the utility of the apple is three times the utility of each of those items. However, with different goods, another distortion effect enters the scene, namely the complementarity or substitutability relationships between them, which also modifies, and in a way not precisely determinable, the utility units. See Čuhel [1907] 1994, 317–318.

individual only needs to judge whether the first kind of pleasure is larger or smaller than the *sum* of the six smaller pleasures, and to make *this* judgment, knowledge of how many times larger is the pleasure of eating the apple than the pleasure of eating the *n*th plum is "completely superfluous" (320).

Analogously, if the individual is indifferent between one apple and six plums, this does not mean that the pleasure of eating one apple is exactly six times greater than the pleasure of eating a plum. In fact, the law of diminishing marginal utility modifies the pleasure we obtain from eating the successive plum units and therefore prevents us from expressing the pleasure of eating the apple as a multiple of the pleasure of eating a plum.

5.2.4. Against Cassel and Willingness to Pay

In his book, Čuhel also briefly criticized the version of the idea of measuring utility by willingness to pay advanced by Swedish economist Gustav Cassel. Like Marshall, whom Čuhel did not discuss, Cassel (1899, 397) had argued that if an individual is willing to pay at most 10 marks for a certain good and at most 20 marks for another good, then for him, the utility of the second good is twice the utility of the first good.

Čuhel ([1907] 1994, 327) insisted that Cassel's inference is unwarranted. In the situation described by Cassel, we are only entitled to say that the utility of the first good is equal to the utility of 10 marks and that the utility of the second good equals the utility of the 20 marks. This, however, tells us nothing about the ratio between these two utilities.

As discussed in chapter 3, section 3.4.1, Marshall avoided this problem by tacitly assuming a proportional relationship between the utility of a good and the willingness to pay for it. Apparently, Cassel made the same tacit assumption. For Čuhel, this assumption was unwarranted.

5.2.5. Čuhel versus Pareto, Marginal Utility versus Total Utility

Although Čuhel made an explicit and extensive case for ordinal utility, he did not mention Pareto. This is probably because Čuhel (1907, viii) finished his book in October 1906, while the Italian edition of Pareto's *Manual* was published only a few months earlier. It is useful to point out some major differences between Čuhel's and Pareto's approaches to ordinal utility and utility measurement.

First of all, while Pareto connected ordinal utility to demand and equilibrium analysis, Čuhel did not. Pareto was interested not in ordinal utility per se but in showing that the main results of demand and equilibrium theory do not depend on the measurability of utility. Čuhel's discussion of utility measurement, in contrast, remained fundamentally in the field of psychology. His lack of interest in a systematic exploration of the implications of an ordinal conception of utility on demand and equilibrium analysis is a characteristic not only of Čuhel's ordinalism but of Austrian ordinalism in general.

A second major difference is that for Čuhel, as for the other early Austrian economists, the basic concept of utility analysis remained that of marginal utility. In contrast, and as discussed in section 5.1 earlier, Pareto started directly with preferences and total utility. As a consequence, in Pareto's approach, the issue discussed by Böhm-Bawerk and Čuhel—"How can the boy decide between one apple and six plums?"—is no longer a problem, as the boy can directly compare the two alternatives without multiplying or summing anything.

In Čuhel's Austrian approach, by contrast, the total utility of a set of goods is not directly given but is derived from the marginal utilities of the items in the set. Therefore, the boy needs first to discover the total utility of the six plums by multiplying (Böhm-Bawerk) or summing (Čuhel) their marginal utilities, and only then can he compare the total utility of the six plums with the total utility of the apple (as the apple is a single item, its total and marginal utilities coincide).

That Čuhel stuck to marginal utility as the primary notion of utility analysis created a number of inconsistencies in his ordinal approach. As we will see in the next section, these inconsistencies were spotted by Böhm-Bawerk, who exploited them to argue that ultimately, he and Čuhel conceived of utility in the same way.

5.3. BÖHM-BAWERK RELOADED

In the third and final edition of *Capital and Interest: The Positive Theory of Capital* (part I, 1909; part II, 1912), Böhm-Bawerk inserted new notes and passages and one excursus (Excursus X) on utility measurement, intended mainly to address Čuhel's objections.[13] He began Excursus X by declaring, in a conciliatory fashion, that "the kernel of this [i.e., Čuhel's] objection is correct" ([1909–1912] 1959, vol. 3, 124) but then counterattacked with two arguments.

5.3.1. Precise versus Imprecise Measurement

Böhm-Bawerk's first argument against Čuhel is based on the distinction between "precise" and "imprecise" measurement. Precise measurement requires the perfect equality of the employed units. However, Böhm-Bawerk observed, we do measure things even when this perfect equality is lacking: "Nothing is more commonplace than to measure distances by steps, whereby the complete equality of each single step . . . cannot be guaranteed" (128). When the units are not perfectly equal, we obtain imprecise measures. However, imprecision does not transform measurement into ordinal ranking: "The lack of accuracy of a procedure does not change measuring into ranking, just as the accuracy of the procedure does not change ranking into measurement" (128).

In relation to utility measurement, Böhm-Bawerk claimed that by making the utility units unequal, the law of diminishing marginal utilities renders utility measurements not

13. A bibliographical note on *The Positive Theory* may be useful here. Part I of the third edition of the work (1909) includes Books I and II and Excursuses I–VI, while part II (1912) includes Books III and IV and Excursuses VII–XIV. Böhm-Bawerk's discussion of utility issues is contained in Book III and Excursus X. See Böhm-Bawerk [1909–1912] 1959, vol. 2, 119–204, 421–432; vol. 3, 124–136, 232–233.

practically impossible, as Čuhel had argued, but only imprecise. For Böhm-Bawerk, these imprecise utility measurements are sufficient for most practical purposes, just as for most practical purposes it is sufficient to measure distances by steps (130–131).

5.3.2. Multiplication Is Summation

With his second argument, Böhm-Bawerk pointed out two inconsistencies in Čuhel's analysis of the measurability of utility that render Čuhel's position on the subject untenable. As we have seen, Čuhel denied the possibility of expressing one utility as a *multiple* of another but considered it meaningful to *sum* the figures representing the utilities. Böhm-Bawerk first pointed out that if these figures represent only a ranking, then summing them would be meaningless. To illustrate the point, he took the example of the Mohs scale that Čuhel had used.

Böhm-Bawerk acknowledged that numbers on the Mohs scale do not allow us to state, for example, that a mineral of the eighth degree of hardness is four times as hard as a mineral of the second degree. But then, he added, the Mohs numbers do not even allow us to express the hardness of one mineral as the sum of the hardness of other minerals: "We can by no means maintain that a mineral of the 8th degree is as hard as three minerals of the 5th, 2nd, and 1st degree together" (131). Similarly, if utility numerals represent only a ranking, we can by no means sum them.

To illustrate the second inconsistency of Čuhel's analysis, Böhm-Bawerk began by observing that multiplication is only a special case of summation, namely summation of equal quantities. But, Böhm-Bawerk insisted, if Čuhel allows for the possibility of summing utilities, then he should allow also for the possibility of expressing one utility as a multiple of another: "In the case of intensities of sensations and 'egences,' according to Čuhel's own concession, summation of unequal quantities is feasible. Therefore summation of equal quantities or, what is the same, the determination of a multiple of a quantity, cannot be unfeasible" (132). In other words, Čuhel summed the numbers representing utility, and this showed that for him, the numerical determination of utilities was different from the numerical determination of mineral hardness. More precisely, Böhm-Bawerk concluded that as multiplication is only a special case of summation, his and Čuhel's numerical determinations of utilities are in fact one and the same.

5.3.3. Čuhel, Böhm-Bawerk, Mises

Böhm-Bawerk exploited the inconsistencies in Čuhel's notion that the comparison of total utilities is dependent on the sum of marginal utilities. But if one allows for the possibility that the individual can directly compare total utilities, such arguments lose their force. In fact, if an individual can directly compare the total utility of the apple with the total utility of the six plums, he does not need to *measure*—not even in an imprecise way—the total utility of the six plums in order to make a choice. The individual does not even need to *sum* the marginal utilities of the plums.

As we will see in the next section, by building on Čuhel's analysis, Mises was able to free himself from the traditional Austrian idea that the comparison of total utilities requires the summation of marginal utilities and thereby to elaborate an ordinal view of utility impervious to arguments like those used by Böhm-Bawerk.

5.4. MISES VERSUS BÖHM-BAWERK AND FISHER

Together with Joseph Schumpeter, Mises (1881–1973) was the most influential member of the so-called third generation of the Austrian School. He enrolled in the University of Vienna in 1900, and when Böhm-Bawerk began running his seminar in 1905, Mises, together with Čuhel, Schumpeter, and others, became a regular participant. Mises graduated in 1906, and in 1912, he published *The Theory of Money and Credit*, a systematic and comprehensive treatise on monetary topics ([1912] 1953). The book was intensively discussed in Böhm-Bawerk's seminar and became a key reference for the Austrian theory of money and credit.

In chapter 2 of his book, Mises broadened the discussion from monetary theory to value theory. Without mentioning Pareto, he argued that subjective value, that is, utility, cannot be measured but only ordered, and he criticized the stances of Böhm-Bawerk and Fisher on utility measurement. As we will see, Mises's arguments were to a large extent a restatement of the arguments Čuhel had used against Böhm-Bawerk.

5.4.1. Against Böhm-Bawerk, Again

Mises adhered to a unit-based understanding of measurement and argued that subjective evaluations concerning the significance of goods do not measure this significance in a unit-based sense. Subjective evaluations only arrange goods in order of their significance. Among the many passages in which Mises made this point, the following is particularly telling:

> It is impossible to measure subjective use-value. . . . We may say, the value of this commodity is greater than the value of that; but it is not permissible for us to assert, this commodity is worth *so much*. Such a way of speaking necessarily implies a definite unit. It really amounts to stating how many times a given unit is contained in the quantity to be defined. But this kind of calculation is quite inapplicable to processes of valuation. ([1912] 1953, 45)

Mises then examined Böhm-Bawerk's 1886 argument in favor of the measurability of utility, namely that if eating one apple is preferred to eating six plums, this means that the pleasure of eating the apple is at least six times greater than the pleasure of eating one plum. Mises dismissed the argument by reiterating Čuhel's point that the law of diminishing marginal utility modifies the pleasure obtained from eating the successive plum units and thus prevents us from concluding that the pleasure of eating an apple is larger than the pleasure of eating a plum multiplied by six. Mises (41) gave full credit to Čuhel for this argument.

The first edition of Mises's book does not contain any reference to Böhm-Bawerk's response to Čuhel's criticisms, for *The Theory of Money and Credit* appeared in the same year as the relevant (and final) edition of *The Positive Theory of Capital* (1912). Note, however, that Böhm-Bawerk's most effective point against Čuhel—that by summing utilities Čuhel was treating them as measurable—does not apply to Mises's position. For Mises, in order to compare the utility of one apple and the utility of six plums, neither multiplication nor summation of utilities is needed. All that is needed is direct and immediate comparison between the two utilities: "There is no value outside the process of valuation. There is no such thing as abstract value. . . . The person making the choice does not have to make use of notions about the value of units of the commodity. His process of valuation . . . is an immediate inference from considerations of the utilities at stake. . . . Like every other act of valuation, this is complete in itself" (47).

In part because Böhm-Bawerk's argument does not apply to his own position, the second edition of *The Theory of Money*, published in 1924, comments on Böhm-Bawerk's rejoinder to Čuhel only in a single sentence in a footnote: "Böhm-Bawerk endeavoured to refute Čuhel's criticism, but did not succeed in putting forward any new considerations that could help towards a solution of the problem [of utility measurement]" (41).

5.4.2. Against Fisher

After rejecting Böhm-Bawerk's case for the measurability of utility, Mises moved on to criticizing the method proposed by Fisher for measuring utility. Fisher had claimed that his method works only under the special assumption that the marginal utility of each commodity is independent of the quantities of other commodities. Mises's critique, however, applies even if this assumption is verified.

As explained earlier here in chapter 3, section 3.3.3, Fisher (1892) imagined an individual who consumes 100 loaves of bread and B gallons of oil per year and assumed that for this individual, the marginal utility of the 100th loaf is equal to the marginal utility of an increment of β gallons over B: U(100th loaf) = U(β). Moreover, Fisher also hypothesized that for the individual, the marginal utility of the 150th loaf equals the marginal utility of an increment of $\beta/2$ gallons over B: U(150th loaf) = U($\beta/2$). Fisher then claimed that the marginal utility of $\beta/2$ is half the marginal utility of β, that is, U($\beta/2$) = U(β)/2, and on the basis of this claim, he concluded that U($\beta/2$) could be taken as the unit of marginal utility, that is, the util. Accordingly, the measures of U(150th loaf) and U(100th loaf) would be, respectively, 1 util and 2 utils.

Mises ([1912] 1953, 43–44) now pointed out that the key passage of Fisher's reasoning—namely that the marginal utility of β is twice the marginal utility of $\beta/2$—is undermined by the law of diminishing marginal utility. Mises's point against Fisher follows quite closely Čuhel's against Böhm-Bawerk: just as the marginal utility of six plums taken together is not equal to the marginal utility of one plum multiplied by six, so the marginal utility of β is not equal to the marginal utility of $\beta/2$ multiplied by two. Rather, because of diminishing marginal utility, the marginal utility of β is smaller than the marginal utility of $\beta/2$ multiplied by two but to an extent not precisely determinable.

Mises considered the defense of Fisher's method based on the argument that since β and β/2 are infinitesimal quantities, the law of diminishing marginal utility does not apply to them. He objected, in the first place, that if β and β/2 are infinitesimal quantities, then they "remain imperceptible to the valuer and cannot therefore affect his judgment" (44). As a consequence, the valuer would judge the marginal utility of β equal to, and not twice as large as, the marginal utility of β/2. Moreover, if β and β/2 are infinitesimal quantities, it is impossible to equate their infinitesimal marginal utilities with the *finite* marginal utilities of the 100th and 150th loaves and thus impossible to express the latter as a ratio of the former.

5.4.3. The Rise of Ordinalism in Austria

In the 1920s and early 1930s, Mises reiterated his criticisms of measurable utility and restated his case for a purely ordinal conception of utility in a number of further publications (see, e.g., [1922] 1951; [1931] 1978; [1932] 1978). His ordinalism, however, always remained more like Čuhel's than like Pareto's. For unlike the Italian economist, Mises did not attempt to investigate in detail if and how the main results of demand and equilibrium analysis are affected by the unmeasurability of utility.

At any rate, and thanks to Mises's influence, in the interwar period, the ordinal approach to utility became dominant among Austrian economists.[14] As discussed here in chapter 6, the interwar Austrian consensus around ordinal utility was enlivened by discussion of the individuals' capability of ranking not only utilities but also utility differences.

5.5. MEASURING UTILITY OR MEASURING PREFERENCES?

To conclude this chapter, I turn to an issue of relevance to the very title of this book. As extensively explained in the previous sections, in Pareto's approach the primary notion is that of preference, while utility is conceived of as a numerical index that expresses the existing preference relations between objects. From this perspective, the actual measurand is preference, not utility. Utility numbers are only measures of the ranking or, possibly, the intensity of preferences. As we will see in chapter 6, beginning in the mid-1930s, the Paretian view of the relationship between preference and utility became dominant in utility analysis, and this may suggest that a more apt title for the book would be *Measuring Preferences* rather than *Measuring Utility*. There are, however, two important reasons why I deem it more appropriate to talk of *utility measurement* rather than *preference measurement*.

First, and as the following chapters show, even after the Paretian view of the relationship between preference and utility became dominant, utility theorists continued to talk about *utility measurement* rather than *preference measurement* and often used the terms *preference* and

14. On Austrian economics in the interwar period, see Morgenstern 1931; Rothbard 1956; Hayek [1968] 1992; High and Bloch 1989; Boehm 1992.

utility interchangeably. The resilience of the expression *utility measurement* seems to be due to the fact that issues concerning preference measurement can be translated into issues concerning utility measurement, and vice versa. Thus, the question of whether there is a unit to measure utility translates into the question of whether there is a unit to measure the intensity of preferences. In the opposite direction, the idea that preferences only rank combinations of goods translates into the idea that utilities can only be ordered. The exact nature of the relationship between the properties of preferences and the properties of the utility index that expresses numerically the preferences is often far from obvious. For instance, and as pointed out in chapter 6, in the 1930s, utility theorists found it difficult to understand the implications for the utility index of the assumption that individuals can rank transitions among different combinations of goods. However, insofar as it is clear how assumptions regarding preferences translate into features of the utility index, and vice versa, it appears fully legitimate to use the traditional and still widely used expression *utility measurement.*

The second reason for continuing to refer to *utility measurement* is that the expression *preference measurement* is ill suited to capture substantial portions of the history told in the book. The expression *measuring preferences* is not a helpful indicator of what Jevons, Menger, and the other early utility theorists were doing. As shown in chapters 1 and 2, the primary concept in their theories was that of utility and, more specifically, marginal utility, not preference. Accordingly, the early utility theorists discussed issues concerning the measurability of utility, not the measurability or intensity of preferences. In most early utility theories, the very notion of preference does not even appear. The expression *measuring preferences* is not even of much help as an indicator of what Frederick Mosteller, Patrick Suppes, and other experimenters were doing in the period 1950–1985. As we will see in chapters 13, 14, and 16, these researchers attempted to measure utility, and more specifically the utility of money, not preferences. Finally, the novel conception of measurement elaborated by Milton Friedman and other utility theorists in the early 1950s and examined in chapter 12 specifically concerns utility measurement rather than the measurement of preferences. Therefore, the expression *utility measurement* appears more appropriate to indicate the general topic of this book.

CHAPTER 6

Cardinal Utility

How It Entered Economic Analysis from Pareto to Samuelson, 1915–1945

Beginning in the mid-1910s, the ordinal approach to utility analysis found an increasing number of supporters. Outside Austria, these supporters typically referred to Vilfredo Pareto's works and, more specifically, to the French edition of his *Manual of Political Economy*. In Austria, the main influence was that of Ludwig von Mises, although beginning in the 1920s, Pareto was also discussed. In the period between 1915 and 1945, two main threads of research can be identified. The first was concerned to work out a fully consistent ordinal approach to demand and equilibrium analysis by correcting some shortcomings detected in Pareto's ordinal theory. The major contributors to this line of research were two junior scholars at the London School of Economics, John Hicks and Roy Allen. The discussion reached its peak between 1934 and 1939, while Hicks's *Value and Capital* (1939b) provided the sought-for improved version of Pareto's ordinal theory.

The second research thread explored the consequences of Pareto's suggestion that individuals are not only able to rank combinations of goods but might even be capable of ranking transitions from one combination to another. The most fervid phase of this debate took place from 1934 to 1938, with a coda that extended until the early 1940s. The discussion involved scholars from different institutions, such as Oskar Lange (University of Chicago), Henry Phelps Brown (Oxford University), Allen (LSE), Franz Alt (University of Vienna), and Paul Samuelson (Harvard University and then MIT).

The second line of research is the more relevant for our narrative. In the first place, discussion of the implications of the idea that individuals can rank transitions led to the definition and stabilization of the current notion of cardinal utility as utility unique up to linear increasing or, equivalently, positive linear transformations. But in the course of the discussion, cardinal utility, that is, utility measurable on an interval scale rather than in the unit-based sense, began to be considered as measurable utility.

6.1. THE RANKING OF TRANSITIONS FROM THE MID-1910S TO THE EARLY 1930S

As pointed out here in chapter 5, section 5.1.6, in his *Manual*, Pareto ([1906/1909] 2014, 132–133) argued that utility would be measurable in a unit-based sense if the following three assumptions hold: (1) individuals are able to rank combinations of goods, (2) they are also capable of ranking transitions from one combination to another, and (3) they are even capable of stating that a given transition is equally or twice as preferable as another. Assumption 1 is the basic assumption of ordinal utility theory, and Pareto took for granted that it was always verified. He considered assumption 2 plausible, at least for adjacent transitions, because it is in accord with the idea of diminishing marginal utility. As we saw in chapter 5, the very notion of diminishing marginal utility is inconsistent with the ordinal approach, but Pareto continued using it nonetheless. For Pareto, the problematic assumption is number 3. Since it is not verified, he concluded, utility is not measurable in a unit-based sense. Nevertheless, he left one issue open: What happens if only assumptions 1 and 2 hold? Is there a chance that utility becomes measurable anyway?

From the mid-1910s to the early 1930s, a number of eminent economists from different quarters picked up on Pareto's discussion about the ranking of transitions and utility differences.[1] They focused on assumptions 1 and 2 only and discarded assumption 3 as far-fetched. Yet, as we will see, they were unable to clarify the exact meanings and implications of assumptions 1 and 2.

In 1915, Francis Ysidro Edgeworth published in the *Economic Journal* a two-part review article in which he discussed some recent publications, such as the economics textbooks by António Horta Osório (1913) and Wladimir Zawadzki (1914) that had adopted Pareto's ordinal approach. Edgeworth (1915, 58) remarked that Osório endorsed Pareto's assumption 2, as well as Pareto's claim that if an individual prefers the transition from combination I to combination II to the transition from combination II to combination III, then for him, $U(II) - U(I) > U(III) - U(II)$. Edgeworth agreed with Osório and thus, implicitly, with Pareto.[2]

In Italy, Luigi Amoroso, a Paretian, also accepted assumption 2 and argued that the capacity to rank transitions makes the comparison of utility differences meaningful (1921, 91–92). This, in turn, would allow preservation of the principle of diminishing marginal utility and the traditional definition of complementarity à la Auspitz–Lieben without returning to the pre-Paretian view that utility is measurable in a unit-based sense.

In 1924, Arthur Bowley, an English economist and statistician based at the London School of Economics, published *The Mathematical Groundwork of Economics*. His presentation of utility theory was the most sympathetic to Pareto's ordinal approach of any work published in England in the 1920s. In particular, Bowley (1924, 1–2) stressed that the principle of diminishing marginal utility and the traditional definition of complementarity

1. I consider here only those who were mentioned in the debate of the mid-1930s. Among others who touched on the ranking of transitions are Alfonso de Pietri-Tonelli (1927) and Ragnar Frisch ([1926] 1971). See more on Frisch in chapter 7.

2. On Osório and Pareto, see Mata 2007.

require the assumption that individuals are able to rank transitions from one combination of goods to another, an assumption that he did not oppose.

Paul Rosenstein-Rodan and Oskar Morgenstern, then two young members of the Austrian School, also discussed the ranking of transitions and utility differences. Rosenstein-Rodan ([1927] 1960, 75) admitted the possibility that individuals are able to rank utility differences (assumption 2) but, like Pareto, denied that individuals are capable of stating "how much larger or smaller the utility difference is" (assumption 3). Given the role played by Morgenstern in our narrative, an account of his background and early positions on utility is in order.

Morgenstern (1902–1977) had studied under Hans Mayer, who then occupied one of the few chairs in economics at the University of Vienna. After graduation and following three years abroad on a Rockefeller fellowship, in 1928, Morgenstern entered the University of Vienna as *Privatdozent* and joined Rosenstein-Rodan as the managing editor of the *Zeitschrift für Nationalökonomie*, a new economic journal edited by Mayer that in the 1930s enjoyed a significant international standing (Rothschild 2004; Leonard 2010).

In 1931, Morgenstern published an essay on "Die drei Grundtypen der Theorie des subjektiven Wertes" (The Three Fundamental Types of the Theory of Subjective Value) in a volume coedited by Mises and German economist Arthur Spiethoff. In this essay, Morgenstern outlined the Austrian version of utility theory and presented the Lausanne version and the Anglo-American version as imperfect variations of the Austrian doctrine. Morgenstern also argued that economic subjects cannot measure utilities but only rank them. In addition, they can "compare the differences . . . between total economic utilities by comparing them two at time" (1931, 13). These two abilities, Morgenstern claimed, are all that individuals need in order to behave rationally in the economy.

Two brief comments on the discussion of transition rankings in the 1910s, 1920s, and early 1930s are in order. First, none of the economists contributing to the discussion employed the expression *cardinal utility*. Second, although these economists often viewed the capacity of ranking transitions as a way of preserving some important notions of pre-Paretian utility theory within the boundaries of Pareto's ordinal framework, the exact meaning and implications of that capacity remained unexplored.

6.2. CARDINAL AND ORDINAL UTILITY BY HICKS AND ALLEN

Discussion of the exact implications of transition ranking underwent a sudden and decisive acceleration in 1934, with the London School of Economics as the epicenter of this new phase of the debate. After becoming director of LSE's economics department in 1929, Lionel Robbins (1898–1984) formed around him a circle of brilliant young scholars who were already or would later become prominent economists. The group met in a weekly seminar that came to be known as the Robbins seminar, which included John Hicks, Roy Allen, Nicholas Kaldor, Abba Lerner, Ursula Webb (who married Hicks in 1935), Rosenstein-Rodan (who left Vienna for London in 1930), and Friedrich Hayek (who joined in 1931, also from Vienna). In the early 1930s, Robbins and his circle managed to introduce Paretian and

Austrian economic theory into an English economics then still dominated by Marshallian orthodoxy.[3]

Of these members of the Robbins seminar, Hicks and Allen are the most important for our narrative. Hicks (1904–1989) had studied at Oxford and joined the LSE in 1926 as a lecturer in economics, whereupon he commenced an intensive study of Pareto, Walras, and Edgeworth. Allen (1906–1983) studied mathematics at Cambridge and in 1928 entered the LSE department of statistics, then directed by Bowley. In 1933, Hicks and Allen cowrote a paper titled "A Reconsideration of the Theory of Value," which, after thorough discussion in Robbins's seminar (Hicks 1981), was published the following year in *Economica*, the senior LSE economics journal.

In their article, Hicks and Allen endorsed Pareto's superseding of measurable utility but argued that the Italian economist had not examined thoroughly what adjustments in demand analysis are made necessary by that superseding. However, and unlike the economists discussed earlier here in section 6.1, Hicks and Allen did not attempt to save pre-Paretian notions, such as diminishing marginal utility, by introducing the additional hypothesis that individuals are capable of ranking transitions from one combination to another. Rather, they accepted only the basic assumption of ordinalism, namely that individuals are able to rank transitions, rejecting all pre-Paretian notions inconsistent with this assumption, and enquiring, "what, if anything, can be put in their place" (Hicks and Allen 1934, 55).

6.2.1. A Utility-Free Approach

In effect, Hicks and Allen eliminated not only diminishing marginal utility but also marginal utility and even utility itself. They attempted to construct demand theory solely on the basis of indifference curves, that is, without introducing utility indices to represent the preference and indifference relations between commodities. The cornerstone of their analysis became the marginal rate of substitution, which corresponds to the slope of the indifference curve. In a utilitarian framework, the marginal rate of substitution between commodities x and y is expressed by the ratio between the marginal utility of x and the marginal utility of y. Hicks and Allen, however, explicitly avoided defining the marginal rate of substitution in this way. They argued that by bringing into play the ratio of marginal utilities, one would end up separating the two marginal utilities and talking of the increasing or diminishing trend of one single marginal utility (Hicks and Allen 1934, 56). Therefore, Hicks and Allen defined the marginal rate of substitution between commodities x and y as the quantity of commodity y that just compensates the individual for the loss of a marginal unit of x. This is a definition in terms of commodity quantities and is independent of utility.

Based on the marginal rate of substitution so defined, Hicks and Allen were able to determine the relationships between the demand for goods, their price, and consumer income in elasticity terms and to decompose the effect of a price change on demand into what in current microeconomics is called the substitution effect (the effect of a price change on demand

3. On Robbins and his circle, see Howson 2011 and also the autobiographical writing of Hayek [1963] 1995.

due to the change of relative prices) and the income effect (the effect of a price change on demand due to the change of purchasing power). They also provided a new and utility-free definition of complementary and competitive goods. The new definition was based on the relative changes of demand for goods y and z determined by a variation of the price of good x. However, as Samuelson would notice (see section 6.7.2), Hicks and Allen's demand analysis depends on the assumption that the marginal rate of substitution is diminishing or, equivalently, that the indifference curves are convex. This assumption, however, seems to rely on introspective considerations about preferences or utilities.[4]

Hicks and Allen's article had an immediate and pronounced impact on economists working on demand analysis and became a standard reference for subsequent discussions of utility theory. It is also relevant for our story because it contributed significantly to the diffusion of the cardinal–ordinal terminology within economics.

6.2.2. Entering Cardinal and Ordinal Utility

As chapter 1, section 1.4.3, pointed out, the distinction between cardinal and ordinal numbers passed from mathematics into economics through Andreas Voigt ([1893] 2008). Among the very few who took notice of Voigt's paper was Edgeworth, who cursorily referred to Voigt's distinction between cardinal and ordinal numbers in some *Economic Journal* articles (Edgeworth 1894; 1900; 1907; 1915). Notably, neither Voigt nor Edgeworth related cardinal numbers to the ranking of differences between objects or to positive linear transformations of mathematical functions. At any rate, before 1934, no economist apart from Edgeworth seems to have employed the cardinal–ordinal terminology.

This situation changed after Hicks and Allen used the terms *cardinal* and *ordinal* in their influential 1934 article. As argued by Schmidt and Weber (2012), these two English economists must have come upon the cardinal–ordinal terminology either by reading Edgeworth or through another member of the Robbins group, Rosenstein-Rodan, who knew Voigt's article. In one passage in their article, Hicks and Allen (1934, 54–55) referred to Pareto's approach to utility theory as "the 'ordinal' conception of utility" and labeled the approaches relying on the measurability of utility as "dependent upon a 'cardinal' conception of utility."

However, because of the nonutilitarian framework of their article, Hicks and Allen did not elaborate on this distinction. While it is evident that by ordinal utility they referred to Paretian utility indices that are unique up to monitonic increasing transformations, Hicks and Allen did not make clear what they meant by cardinal utility. Apparently, they used *cardinal* as a residual notion, in the sense that they considered cardinal everything not ordinal, that is, not invariant to monitonic increasing transformations of the utility function. Certainly, Hicks and Allen did not associate cardinal utility with the ranking of utility differences or positive linear transformations of the utility function, not least because in their article there is no sign of the latter.

4. For more on Hicks and Allen's approach to demand analysis and its possible internal inconsistencies, see Fernandez-Grela 2006; Moscati 2007b.

Despite the fact that the terms *ordinal* and *cardinal* occurred only once in their paper, Hicks and Allen contributed immediately to the diffusion of these terms, at least within the Robbins group. Two other members of the group, Hayek and Frederic Benham, separately published in the November 1934 issue of *Economica* articles in which the terms are used (once in each). However, neither Hayek nor Benham associated the term *cardinal* with the ranking of utility differences.[5]

6.3. LANGE AND THE DETERMINATENESS OF THE UTILITY FUNCTION

The meaning and implications of the utility-difference ranking were thoroughly investigated in a debate initiated in 1934 by Polish economist Oskar Lange. Lange (1904–1965) studied at the University of Cracow, where in 1927 he became a lecturer in statistics. In 1934, he left Poland on a two-year Rockefeller fellowship that brought him first to the LSE and then to Harvard, where he studied under Austrian economist Joseph Schumpeter. Between 1936 and 1938, he lectured at Michigan, California, and Stanford Universities, and in 1939 he was appointed professor at the University of Chicago (Dobb 1966).

Lange was prompted to reconsider the discussions on transition rankings by Hicks and Allen's claim that ordinal utility implies the abandonment of diminishing marginal utility. His article was published in the June 1934 issue of the *Review of Economic Studies*, the junior LSE economics journal. The *Review* had been founded in 1933 by Ursula Webb and Abba Lerner, two members of the Robbins circle, and Paul Sweezy, a Harvard graduate student who visited the LSE in the academic year 1932–1933. The article was titled "The Determinateness of the Utility Function" (Lange 1934a), where by "determinate" Lange, as we will see, meant measurable.

6.3.1. The Hidden Implications of Postulate 2

In his article, Lange first summarized the discussion of the implications of the immeasurability of utility from Pareto to Hicks and Allen. He relabeled Pareto's assumption 1, according to which individuals are only able to rank combinations of goods, "postulate 1." Pareto's assumption 2, according to which individuals are also capable of ranking transitions over combinations, became "postulate 2." For Lange, none of the economists who admitted postulate 2, namely Pareto, Edgeworth, Osório, Amoroso, Bowley, Rosenstein-Rodan, and Morgenstern, seemed to have realized that it implies something that they discarded as implausible, namely Pareto's assumption 3, which states that individuals are also capable of stating how many times a given transition is preferable to another: "From the assumption that the individual is able to know whether one increase of utility is greater than another

5. Hayek (1934, 401) claimed that Carl Menger understood the numbers he used to express the marginal utility of goods "not as cardinal but as ordinal figures." Benham (1934, 446) argued that utility and welfare preclude "objective measurement (whether in 'cardinal' or 'ordinal' numbers)."

increase of utility the possibility of saying how many times this increase is greater than another one follows necessarily" (220). In fact, Lange reasoned, if postulate 2 holds, we can vary combination III until the individual perceives the change of utility due to transition from II to III as equally preferable to the change of utility due to transition from combination I to combination II; that is, we can vary combination III until U(III) – U(II) = U(II) – U(I). Rearranging this equation, we obtain U(III) – U(I) = 2[U(II) – U(I)] and thus that "the change of utility due to transition from I to III is twice the change of utility due to transition from I to II" (222). Therefore, Lange concluded, postulates 1 and 2 imply a return to "determinate," that is, measurable, utility: "The two fundamental assumptions used by Pareto and other writers of his and of the Austrian school (and by Professor Bowley) are equivalent to the assumption that utility is measurable" (223).

6.3.2. Positive Linear Transformations

In making this point, Lange also ushered onto the stage the positive linear transformations of the utility function. As Pareto had shown in his *Manual* (see here chapter 5, section 5.1.5), postulate 1 restricts the admissible transformations of U to the increasing ones, that is, to F(U) having a positive first derivative: $F' > 0$. Postulate 2, Lange argued, further restricts the admissible transformations of U by implying that the second derivative of F(U) is equal to zero: $F'' = 0$. However, the transformations F that display a positive first derivative and a null second derivative are the positive linear ones, that is, those of the form $F(U) = \alpha U + \beta$, where $\alpha > 0$. This means that "the different systems of utility indices can differ only by a constant multiplier [α] which fixes the unit of measurement and by an additive constant [β] fixing the zero point of measurement," as is also the case in "the difference between the centigrade and the Fahrenheit thermometer scales" (221).

6.3.3. Equilibrium versus Welfare, Choices versus Introspection

Based on the conviction that postulate 2 restores the measurability of the utility function, Lange indicated two alternative approaches to demand and equilibrium analysis. The first, based on postulate 1 alone, is sufficient to establish all equations of demand and equilibrium analysis. Moreover, postulate 1 "can be expressed in terms of objective human *behaviour*, i.e. in terms of choice" (224). The idea is that if an individual chooses alternative x over alternative y, this choice can be interpreted as an indication that he prefers x to y. (I postpone to chapter 7 a discussion of the relationship between preference and choice.)

The second approach is based on postulates 1 and 2. For Lange, postulate 2, although superfluous for the theory of economic equilibrium, has the merit of allowing for a psychological interpretation of the equations of demand theory in terms of intuitive concepts such as diminishing marginal utility. In this way, postulate 2 permits the interpretation of economic equilibrium "in terms of *human welfare*" (224). Postulate 2, however, cannot be expressed by referring to choice behavior, and in order to have some insight into which transition an individual prefers, we have to rely on the individual's communication of the result of "psychological *introspection*" (224). For Lange, both approaches are scientifically legitimate.

6.3.4. A Novel Understanding of Measurement

This discussion of Lange's views reveals a novel understanding of which forms of quantitative assessment of utility count as utility measurement. He did not consider the availability of a utility unit and the possibility of assessing utility ratios as necessary conditions for the measurability of utility. Rather, for him, the restriction of the admissible transformations of the utility function to the positive linear transformations is sufficient to make utility measurable.

It is useful to distinguish between two slightly different aspects of Lange's novel understanding of measurement. First, he identified measurement with what in current measurement theory is called interval-scale measurement rather than with the more restrictive ratio-scale (or unit-based) measurement. As we will see in the next section, not all the contributors to the debate on the determinateness of the utility function shared this view.

The shift of focus from the ratio-scale to the interval-scale measurement of utility is at least in part a consequence of the developments in utility theory that occurred during the period 1870–1934. These developments made clear that, contrary to what the early marginalists believed, the results of utility analysis do not depend on the unit-based measurability of utility. For many of these results, as Pareto, Hicks, and Allen showed, the ordinal-scale measurement of utility suffices. For other types of considerations, such as those Lange mentioned, the more demanding interval scale of measurement might be necessary. However, in 1934 (and, in fact, also in the following decades), none of the relevant results of utility analysis appeared to require the even more demanding ratio-scale measurement of utility.

Second, Lange strictly associated the measurability or unmeasurability of utility with the uniqueness or nonuniqueness of the utility numbers to some set of mathematical transformations. For Lange, if utility numbers are unique only to increasing transformations, utility is not measurable. If, instead, utility numbers are unique only to linear increasing transformations (which also means to a subset of these transformations such as the proportional transformations), then utility is measurable.

As chapter 5, section 5.1.5, explained, the characterization of the different forms of utility in terms of the mathematical transformations the utility numbers can be subjected to was initiated by Pareto in the mathematical appendix of his *Manual*. As we will see in the next sections and chapters, this "characterization approach" to utility measurement became increasingly popular among utility theorists.

Two final comments on Lange are in order. First, while he was the first to connect explicitly and formally the ranking of utility differences with positive linear transformations of the utility function, Lange did not employ the expression *cardinal utility*. Second, like Pareto, Amoroso, and the other economists who admitted postulate 2, Lange took for granted that the ranking of transitions from one combination to another and the ranking of utility differences are one and the same thing. As we shall now see, Henry Phelps Brown's comment on Lange's article showed that this is not the case.

6.4. THE ANALOGY OF QUANTITY AND PHELPS BROWN'S CRITIQUE

Like Hicks, Phelps Brown (1906–1994) studied at Oxford, where he was taught by Robbins, whom he replaced as lecturer in economics at New College when the latter moved to the LSE. Like Hicks, Allen, and Lange, Phelps Brown was a member of the Econometric Society, which had been founded in 1930 by Irving Fisher, Ragnar Frisch, and other prominent economists with the aim of advancing economic theory by consolidating its mathematical and statistical dimensions (see more on the creation of the Econometric Society in chapter 7). Through the European meetings of the Econometric Society, Phelps Brown became acquainted with Hicks, Allen, Lange, and other members of the Robbins circle (Hancock and Isaac 1998).

In his three-and-half-page comment on Lange's article, Phelps Brown (1934) showed that the implications of postulate 2 are much weaker than those supposed by all its supporters, from Pareto to Lange, and that, in particular, Lange's claim that postulate 2 restricts the admissible transformations of the utility function to the positive linear ones is unwarranted.

6.4.1. Back to Unit-Based Measurement

Before discussing Lange's claim, Phelps Brown explicitly stated which forms of quantitative assessment he considered to constitute measurement. In contrast to Lange, Phelps Brown stuck to the unit-based understanding of measurement: "We should here first clear our minds as to what measurability means, and we may perhaps agree that it consists in the possibility of expressing one magnitude as a multiple of another. . . . [Measuring lies in] the possibility of relating the magnitudes one to another by division and multiplication" (66).

6.4.2. Two Different Preference Orders

On turning to Lange's article, Phelps Brown began by noticing that both postulates 1 and 2 concern preference order. Postulate 1 refers to preference order over combinations of goods and allows for the introduction of a numerical index U that assigns larger numbers to more preferred combinations. Postulate 2 refers to the preference order over transitions from one combination to another and allows for the introduction of another index, let us call it G, that assigns larger numbers to more preferred transitions. However, Phelps Brown stressed, the numbers associated by G to transitions need not be equal to the differences between the numbers associated by U to combinations (67).

Thus, if an individual prefers combination III to combination II, and combination II to combination I, then postulate 1 implies that U(III) > U(II) > U(I). If, in addition, the individual prefers transition from I to II to transition from II to III, then postulate 2 implies that G(I, II) > G(II, III). But postulate 2 does not imply that G(I, II) = U(II) – U(I) or that G(II, III) = U(III) – U(II).[6] Moreover, since postulate 2 refers only to the ranking of transitions

6. Consider the following numerical example. If the individual prefers III to II, and II to I, we can assign the following U numbers to the three combinations: U(III) = 10, U(II) = 3, and U(I) = 1.

and G numbers and has no implications for the differences between the U numbers, then Lange's proof that postulate 2 restricts the admissible transformations of utility function U to the positive linear ones cannot be correct.

Phelps Brown (68) pointed out a second problem, strictly connected to the previous one. If postulate 2 has no implication for the U numbers, it also cannot have implications for the variation of marginal utilities as expressed by the differences between those U numbers. Therefore, postulate 2 does not allow us to talk meaningfully of diminishing marginal utility or to employ the traditional definition of complementarity.

6.4.3. No Summation of Ordinal Magnitudes

Finally, Phelps Brown called attention to a third problem, one already emphasized by Eugen Böhm-Bawerk in his reply to Franz Čuhel (see chapter 5, section 5.3.2), namely that the summation of ordinal magnitudes makes little sense.[7] Yet the G numbers have in effect only an ordinal meaning.[8] Thus, for instance, if the individual considers transition from I to II equally preferable to transition from II to III, then the G number associated with both transitions is the same, say, 7. What will be the G number associated with the transition from I to III? Since the transition from I to III is obtained by making two equally preferable transitions associated with the G number 7, it is tempting to answer 7 + 7 = 14. But this temptation, Phelps Brown argued, should be resisted, for it arises from the fact that in representing preferences by numbers, we tend illegitimately to extend the additive properties of numbers to preferences.

If we avoid numbers and, for instance, represent preference orders by the order of words, the temptation to sum what cannot be summed disappears: "The two included transitions [from I to II and from II to III] are indistinguishable, and to each will therefore correspond the same term . . . *maison*. We have then no temptation to suppose that if the consumer makes the transition represented by *maison* once and then once again, he has made in all a transition to be represented by 2(*maison*)" (68).

Therefore, Lange's claim that postulate 2 allows us to say that the change of utility due to a transition is twice the change of utility due to another transition is unwarranted, as his conclusion is that postulate 2 implies a return to determinate or measurable utility.

6.4.4. The Analogy of Quantity and Its Perils

To sum up, Phelps Brown showed that the power of postulate 2 is much more limited than had been previously supposed and that all the nice implications that Pareto, Lange, and

If the individual prefers transition from I to II to transition from II to III, we can assign to the two transitions the G numbers G(I, II) = 5 and G(II, III) = 2. Although these U numbers and G numbers are perfectly consistent with postulates 1 and 2, it turns out that U(II) – U(I) = 2 while G(I, II) = 5, and U(III) – U(II) = 7 while G(II, III) = 2.

7. Phelps Brown, however, did not even mention Böhm-Bawerk and Čuhel.

8. The same holds for the summation of the U numbers, but Phelps Brown did not discuss this point, as it was not relevant to his argument.

others imagined they had drawn from it had in fact been illusory. For Phelps Brown, the illusion is caused by "the analogy of quantity" (68), that is, by representing psychological phenomena such as preferences through numbers, without keeping in mind that not all properties of numbers extend to preferences: the analogy of quantity, "though permissible, is dangerous, because quantities have properties which we cannot easily banish from our thoughts, and some of these properties have no part in the just analogy. It is by the unnoticed intrusion of such properties that the semblance of measurable utility has appeared" (69).

6.4.5. Lange's Reply and Open Problems

Phelps Brown's article was followed by a note by Lange (1934b) in which he refined his proof that the comparability of differences between the U numbers restricts the admissible transformations of U to those of the form $F(U) = \alpha U + \beta$. But Lange did not address Phelps Brown's point that postulate 2 does not warrant the comparability of the differences between the U numbers. It appears that Lange wrote his note before reading Phelps Brown's comment. Nevertheless, in a letter sent to Samuelson on May 10, 1938, Lange acknowledged that Phelps Brown's objections were correct (see section 6.7.4).

Two brief final comments on Phelps Brown's contribution are in order. First, he did not use the cardinal–ordinal terminology. Second, he did not investigate what missing assumptions, if any, should be added to postulates 1 and 2 to make sense of the sum of the G numbers or ensure that the G numbers coincide with the differences between U numbers.

6.5. ALLEN'S CRITICISM OF POSTULATE 2 AND HIS UNDERSTANDING OF MEASUREMENT

Lange's article and Phelps Brown's comment prompted different reactions among the affiliates of the Robbins group. Here I focus on the most significant of those reactions, namely that of Allen.[9] While Allen criticized postulate 2 and Lange's acceptance of it, Allen's and Lange's understandings of measurement were similar: both identified measurement with interval-scale measurement rather than unit-based measurement.

6.5.1. Allen's Criticism of Postulate 2

With a brief note in the February 1935 issue of the *Review of Economic Studies*, Allen also entered the fray, denying the usefulness of postulate 2. He argued that since the theory of value can be developed on the basis of postulate 1 alone, and given that postulate 2 "cannot be expressed in terms of the individual's acts of choice," it would be futile to complicate the analysis with postulate 2 unless it "works its passage" (1935, 155–156).

9. In Moscati 2013a, I also discuss the reaction of Harro Bernardelli (1934), another member of the Robbins circle.

Notably, Allen took into account Phelps Brown's criticism of Lange but circumvented the difficulties raised by reinterpreting postulate 2 as directly concerned with the capacity to rank utility increments, that is, of stating whether U(II) – U(I) is larger, smaller, or equal to U(III) – U(II), rather than the capacity to rank transitions of the original formulation.

In opposition to Lange, who had argued that postulate 2 is necessary to understand complementarity and for welfare analysis, Allen claimed that this was not the case. The new definition of complementarity that he and Hicks had proposed in their 1934 article was not only independent of postulate 2 but showed that the distinction between complementary and substitute goods "has nothing to do with utility or intensities of preference" and is rather based on "the inter-relations of individual demands under market conditions" (Allen 1935, 158). Postulate 2 does not even warrant welfare analysis, for which "additional, and far more serious, assumptions about the relations between the preference scales of *different* individuals are necessary" (158). For Allen, therefore, postulate 2 does not work its passage and should be discarded.[10]

6.5.2. Allen's Understanding of Measurement

This criticism of postulate 2 notwithstanding, Allen shared with Lange the view that if postulate 2 were verified, utility would be measurable. Allen went on to claim that if postulate 2 were verified, utility would be measurable in the same sense as length is measurable.

Allen (1935, 155) began by rejecting Phelps Brown's unit-based view of measurement: "It is sometimes maintained . . . that the measurability of utility necessarily implies that one utility can be definitely spoken of as a multiple of another. . . . This is not the case." Like Lange, Allen also deemed that utility is measurable if numerical measures of utility are unique up to linear increasing transformations, that is, if not only the unit of measurement (as in the ratio scale) but also the zero point of measurement are arbitrary. In current measurement-theoretic terminology, for Allen, utility is measurable if it is measurable on an interval scale.

Allen stressed that the arbitrariness of the zero point makes the assessment of utility ratios meaningless: "If it is found that one utility is double another relative to one zero

10. In the mid-1930s, the leader of the group to which Allen was affiliated, Robbins, did not take an explicit stance on postulate 2 or the debate it generated. However, it seems likely that Robbins did not share Allen's position. At a general methodological level, in fact, Robbins was opposed to behaviorist approaches in economics and defended reference to psychological variables in the explanation of economic phenomena not only as scientifically legitimate but also as scientifically necessary (see, e.g., Robbins 1935, 86–88). Based on this methodological stance, Robbins may well have considered postulate 2 as acceptable, at least in principle. Certainly, in an article dealing with utility theory that he wrote almost twenty years later, Robbins (1953) explicitly argued that individuals are capable of ranking transitions among different combinations of goods: "I am quite sure that I can and do judge differences. The proposition that my preference for the Rembrandt over the Holbein is less than my preference for the Holbein over, let us say, a Munnings, is perfectly intelligible to me" (104). This statement may reflect views Robbins arrived at only after the mid-1930s, but it suggests that even in that period, he could have considered postulate 2 as scientifically legitimate and psychologically plausible.

mark, then alteration of the mark completely destroys this relation" (156). This fact, however, does not impinge on the measurability of utility: "Statements relating to one utility as a multiple of another . . . are not essential to the notion of utility as a measurable quantity" (156).

Allen proceeded to argue that, in effect, the measurement of utility is akin to the measurement of length, which he considered measurable on an interval scale rather than a ratio scale. For Allen, in fact, the zero point for measurement of length is also arbitrary. While the use of different units, such as inches or millimeters, makes the arbitrariness of the length unit apparent, the arbitrariness of the zero-length point is obscured by the circumstance that everybody accepts one particular zero mark, namely the null length. However, Allen observed, "there is no theoretical . . . reason why a definite length such as 6 inches should not be taken as a zero mark" (158). In this case, all lengths measured in inch units would have measures reduced by six, while the ratios between length measures would be different. Therefore, Allen concluded, "the measure of utility . . . is in no essential way different from that of a physical magnitude such as length" (158).

One may wonder whether it really makes sense to choose any positive length as the zero point of length measurement. For our purposes, however, this is not the relevant point. The relevant point is that Allen, like Lange but in contrast to Phelps Brown, displayed a novel understanding of utility measurement according to which utility is measurable if it is measurable on an interval scale rather than on a ratio scale.

Two final comments on Allen are in order. First, like Lange and Phelps Brown, Allen in his note did not use the expression *cardinal utility*. Second, while Phelps Brown did not investigate what additional assumptions should be added to postulates 1 and 2 to warrant the passage from the ranking of transitions to the ranking of utility differences, Allen begged this question by reinterpreting postulate 2 as directly concerned with the capacity to rank utility differences. The man who did solve the problem opened up by Phelps Brown was Franz Alt, a young Viennese mathematician and economist who, like Čuhel, is little known in the history of economics.

6.6. THE MAN WHO CAME IN FROM MATHEMATICS: ALT'S 1936 CONTRIBUTION

6.6.1. A Biographical Sketch

Alt (1910–2011) graduated in mathematics in 1932 with a dissertation under Karl Menger, the son of the founder of the Austrian School of economics, and became a regular participant in the younger Menger's seminar, the *Mathematische Kolloquium*. As a Jew, Alt failed to obtain an academic position, but on Menger's recommendation, he was hired by Morgenstern as a private tutor when the latter decided to improve his mathematical skills. Through participation in the *Kolloquium* and his tutoring of Morgenstern, Alt became interested in the mathematical aspects of economics.

Through Morgenstern and at some point between late 1934 and early 1935, Alt became involved in the debate over the determinateness of the utility function. At an afternoon tea at Morgenstern's house, he met Paul Sweezy, one of the three editors of the *Review of Economic*

Studies, who showed him a reprint of Lange's paper. Alt had been trained in the axiomatic mathematical tradition of David Hilbert, which was also the standard approach of Menger and other *Kolloquium* participants.[11] From the perspective of the standards of proof accepted in mathematics, Alt found Lange's demonstration that postulates 1 and 2 imply the measurability of utility unsatisfactory and began writing a letter to Lange that ended up becoming a paper: "Lange said if you had these two conditions [postulates 1 and 2] then that's sufficient to assign a number to every commodity by itself. . . . I read that, and I was a very theoretical mathematician. That's not mathematics. That's not a proof, I thought. I began to write a letter to Oskar Lange . . . , and the letter grew to be 10 pages long. And I realized I was writing a paper" (Alt and Akera 2006, 8–9). Originally written in English, Alt translated his paper into German and gave it to Morgenstern to read. In June 1936, it was published as "Über die Messbarkeit des Nutzens" (On the Measurability of Utility) in Morgenstern's *Zeitschrift für Nationalökonomie*.[12] In this article, Alt proved what today we would call a representation theorem, analogous to that demonstrated by Otto Hölder in 1901 (see chapter 1, section 1.4.1). But while Hölder's axioms provide conditions for measurability on a ratio scale, Alt's axioms provide conditions for measurability on an interval scale.

6.6.2. Alt's Representation Theorem

Alt knew Phelps Brown's article and agreed with him that the key flaws of Lange's argument consisted in the unwarranted intermingling of the preference order over combinations with the preference order over transitions and also in the tacit attribution of additive properties to the latter (Alt [1936] 1971, 431).

In the spirit of the axiomatic method, Alt added to Lange's two postulates five additional postulates concerning the properties of the two preference orders and their relationships. Alt's postulates 3 and 6 require that both preference orders are transitive and continuous.[13] Postulate 4 and postulate 7 connect the two preference orders.[14] Postulate 5 provides the preference order over transitions with an additive structure.[15]

11. On the different aspects of Hilbert's axiomatic method, see Weintraub 2002.

12. For more on Alt, see Alt and Akera 2006; Moscati 2013a.

13. A preference relation is continuous if it is preserved under limits. In the 1930s, requiring the continuity of the preference relation was quite exceptional. The importance of this assumption for the existence of a utility function representing the preference relation came to be appreciated only in the early 1950s (Debreu 1954). See more on this in Moscati 2007b.

14. Postulate 4 states that the individual prefers combination x to combination y if and only if he prefers the transition to x to the transition to y whatever the starting combination z is, and at the same time, he prefers reaching whatever combination w by starting from y rather than by starting from x. Postulate 7 is an Archimedean requirement: if x is preferred to y, there exists a finite sequence of equivalent transitions to more preferred combinations such that the last element of the sequence is at least as preferred as x.

15. Postulate 5 requires that if transition from x to y is preferred to transition from x′ to y′, and transition from y to z is preferred to transition from y′ to z′, then transition from x to z is preferred to transition from x′ to z′.

Alt proved that these seven postulates are necessary and sufficient for the existence of a utility function U over combinations of goods such that (1) combination x is preferred to combination y if and only if U(x) > U(y); (2) the transition from y to x is preferred to the transition from w to z if and only if U(x) – U(y) is larger than U(z) – U(w); and (3) U is unique up to positive linear transformations. Alt thus provided an analytically rigorous answer to the question concerning the exact conditions that make utility measurable in the sense envisaged by Lange.

Alt also addressed the validity and empirical verifiability of the seven postulates. He believed that postulate 1 "can be verified *by economic observations*" and is therefore well founded (431). He found postulate 2 more problematic, because it is not clear "whether it is at all possible to make comparisons between transitions . . . on the basis of experience" (431). With respect to the other five postulates, Alt left the issue concerning their validity open, arguing that they "can (and must) be tested against experience" (431).

6.6.3. Alt's Understanding of Measurement

Alt's understanding of which forms of quantitative assessment of utility count as utility measurement was very similar to that of Lange and Allen, although Alt did not cite Allen's 1935 note. Alt argued that if the utility numbers are arbitrary only with respect to unit and zero point of measurement, as is indeed the case when his seven postulates hold, then utility is properly measurable: "When we say that the utility of a commodity is 'measurable' or 'numerically representable' we mean that we can assign a real number . . . to each set of commodities . . . in such a way that this assignment is unique for choice of origin and unit of measurement" (424–425).

6.6.4. The Fortunes of Alt's Article

The fact that Alt's article was published in German in an Austrian journal seems to have hindered its appreciation in the English-speaking academic world. It was known by a number of important Austrians who emigrated to the United States in the early or mid-1930s, such as Schumpeter and Gerhard Tintner, as well as by Menger and Morgenstern, who both left Vienna for the United States shortly before the annexation of Austria by Nazi Germany in 1938 (Alt and his wife also eventually managed to flee to New York). In section 6.7.4, we will discover that Lange, who was Polish but fluent in German, also read Alt's paper. However, in the journals and books collected in the JSTOR database, in the ten years after its publication, Alt's article was cited only a few times and then only in footnotes. This faint appreciation of Alt's article in the English-speaking academic world plays some role in the events reconstructed in the next section.

A final comment: like Lange, Phelps Brown, and Allen, Alt did not associate utility that is unique up to positive linear transformations with the expression *cardinal utility*. The economist responsible for this association was a Harvard Ph.D. student named Paul Samuelson.

6.7. SAMUELSON'S CARDINAL UTILITY

6.7.1. Discounted Utility

Samuelson (1915–2009) entered the University of Chicago in 1932 and then moved on to graduate school at Harvard, where he studied under, among others, Schumpeter.[16] In 1937 and only twenty-one years old, Samuelson published in the *Review of Economic Studies* his first scientific article, "A Note on Measurement of Utility." Here he put forward a model of intertemporal choice where the individual behaves so as to maximize the discounted sum of all future utilities.[17] Given our concerns, it is important to notice that for Samuelson, the maximization of the discounted sum of future utilities implies that the individual is able to rank utility differences, that is, Pareto's assumption 2: "Reflection as to the meaning of our Assumption Two [that the individual maximizes the sum of future utilities] will reveal that the individual must make preferences in the Utility dimension itself, that is to say, we must invoke Pareto's postulate Two, which relates to the possibility of ordering *differences* in utility by the individual" (Samuelson 1937, 160–161).

This quotation also shows that, following Lange and ignoring the contributions of Phelps Brown and Alt, Samuelson in 1937 identified postulate 2 with the possibility of ranking utility differences. Accordingly, he claimed that postulate 2 restricts the admissible transformations of the utility function to the positive linear ones. In his first publication, Samuelson did not use the cardinal–ordinal terminology.

6.7.2. "Note" on Consumer's Behavior

The 1937 article was the first of an exceptionally copious and long-lasting series. In 1938 alone, Samuelson published four articles in major economics journals, three of which were related to utility theory and demand analysis, while the fourth addressed welfare economics.

The first 1938 article is Samuelson's celebrated "A Note on the Pure Theory of Consumer's Behaviour" (1938b). Here the Harvard Ph.D. student criticized Hicks and Allen's demand analysis as not properly behaviorist and put forward his own brand of behaviorism, later called the revealed preference approach to consumer demand. For Samuelson, Hicks and Allen's theory is not sound, because it relies on the assumption that the marginal rate of substitution is diminishing, that is, that the indifference curves are convex. This assumption, however, depends on introspective considerations: "Just as we do not claim to know by introspection the behaviour of utility, many will argue we cannot know the behaviour

16. On Samuelson's years at Chicago and Harvard, see Backhouse 2017.

17. That is, if $(x_0, x_1, x_2, \ldots, x_T)$ is a stream of monetary payments from the present time $t = 0$ until a future time $t = T$, Samuelson's discounted-utility model states that the individual behaves so as to maximize the discounted sum of all future utilities $\sum_{t=0}^{T} \delta^t U(x_t)$, whereby δ is the subjective discount factor. In the 1960s, the discounted-utility model became the standard neoclassical formalization of intertemporal choice. See more on the history and limitations of the discounted-utility model in Frederick, Loewenstein, and O'Donoghue 2002.

of . . . indifference directions. Why should one believe in the [*diminishing*] *rate of marginal substitution*?" (61).[18]

Since the goal of the "Note" was to show that demand analysis requires no reference to utility, Samuelson did not dwell on issues concerning the notion of utility. However, and this is important for the terminological aspect of our narrative, he here employed the expression *cardinal utility* for the first time in print. In reviewing the history of demand analysis based on utility, Samuelson argued that it had progressively ruled out unnecessarily restrictive conditions such as "the assumption of the measurability of utility in a cardinal sense" (61). It is not clear, however, what Samuelson meant by "measurability of utility in a cardinal sense." Certainly, he did not associate the expression with utility unique up to positive linear transformations.

In the second of the four articles published in 1938, "The Empirical Implications of Utility Analysis," Samuelson (1938a) argued that the ordinal utility theory initiated by Pareto does have refutable implications in terms of demand behavior, such as the negativity of the substitution effect, and attempted to provide a complete list of these implications. However, Samuelson claimed, the same implications can be derived more easily and directly from the postulates on choices he had put forward in the "Note." In this article, Samuelson twice employed the expression *ordinal preference* (345) but not the term *cardinal utility*.

6.7.3. Naming Cardinal Utility

Samuelson's third article of 1938, "The Numerical Representation of Ordered Classifications and the Concept of Utility," appeared in the October issue of the *Review of Economic Studies* (1938c) and is the most relevant one for our story. Samuelson here provided his solution to the problem concerning the conditions restricting the admissible transformations of the utility function to the positive linear ones and consistently coupled the expression *cardinal utility* with utility unique up to those transformations.

At the outset of the article, Samuelson acknowledged that Phelps Brown was right in criticizing Lange's results because they were based on an unwarranted identification of the G numbers representing the ranking of transitions with the difference between the U numbers representing the ranking of combinations (65). Samuelson saw that this identification cannot be taken for granted and accordingly investigated under what conditions it is valid.

In effect, the issue concerning the hypotheses that warrant the identification of the G numbers with the difference between the U numbers is exactly the problem that Alt had already addressed and solved in his 1936 article. However, Samuelson did not mention Alt's article.

Following Phelps Brown, Samuelson began by noting that postulates 1 and 2 concern only preference order, that postulate 1 allows for the introduction of an index U that assigns larger numbers to more preferred combinations, and that postulate 2 allows for the introduction of another index G assigning larger numbers to more preferred transitions (65–68). Samuelson then assumed that both preference orders are transitive and informally connected

18. For more on Samuelson and his revealed preference approach, see Mongin 2000; Moscati 2007b; Hands 2013a; Hands 2014; Hands 2017.

them by arguing that if an individual prefers the transition from x to y to the transitions from x to z, that is, if G(x, y) > G(x, z), then combination y must be preferred to combination z, that is, U(y) > U(z). This informal assumption corresponds to Alt's postulate 4.

Subsequently, Samuelson introduced the key postulate of his article as equation 15 (68). I noted in section 6.4.3 that Phelps Brown had also showed that postulate 2 does not warrant the possibility of summing G numbers. Samuelson's postulate overcomes the problem by simply assuming that G numbers can indeed be summed. That is, if G(x, y) is the number associated with the transition from x to y, and G(y, z) is the number associated with the transition from y to z, the postulate requires that the number G(x, z) associated with the transition from x to z must be equal to the sum of G(x, y) and G(y, z), that is, G(x, y) + G(y, z) = G(x, z). This postulate corresponds to Alt's postulates 5 and 7. However, while Alt's postulates concerned the preference orders over combinations and transitions, Samuelson's assumption refers directly to the G numbers and therefore does not make clear what features of the preference orders may be behind it.

At any rate, Samuelson showed that this postulate, together with the other assumptions mentioned above, is necessary and sufficient to make the G numbers associated with transitions equal to the difference between the U numbers associated with combinations, that is, to have G(x, y) = U(y) − U(x). In turn, and as Lange had already showed, G(x, y) = U(y) − U(x) if and only if the utility function U is unique only up to linear increasing transformations (69–70).

In the final part of his paper, Samuelson discussed the plausibility of the condition G(x, y) + G(y, z) = G(x, z) and argued that it is an "arbitrary restriction" that must be regarded as "infinitely improbable" (70). Therefore, he concluded, the uniqueness of the utility function up to positive linear transformations should also be considered as arbitrary and infinitely improbable.

Thus, Samuelson's confidence in the plausibility of cardinal utility shifted from the agnosticism of his discounted-utility article of 1937 (where, in effect, cardinal utility was necessary to make sense of the discounted-utility model) to the disbelief expressed in the 1938 paper under examination.

This last work also contains a terminological novelty that is central to our story: for the first time, utility unique up to positive linear transformations was explicitly and consistently coupled with the terms *cardinal* and *cardinal measurability*. This association occurs ten times in Samuelson's paper, and one example is as follows:[19] "Dr. Lange has not proved satisfactorily that from these two assumptions [Pareto's assumptions 1 and 2] can be derived the cardinal measurability of utility (subject to a linear transformation involving scale and origin constants)" (66). I argue, therefore, that *cardinal utility* acquired its current technical meaning in Samuelson's 1938 article.

6.7.4. Samuelson, Lange, and Alt

One question that naturally arises at this point is whether Samuelson knew of Alt's 1936 article. We can say that he was at least aware of its existence.

19. The other nine occurrences can be found at pp. 65, 68, and 70 of Samuelson 1938c.

Presumably in early 1938, Samuelson sent a draft of his cardinal utility paper to Lange, who replied in the letter of May 10, 1938, mentioned in section 6.4.5. Lange declared Samuelson's manuscript "a contribution which really helps to clarify the subject" and judged Samuelson's equation 15, that is, his postulate $G(x, y) + G(y, z) = G(x, z)$, a satisfactory solution to the problems Phelps Brown had called attention to:

> I agree with your argument and particularly that the functional equation (15) is necessary to establish measurability. It was contained implicitly in my formulation of postulate (2) . . . . It was exactly (15) that Phelps Brown had in mind when he objected to my argument. The formulation of the postulate 2 given by me was simply that of Pareto, Bowley, etc. since I was chiefly concerned with the inconsistency of their argument. (Samuelson papers, box 48)

In his letter, Lange also explicitly invited Samuelson to look at Alt's article and pointed out the possible relationship between Samuelson's postulate 15 and Alt's postulates: "I would suggest that you look up the article of Alt, Über die Messbarkeit des Nutzens, Zeitschr. F. Nat.- Oeconomie, Bd. VII (1936). If I am not mistaken your equation (15) corresponds to his postulates IV and V."

We know from a letter of Ursula Webb Hicks to Samuelson that Samuelson did not see the proofs of his article.[20] Therefore, even if he did look at Alt's article between May and October 1938, he could not have added a reference to Alt. Be that as it may, in his subsequent writings of the 1930s and 1940s, Samuelson did not refer to Alt's 1936 article.

6.8. HICKS'S *VALUE AND CAPITAL* AND SAMUELSON'S *FOUNDATIONS OF ECONOMIC ANALYSIS*

After the publication of Hicks and Allen's 1934 article and in parallel with the debate about the ranking of transitions, other significant developments were taking place in utility analysis. These developments found their culmination in the systematized version of the ordinal approach based on utility indices provided by Hicks in *Value and Capital* (1939b) and by Samuelson in his *Foundations of Economic Analysis* (1947).

6.8.1. Slutsky and Allen

Russian economist and statistician Eugen Slutsky was an admirer of Pareto. In 1915, he published in the *Giornale degli Economisti*, the Italian journal in which Pareto had published most of his contributions, an article in which he anticipated many of the results later obtained by Hicks and Allen. Unlike the two LSE economists, however, Slutsky ([1915] 1952) expressed his theory in terms of a utility function and its derivatives. Moreover, Slutsky did not make clear whether his results were ordinal in nature, that is, whether they were invariant to increasing transformations of the utility function. At any rate, for reasons

20. Ursula Webb Hicks to Samuelson, October 4, 1938, Samuelson papers, box 37.

about which we can only speculate, for almost twenty years, Slutsky's paper was completely neglected. It was rediscovered only in the early 1930s, by Valentino Dominedò (1933) in Italy, Henry Schultz (1935) in the United States, and Allen in England.[21]

In an article published in the *Review of Economic Studies*, Allen (1936) called attention to Slutsky's paper, acknowledged his priority with respect to a number of results, and stressed the differences between Slutsky's utility-based approach and the utility-free approach he and Hicks had put forward in their 1934 article: "Slutsky's starting point is different from that of Hicks and myself. Our theory was constructed so as to be independent of the existence of an index of utility.... Slutsky expresses his theory in terms of one selected utility function and its partial derivatives" (127). Allen showed, however, that Slutsky's results are in fact independent from measurability assumptions on the utility function and hold also in a purely ordinal framework.

6.8.2. Hicks the Ordinalist

Allen's article paved the way for the ordinal restatement of Slutsky's findings and the subsequent establishment of ordinal utility theory as the mainstream approach to demand analysis. Although for a while, Allen (1938) insisted on the utility-free approach, after 1936, Hicks (1937, 1939b) set forth his analysis in terms of ordinal utility indices.

Most notably, in *Value and Capital* (1939b), Hicks fine-tuned the ordinal approach to utility theory. He now re-presented Slutsky's results in a systematic and mathematically clear way and demonstrated, more thoroughly than Allen had, that these results are ordinal in nature. Hicks also showed that the results he and Allen had obtained in 1934 using the marginal rate of substitution could be obtained through ordinal utility indices in a theoretically rigorous and much simpler way. The marginal rate of substitution itself returned to being expressed as the ratio between the partial derivatives of the utility function.

It is notable that in *Value and Capital*, Hicks did not discuss any of the issues associated with the emergence of the notion of cardinal utility. There is in his book no mention of the ranking of transitions, postulate 2, determinateness of the utility function, or utility unique up to positive linear transformations. In other words, cardinal utility plays no role in *Value and Capital*, and the very expression *cardinal utility*, which Hicks had used in the article coauthored with Allen, does not even appear in the book. In chapter 1, Hicks (1939b, 18) mentioned issues related to the "quantitative measure of utility" but only to stress that "the quantitative concept of utility is not necessary in order to explain market phenomena." Therefore, Hicks concluded, on the basis of the methodological "principle of Occam's razor, it is better to do without it" (18). As I observed in section 6.5.1, Allen (1935) had expressed a similar idea by stating that Pareto's assumption 2 does not work its passage in utility theory.

6.8.3. Samuelson's *Foundations*

As mentioned in section 6.7.3, Samuelson (1938c, 70) argued that the key condition implying cardinal utility, namely the condition $G(x, y) + G(y, z) = G(x, z)$, is an "arbitrary

21. On the rediscovery of Slutsky's 1915 article, see Chipman and Lenfant 2002.

restriction" that must be regarded as "infinitely improbable." Samuelson's skepticism about cardinal utility found full expression in his Harvard Ph.D. dissertation, which he submitted in November 1940 after he had already left Harvard for MIT.[22]

The dissertation was entitled "Foundations of Analytical Economics" (Samuelson 1940), and it became, seven years later, *Foundations of Economic Analysis* (Samuelson 1947).[23] *Foundations* quickly became a reference book for postwar economic theorists of no less importance than Hicks's *Value and Capital*, and it consolidated Samuelson's position as a leading internationally recognized economist. In the Ph.D. dissertation and, in identical form, in *Foundations*, Samuelson downplayed the utility-free approach he had proposed in his 1938 "Note" and presented the theory of consumer demand following an ordinal utility approach substantially equivalent to that used by Hicks in *Value and Capital*.

Accordingly, Samuelson argued that "the content of utility analysis in its most general form [involves] only an ordinal preference field" and dismissed "the cardinal measure of utility" as a "special and extra" assumption by which "nothing at all is gained" (Samuelson 1940, 147–150; 1947, 172–173). Samuelson then discussed other special and extra assumptions of utility theory, such as the additive separability of the utility function and the constancy of the marginal utility of income and showed that they often imply cardinal utility. However, Samuelson rejected these other special assumptions, too, judging them "not generally applicable," "arbitrary," "dubious," "highly unrealistic," "superfluous," and leading to "really fantastic conclusions" (1940, 150–189; 1947, 174–202). Also in other works of the same period, Samuelson (1939a; 1942) maintained a skeptical stance on the empirical validity and theoretical usefulness of cardinal utility.

6.8.4. The Fortunes of Cardinal Utility from 1940 to 1945

From 1940 to 1945, other economists began to refer to cardinal utility in the sense established by Samuelson. Frank Knight, one of the leaders of the Chicago School, referred approvingly to cardinal utility in two articles where he criticized the ordinal approach to demand analysis epitomized by Hicks's *Value and Capital* (Knight 1940; Knight 1944). In 1943, Robert L. Bishop, a young colleague of Samuelson at MIT, published the first economics article containing the expression *cardinal utility* in its title. Bishop (1943) argued that cardinal utility is necessary to make sense of the notion of consumer surplus, which he considered useful for welfare analysis.

At any rate, we can say that before 1945, cardinal utility in the specific sense established by Samuelson, that is, as utility unique up to positive linear transformations, remained peripheral in economic theory. In effect, it was at odds with the ordinal approach that, especially after the publication of Hicks's *Value and Capital*, dominated demand analysis. From a terminological perspective, however, Samuelson's use of the expression *cardinal utility* stabilized. For while Samuelson himself remained highly critical of utility unique up to positive linear

22. More on Samuelson's move to MIT in Backhouse 2014.
23. See more on the relationships between the dissertation and the book and the reasons for the book's delayed publication in Samuelson 1998; Backhouse 2015.

transformations, by consistently referring to it as cardinal utility, he contributed to the stabilization of the meaning of the expression.

As I discuss in part III, the fortunes of cardinal utility changed after 1945, when von Neumann and Morgenstern's axiomatic version of expected utility theory generated a debate that eventually brought about a rehabilitation of the concept of cardinal utility. The rehabilitated cardinal utility of the 1950s, however, was significantly different from the cardinal utility of the 1930s.

CHAPTER 7

Going Empirical

The Econometric and Experimental Approaches to Utility Measurement of Frisch and Thurstone, 1925–1945

Between the mid-1920s and the final phase of the ordinal revolution initiated with the publication of Hicks and Allen's 1934 article, two early attempts to give the notion of utility an empirical content were made. In 1926 Norwegian Ragnar Frisch published an article in which he coined the term *econometrics* and applied an econometric approach to measuring the marginal utility of money on the basis of demand data collected in France from 1920 to 1922. In his *New Methods of Measuring Marginal Utility* (1932), Frisch provided a more extensive presentation of his econometric method of measuring the marginal utility of money and also advanced two further procedures to measure utility. The second attempt to give an empirical content to the notion of utility was carried out by Louis Leon Thurstone, an American psychologist encountered in chapter 4. In 1930, Thurstone conducted a laboratory experiment to elicit the indifference curves of an individual on the basis of choices between bundles containing hats, shoes, and overcoats. Notably, both Frisch and Thurstone intended measurement in the unit-based sense.

Most commentators of the 1930s and early 1940s judged the assumptions underlying both Frisch's and Thurstone's utility measurements to be highly problematic and therefore remained skeptical about the significance of their respective measurements. Moreover, after the mid-1930s and the completion of the ordinal revolution, most utility theorists lost interest in measuring utility in a more than ordinal sense. The limited impact of Frisch's and Thurstone's pioneering studies notwithstanding, they nevertheless represent significant episodes in the history of the empirical measurement of utility.[1] In addition, their two

1. For a broader picture of the attempts to give empirical content to ordinal utility theory that looks beyond issues concerning utility measurement, see Hands 2017.

studies stand at the origin of two important areas of empirical economics, namely econometrics and experimental economics.

In the main part of this chapter, I review Frisch's and Thurstone's studies and the discussions they initiated in the 1930s and early 1940s. In the final section, which also concludes part II of the book, I reconsider the history of utility measurement between 1900 and 1945 with respect to the five dimensions of the problem of utility measurement set out in the prologue.

7.1. FRISCH'S ECONOMETRIC MEASUREMENT OF THE MARGINAL UTILITY OF MONEY

7.1.1. A New Discipline Called Econometrics

Frisch (1895–1973) graduated in economics from the University of Oslo in 1919, and from 1921 to 1923, he studied in Paris, where he became familiar with the works of Irving Fisher and Vilfredo Pareto. Returning to Oslo, he completed his doctoral dissertation in mathematical statistics, which he successfully defended in 1926. In the same year, he published in the Norwegian journal *Norsk Matematisk Forenings Skrifter* his first economic article, "Sur un problème d'économie pure" (On a Problem in Pure Economics).[2]

In the first paragraph of this article, Frisch ([1926] 1971, 386) coined the term *econometrics* (*économetrié*) to designate a new discipline "intermediate between mathematics, statistics, and economics." For Frisch, the aim of the new discipline should be "to subject abstract laws of . . . 'pure' economics to experimental and numerical verification, and thus to turn pure economics, as far as is possible, into a science in the strict sense of the word" (386).

Frisch immediately applied his econometric approach to a traditional problem of economics, namely that of measuring utility. More specifically, Frisch focused on the problem of measuring the marginal utility of money, that is, the marginal change in total utility arising from a marginal increase in the consumer's income: "The econometric study that I shall present is an attempt to realize the dream of Jevons: to measure the variation in the marginal utility of economic goods. I shall give special attention to the variation in the marginal utility of money" (386).

As we will see, what Frisch in fact attempted to measure was the elasticity of the marginal utility of real income.

7.1.2. Utility as a Quantity

Frisch reasoned that before making any attempt to measure utility empirically, it is first necessary to define exactly the concept of utility. Moreover, the definition should warrant that marginal utility is in fact a measurable magnitude, that is, "a quantity" (387). Following the tradition initiated by Aristotle and Euclid (see chapter 1, section 1.1), Frisch meant by quantity a magnitude for which a unit of measurement is available and that is therefore

2. See more on Frisch in Arrow 1960; Strøm 1998; Bjerkholt and Dupont 2010.

measurable on a ratio scale. In the first section of his article, therefore, he put forward a series of axioms that define the utility concept so that "the unit of measurement for marginal utility" (394) is well defined.[3]

7.1.3. The Basic Equation

In sections 2 and 3 of his article, Frisch constructed the equation featuring the marginal utility of money that, in section 4, he estimated using his statistical data on demand. A basic implication of utility analysis (see, e.g., Marshall 1890, 737–738) is that for a consumer who has a fixed income I and spends it on commodities $x_1, x_2, x_3, \ldots$, whose fixed prices are $p_1, p_2, p_3, \ldots$, at the equilibrium point the marginal utility of money λ is equal to the common ratio between the marginal utility U'_i of commodity i and the commodity price p_i:

$$\frac{U'_1}{p_1}=\frac{U'_2}{p_2}=\frac{U'_3}{p_3}=\ldots=\lambda \tag{1}$$

Since in equilibrium, the U'_i/p_i ratio is common for all commodities, we can focus on a single commodity, say commodity 1:

$$\frac{U'_1}{p_1}=\lambda \tag{2}$$

This is the general equation from which Frisch started.

Frisch next assumed that the marginal utility of each commodity depends only on the quantity consumed of that commodity, that is, that the (total) utility function is additively separable. Based on this additivity assumption but also on a number of implicit hypotheses that became clear only in the subsequent discussion of his work, from equation (2), Frisch derived equation (3):

$$\frac{U'_1(x_1)}{p_1}=\frac{1}{P}g\left(\frac{I}{P}\right) \tag{3}$$

where P is an index of the general price level and g a function expressing the marginal utility of real income I/P. In this equation, the numerical values of x_1, p_1, I, and P are, at least in principle, obtainable from market data. According to Frisch, these numerical values allow us to estimate how the marginal utility of real income, that is, g, varies when real income I/P varies.

3. Apparently, Frisch's is the first axiomatic treatment of utility. However, since Frisch's axiomatization had little impact on the subsequent literature and because my main concern here is the econometric part of his article, I do not here enter into Frisch's axioms on utility. See more on this in Arrow 1960; Chipman 1971.

7.1.4. Measuring Elasticity

In section 4 of his article, Frisch implemented his econometric model using statistical data furnished by the Union des Coopérateurs Parisiens about the price of sugar (which was used as the reference commodity 1), the quantity of sugar sold, the number of members of the cooperative, and the value of the cooperative's total sales from June 1920 to December 1922. In particular, Frisch determined the percentage variation in the marginal utility of real income determined by a given percentage variation in the real income, that is, the elasticity of the marginal utility of real income.

In accord with the marginalist idea that the marginal utility of all commodities, including money, is diminishing, that is, that their elasticity is negative, Frisch found that when real income increased, its marginal utility decreased, and vice versa. Thus, for instance, he found that a 5 percent increase in real income determined a 9.6 percent decrease in the marginal utility of real income, while a 5 percent decrease in real income determined a 13 percent increase in the marginal utility of real income (416, tab. 2).

Frisch's 1926 article went largely unnoticed among economists, arguably because it was published in a mathematical Norwegian journal by a scholar who, at that time, had only just completed his Ph.D.

7.2. FROM OSLO TO YALE

7.2.1. Frisch and Fisher

From February 1927 to March 1928, Frisch was in the United States on a Rockefeller fellowship. During this time, he promoted the creation of an international scientific society that could advance the new discipline of econometrics. He discussed the project with a number of leading economists based in the United States, including Joseph Schumpeter at Harvard and Irving Fisher at Yale.

As discussed in chapter 3, section 3.3.3, in his *Mathematical Investigations*, Fisher (1892) had imagined an experimental method to measure the marginal utility of commodities. In the following years, he attempted to implement a modified version of this method using actual statistical data, but he judged the results obtained unsatisfactory. In 1927, Fisher decided to present at least the structure of his statistical method for measuring marginal utility but left to others the problem of applying it to actual demand data: "I am here offering no statistics but only a statistical method. . . . If someone else than I will perform this arduous task [that of applying the method] I shall be more than pleased" (Fisher 1927, 193).

Fisher's method was tricky. In the first place, it was based on demanding theoretical assumptions, such as that different groups of individuals have the same utility function and that this function is additively separable. Moreover, it required data difficult to find, such as data about the prices of commodities in different localities at the same moment. When Frisch and Fisher met in 1927 to talk about the creation of a society that could promote econometrics, they also discussed their common interest in measuring utility using statistical data. In 1929, Fisher invited Frisch to Yale as a visiting professor so that they could work together on this topic.[4]

4. See Bjerkholt and Dupont 2010; Frisch 1932, 2–6.

7.2.2. Utility Measurement and the Founding of the Econometric Society

Frisch visited Yale from February 1930 to June 1931. In spring and summer 1930, Frisch, Fisher, and Charles F. Roos, a mathematical economist based at Cornell University, worked to establish the scientific society promoting econometrics that came to be named the Econometric Society, and Frisch wrote a draft of its constitution. The society was officially founded in Cleveland in December 1930 during the annual joint meetings of the American Economic Association and the American Statistical Association. Fisher was elected president of the society, while Frisch, Roos, and Schumpeter were elected to the society's council.[5] Among the other scholars involved in the creation of the Econometric Society were the Europeans Luigi Amoroso, Arthur Bowley, Karl Menger, and Wladimir Zawadzki (see chapter 6), as well as Harold Hotelling, an eminent economist and statistician based at Columbia University, and Henry Schultz, another leading economist and statistician who worked at the University of Chicago (see more on Schultz in sections 7.3 and 7.4.2).

With respect to issues relating to utility measurement, during the first part of Frisch's stay at Yale, he and Fisher attempted to apply Fisher's measurement method to American statistical data. However, as Frisch later explained, they were not successful. The difficulty arose from the lack of adequate price data: "We were unable to secure reliable data by which to make the *geographical* price comparisons needed in our study" (Frisch 1932, 6).

At this point, Fisher lost interest in the project, while Frisch decided to expand his 1926 study on the econometric measurement of the marginal utility of money. During the remaining part of his stay at Yale, Frisch worked on this project, and in May 1931, he completed his book on *New Methods of Measuring Marginal Utility*. The book was dedicated to "Irving Fisher, the pioneer of utility measurement," and was published in 1932. By this date, Frisch had returned to Norway to become professor of economics and statistics and also director of the newly established Institute of Economics at Oslo University.

7.3. *NEW METHODS* AND REACTIONS TO IT

In the first part of *New Methods of Measuring Marginal Utility*, Frisch (1932, 8–32) represented the method of measuring the elasticity of the marginal utility of real income which he had put forward in his 1926 article. He now called it the "isoquant method." In the second part of the book (33–58), Frisch set out two variations of the isoquant method, which he called the "quantity variation method" and the "translation method." Finally, he applied the translation method to budget data collected by the US Bureau of Labor Statistics for the years 1918 and 1919. Frisch found that the elasticity of the marginal utility of real income was negative and inferior to one in absolute value (64, tab. 5).

Frisch's 1932 book was widely discussed. The role played by Frisch in the creation of the Econometric Society and the fact that in 1933 he had become the editor of *Econometrica*, the society's journal, certainly helped in getting the attention of his fellow economists. Although

5. See more on the foundation of the Econometric Society in Bjerkholt 1998.

most commentators appreciated Frisch's general approach to giving empirical content to the notion of marginal utility, they also stressed that the additive-utility assumption as well as other assumptions underlying Frisch's study were doubtful.

For example, reviewing the book in the *Economic Journal*, Bowley (1932, 252) argued that "in the end it will be the non-numerical part of this treatment that will prove the most important," because that part is independent of "the troublesome and doubtful hypotheses that are necessary in handling existing data." In a similar vein, Hotelling (1932, 452) claimed that Frisch's book was "more concerned with telling how to work them out [the marginal utility functions] than showing the numerical results accomplished."

Schultz devoted to Frisch's book a full review article in the *Journal of Political Economy*. On the one hand, Schultz (1933, 111) agreed with Frisch that his method fulfilled Jevons's vision of measuring utility indirectly: "A method is now at hand which, while it does not directly measure [Jevons's] pleasure and pain . . . at least determines their comparative intensity from the quantitative effects of these feelings." Yet on the other hand, Schultz stressed that Frisch's method relied on several implausible assumptions, such as that "the utility which an individual derives from a commodity is a function only of the quantity of that commodity" (111) and that "the marginal-utility functions . . . are of the same shape for all persons of the group" (112). Finally, Schultz argued that all manipulations Frisch made to pass from the theoretical equation expressing the marginal utility of money, that is, $\frac{U_1'}{p_1} = \lambda$, to the equation estimated using the statistical data, that is, $\frac{U_1'(x_1)}{p_1} = \frac{1}{P} g\left(\frac{I}{P}\right)$, obscured the actual economic meaning of what is measured. Why, Schultz asked, call the function g "a curve of marginal utility of money?" (112).

In a critical article published in *Economica*, Roy Allen (1933) made a similar point. He claimed that in passing from the marginal utility of money as defined in utility theory, that is, as a function of the consumer's income I and the prices $p_1, p_2, p_3, \ldots,$ of all commodities, to the marginal utility of money as defined by Frisch, that is, as a function of the consumer's income I and the general price level P, Frisch was taking "from the notion of money marginal utility most of its essential and distinctive meaning" (187).

Frisch (1936) replied to some of these criticisms, but commentators such as Abram Burk (who later changed his surname and came to be known as Abram Bergson) remained unconvinced (Burk 1936). In general, after the mid-1930s, interest among utility theorists in Frisch's econometric measurements of marginal utility faded away. This seems to have been due to various compounding factors. In the first place, and as already discussed, the assumptions underlying Frisch's measurement methods appeared implausible to most utility theorists. Moreover, after the completion of the ordinal revolution in the mid-1930s, utility theorists lost interest in measuring the marginal utility of money, for this concept plays only a minor role in the ordinal approach.

7.4. THURSTONE, PARETO, SCHULTZ

Around the same period when Frisch was working on his econometric approach to utility measurement, another attempt to give an empirical content to the notion of utility was carried out by American psychologist Louis Leon Thurstone. To measure utility, Thurstone did not use real market data. Rather, he imported into economics the experimental approach that psychologists had been using since the rise of psychophysics in the late nineteenth century (see chapters 1 and 4). In this approach, the data are generated in a controlled environment, that is, in a "laboratory," by asking one or more individuals to perform certain tasks. According to all available evidence (Roth 1993; Moscati 2007a), Thurstone's study was the first actual lab experiment in economics.

7.4.1. From Pareto to Thurstone

As discussed in chapter 5, section 5.1.5, indifference curves play a central role in Pareto's utility analysis. He conceived of them as lines collecting all combinations of goods among which the individual is indifferent and associated each indifference curve with an ordinal utility index, whereby higher indifference curves correspond to larger utility indices. To elicit the indifference curves of an individual, Pareto ([1900] 2008, 453–454; [1906/1909] 2014, 118–119) imagined an experiment in which the individual is asked to choose between two commodity bundles x and y. If the individual chooses bundle x, the composition of y is changed up to the point where the individual becomes indifferent between x and y, thus determining two points on the indifference curve. This procedure can be repeated until a sufficient number of points on the same indifference curve are identified.

Pareto's experiment, however, was hypothetical; there was no actual experimental subject and no commodity bundles. Thurstone carried out the first experimental study to determine the indifference curves of a real individual in 1930, and his results were published in the *Journal of Social Psychology* a year later (Thurstone 1931).

7.4.2. Thurstone and Schultz

As chapter 4 described, Thurstone was a central figure in experimental psychology in America from the early 1920s to the mid-1950s and made important contributions to the development of psychometric techniques and the study of intelligence. From 1924, he was a professor at the University of Chicago, where in the early 1930s he established the Psychometric Laboratory. A colleague of Thurstone's at Chicago was Schultz, an economist and statistician who had a particular interest in the quantitative estimation of economic variables, especially demand (Schultz 1928; 1938). As mentioned earlier in section 7.2.2, Schultz was among the founding members of the Econometric Society. He was also one of the rediscoverers of Slutsky's neglected paper (see chapter 6, section 6.8.1) and a major expert on and admirer of Pareto.

As Thurstone (1931, 139) recalled, it was Schultz who suggested that he apply the experimental methods used in his psychological research to estimate an individual's indifference curve: "The formulation of this problem is due to numerous conversations about psychophysics with my friend Professor Henry Schultz. . . . It was at his suggestion that experimental methods were applied to this problem in economic theory."

At that time, Schultz appears to have been Thurstone's only source of knowledge of economic theory. In fact, at the beginning of his paper, Thurstone cautiously attributed to

Schultz the opinion that the indifference curves had never before been subjected to experimental study, emphasizing that "the writer dares not venture far into economic theory" (139). Apart from Schultz, in his article, Thurstone cited neither Frisch nor any other economist. The only explicit hint to the economic literature was the listing of Fisher's *Mathematical Investigations* in the references section.

7.5. THURSTONE'S EXPERIMENTAL INDIFFERENCE CURVES

7.5.1. Goals and Approach

The supposition that Thurstone was not acquainted with economic theory fits well with the fact that his approach to utility analysis and the ultimate goals of his experiment were quite at odds with the antipsychological stance of Fisher and Pareto. Thurstone was not interested in abandoning the mental variables *utility* and *marginal utility,* for which he used the psychologically tinged expressions *satisfaction* and *motivation*. The problem for him was rather to give the satisfaction curve, that is, the utility curve, and the indifference curve an exact quantitative determination.

To attain this goal, he first put forward a model of utility based on some "fundamental psychological postulates" (141). Then he measured the parameters of that model by using the data obtained in the first part of his experiment. Finally, based on the parametrized model, he made some predictions about the behavior of the experimental subject, checked whether these predictions were correct, and thus tested the descriptive validity of the parametrized model.

7.5.2. Thurstone's Utility Model

The assumptions of Thurstone's utility model are much more in line with the marginal utility theory of the 1870s than with the ordinal approach of the 1930s. In the first place, Thurstone hypothesized that satisfaction, that is, utility, is measurable on a unit-based scale. As a unit, he used the "standard discriminal error" that he had defined in 1927 within his method of comparative judgment (Thurstone 1927a; 1927b; see chapter 4, section 4.2.2): "In the measurement of satisfaction we shall imply throughout that it is accomplished in terms of the subjective unit of measurement, the discriminal error" (Thurstone 1931, 140–141). Second, like the early utility theorists but also like Frisch, Thurstone assumed that the utility of each commodity is independent of the quantities of other commodities. Third, in accord with the Weber–Fechner assumption about the relation between physical stimulus and corresponding sensation (see chapter 1, section 1.3.1), Thurstone posited that "motivation," that is, marginal utility, is proportional to the quantity of the good already possessed. This assumption implies that the utility function has a logarithmic form: $U(x_i) = k_i \log(x_i)$, where k_i is a constant characterizing each commodity i. Accordingly, the indifference curves are hyperbolas with equation $\bar{U} = k_1 \log(x_1) + k_2 \log(x_2)$, where $\bar{U}$ is a fixed level of satisfaction or utility.

7.5.3. Measuring the Parameters of the Utility Model

Thurstone considered three different commodities, namely hats, shoes, and overcoats. In the experiment, a female subject was presented with a hypothetical bundle containing a certain number of two commodities, for example, eight hats and eight pairs of shoes.[6] Each commodity bundle was plotted on a Cartesian plane with the commodity quantities on the axes. Subsequently, in random order, the subject was presented with other hypothetical combinations (more than two hundred) of the same commodities and asked to choose her preferred one.

It is important to note that this is not the procedure originally suggested by Pareto. As recalled in section 7.4.1, Pareto had imagined asking the subject to identify a bundle indifferent to a reference bundle. This means that the subject could be presented with a series of choices of the form "eight hats and eight pairs of shoes, or six hats and *n* pairs of shoes," and asked to indicate the number *n* that would render him indifferent between the two commodity bundles.

Thurstone judged Pareto's hypothetical procedure, which he called "the method of reproduction," unreliable. For him, indeed, the statements required by the reproduction method would be "so unstable and so markedly influenced by the desire for numerical consistency" that indifference curves obtained through these statements would be "of doubtful value" (151). Thurstone considered asking the subject to choose between a reference bundle and another bundle a less problematic procedure and called it "the constant method."

Based on the constant method, Thurstone built up two fields in the plane: one containing the bundles preferred to the initial one (indicated with a black circle), the other containing the bundles less preferred (indicated with a white sign). At this point, Thurstone drew the indifference curve so that, as far as possible, all the preferred bundles lay above the curve and all the less preferred bundles lay below it. The as-far-as-possible clause means that in practice, Thurstone discounted some anomalous preferences in order to draw a hyperbolic curve through the black (preferred) and the white (less preferred) fields. Following the described procedure, Thurstone constructed four hyperbolic indifference curves for hats and shoes. Similarly, he constructed four curves for hats and overcoats. In figure 7.1, one of Thurstone's indifference curves for hats and shoes is reproduced.

By using the method of averages, Thurstone estimated from the data the values of the parameters k_i for hats, shoes, and overcoats. In particular, he found that for hats $k_1 = 1.00$, for shoes $k_2 = 1.26$, and for coats $k_3 = 1.32$.

7.5.4. Testing the Utility Model

Parameters k_2 and k_3 are derived, respectively, from hats–shoes and hats–overcoats comparisons. Within Thurstone's utility model, they imply that the subject's indifference

6. In a letter to experimental psychologist Ward Edwards dated December 7, 1953, Thurstone specified: "I selected as subject a research assistant in my laboratory who knew nothing about psychophysics. . . . She had a very even disposition, and I instructed her to take an even motivational attitude on the successive occasions" (quoted in Edwards 1954c, 387).

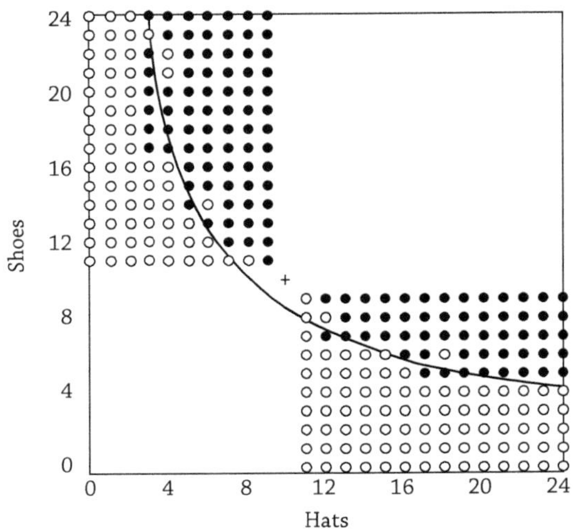

Figure 7.1. Indifference curve elicited by Thurstone
An experimental indifference curve for shoes and hats built using as reference the bundle containing ten hats and ten pairs of shoes. The black circles below the curve and the white circles above the curve are discounted as anomalous preferences.
Source: Thurstone 1931, 156. Reproduced with permission of Taylor & Francis.

curves regarding shoes and overcoats have the form $\bar{U} = 1.26 \log(x_1) + 1.32 \log(x_2)$. In the final part of his experiment, Thurstone elicited four indifference curves for shoes and overcoats using the constant method, checked whether the equation had predicted the elicited curves in a satisfactory way, and argued that this was in fact the case (163–164). He concluded his article with the claim: "It is possible to reduce the indifference function to experimental treatment and . . . it is possible to write a rational equation for the indifference function which is based on plausible psychological postulates" (165).

A final comment concerning the relationship between Pareto's thought experiment and Thurstone's actual study is in order. With respect to Pareto's mental exercise, in Thurstone's experiment, there is indeed a real subject but still no bundles: the subject chose between imaginary bundles containing imaginary hats, shoes, and overcoats. Many commentators on Thurstone's experiment criticized this aspect of its design.

7.6. THE RECEPTION OF THURSTONE'S EXPERIMENT, 1932–1942

7.6.1. The 1930s

Despite the fact that Thurstone's paper was published in a psychological journal, it became known to a number of prominent utility theorists, for in June 1932, he presented his experimental study at the meeting of the Econometric Society held in Syracuse, New York. Among others, Frisch and Hotelling were in attendance. In the discussion following Thurstone's presentation, the comments were mainly critical.

Applied economist and statistician Mordecai Ezekiel pointed out the difference between answers individuals give to questions or questionnaires and their actual behavior, and he argued that the latter often contradicts the former: "Housewives' answers, for example, indicated an elastic demand for milk, while objective studies showed the demand to be inelastic" (Mayer 1933, 97). Another participant in the session, economist and methodologist Joseph Mayer, stressed the distinction between "order of preference and measure of preference" and remained skeptical about the possibility of an "actual quantitative measurement of satisfactions" (Mayer 1933, 98).

In the published literature, Thurstone's paper did not fare much better, for references to it were quite cursory. In his 1936 paper on the theory of consumer behavior, Nicholas Georgescu-Roegen of Romania (at Harvard from 1934 to 1936) cited Thurstone's experiment in a footnote but only to observe that it could not "be relevant to a theory concerned with an actual choice" (Georgescu-Roegen 1936, 585 n. 3). Basically, Georgescu-Roegen was critical of the hypothetical nature of the subject's decisions in Thurstone's study. Hotelling cited Thurstone's experiment just once, writing only that the psychologist had "succeeded in mapping out in a tentative manner the indifference loci" (Hotelling 1938, 248). Schultz himself recalled Thurstone's experiment only casually in two footnotes (Schultz 1931, 78 n. 5; 1938, 15 n. 18).

In conclusion, Thurstone's paper had a negligible impact on the development of utility theory in the 1930s. This does not seem to be due to ignorance of his work. More crucial is the fact that Thurstone's approach to utility theory was at odds with the ordinalist ideas of the period. In particular, Thurstone's preordinal conception of utility and the fact that his experiment did not bear on the actual choices of individuals undermined the impact on economics of his pioneering study.

7.6.2. The Wallis–Friedman Critique of Thurstone's Experiment

Probably the most thorough criticism of Thurstone's experiment was published in 1942, that is, more than a decade after the publication of his article in 1931. The critics were W. Allen Wallis and Milton Friedman, then two young economists and statisticians who had studied at the University of Chicago. Their article appeared in an important volume of essays published in memory of Schultz, who had died in a car accident in 1938. Given the role played by Wallis and Friedman in our narrative, a discussion of their careers prior to the early 1940s is in order.

Wallis (1912–1998) studied psychology (B.A. 1932) and then economics at the University of Minnesota. In 1933–1934, he pursued his graduate studies at the University of Chicago, where he met Friedman, with whom he formed a lifelong friendship. Unsatisfied with Schultz's approach to statistics, in 1935–1936, Wallis went to Columbia University to study under Hotelling. After holding one-year positions first at the National Resources Committee in Washington and then at Yale University, in 1938, Wallis was appointed assistant professor at Stanford University. In July 1942, he was named director of the Statistical

Research Group (SRG), a wartime think tank providing statistical analysis for the US Army and based at Columbia University. Several characters in our story, including Hotelling, Friedman, Leonard Jimmie Savage, and Frederick Mosteller worked at SRG during the war (see chapters 10 and 13).[7]

Friedman (1912–2006) is today usually remembered as a monetary theorist, but he began his career as a consumption theorist and an applied statistician. He studied economics and mathematics at Rutgers University (B.A. 1932), moved to the University of Chicago for a master's degree in economics (1933), and then transferred to Columbia to continue his studies in mathematical economics under Hotelling. In 1934–1935, he returned to Chicago as a research assistant to Schultz and helped him in the completion of the book *The Theory and Measurement of Demand* (Schultz 1938). In 1935, Friedman joined the staff of the National Resources Committee in Washington, where he designed sampling techniques for a large study on consumer purchases. In 1937, he moved to the National Bureau of Economic Research (NBER) in New York to collaborate with economist and statistician Simon Kuznets on a statistical study of income distribution. After holding positions at the University of Wisconsin (1940–1941) and the Treasury Department in Washington (1941–1943), in March 1943, Friedman joined Wallis at the SRG.[8]

In their joint paper, Wallis and Friedman (1942) first pointed out some flaws in Thurstone's statistical techniques that marred his estimation of the k_i parameters. More fundamentally, and similarly to Ezekiel and Georgescu-Roegen, they criticized Thurstone's experiment for the hypothetical nature of the subject's choices: "For a satisfactory experiment it is essential that the subject give actual reactions to actual stimuli. . . . Questionnaires or other devices based on conjectural responses to hypothetical stimuli do not satisfy this requirement" (179–180).

The conjectural nature of Thurstone's test, however, does not preclude the possibility of experiments with real stimuli. To discuss this point, Wallis and Friedman imagined a different experiment, in which a child can choose among different combinations of candy and ice cream but has to consume the chosen combination. If different combinations of candy and ice cream are offered to the child, "it would clearly be necessary to offer the same combinations day after day, to give the subject an opportunity to experiment" (180). The attractiveness of variety can lead to alterations in the pattern of choices, so that it may be necessary to wait some time between offering different combinations. At the end of this process, only a single observation would be obtained, and it would be necessary to repeat the procedure in order to get additional data for the estimation of the child's indifference curve. Wallis and Friedman argued that in the course of such a prolonged process of data recording, the individual's preferences would change so that the entire estimating procedure would fail.

Their conclusion regarding the experimental derivation of the indifference curves was therefore skeptical: "These are more than technical or practical obstacles and indicate that it is probably not possible to design a satisfactory experiment for deriving indifference curves from economic stimuli" (181).[9]

7. See more on Wallis and the SRG in Wallis 1980; Olkin 1991.
8. See more on Friedman's early career in Hammond 2006; Hammond 2010.
9. In their paper, Wallis and Friedman also criticized the possibility of deriving indifference curves using statistical techniques. On this part of their paper, see Moscati 2007a.

As we will see in chapter 13, this earlier skeptical conclusion notwithstanding, in 1948–1950, Wallis and Friedman contributed as supportive discussants to an experiment to measure the utility of money performed by Frederick Mosteller and Philip Nogee. Notably, Mosteller and Nogee's decision to use real money in their experiment agrees with Friedman and Wallis's claim that experiments in which subjects give "conjectural responses to hypothetical stimuli" are of little interest for economists.

7.7. EPISTEMOLOGICAL ANALYSIS

In this concluding section of part II, I review the debates of the period 1900–1945 with respect to the five dimensions of the problem of utility measurement set out in the prologue.

7.7.1. The Understanding of Measurement

By showing that the main results of demand and equilibrium analysis are independent of the unit-based measurability of utility, Pareto and the other ordinalists solved most of the problems that had worried Jevons, Walras, and the other early marginalists. Notably, the ordinal solution to the issue of the unmeasurability of utility did not require any reconceptualization of the notion of measurement. In fact, Pareto, Čuhel, Mises, Phelps Brown, and other ordinalists stuck to the unit-based understanding of measurement and, accordingly, conceived of ordinal utility as unmeasurable utility. In this respect, the situation in utility theory during the period 1900–1945 was quite different from the contemporary situation in psychology. As discussed in chapter 4, in psychology, the lack of any consensual solution to the problem of the apparent unmeasurability of sensations motivated a fundamental rediscussion of the very notion of measurement. In utility theory, such rediscussion took place only some years later, in the early 1950s, as an eventual outcome of the discussion of von Neumann and Morgenstern's expected utility theory (chapter 12).

A significant similarity between utility analysis and psychology during the period 1900–1945 is that in both fields, the debate about measurement involved a discussion about the assessment of differences, that is, of utility differences in utility theory and sensation differences in psychology. In particular, in utility analysis, the discussion about utility differences was associated with the definition and stabilization, from the mid-1930s onward, of the notion of cardinal utility as utility unique up to positive linear transformations.

For our story, the discussions leading to the definition of cardinal utility are important for at least two reasons. First, a novel understanding of "measurable utility" emerged in the contributions of Lange, Allen, and Alt to the debate on utility differences. For the early marginalists but also, as just mentioned, for many ordinalists, utility is measurable when a unit of utility warranting the possibility of assessing utility ratios is available; that is, utility is measurable when utility numbers U are invariant to proportional transformations of the form $\alpha U(x)$. In chapter 2, I called this type of utility "ratio-scale utility." For Lange, Allen, and Alt, by contrast, utility is measurable when it is measurable on the less restrictive interval scale, that is, when utility numbers are invariant to positive linear transformations of the form $\alpha U(x) + \beta$. Accordingly, Lange, Allen, and Alt conceived of cardinal utility as measurable utility. As we will see in part III, the view according to which utility is measurable when it is measurable on an interval scale quickly became the dominant one, and after 1945, most utility theorists talked of "cardinal utility" and "measurable utility" interchangeably.

Second, the discussions leading to the definition of cardinal utility showed that even if a utility theorist wants to go beyond ordinal utility, which itself is sufficient for demand and equilibrium analysis, he or she need not go all the way to ratio-scale utility but can stop at the less demanding cardinal utility station. In fact, cardinal utility is sufficient to talk about traditional topics such as diminishing marginal utility as well as new topics of economic interest such as intertemporal choice (Samuelson 1937) and welfare analysis (Lange 1934a; Bishop 1943).

After the stabilization of the notion of cardinal utility as utility unique up to linear transformations, discussions in utility theory centered on the opposition between ordinal and cardinal utility, while the problems associated with ratio-scale utility and the identification of a utility unit that had occupied Jevons, Walras, and the other early marginalists faded away. A consequence of the rise of cardinal utility and the wane of ratio-scale utility was that, as argued in chapter 2, utility theorists and historians of economics began to retrospectively project the new notion of cardinal utility onto the old notion of ratio-scale utility and to identify the latter with the former.

However, Lange's, Allen's, and Alt's novel understandings of measurable utility and the notion of cardinal utility were not associated with an explicit redefinition of the very concept of measurement. These three economists claimed that utility is measurable not only when a unit of utility is available but also when utility differences are comparable. But they did not discuss whether this idea entails a modification in the traditional, unit-based notion of measurement.

An important point at which the 1900–1945 discussions about the measurability of utility touched the measurement-theoretic issue of what should be meant by measurement was with Phelps Brown's warning against the "analogy of quantity." As discussed in chapter 6, section 6.4.4, Phelps Brown (1934) argued that representing psychological phenomena through numbers is dangerous, because we unintentionally tend to attribute the properties of numbers to the represented psychological phenomena, even when the latter do not possess numerical properties.

Phelps Brown conceived of measurement in the traditional unit-based sense and explicitly argued that measuring relies on the possibility of "expressing one magnitude as a multiple of another" (1934, 66). However, in his warning against the "analogy of quantity," we can find a very different idea, namely that measurement does not deal primarily with units and ratios but rather with the similarity between certain properties of preferences or other entities and certain properties of numbers. Although I have been unable to find any direct link between Phelps Brown and the literature on the philosophy of measurement discussed in chapter 4, this idea of measurement recalls the broad definition of measurement that Campbell (1920, 267) and Nagel (1931, 313) had put forward, according to which measurement is the process of assigning numbers to entities in order to represent certain properties of these entities. Chapters 8 and 9 describe how in the 1940s, von Neumann, Morgenstern, and Stevens associated the idea of measurement with the mathematical notion of isomorphism. With hindsight, it is tempting to identify some similarity between Phelps Brown's "analogy of quantity" and the notion of isomorphism employed by Stevens, von Neumann, and Morgenstern.

At any rate, during the period 1900–1940, neither Phelps Brown nor any other utility theorist worked out a theory of measurement based on the idea that measurement primarily deals with the "analogy" or "isomorphism" between certain properties of objects and certain properties of numbers. As part III shows, this approach to measurement was expounded by von Neumann and Morgenstern in the first chapter of their *Theory of Games and Economic Behavior* ([1944] 1953) and was subsequently elaborated by other economists over the course of the debate on von Neumann and Morgenstern's axiomatic version of expected utility theory.

7.7.2. The Scope of the Utility Concept

As seen in chapters 5 and 6, in the period 1900–1945, the primary notion of utility analysis became that of preference, while utility began to be conceived of as a numerical index expressing the preexisting preference relations between objects. This holds not only within the strictly ordinal approach of Pareto, Hicks, and Allen but also for the utility theorists who discussed the conditions under which utility is cardinal. In the works of Lange, Phelps Brown, Alt, and Samuelson, in fact, the cardinal restrictions on the utility function are derived from axioms concerning preferences regarding combinations of goods *and* axioms concerning preferences regarding transitions from one combination to another.

In both the ordinal and the cardinal case, preferences are conceived of in a broad way, so as to encompass all possible psychological motivations that may induce an individual to prefer combination x to combination y or to prefer the transition from combination x to combination y to the transition from y to z. Using the terminology introduced in chapter 3, preferences are "preferences all things considered," and the utility representing these preferences, whether ordinal or cardinal, is an "all-things-considered utility."

In this approach, the diverse psychological motivations underlying preferences are not directly relevant for economic theory. As Pareto wrote ([1900] 2008, 454), once we know the preferences of an individual, "the *reasons* for the preferences . . . no longer interest us." And this holds not only for the preferences Pareto referred to in this sentence, namely preferences between combinations of goods that lead to ordinal utility, but also for the preferences between transitions from one combination to another that lead to cardinal utility.

7.7.3. The Status of Utility

The fact that in the period 1900–1945, the primitive notion of utility analysis became that of preference does not change in any substantial way the issue concerning the epistemological status of preference and utility. We can still contrast two main possible interpretations, namely the mentalist view, according to which the concept of preference refers to some entity existing in the mind of the decision maker, and the instrumentalist view, according to which preference is a purely theoretical construct that proves useful for explaining or predicting economic behavior but does not necessarily have any real correlate in the decision maker's mind. All utility theorists considered in part II, namely Pareto, Čuhel, Mises, Hicks, Allen, Lange, Phelps Brown, Alt, and Frisch, more or less tacitly adhered to a mentalist view of preferences, and I was unable to find any passage hinting at an instrumentalist position in their writings. As Wade Hands (2017, 556) has aptly put it: "Ordinal utility remained in the mind of the agent."

Not even Samuelson denied the psychological existence of preferences. In his famous "A Note on the Pure Theory of Consumer's Behavior," Samuelson (1938b, 62) did not argue against the existence of preferences but only claimed that "the analysis [of consumer's behavior] can be carried out more directly, and from a different set of postulates" than those concerning preferences. Samuelson's mentalism about preferences will become even more evident in the debate about von Neumann and Morgenstern's expected utility theory (see chapters 10 and 11).

When we move from the issue concerning the status of preferences to that concerning the status of utility, it is useful to distinguish between the informal usage of the terms *utility* and *preference* and their precise technical meaning. As noted in chapter 5, in informal usage, utility theorists often employ the terms *utility* and *preference* interchangeably. When this is the case, that is, when *utility* is used as a synonym for *preference*, the epistemological status of utility simply coincides with the epistemological status of preference. Therefore, if the concept of preference is conceived of as referring to some entity existing in the mind of the decision maker, so is the concept of utility. In this specific sense, we can say that Pareto, Čuhel, Mises, Hicks, Allen, Lange, Phelps Brown, Alt, Samuelson, and Frisch all adhered to a mentalist view of utility.

In its precise, technical meaning, however, utility is just an index that expresses numerically the decision maker's preferences between objects. According to this meaning, utility does not exist in the mind of the decision maker. At most, utility exists in the mind of the utility theorist who makes use of the utility index to explain or predict the behavior of the decision maker. In this second, technical sense, the utility theorists considered in part II were instrumentalists about utility.

As explained at the end of chapter 5, I contend that for most of the purposes of the present investigation, there is no need to continually distinguish *preference* from *utility*, and that we can accept the common identification of the two terms. The distinction between preference and utility will be emphasized only when it is important for our narrative.

7.7.4. The Data for Utility Measurement

The fourth dimension of the problem of utility measurement concerns the kind of data that can be legitimately used to measure utility. Generally speaking, with the rise of the ordinal approach, psychological data obtained by introspection lost importance in favor of choice data that, in principle, can be retrieved by experimental or statistical observations. This change of emphasis was consistent with the rise of positivistic ideas in the philosophy of science, a rise that had begun in the second half of the nineteenth century with the spread of Auguste Comte's *philosophie positive*, and reached its peak in the 1920s and 1930s with the ascent of logical positivism in Austria. Broadly speaking, positivistic philosophies contend that scientific theories should be based on experience and related to observable entities, and that scientific statements should be empirically verifiable, at least in principle.[10]

However, in the period 1900–1945, distinctions between introspection and observation, preference and choice, and mind and behavior remained very much abstract. In fact, in this period, only two attempts to empirically measure utility were conducted, by Thurstone and by Frisch, and neither made more than a very limited impact on utility analysis. For the most part, discussion about introspection versus observation remained at the methodological or, one may say, rhetorical level.[11]

In the period 1900–1945, utility theorists confidently referred to the binary introspective judgments associated with Pareto's postulate 1—judgments such as "I prefer commodity bundle x to commodity bundle y"—in order to rank alternatives and thus determine an ordinal utility function. Utility theorists took these judgments as psychologically plausible, even if they referred to preference or utility "all things considered." For utility theorists with a behaviorist leaning, such as Allen, binary introspective judgments of the postulate 1 type were reliable also because they could be mapped onto choice behavior by a one-to-one correspondence: if the individual prefers x to y, then, when given the possibility, he will choose x over y; conversely, if the individual chooses x when y is also available, we can infer from this act that he prefers x to y.[12]

Prior to the publication of the Hicks–Allen article of 1934, utility theorists such as Bowley, Rosenstein-Rodan, and Morgenstern also accepted quaternary introspective judgments associated with Pareto's postulate 2, that is, judgments such as "I prefer the transition from bundle x to bundle y to the transition from bundle w to bundle z." After 1934 and specifically over the course of the debate that led to the definition of cardinal utility, utility theorists became increasingly skeptical about the psychological plausibility of quaternary introspective judgments of the postulate 2 type. Moreover, as Allen (1935, 155) stressed, such judgments "cannot be expressed in term of the individual's acts of choice."

Introspective judgments did not only play a role with respect to postulates 1 and 2. As remarked by Samuelson (1938b, 61), the standard assumption that the marginal rate of substitution is diminishing, that is, that the indifference curves are convex, also appears to rely on some introspective judgment. In principle, the convexity of the indifference curves can be checked in a choice experiment, but neither Pareto nor Hicks nor any of the other ordinalists active in the period 1900–1945 attempted to conduct such an experiment.[13]

10. On Comte's positivism, see Bourdeau 2015. On the influence of positivism on Pareto, see Bruni 2002. On the influence of logical positivism on economic methodology in the 1930s, see Hands 2001.

11. See more on this rhetorical aspect of the ordinal revolution in Hands 2010; Hands 2011.

12. As a number of economists, psychologists, and philosophers of science have argued since 1970, the relationship between preference and choice is far from straightforward. See in particular Sen 1973; Sen 1997; the essays by Hausman, Spiegler, Rubinstein and Salant, and Caplin, in Caplin and Schotter 2008; and Hausman 2012. The utility theorists of the period 1900–1945, however, did not call this relationship into question.

13. Apparently, the first experiment specifically aimed at testing the convexity of indifference curves for commodity bundles was performed by Kenneth MacCrimmon and Masanao Toda in the late 1960s. MacCrimmon and Toda (1969) found that the indifference curves of their seven experimental subjects were generally convex, although concave parts were recorded for two subjects. See more on this experiment in Moscati 2007a.

In this period, only Frisch and Thurstone attempted to measure utility empirically, and in both cases, the utility measurements were indirect. Frisch tried to measure the elasticity of the marginal utility of real income from market data on prices, purchases, and incomes. Thurstone attempted to identify the indifference curves of a real subject from experimental choices between hypothetical bundles of commodities.

However, Frisch's and Thurstone's early attempts on the empirical measurement of utility had little impact on utility analysis. In the first place, utility theorists lacked confidence in the models Frisch and Thurstone had employed to connect observable data to utility. These models, in fact, relied on assumptions, such as that the utility of each commodity is independent of the quantities of other commodities, that appeared far-fetched to most utility theorists of the period. Moreover, the data used to measure utility were considered either incomplete, as in the case of Frisch's market data on the sales of sugar, or unreliable, as with Thurstone's experimental data. In particular, many commentators remarked that Thurstone's data concerned hypothetical rather than actual choices. More radically, Wallis and Friedman (1942) cast doubts on the very possibility of obtaining reliable choice data using experimental techniques.

As part IV shows, later attempts to measure utility using experimental choice data were received much more favorably by utility theorists, including Friedman.

7.7.5. The Aims of Utility Theory

As explained in chapter 3, utility theory has multiple aims: explanation, descriptive validity, and prediction on the descriptive side and evaluation, advice, and intervention on the normative side. With respect to the descriptive dimension, like the early utility theorists considered in part I, those studied in part II also were mainly interested in explanation of the demand for commodities and the equilibrium of the market. In particular, Pareto, Hicks, and the other ordinalists showed that to explain demand and equilibrium, ordinal utility suffices. Samuelson's discounted-utility model of 1937 (see chapter 6, section 6.7.1) explained intertemporal choices using cardinal utility. However, in the late 1930s and the 1940s, utility theorists, including Samuelson, were skeptical about the plausibility of the assumptions underlying the model.[14] Therefore, the discounted-utility model did not modify the general opinion that cardinal utility was dispensable for the explanatory or descriptive aims of utility theory.

With respect to the normative aims of the theory, many utility theorists of the 1900–1945 period were interested in the evaluation of market equilibria with respect to social welfare. Pareto ([1906/1909] 2014, 179) proposed his famous criterion of optimality, according to which a certain allocation of resources is optimal if there is no way of reallocating the resources so as to increase the utility of some individuals without reducing the utility

14. For instance, in an article published in *Econometrica*, William Vickrey (1945, 324) argued that Samuelson's discounted-utility model "rests on assumptions that the utility at one point of time is independent of consumption at other points of time, that the utility function is not subject to change through time, and that some schedule of subjective discounts of future utilities can be postulated a priori. These assumptions are by no means easy to justify."

of some other individuals. Since Pareto's criterion refers only to increases or decreases of utility and does not require any assessment of how much utility is increased or decreased, it is fully consistent with the ordinal approach to utility. Moreover, since the criterion does not necessitate comparisons of the utility loss of one individual with the utility gain of another, it is independent of interpersonal comparisons of utilities. As is well known, the main disadvantage of Pareto's criterion is that it is too coarse, in the sense that there are too many allocations that are Pareto optima, and the criterion does not offer any way to discriminate among them.

Beginning in the mid-1930s, Pareto optimality became the key concept of a rising approach to social welfare based on ordinal utility and the rejection of interpersonal comparisons of utility. In opposition to the traditional, Marshallian approach based on consumers' surplus, this approach came to be known as New Welfare Economics. Several economists encountered in our narrative contributed to it, including Robbins (1935; 1938), Bergson (1938), Hicks (1939a), Samuelson (1939b; 1947, chap. 8), and Lange (1942).[15]

For our narrative, the important aspect of the rise of New Welfare Economics is that between the mid-1930s and the mid-1940s, ordinal utility appeared sufficient, not only for the positive goal of explaining or describing demand and equilibrium but also for the normative goal of evaluating social welfare. Hence, to repeat Allen's point, cardinal utility did not appear to work its passage. The so-called Impossibility Theorem demonstrated by Kenneth Arrow in his *Social Choice and Individual Welfare* (1951b) and the rise of von Neumann and Morgenstern's version of expected utility theory changed this situation.

15. For a survey of New Welfare Economics, see Graaff 1957; Mishan 1960.

PART THREE

From Debating Expected Utility Theory to Redefining Utility Measurement, 1945–1955

CHAPTER 8

Stevens and the Operational Definition of Measurement in Psychology, 1935–1950

Like chapters 1 and 4, chapter 8 broadens the narrative beyond utility measurement. Specifically, I focus here on an important outcome of the British controversy about psychological measurement of the 1930s discussed in chapter 4, namely the operational definition of measurement put forward by Harvard experimental psychologist Stanley Smith Stevens in the early 1940s.

As observed in chapter 4, section 4.3.2, in an attempt to find some common ground for discussion between physicists and psychologists, the Ferguson committee in its final report of 1940 chose to focus on a concrete example of psychological measurement, namely the measurement of loudness sensations provided by Stevens and his Harvard colleague Hallowell Davis in their book *Hearing: Its Psychology and Physiology* (Davis and Stevens 1938). As in their earlier discussions, however, these British physicists and psychologists were unable to find agreement on what should be meant by measurement and, consequently, on whether Davis and Stevens had actually measured loudness sensations. The physicists, led by Norman Robert Campbell, stuck to a unit-based conception of measurement and argued that the quantification practices of experimental psychology do not constitute real measurement because loudness and other sensations cannot be added. For their part, Kenneth Craik, Lewis Fry Richardson, and other psychologists attacked the physicists' conception of measurement as too narrow and thus incapable of accounting for psychological measurement. However, they were unable to provide a broader theory of measurement that could compete with Campbell's measurement theory. This impasse was broken by Stevens in the early 1940s, when he proposed an operational definition of measurement that made room for the psychologists' quantification practices and quickly became canonical in psychology.

8.1. STEVENS AND OPERATIONALISM IN PSYCHOLOGY

Stevens (1906–1973) received a Ph.D. in psychology from Harvard in 1933. His supervisor had been Edwin Garrigues "Gary" Boring, a leading American experimental psychologist who had also published an influential book on the history of experimental psychology (Boring 1929). After graduation, Stevens moved to Harvard Medical School and worked on the physiology of hearing under Davis. In 1936, he returned as an instructor in experimental psychology to the newly independent department of psychology at Harvard, which was directed by Boring. He was promoted to assistant professor in 1938 and later to associate and full professor of psychology. In 1940, the US Air Force supported the creation of the Harvard Psycho-Acoustic Laboratory to study the effects of intense noise in military aircraft, and Stevens was named its director. The emergence of Stevens's theory of measurement was intimately bound to his interaction with Boring and his own work on loudness measurement.[1]

In the first half of the 1930s, Boring had struggled with methodological questions that concerned both the relationship between consciousness and physiology and the meaning of psychological measurement. Boring discussed these problems with Stevens and Douglas McGregor, another student of his who later became a management professor at MIT. Boring, Stevens, and McGregor found a solution to their methodological problems by way of a restatement of psychological concepts inspired by the operational epistemology put forward by Harvard physicist Percy Williams Bridgman in his book *The Logic of Modern Physics* (1927).

The key idea of operationalism is that the meaning of a scientific concept is defined by the set of concrete operations through which the concept is identified. In a series of articles to which Boring contributed in a significant way, Stevens (1935a; 1935b; 1936a; 1939) and McGregor (1935) applied the operational point of view to psychology. Their operational approach was critically discussed in a number of articles appearing in psychology journals from the second half of the 1930s to the early 1940s. The debate culminated in a symposium on operationalism that was published in the *Psychological Review* in 1945 and to which Boring and Bridgman also contributed.[2] Here we focus on the aspects of Stevens's and McGregor's articles that relate most directly to measurement issues.

In an article titled "The Operational Basis of Psychology," Stevens (1935a) illustrated the meaning of operationalism by taking as an example the measurement of length.[3] The length of an object such as a table, he noted, is determined by applying to the table a measuring stick. In this case, "what we mean by the length of the object is that the ends of the object coincide with certain marks on the measuring rod" (1935a, 324). However, the length of the path of light from a star to the earth is determined not by using a measuring stick but through a different set of concrete operations. Therefore, Stevens argued: "The length in this

1. See more on Stevens's biography and career in Stevens 1974; Miller 1975.

2. See more on the origins of the operational approach to psychology and the early debate on it in Miller 1975; Hardcastle 1995; Feest 2005.

3. Stevens's illustration is based on Bridgman's detailed discussion of the concept of length; see Bridgman 1927, 9–25.

latter case is a different concept from that of length when applied to the edge of the table. Other concrete operations can be performed to determine the relation between these two concepts of length; but the concept of their relation depends upon these 'other operations' and the two 'lengths' cannot be considered identical" (324).

McGregor devoted the first part of his article on "Scientific Measurement and Psychology" (1935) to an illustration of the theory of physical measurement as expounded by Campbell (1920) and by Cohen and Nagel (1934; see chapter 4, section 4.1). He then introduced the operational point of view by arguing that since both physical and psychological measurement are defined by a set of specific operations, there is no substantial difference between them. In particular, for McGregor, some of the operations performed in psychological measurement are analogous to the operations of addition used in physical measurement. Therefore, "fundamental" and "derived" measurement (in Campbell's sense) are possible not only for physical but also for psychological magnitudes. In concluding his article, McGregor boldly claimed that "psychological measurement, understood in operational terms, is a *fait accompli*" (265).

McGregor's operational approach to measurement, however, was too generic to constitute a viable alternative to Campbell's articulated theory of measurement.

8.2. STEVENS'S THEORY OF MEASUREMENT

8.2.1. Overview

Stevens believed that the scale of loudness that he and Davis had expounded in *Hearing* did have the formal properties of other basic scales, such as those used to measure length and weight. He was therefore dissatisfied with the dismissive attitudes of the physicists on the Ferguson committee toward the psychologists' efforts to measure loudness and other sensations. Drawing on his operationalism, from 1940 to 1941, he elaborated a theory of measurement that was broad enough to include the quantification practices developed by experimental psychologists yet precise enough to compete with Campbell's measurement theory. Stevens presented a first version of his theory in 1941 at the Chicago Congress of the Unity of Science Movement, an association of philosophers and scientists influenced by logical empiricism that included Nagel and Bridgman. The 1941 paper was mimeographed and given some limited distribution, but Stevens only published his measurement theory in a journal, *Science*, in 1946. He gave his article the title "On the Theory of Scales of Measurement."[4]

As discussed in chapter 4, section 4.1, both Campbell and Nagel had defined measurement in a broad way as, respectively, "the process of assigning numbers to represent properties" (Campbell 1920, 267) and "the correlation with numbers of entities which are not numbers" (Nagel 1931, 313). In these works, however, Campbell and Nagel had implicitly identified measurement with unit-based measurement. Stevens retrieved the broad definition of measurement given by Campbell and Nagel: "Paraphrasing N. R. Campbell, we

4. See more on the genesis of Stevens's 1946 article in Stevens 1974; Newman 1974; Miller 1975.

may say that measurement, in the broadest sense, is defined as the assignment of numerals to objects or events according to rules" (1946, 677).

However, unlike Campbell and Nagel, Stevens did not proceed to undermine this broad definition and did not return to unit-based measurement. For Stevens, since there are various rules for assigning numbers to objects, there are various forms, or scales, of measurement. Each scale is identified by the empirical operations that are used to create it and by the class of mathematical transformations that the numbers in each scale can be subjected to without altering the scale's character.

Stevens connected this view of measurement with the mathematical notions of "isomorphism" and "group." He argued that measurement is possible in the first place because there is "a certain isomorphism" (677), that is, a certain similarity or, as Phelps Brown might have said (see chapters 6, section 6.4.4, and 7, section 7.7.1), a certain "analogy," between some empirical relations between the objects to be measured and some formal relations between the numbers assigned to those objects. Thus, for example, there exists an isomorphism between the empirical relation *heavier than* between bodies and the formal relation *greater than* between numbers. In mathematics, a group consists of a set S of elements together with an operation $\circ$ defined on S. In particular, the set S must be closed under operation $\circ$; that is, if elements a and b belong to S, also $a \circ b$ is an element of S.[5] Each scale of measurement may be seen as a group in the sense that its numbers are closed under some operation $\circ$; that is, the transformation of the scale's numbers through operation $\circ$ does not alter the isomorphic properties of the scale. In other words, the empirical relations between the objects are still mirrored by the formal relations between the numbers transformed by operation $\circ$.

According to Stevens, there exist four basic scales of measurement, each of which is associated with a basic empirical operation, a set of admissible mathematical transformations, and a group structure. Introducing the terminology that later became standard, Stevens labeled these scales the *nominal, ordinal, interval,* and *ratio* scales of measurement. Each scale is more restrictive than the preceding one in the series, in the sense that it requires the performing of an additional empirical operation, and its numbers can be subjected to a smaller class of mathematical transformations.

Two final general remarks on Stevens's measurement theory are in order. First, his was not an axiomatic theory. He associated each scale of measurement with a set of empirical operations and a class of mathematical transformations but did not attempt to specify under what exact conditions, that is, axioms, certain operations are feasible while others are not. Second, in Stevens's measurement theory, there are no representation theorems, that is, theorems like those of Hölder (chapter 1, section 1.4.1) that explicitly connect certain assumptions about the relations and operations between objects with certain mathematical relations and operations between numbers. In this sense, the label *representational* that is usually associated with Stevens's theory in the measurement-theoretic literature appears questionable. As chapter 9 discusses, the absence of axioms and representation theorems in Stevens's measurement theory follows from his operationalism.

5. The other three properties a group must satisfy are (1) associativity: $a \circ (b \circ c) = (a \circ b) \circ c$, for each a, b, c in S; (2) existence of an identity element, that is, of an element e of S such that $a \circ e = e \circ a = a$, for each a in S; (3) existence, for each element of S, of an inverse element d, that is, of an element d such that $a \circ d = d \circ a = e$, whereby e is the identity element.

8.2.2. Detailed Presentation

I now present Stevens's measurement theory in greater detail. In the nominal scale of measurement, numbers serve only as labels to identify classes of objects or individuals, as when, for instance, number 1 is associated with males and number 2 with females. The nominal scale is based on the operation that Stevens calls "determination of equality," which consists of determining whether the objects under consideration are equal in respect to some trait (e.g., gender) and then classifying them accordingly. The rule for assigning numbers to objects is that objects in the same class must be assigned the same number. Any one-to-one mathematical function F(x) that transforms the numbers in the nominal scale does not alter the scale's character. For instance, if $F(x) = -x$, males are associated with –1 and females with –2, but this does not modify the classification already obtained. Stevens called the mathematical group coupled with this scale the "permutation group."

The ordinal scale arises when, besides operation (1), the operation of (2) rank ordering can also be performed. The assignment of numbers follows the rule that greater numbers are associated with higher-ranked objects. As we already know (see chapters 2 and 5), in this case, the class of the permissible transformations is constituted by the monotonic increasing transformations. The mathematical group associated with these transformations was called by Stevens "isotonic." As examples of ordinal scales, Stevens (1946, 679) referred to the Mohs scale of mineral hardness, the scale of intelligence, and the scale of leather quality, but he did not mention ordinal utility.

The third form of measurement, in order of increasing restrictiveness, is provided by the interval scale, which is based on operations (1), (2), and (3), the determination of equality of intervals or differences. For interval scales, the class of permissible transformations is constituted by the positive linear transformations, that is, by transformations of the form $F(x) = \alpha x + \beta$. The associated mathematical group is called the "general linear group." As examples of physical interval scales, Stevens took the usual Celsius and Fahrenheit scales of temperature. For psychology, he argued that "most psychological measurement aspires to create interval scale, and it sometimes succeeds" (679). He did not mention cardinal utility as an instance of interval scale.

With the fourth and strictest scale identified by Stevens, namely the ratio scale, we are back to unit-based measurement (see chapter 1). The ratio scale is based on operations (1), (2), (3), and (4), the determination of equality of ratios. The mathematical group associated with the ratio scale is the "similarity group," while the permissible transformations are the proportional ones, that is, the transformations of the form $F(x) = \alpha x$. For Stevens, fundamental and derived measurements in Campbell's sense are a subset of ratio scales. For him, in fact, the operation of addition, on which fundamental and derived measurements rest, provides *one possible* procedure to determine the equality of ratios but certainly not the only one. The passage of the 1946 article in which Stevens makes this point is worth quoting at length:

> Weights, lengths, and resistances can be added in the physical sense, but this important empirical fact is generally accorded more prominence in the theory of measurement than it deserves. The so-called fundamental scales are important instances of ratio scales, but they are only instances. As a matter of fact, . . . the fundamental scales could be set up even if the physical operation of addition were ruled out as impossible of performance. (680)

Stevens noted that ratio scales are "those most commonly encountered in physics" (679). In mathematics, the scale of numbers, that is, "the scale we use when we count such things as eggs, pennies, and apples," provides another example of ratio scale. Following the mathematical distinction between cardinal and ordinal numbers (see chapter 1, section 1.4.2), Stevens (680) labeled numbers used to count "cardinal numbers." In psychology, ratio scales are rare but, Stevens argued, "not entirely unknown." In particular, for Stevens, the scale of loudness that he and Davis had constructed in their 1938 book on *Hearing*, and which had been discussed by the Ferguson committee, "ought properly to be classed as a ratio scale" (680). The Stevens–Davis ratio scale was based not on the addition of tones but on the direct ratio judgments made by the experimental subjects, who were asked to adjust one tone until it sounded half as loud as another tone.

Stevens concluded his article in a cuttingly provocative manner by suggesting that the Ferguson committee accept Campbell's broad definition of measurement and evaluate the quantification practices of experimental psychology accordingly:

> To the British committee, then, we may venture to suggest by way of conclusion that the most liberal and useful definition of measurement is, as one of its members [i.e., Campbell] advised, "the assignment of numerals to things so as to represent facts and conventions about them." The problem as to what is and is not measurement then reduces to the simple question: What are the rules, if any, under which numerals are assigned? If we can point to a consistent set of rules, we are obviously concerned with measurement of some sort, and we can then proceed to the more interesting question as to the kind of measurement it is. (680)

8.3. STEVENS'S THEORY OF MEASUREMENT: DISCUSSION AND A LOOK AHEAD

8.3.1. Open Issues

Stevens's operational theory of measurement can be, and has been, criticized in several respects.[6] At the most basic level, one may wonder whether Stevens's classification of measurement scales is complete. Are there further measurement scales, invariant to different classes of mathematical transformations beyond, or between, the nominal, ordinal, interval, and ratio scales?

More fundamentally, one may argue that Stevens simply begged the question at the center of discussions of measurement theory from the late nineteenth century to Campbell, namely the conditions that make an object measurable in one way rather than another. For instance, Stevens argued that an object is measurable according to the interval scale when the operations of equality determination, order determination, and determination of equality of intervals are feasible. But when—that is, under what conditions—are these operations feasible? Why can certain objects be measured only on the interval scale, while others can be measured on the ratio scale?

6. See, e.g., Michell 1999.

From an operational viewpoint, one may reply that these are ill-posed questions relying on a realist metaphysics, in the sense that they implicitly assume that there is something "out there in the world" that can be defined independently of the concrete operations by which it is measured. From an operational viewpoint, however, what is "out there in the world" is determined by just these operations.

The counterreply calls into question the very operational philosophy underlying Stevens's theory of measurement. If the operations completely define the concept or, in the concrete illustration given by Boring, if "intelligence is simply what the tests of intelligence test" (1923, 35), then it becomes unclear how measurement contributes to our knowledge of the world and what might be the practical use of our measures. If intelligence simply is what the tests of intelligence test, why would we be interested in finding out that one man has an IQ of 150 and another of 75? And according to what criteria should we judge whether an intelligence test is valid or try to improve it if it is deemed invalid? Furthermore, can we construct different tests to measure intelligence? Or would different tests inevitably measure different intellectual abilities and so produce unrelated outcomes? The general problem to which these questions point is that the operational approach to measurement risks generating an uncontrollable proliferation of measures and concepts that are tricky to relate to one another.[7]

In chapter 16, we will see how similar problems to those just mentioned emerged in utility analysis when it became apparent that different operations to measure utility produce different utility measures, which are difficult to relate to one another and possibly identify different utility concepts.

8.3.2. Stevens, von Neumann, and Morgenstern

In 1951, Stevens edited the first *Handbook of Experimental Psychology*, which quickly became a key reference for experimental psychologists. In the first chapter of the *Handbook*, titled "Mathematics, Measurement, and Psychophysics," Stevens re-presented his theory of measurement. Although now put forward in the context of an extended discussion of the nature and history of mathematics, the 1951 version of the theory was substantially identical to that which had appeared in the *Science* article of 1946. Especially through the *Handbook*, Stevens's theory became established as the canonical view of measurement in post–World War II psychology. His fourfold taxonomy of measurement scales became so ingrained in the practices of psychologists that by the mid-1970s, Stevens (1974, 437) would lament that many psychologists used it without feeling the need to cite its origin.

Albeit incidentally, in the *Handbook*, Stevens referred to the theory of measurement that von Neumann and Morgenstern had presented in 1944 in their *Theory of Games and Economic Behavior*. As chapter 9 points out, despite some substantial differences, there exist also some significant similarities between von Neumann and Morgenstern's measurement theory and that of Stevens. In particular, von Neumann and Morgenstern also connected

7. Chang 2009 provides a useful overview of the main philosophical objections to operationalism.

different types of measurement with different classes of mathematical transformations and conceived of these transformations in terms of the mathematical theory of groups.

In his *Science* article, Stevens did not cite von Neumann and Morgenstern. In the *Handbook*, however, Stevens acknowledged in a footnote the similarities of his measurement theory with that put forward by the authors of *Theory of Games*: "The gist of [my] notion of relating scales of measurement to transformation groups is also contained in the recent book by von Neumann and Morgenstern on games and economic behavior" (Stevens 1951, 23). Anticipating possible priority issues, Stevens specified that he had already presented his theory "before the International Congress for the Unity of Science, September 1941," that is, three years before the publication of *Theory of Games*.

I have found no evidence against this claim of Stevens. Apparently, he and the von Neumann–Morgenstern team arrived at similar theories of measurement in an independent way around the same time. We now move to von Neumann and Morgenstern's measurement and utility theory.

CHAPTER 9

The Expected Utility Theory and Measurement Theory of von Neumann and Morgenstern, 1944–1947

As explained in part II of this book, the ordinal revolution inaugurated by Vilfredo Pareto in 1900 was completed in the second half of the 1930s, and in the formulation provided by John Hicks's *Value and Capital* (1939b), the ordinal approach to demand and equilibrium analysis now became dominant. We have also seen that in the second half of the 1930s, the notion of cardinal utility as utility unique up to positive linear transformations entered economic theory but remained peripheral.

Before and during the ordinal revolution, discussion of the measurability of utility focused on decisions not involving risk, that is, on decisions concerning riskless alternatives. When Pareto and other ordinalists assumed that individuals are able to state whether they prefer, say, a liter of wine to a kilogram of bread, it was implicit that the comparison was between a liter of wine *for sure* and a kilo of bread *for sure*. Similarly, when Oskar Lange, Franz Alt, and Paul Samuelson discussed the possibility of comparing utility differences between alternatives as a way of obtaining cardinal utility, they had in mind *risk-free* alternatives.

Economists did have a theory for analyzing decision-making under risk, namely the expected utility hypothesis advanced by Daniel Bernoulli in the eighteenth century. According to this hypothesis, individuals prefer the risky prospect with the highest expected utility. The latter is given by the average of the utilities U of the possible outcomes of the prospect, each weighted by the probability that the outcome will occur. Thus, for example, the expected utility of a prospect yielding either outcome x_1 with probability p or outcome x_2 with probability $(1 - p)$ is given by $U(x_1) \times p + U(x_2) \times (1 - p)$.

In the nineteenth century, the expected utility hypothesis was adopted by some leading marginalists, such as William Stanley Jevons and Alfred Marshall, but in the 1920s and 1930s, it came under sustained criticism from various quarters. By the late 1930s and early 1940s, the fortunes of expected utility theory were so low that in the two major economic treatises written in this period—Hicks's *Value and Capital* and Samuelson's *Foundations of Economic Analysis*—the theory is not even mentioned.[1]

The fortunes of expected utility theory (EUT) began to recover in 1944, when John von Neumann and Oskar Morgenstern published their *Theory of Games and Economic Behavior*. This book made several seminal contributions to economic theory. First, it gave birth to the economic analysis of strategic behavior, that is, to game theory. Second, it introduced into economics the axiomatic approach that David Hilbert had promoted in mathematics since 1900, as well as convex analysis, fixed-point theorems, and other mathematical tools that added to the economist's traditional toolbox based on the differential calculus.

Third, and this is the most important contribution of *Theory of Games* for our narrative, in their book, von Neumann and Morgenstern put forward an axiomatic version of EUT. They showed that if the preferences of the decision maker between risky alternatives satisfy certain axioms, then he or she will prefer the risky alternative with the highest expected utility. Expected utility is calculated by using a cardinal utility function whose existence is warranted by the axioms. Beginning in the late 1940s and until the mid-1950s, the normative plausibility of von Neumann and Morgenstern's axioms for EUT, the descriptive power of the theory, and the nature of the cardinal utility function featured in the expected utility formula became the subject of intense debate in which all major utility theorists of the period took part. As discussed here in chapters 10 to 12, the major outcomes of this debate were the acceptance of EUT by the large majority of utility theorists, a reconceptualization of the very notion of utility measurement, and the rehabilitation of cardinal utility in the economic theory of decision-making.

The fourth important contribution of *Theory of Games* consists in the theory of measurement presented in the first chapter of the book. Von Neumann and Morgenstern embedded their discussion of the EUT axioms and cardinal utility in an extended discussion of what it means, in general, to measure a thing. Although von Neumann and Morgenstern did not cite Norman Robert Campbell (1920) or Ernest Nagel (1931), it is possible to find in their measurement theory several echoes of the views on measurement expressed by these two scholars, as well as of the views on measurement that emerged in the 1930s in discussions of cardinal utility. Von Neumann and Morgenstern did not cite Stanley Smith Stevens's measurement theory, but this simply reflects the fact that Stevens's 1946 *Science* article was published two years after the first edition of *Theory of Games*.

In the late 1940s and early 1950s, von Neumann and Morgenstern's measurement theory did not have any significant impact on utility analysis or on measurement theory. The lack of impact on utility analysis appears to be due to the fact that von Neumann and Morgenstern presented their measurement theory in terms that were too abstract for economists and focused on examples taken from physics or mathematics rather than economics. Beginning in the mid-1950s, however, von Neumann and Morgenstern's measurement theory became, together with that of Stevens, a main source of inspiration for the axiomatic theory of measurement that Patrick Suppes and his coauthors were then beginning to develop, which would eventually become the dominant approach to measurement within measurement theory.

1. As discussed in chapter 6, although *Foundations* was published in 1947, Samuelson had fundamentally completed the book by 1940; see Samuelson 1998; Backhouse 2015.

In this chapter, I discuss von Neumann and Morgenstern's axiomatic version of EUT as well as their theory of measurement. Chapters 10 to 12 are devoted to the debate generated by their axiomatic version of EUT. The way in which von Neumann and Morgenstern's theory of measurement and, more generally, utility analysis influenced the development of Suppes's theory of measurement is addressed in chapter 15.

9.1. EXPECTED UTILITY THEORY BEFORE 1944

9.1.1. From Expected Payoff to Expected Utility

Decisions involve risk when their outcomes depend on whether certain events occur or not. For instance, the decision to buy a lottery ticket involves risk because its outcome depends on whether the purchased ticket is drawn. Questions related to lotteries and other forms of gambling had been addressed by scholars dealing with probability theory such as Blaise Pascal and Christiaan Huygens since the mid-seventeenth century. Initially, the accepted answer to the question "What is the fair price to pay to participate in a lottery?" was "Its expected monetary payoff." According to this hypothesis, the fair price to pay to participate in a lottery that pays, say, 50 ducats with probability 0.5 and 100 ducats with probability 0.5 would be 75 ducats.

In the early 1710s, Swiss mathematician Nicholas Bernoulli showed that the expected-payoff hypothesis has implausible consequences. He proposed a game, which came to be known as the St. Petersburg game, that has an infinite expected payoff. According to the expected-payoff hypothesis, individuals should be willing to pay any sum, however large, to play it. It turns out, however, that this is not the case. As discussed in chapter 1, section 1.5, in 1738 Daniel Bernoulli, another Swiss mathematician and a cousin of Nicholas, suggested that individuals evaluate a gamble not on the basis of its expected monetary payoff but by taking into account the average utility of the gamble's payoffs. According to this hypothesis, the value of a lottery paying 50 ducats with probability 0.5 and 100 ducats with probability 0.5 would be $0.5 \times U(50 \text{ ducats}) + 0.5 \times U(100 \text{ ducats})$. In particular, Daniel Bernoulli assumed that "any increase in wealth . . . will always result in an increase in utility which is inversely proportionate to the quantity of goods already possessed" ([1738] 1954, 25). This assumption implies not only that the marginal utility of money is diminishing but more specifically that the utility function of money has the logarithmic form $U(x) = \alpha\log(x)$, which we have encountered often in our narrative (see chapters 1, section 1.3.1, and 7, section 7.5.2). Under the logarithmic-utility assumption, Bernoulli showed that a person with an initial wealth of 1,000 ducats should pay only 6 ducats to play the St. Petersburg game.[2]

As already pointed out in chapter 1, Bernoulli did not discuss the possible issues related to the measuring and averaging of utilities and simply treated utility as if it were readily measurable in the unit-based sense.

2. See more on the St. Petersburg game and the origins of the expected-utility hypothesis in Samuelson 1977; Jorland 1987; Giocoli 1998.

9.1.2. Expected Utility and Marginal Utility Analysis

Bernoulli's EUT was the subject of extensive commentaries by mathematicians in the eighteenth and nineteenth centuries. In economics, however, it passed almost unnoticed prior to the marginal revolution of the 1870s. In his *Theory of Political Economy*, Jevons (1871, 154–155) referred explicitly to Bernoulli's EUT and based his succinct analysis of decisions under uncertainty on it. After Jevons, Marshall (1890, 180 n. 2, 741–742) and other marginalists also used EUT to discuss decisions involving risk.[3]

However, a number of problems remained open. The first involved gambling. As both Jevons and Marshall noted, if the expected utility hypothesis is true and the marginal utility of money is diminishing, as they both assumed it was, individuals should never gamble or buy lotteries. Basically, this is due to the diminishing marginal utility of money, for the utility of the additional sum that may be gained is always smaller than the utility of the sum that may be lost. However, people do gamble and buy lottery tickets. To solve the problem, Jevons and Marshall suggested that gambling could be explained by taking into account the pleasure or utility derived from the very activity of gambling. Yet this solution was at odds with utility theory itself: if the utility derived from the activity of gambling is relevant, should it not be explicitly included in a utility-based theory of decision under risk?

A second albeit much less severe problem concerned Bernoulli's specification of the utility function for money. Pareto (1896, 51–53), for instance, agreed with Bernoulli's EUT but argued that there is no reason to assume that the money utility function has a logarithmic form.

9.1.3. Expected Utility in the Early Decades of the Twentieth Century

In the early decades of the twentieth century, skepticism about EUT increased. Both Frank Knight (1921) and John Maynard Keynes (1921) doubted that numerical probabilities completely capture the way in which individuals judge risk and therefore had reservations about the possibility that the expected utility formula, which is based on numerical probabilities, can completely explain decisions under risk. Austrian mathematician Karl Menger (see chapter 6, section 6.6.1) showed that EUT may have consequences as implausible as those of the expected-payoff hypothesis ([1934] 1967). Menger considered a modified version of the St. Petersburg game and proved that if the amounts of money to be won in the game are increased opportunely, an individual who maximizes expected utility may be willing to pay any sum, however large, to play the game. And, again, this appears implausible.

Other economists, such as John Hicks (1931), Jacob Marschak (1938), and Oskar Lange (1944), assumed that individuals evaluate risky alternatives by looking at the mean, the variance, and possibly other elements of the distribution of the uncertain payoffs rather than the expected utility of the payoffs. Hicks (1934) and Gerhard Tintner (1942) also noted that

3. See more on the use of the expected utility hypothesis by Jevons, Marshall, and other marginalists in Friedman and Savage 1948; Schlee 1992.

calculating the average of utilities implies the cardinal measurability of utility, which stood in contrast with the then-dominant ordinal conception of utility. As already mentioned, EUT is totally absent from the two major economic treatises written in this period, Hicks's *Value and Capital* and Samuelson's *Foundations of Economic Analysis*.

9.1.4. The Explanatory Structure of Pre-1944 Expected Utility Theory

Before concluding this overview of the pre-1944 history of EUT, it is important to call attention to the causal explanatory structure of Bernoulli's version of the theory. Bernoulli and his followers explained the utility of a risky prospect such as a lottery as causally derived from (1) the utilities U of the alternative possible outcomes of the lottery and (2) the (fixed) probabilities of the lottery's outcomes. In other words, given the probabilities, the utilities of the outcomes constitute the *explanans* of Bernoulli's theory, while the utility of the lottery is the *explanandum*. Similarly, in the Bernoullian approach, the individual's attitude toward risk is *explained* by the trend of his marginal utility over outcomes. For instance, the individual is (or should be) averse to gambling *because* the marginal utility of money is diminishing. Insofar as utilities and preferences between riskless outcomes appear more straightforward than utilities and preferences between combinations of riskless payoffs *and* probabilities, Bernoulli's theory appears to be an intuitive explanatory approach.

As we will see, in von Neumann and Morgenstern's version of EUT, things are more complicated. To anticipate the key point, in von Neumann and Morgenstern's EUT, the preferences between risky lotteries are the primitive element of the analysis, and accordingly, they are *not* causally explained by the utilities or preferences between riskless outcomes (combined with probabilities). This difference generated, and to some extent still generates, some confusion about EUT and the nature of the cardinal utility featured in the expected utility formula.

Having reviewed the fortunes of EUT before 1944, we can now move to the early 1940s and the genesis of *Theory of Games and Economic Behavior*.

9.2. GENESIS

János von Neumann (1903–1957) was a Hungarian-born Jewish mathematician who embraced Hilbert's axiomatic approach and made fundamental contributions to fields as diverse as set theory, mathematical logic, geometry, physics, and economics. In particular, in 1928, von Neumann published an article on the theory of games that constituted the starting point of the theory of strategic behavior that he later developed with Morgenstern (von Neumann [1928] 1959). After holding positions at the Universities of Göttingen and Berlin, at the beginning of the 1930s, he moved to Princeton, where he became a member, along with Albert Einstein, of the newly founded Institute for Advanced Study. In the United States, von Neumann anglicized his first name to John.[4]

4. On von Neumann's scientific contributions and personality, see Mirowski 2002; Giocoli 2003a; Israel and Gasca 2009; Leonard 2010.

As we know from chapter 6, Morgenstern was a Viennese economist who, in an article published in 1931, supported the idea that economic subjects are able to rank the differences between utilities. As an editor of the *Zeitschrift für Nationalökonomie*, in 1936 Morgenstern was also responsible for the publication of the article in which his private tutor in mathematics, Alt, axiomatized cardinal utility using postulates about preferences regarding transition rankings. Morgenstern's main research topic in the 1920s and 1930s, however, was not utility theory but the role of predictions in economics and the paradoxes associated with situations in which the actions of two agents depend on the prediction of each regarding the other's action (1928; 1935).[5]

In January 1938, just two months before Nazi Germany annexed Austria, Morgenstern left Vienna for the United States, and, shortly thereafter, he joined Princeton University. He and von Neumann met at Princeton at some point in the fall of 1938, and from early 1939 to mid-1941, they engaged in several discussions about strategic behavior and other aspects of economic theory. Meanwhile, von Neumann had resumed his work on game theory. In the summer of 1941, von Neumann proposed that he and Morgenstern collaborate on a joint research project, which eventually became *Theory of Games*. Morgenstern began writing a paper that was to serve as an introduction to the project and ended up being chapter 1 of the book.[6]

Among the things von Neumann and Morgenstern discussed was the interpretation to give to payoffs in the matrices representing the games. As a noneconomist, von Neumann did not care much for utility and was content to consider payoffs simply as money. Morgenstern, however, believed that the majority of his fellow economists would not accept this approach, first because they believed that individuals maximize utility rather than money and second because they had an ordinal conception of utility. As Morgenstern (1976, 809) later recalled:

> We were in need of a number for the pay-off matrices. We had the choice of merely putting in a number, [and] calling it money. . . . I was not very happy about this, knowing the importance of the utility concept, and I insisted that we do more. At first, we were intending merely to postulate a numerical utility, but then I said that, as I knew my fellow economists, they would find this impossible to accept and old-fashioned, in view of the predominance of indifference curve analysis, which neither of us liked.

In the end, Morgenstern persuaded von Neumann to provide a demonstration of how "numerical utility," that is, utility invariant to positive linear transformations, that is, cardinal utility, draws from a set of apparently plausible axioms. The axiomatization of cardinal utility was carried out quite quickly on April 14, 1942, when Morgenstern noted in his diary: "Today at Johnny's: axiomatization of measurable utility. . . . It developed slowly, more and more quickly, and at the end, after two hours (!) it was nearly completely finished" (quoted in Leonard 2010, 232 n. 20).

5. On Morgenstern in the Vienna years, see Leonard 2004.
6. This reconstruction of the relationship between von Neumann and Morgenstern is based on Morgenstern 1976; Shubik 1978; Rellstab 1992; Leonard 1995.

Von Neumann and Morgenstern's theory of cardinal utility is set out in the third section of the first chapter of *Theory of Games* ([1944] 1953, 15–31), on "The Notion of Utility." The first edition of the book did not contain a formal proof of how cardinal utility could be derived from the axioms. The proof was provided in an appendix added to the second edition, published in 1947.

9.3. VON NEUMANN AND MORGENSTERN'S MEASUREMENT THEORY

In the third section of chapter 1 of their book, von Neumann and Morgenstern introduced cardinal utility in the context of a general discussion of the nature of measurement. A brief review of von Neumann and Morgenstern's theory of measurement is helpful for understanding not only their version of EUT but also the origins of the axiomatic theory of measurement later developed by Suppes and his coauthors, which will be discussed here in chapter 15.

9.3.1. Numbers and Natural Relations

Von Neumann and Morgenstern argued that scientific theories provide mathematical models for certain domains of the existing reality. In order to perform this function, scientific theories first correlate the objects of a given domain with numbers. Scientific theories then correlate certain "natural" ([1944] 1953, 21) relations and operations between the objects under study with certain mathematical relations and operations between the numbers associated with those objects.

The examples von Neumann and Morgenstern used to clarify this point came from physics and, by this point in our narrative, should sound familiar. In the theory of heat, the natural relation of *warmer* between two bodies is correlated with the mathematical relation of *greater* between the numbers associated with the bodies. In physics, the natural operation of "adding" masses by placing them on the same pan of a balance is correlated with the mathematical operation of addition between the numbers associated with the masses.

9.3.2. Transformations and Groups

Von Neumann and Morgenstern stressed that the numbers a mathematical model associates with the objects of its domain are not unique but can be transformed, within certain limits, into other numbers. In particular, we can identify a family or system of transformations to which the numbers can be subjected without changing the empirical meaning of the model. We then say that the objects in a given domain "are described by numbers *up to* that system of transformations" (22).

Like Stevens (see chapter 8, section 8.2.1), von Neumann and Morgenstern associated the system of admissible transformations with the mathematical theory of groups: "The mathematical name of such transformation systems is *groups*" (22). In footnotes, they provided some references to group theory, but they did not indicate other possible sources for their view of measurement.[7]

Von Neumann and Morgenstern then offered various examples of accepted transformation systems. When the objects of a domain can be subjected only to the natural relation of *greater*, then the numbers in the mathematical model are unique up to any increasing transformation: "This was the case for temperature as long as only the concept of 'warmer' was known" (23). At the opposite extreme are mathematical theories within which no transformation is tolerated. This is the case with the absolute value of velocity in James Clerk Maxwell's electrodynamics and Einstein's special relativity theory (23 n. 2).

The narrowing of the system of acceptable transformations within a mathematical model depends on the existence of further natural relations and operations between the objects the model represents. Thus, the existence of a natural operation of addition between masses makes the numbers associated with masses unique up to multiplication by a positive constant factor.

9.3.3. Measurement and Additivity

For von Neumann and Morgenstern, not every assignment of numbers to objects within a scientific theory counts as measurement. Measurement requires that the transformations the numbers of the mathematical model can be subjected to are narrowed at least to the system of linear transformations, that is, the transformations for which only the unit and zero point of measurement are arbitrary. Although von Neumann and Morgenstern did not mention Lange, Roy Allen, or Alt, this is also the understanding of measurement these three economists had displayed in their discussions of cardinal utility in the 1930s (see chapter 6, sections 6.3.4, 6.5.2, and 6.6.3).

Like Campbell and Nagel, among the various natural operations capable of narrowing the system of acceptable transformations to the linear ones, von Neumann and Morgenstern focused on addition. In particular, they argued that additivity and thus measurability could be obtained either directly or indirectly. For example, they contended, when heat could be subjected only to the natural relation of *warmer*, it was not measurable. It became measurable only when the quantity of heat of a body was distinguished from its temperature, and both turned out to be directly or indirectly additive (17). The prominent role von Neumann and Morgenstern attributed to additivity becomes apparent in their utility theory. Before turning to that, however, some final comments on the relationships between von Neumann and Morgenstern's theory of measurement and the theories of Campbell, Nagel, and Stevens are in order.

7. The references provided by von Neumann and Morgenstern ([1944] 1953, 22, 256) are Burnside 1911; Mathewson 1930; Speiser 1937; Weyl 1938.

9.3.4. Von Neumann and Morgenstern versus Campbell, Nagel, and Stevens

As already mentioned, von Neumann and Morgenstern did not connect their discussion of measurement to the previous literature on the topic, not even in the second (1947) and third (1953) editions of *Theory of Games*. They did not refer to Campbell or to Nagel, Cohen, and Stevens. As I noted in section 9.3.2, they cited in footnotes some mathematical works on group theory, but they did not indicate other possible sources for their measurement theory. In his *Mathematical Foundations of Quantum Mechanics* ([1932] 1955), von Neumann had discussed measurement issues related to the fact that in quantum physics, the very act of measuring modifies the object to be measured. However, these are not the kinds of problems addressed in the parts of *Theory of Games* devoted to measurement.

The absence of explicit references notwithstanding, in von Neumann and Morgenstern's account of measurement, it is possible to find several echoes of previous discussions on the topic. Thus, like Campbell, they associated the possibility of proper measurement with the possibility of identifying some operation of addition between the objects to be measured. They also employed the distinction between direct and indirect measurement introduced by Campbell. Moreover, their axiomatic approach to utility measurement, which will be illustrated shortly, is analogous to the axiomatic approach to measurement originally put forward by Otto Hölder (see chapter 1, section 1.4.1) and later employed by Nagel (see chapter 4, section 4.1.4). These elements give a traditional—that is, measurement equals-ratio-scale measurement—flavor to von Neumann and Morgenstern's measurement theory.

There is, however, one major difference between von Neumann and Morgenstern's measurement theory and those of Campbell and Nagel. As discussed here in chapter 6, utility unique up to linear increasing transformations, that is, cardinal utility, is not measurable in the ratio-scale sense, because it is not possible to state that one utility is, for example, two or three times greater than another. This notwithstanding, von Neumann and Morgenstern explicitly considered cardinal utility, which they called "numerical utility," as measurable utility.

With respect to Stevens, there are certainly a number of analogies between his measurement theory and von Neumann and Morgenstern's. Like von Neumann and Morgenstern, Stevens related measurement to the assignment of numbers to objects, connected different types of measurement with different classes of mathematical transformations, and conceived of these transformations in terms of the mathematical theory of groups. Nevertheless, there are two major differences between the two measurement theories.

First, when von Neumann and Morgenstern ([1944] 1953, 24–29) applied their general theory of measurement to the specific case of utility, they defined the "natural" relations and operations between the objects under study by a set of axioms. As observed here in chapter 8, Stevens's theory of measurement was not axiomatic. Second, von Neumann and Morgenstern provided an explicit representation theorem establishing how the (axiomatically defined) relations and operations between objects correlate with certain mathematical relations and operations between numbers. Their representation theorem also identified the admissible transformations those numbers can be subjected to and, accordingly, the mathematical group associated with these transformations. In Stevens's theory of measurement, representation theorems are, by contrast, absent.

These two differences are not accidental but arise from the fact that, unlike von Neumann and Morgenstern, Stevens was, and remained throughout his scientific career, an operationalist. Accordingly, for Stevens, it is impossible to define the "natural" relations between the objects under study in an abstract, axiomatic way, independently of the concrete operations through which these relations are identified. For Stevens, insofar as these concrete operations, such as the operation of "determination of equality," and the rules to assign numbers to objects based on these operations, such as the rule of assigning the same number to two objects that have been identified as "equal," are empirically well defined, they do not require any axioms or representations theorems. In fact, and as discussed here in chapter 15, when the axiomatic approach to measurement began to become prominent, Stevens took an explicit stance against it.

In the late 1940s and early 1950s, von Neumann and Morgenstern's measurement theory did not have any significant impact on utility analysis. The readers of *Theory of Games* took from it the axiomatic treatment of utility but neglected the theory of measurement in which the axiomatization of utility was embedded. Arguably, this is due to the facts that von Neumann and Morgenstern presented their theory of measurement in terms that were too abstract for economists, such as the mathematical theory of groups, and that their exemplifications of measurement were taken from physics and mathematics rather than economics.

After this foray into von Neumann and Morgenstern's measurement theory, we can return to their utility analysis.

9.4. VON NEUMANN AND MORGENSTERN'S EXPECTED UTILITY THEORY

For von Neumann and Morgenstern, the state of the notion of utility in the early 1940s was analogous to the state of the notion of heat before it became measurable. As with heat, there exists for utility a natural relation of *greater* based on "the immediate sensation of preference," but "there is no intuitively significant way to add two utilities" ([1944] 1953, 16). This state of affairs justifies the ordinal approach to utility, which von Neumann and Morgenstern identified with indifference curve analysis.[8] However, von Neumann and Morgenstern argued, if some natural operation of addition for utilities could be identified, the history of the theory of heat could repeat itself, and utility numbers could become unique up to linear transformations. That is, utility could become measurable.

9.4.1. Against Pareto's Postulate 2

Before introducing their natural operation of addition for utilities, von Neumann and Morgenstern discussed another possible method of narrowing the system of acceptable

8. See von Neumann and Morgenstern [1944] 1953, 19–20, 29, 632; Morgenstern 1941; Morgenstern 1976, 809.

transformations of utility numbers to linear ones, namely the method based on Pareto's postulate 2 (see chapter 6, section 6.1, in this book):

> [Assume that] there is a criterion with which to compare the preference of C over A with the preference of A over B. It is well known that thereby utilities . . . become numerically measurable. That the possibility of comparison between A, B, and C only to this extent is already sufficient for a numerical measurement of "distances" was first observed in economics by Pareto. (18)

As already mentioned, von Neumann and Morgenstern did not cite Lange, Alt, or the other contributors to the debate of the 1930s that led to the definition of cardinal utility. However, we saw in chapter 6 that Morgenstern at least was well aware of that debate. In 1931, he had contributed to the discussion on the ranking of transitions and even argued that individuals are capable of comparing utility differences. Moreover, he was familiar with the 1936 article in which Alt had axiomatized cardinal utility on the basis of transition ranking. However, Morgenstern had now become skeptical about Pareto's postulate 2.

Like Allen (1935), Morgenstern and von Neumann criticized postulate 2 because it cannot be verified by "reproducible observations" of individual behavior ([1944] 1953, 24). Fortunately, they argued, the admissible transformations of the utility function can be reduced to linear ones in a different way, namely by introducing a novel but "natural" operation involving utilities: "The failure of one particular device [i.e., Pareto's postulate 2] need not exclude the possibility of achieving the same end by another device. Our contention is that the domain of utility contains a 'natural' operation which narrows the system of transformations to precisely the same extent as the other device would have done" (24).

9.4.2. Combining Lotteries

This natural operation has to do with "combinations of events with stated probabilities" (17).[9] For instance, given outcomes x and y, a possible combination is the prospect of seeing x occur with a probability of 50 percent and y with the (remaining) probability of 50 percent. These combinations came later to be known as "prospects" or "lotteries." Here I use the latter name and adopt the following notational convention to indicate lotteries in a concise way: a lottery yielding outcome x with probability p and outcome y with probability (1 – p) is indicated as [x, p; y, 1 – p]. In this notation, the 50 percent—50 percent described above will be indicated as [x, 0.5; y, 0.5].

Von Neumann and Morgenstern stressed that the events or outcomes of a lottery are "mutually exclusive" (18); that is, in a lottery like the one just introduced, *either* x *or* y occurs but not both. This mutual exclusivity rules out issues related to the possible complementarity or substitutability between x and y, that is, to the circumstance that the utility of x may

9. In what follows, I attempt to keep things as simple and concise as possible; more technical and extensive treatments of von Neumann and Morgenstern's axiomatization of utility can be found in Fishburn 1970; Fishburn 1989; Kreps 1988; Mas-Colell, Whinston, and Green 1995; Gilboa 2009.

depend on the concurrent availability of y (and vice versa). The authors of *Theory of Games* insisted on the mutual exclusivity of x and y because they wanted to avoid their natural operation of addition being confused with the addition of utilities drawing from the discarded hypothesis that the utilities of different goods are additively separable (see chapters 6 and 7 in this book).

9.4.3. Preferences between Lotteries

Von Neumann and Morgenstern assumed that individuals have complete and transitive preferences between risky alternatives, that is, lotteries, and required that, as in the case of preferences between riskless alternatives, the order of the utility numbers associated with the lotteries mirrors the order of preference between lotteries. If we indicate the von Neumann–Morgenstern utility function with the lower-case letter u, and if lottery L_1 is preferred to lottery L_2, it must be that $u(L_1) > u(L_2)$. Here and in the rest of this book, I use the lower-case letter u to designate the utility function featured in von Neumann–Morgenstern expected utility theory and the capital letter U to designate the traditional utility function that expresses the individual's preferences between riskless alternatives.

Von Neumann and Morgenstern next considered a "natural" operation of addition between lotteries that consists in combining two or more other lotteries to form a compound lottery. Call L_1 the lottery [x, 0.5; y, 0.5], and imagine a second lottery [x, 0.8; y, 0.2] called L_2. A compound lottery—call it L_3—is one yielding lottery L_1 with some probability p and lottery L_2 with the remaining probability $(1 - p)$. L_3 can thus be expressed as $[L_1, p; L_2, (1 - p)]$.[10]

The combining of lotteries can be seen as an addition operation because the probability of each outcome in the compound lottery L_3 is equal to the weighted sum of the probabilities of that outcome in L_1 and L_2, where the weights are given by probabilities p and $(1 - p)$. More concretely, the probability of getting x and y in L_3 is equal to, respectively, $p \times 0.5 + (1 - p) \times 0.8$ and $p \times 0.5 + (1 - p) \times 0.2$. In other words, the compound lottery L_3 can be obtained by the weighted vectorial addition of L_1 and L_2: $L_3 = p \times L_1 + (1 - p) \times L_2$.

This is a probabilistic fact concerning the combination of lotteries that does not require any additional assumption. But von Neumann and Morgenstern wanted to extend the additive properties of the vectorial combination of lotteries, namely that $L_3 = p \times L_1 + (1 - p) \times L_2$, to the utility numbers $u(L_1)$, $u(L_2)$, and $u(L_3)$ associated with the lotteries. Thus, they required that $u(L_3) = p \times u(L_1) + (1 - p) \times u(L_2)$.

To sum up, von Neumann and Morgenstern required that for all lotteries L_1, L_2, L_3 and any probability p, the utility numbers u associated with the lotteries satisfy two properties (24):

(1) L_1 is preferred to L_2, if and only if $u(L_1) > u(L_2)$;
(2) if $L_3 = p \times L_1 + (1 - p) \times L_2$, then $u(L_3) = p \times u(L_1) + (1 - p) \times u(L_2)$.

10. Notice that the outcomes x and y may be themselves lotteries, so that L_3 may be a "hyper-compound" lottery.

They also showed that if these two requirements are satisfied, the utility numbers u associated with the lotteries are "determined up to a linear transformation. I.e. then utility is a number up to a linear transformation" (25). Thus, apparently, we are back to cardinal utility.

Von Neumann and Morgenstern put forward a set of eight axioms about the individual's preferences between classes of lotteries that the individual judges as indifferent, attempted to justify these axioms, and proved that they imply the existence of a utility function over lotteries with properties (1) and (2).[11] As already noted, the proof of this result was provided in an appendix to the second edition of *Theory of Games* (1947).

9.4.4. Open Issues

From around the mid-1940s to the mid-1950s, von Neumann and Morgenstern's axiomatic version of EUT was the subject of an intense debate in which all major utility theorists of the period took part. Among the questions addressed in the debate were: What is the exact content of von Neumann and Morgenstern's axiomatic system? Can EUT be axiomatized on the basis of a different set of axioms, possibly more transparent than those introduced by von Neumann and Morgenstern? Are the axioms implying EUT descriptively plausible, or, instead, have they a purely normative nature? Irrespective of the descriptive or normative validity of the axioms underlying it, does EUT allow us to describe or predict important economic phenomena? How should the cardinal utility function featured in the EUT formula be interpreted? Although it is derived from preferences between risky alternatives, that is, lotteries, can the cardinal utility function featured in EUT also be used to analyze decisions between riskless alternatives, such as consumption bundles? If so, can we abandon the ordinal utility approach, build utility analysis on cardinal utility, and thus recover nonordinal notions such as diminishing marginal utility?

In chapters 10 and 11, we will see how the economists involved in the debate on EUT addressed these issues, particularly those concerning the interpretation of the cardinal utility function u featured in the expected utility formula. Here we focus on von Neumann and Morgenstern's stance on this latter issue.

9.5. VON NEUMANN AND MORGENSTERN ON CARDINAL UTILITY

9.5.1. Tricky Questions

The pertinent issue concerns the exact relationship between the "new" cardinal utility function u that, within von Neumann and Morgenstern's EUT, can be derived from

11. As became clear in the debate on EUT of the 1950s, the von Neumann–Morgenstern axioms are ordinal in nature, and the cardinal character of the utility function u depends on the circumstance that the theory is expressed in terms of the arithmetic mean of u. If the theory were expressed using some other mean, such as the geometric or the harmonic mean, a monotonic but not necessarily linear transformation of u, such as $v = e^u$, should be used. See more on this point in chapter 11 of this book, footnote 3; Montesano 1982; Montesano 1985.

preferences between risky alternatives and the "old" utility function U that utility theorists from Jevons to Hicks used to analyze choices between riskless alternatives such as consumption bundles.

It seems natural to assume that individuals consider a riskless option x as equivalent to a lottery L_x that assigns probability 1 to outcome x: $x \sim L_x$. Accordingly, individuals rank two riskless options x and y in the same way as they rank two lotteries L_x and L_y that assign probability 1 to, respectively, outcome x and outcome y. That is, $U(x) > U(y)$ if and only if $u(L_x) > u(L_y)$. But since $x \sim L_x$, $U(x) > U(y)$ if and only if $u(x) > u(y)$. In nonmathematical terms, the old utility function U and the new von Neumann–Morgenstern utility function u rank any two riskless alternatives x and y in the same way. This implies that the numbers that functions U and u assign to riskless alternatives are the same up to increasing transformations, that is, $u = F(U)$, with $F' > 0$. The question is whether the similarity between u and U is stronger than this "ordinal similarity."

More specifically, would it be possible to further restrict the system of transformations linking u and U to the system of linear increasing transformations? That is, would it be possible to say that $u = \alpha U + \beta$, where $\alpha > 0$? If this were possible, the utility differences calculated by using the new von Neumann–Morgenstern utility function u could be interpreted as the utility differences discussed by Pareto, Lange, Alt, and Samuelson with respect to the old utility function U. If, however, it is not possible to restrict the transformations linking u and U to the linear transformations, such an interpretation would be unwarranted.

That these are tricky questions became gradually clearer over the course of the decade-long debate on EUT. It is not, therefore, completely surprising that, as many commentators have noticed, von Neumann and Morgenstern's own stance on these questions was ambiguous.[12]

9.5.2. Ambiguities

In some passages of their book, von Neumann and Morgenstern argued that their approach could indeed be used to calculate utility differences between riskless alternatives. Here is one such passage: "If he [the individual] now prefers [the riskless] outcome A to the 50–50 combination of B and C, this provides a plausible base for the numerical estimate that his preference of A over B is in excess of his preference of C over A" ([1944] 1953, 18). In a first footnote appended to this passage, von Neumann and Morgenstern made the point even clearer:

> Assume that an individual prefers the consumption of a glass of tea to that of a cup of coffee, and the cup of coffee to a glass of milk. If we now want to know whether the last preference—i.e., difference in utilities—exceeds the former, it suffices to place him in a situation where he must decide this: Does he prefer a cup of coffee to a glass the content of which will be determined by a 50%–50% chance device as tea or milk [?]. (18 n. 1)

12. See, among others, Ellsberg 1954; Fishburn 1989.

However, in a second footnote appended to the *same* passage, a retreat was made from this interpretation: "We have not directly postulated any intuitive estimate of the relative sizes of two preferences i.e. . . . of two differences of utilities" (18 n. 2).

In another passage, von Neumann and Morgenstern suggested that their axioms provide a rigorous foundation to Bernoulli's theory, in the sense that if the axioms hold, individuals prefer the lottery maximizing the mathematical expectation of the utility function U for riskless payoffs. In this interpretation, as in Bernoulli's theory, the preferences between (risky) lotteries derive from preferences between (riskless) payoffs, and not vice versa. In a subsequent passage, however, von Neumann and Morgenstern dismissed this interpretation and argued that the preferences between lotteries are the primitives of their theory (which is correct) and that the utility function u that can be derived from these preferences cannot be identified with the traditional utility function U. Rather, u is defined as the function such that if lottery L_1 is preferred to lottery L_2, then the weighted average of u over the outcomes of L_1 is larger than the weighted average of u over the outcomes of L_2. They claimed: "We have practically defined numerical utility as being that thing for which the calculus of mathematical expectations is legitimate" (28).

Finally, in the text of the appendix added to *Theory of Games* in 1947, von Neumann and Morgenstern (630) talked of how much one utility exceeds or is exceeded by another utility. In a footnote, however, they claimed that they were talking of utility differences "merely to facilitate the verbal discussion—they are not part of our rigorous, axiomatic system" (631 n. 1).

9.5.3. Von Neumann versus Morgenstern?

The ambiguities in von Neumann and Morgenstern's interpretation of the relationship between the utility function u featured in their formulas and the riskless utility function U of traditional utility theory can seem unsurprising when we take account of the difficulty of the problem they faced. As we will see in the next two chapters, in mixing up the two functions, von Neumann and Morgenstern were in very good company. Nevertheless, it is possible to advance also a slightly different explanation.

I surmise that the ambiguities in von Neumann and Morgenstern's interpretation of the relationship between the utility functions u and U are at least in part due to their different scientific backgrounds and priorities. Conceiving of the function u as "that thing for which the calculus of mathematical expectations is legitimate" might have been acceptable for von Neumann, who was a mathematician and, as mentioned, did not care much about the economists' struggles with the utility concept. But this solution was less acceptable for Morgenstern. As an economist and, more specifically, as an Austrian economist educated in the tradition of Carl Menger, Morgenstern sought a clear economic interpretation of the utility function u. And the most obvious interpretation was that u is the same utility function through which marginal economists since Menger had explained economic decisions, independently of whether they involve risk or not.

If we accept this viewpoint, we may attribute to Morgenstern the passages of *Theory of Games* that identify the risky utility function u and the riskless utility function U and attribute to von Neumann the passages retreating from this interpretation. This supposition is supported by the fact that the passages of the first type are mainly in the text, while those of the second type are primarily in footnotes. As mentioned earlier here in section 9.2, the chapter of *Theory of Games* dealing with utility theory, chapter 1, was written chiefly by Morgenstern.

Therefore, the following scenario seems plausible. Initially, Morgenstern wrote the chapter and in doing so composed passages claiming that the risky utility function u coincides with the riskless utility function U; afterward, von Neumann pointed out that such claims "are not part of our rigorous, axiomatic system," but his critical comments entered the book only in footnotes and did not lead to revision of the main text.

I attempted to substantiate this supposition by examining the drafts of the chapters of *Theory of Games* collected in the Morgenstern papers. Unfortunately, the drafts of the first chapter of the book are missing, and therefore this suggestion remains supposition. Nonetheless, it is still useful to connect different possible interpretations of the nature of the utility function u featured in EUT with different scientific backgrounds and priorities. As we will see in chapters 12 and 13, from the early 1950s, the majority of economists accepted the interpretation of the utility function u that I have attributed to von Neumann. By contrast, philosophers, psychologists, and other noneconomists, who in the 1950s began using EUT as a handy tool for a variety of disciplinary goals, interpreted the utility function u in a way analogous to the one I have attributed to Morgenstern.

9.6. EXIT THE GAME

As mentioned, in the years following the publication of *Theory of Games*, von Neumann and Morgenstern's EUT and the nature of their "new" cardinal utility function became the topic of an intense debate in which the major economic theorists of the day took part. Von Neumann and Morgenstern, however, did not join in this discussion.

From 1942, that is, before the completion of the manuscript of *Theory of Games* in January 1943, von Neumann had become increasingly involved in consultancy work with the National Defense Research Committee, the Navy, and other military agencies. He also actively participated in the Manhattan Project and the design of the atomic bomb at Los Alamos. After World War II, his interests shifted to operations research and computer science. During the war, Morgenstern was not involved in military consultancy. From 1943 until the late 1940s, he tried to promote game theory among economists but without much success. In the 1940s and 1950s, he published several introductory articles on game theory and wrote on such disparate subjects as oligopoly theory, input-output analysis, the international spread of business cycles, and national security but not on utility measurement.

Apparently, von Neumann and Morgenstern's sole comment on the debate generated by their utility analysis is represented by the few lines they dedicated to the topic in the preface to the third edition of *Theory of Games* ([1944] 1953). They here noticed that since 1944, their theory of utility had "undergone considerable development theoretically, as well as experimentally, and in various discussions" (vii), mentioned some contributions to these discussions, but took no specific stance on them.[13]

13. On von Neumann and Morgenstern's research after their completion of *Theory of Games*, see Giocoli 2003b; Israel and Gasca 2009; Leonard 2010.

CHAPTER 10

What Is That Function?

Friedman, Savage, Marschak, Samuelson, and Baumol on EUT, 1947–1950

The publication of *Theory of Games and Economic Behavior* gave expected utility theory (EUT) a new bounce, but around 1950, it was still only one among several alternative theories of decision under risk on the table. In a comprehensive review article completed in 1950 and published the following year, Kenneth Arrow (1951a) discussed several alternative approaches to the theory of decisions under risk. Besides EUT, approaches examined included theories based on the mean, variance, and possibly other elements of the distribution of the payoffs (Hicks 1931; Hicks 1934; Marschak 1938; Lange 1944), models based on the minimax criterion, that is, the supposition that individuals choose the risky option whose minimum payoff is the highest (Wald 1950) or on the idea that individuals focus only on the best possible and the worst possible outcomes of uncertain alternatives (Shackle 1949). Nevertheless, the debate on EUT intensified in different quarters in this period, especially after the publication in 1947 of the second edition of *Theory of Games*, which contained the proof of the expected utility theorem.

For instance, Cambridge economist Dennis Robertson argued that EUT warranted a return to cardinal utility. In *Value and Capital*, Hicks (1939b, 18) had claimed that since cardinal utility is not necessary to explain market phenomena, it should be set aside on the grounds of the methodological principle of Occam's razor (see chapter 6, section 6.8.2). Now Robertson joked that thanks to EUT, the dark ages when Pareto, Hicks, and the other ordinalists had borrowed the razor "from old Occam to slit the throat of cardinal utility" had come to an end, and it was now time "to restore the old lady to life" (Robertson 1951, 121; 1952, 22). In Paris, from 1949 to 1952, a debate took place between, on the one side, a group of economists with a background in engineering and led by Maurice Allais, who opposed EUT, and, on the other side, a group of mathematicians led by Georges Guilbaud, who favored it.[1] In chapters 10, 11, and 12, however, I focus on the American discussion of EUT from 1947 to 1954, in which participants included such eminent economists as Milton

1. See more on the debate on EUT in France in Jallais and Pradier 2005.

Friedman, Leonard Jimmie Savage, Jacob Marschak, Paul Samuelson, William Baumol, Robert Strotz, Armen Alchian, and Daniel Ellsberg.

This American debate can be divided into three main phases. The first, which is reconstructed in this chapter, ranges from the publication of the second edition of *Theory of Games* in 1947 to April 1950. In this period, Friedman and Savage (1948), Marschak (1950), Samuelson (1950b), and Baumol (1951) wrote papers in which they took stances on the validity of EUT and the nature of the cardinal utility function u featured in the expected utility formula. Friedman, Savage, and Marschak supported EUT, although for different reasons, while Samuelson and Baumol rejected it. Regarding the interpretation of the nature of the von Neumann–Morgenstern utility function u, however, they all shared the view that in chapter 9 I attributed to Morgenstern, namely that the utility function u and the utility function U (which the earlier utility theorists had used to analyze choices between riskless alternatives) are equivalent, at least in the specific sense that one is a linear transformation of the other.

In the first phase of the debate, the various subgroups among these scholars—Friedman and Savage, Samuelson and Baumol, Marschak and his colleagues at the Cowles Commission—reached their conclusions about the validity of EUT and the nature of u without much interaction with the other subgroups. The second phase commenced in May 1950, when Samuelson, Savage, Marschak, Friedman, and Baumol began an intense exchange of letters. In their correspondence, these economists addressed several fundamental issues concerning EUT. In the first place, they argued about the exact assumptions underlying EUT. They also quarreled over whether these assumptions should be considered compelling requisites for rational behavior under risk. Furthermore, they discussed the descriptive validity and simplicity of EUT, which they compared with the descriptive validity and simplicity of alternative theories of risky choices. Finally, they debated the nature of the von Neumann–Morgenstern utility function u featured in EUT.

This correspondence modified the views of all five economists involved. Elsewhere (Moscati 2016a), I have reconstructed their discussions on the first three issues and identified the way they changed Samuelson's and Savage's thinking about EUT. In chapter 11, I focus on the discussions on the nature of the utility function u and enlarge the picture to include Friedman, Marschak, and Baumol. For our narrative, the most important exchange is probably that between Friedman and Baumol, for over the course of it, Friedman argued that the utility functions u and U are not linear transformations of each other and that, accordingly, the curvature of u cannot be interpreted as indicating diminishing or increasing marginal utility, and the expected value of U, even if available, cannot be used to make predictions about choice behavior under risk. Friedman's interpretation was quickly adopted by Baumol and Samuelson and later became standard in economics.

After the epistolary exchange of 1950–1951, the American advocates of EUT, new and old, went public. The first main occasion was a prominent conference on the theory of decisions under uncertainty that took place in Paris in May 1952, where Friedman, Savage, Marschak, and Samuelson advocated EUT in the face of attacks from Allais and other opponents of the theory. Later in the year, a symposium on EUT featuring contributions by Samuelson and Savage in support of the theory was published in the October 1952 issue of *Econometrica*. The Paris conference and the *Econometrica* symposium saw the emergence of EUT as the mainstream economic model of decision-making under risk, and so October 1952 can be taken as marking the conclusion of the second phase of the debate on EUT.

In the third phase, which ranged from the end of 1952 to 1955, further contributions to understanding the nature of the utility function featured in EUT emerged, such as those by Friedman and Savage (1952), Strotz (1953), Alchian (1953), Ellsberg (1954), Savage ([1954] 1972), and Friedman (1955). In these contributions, however, the issues concerning utility measurement gained an autonomous status, and the discussion shifted from the question "What does the utility function u featured in EUT measure?" to the question "What does it mean, in general, to measure utility?" In particular, Friedman, Savage, Strotz, and Alchian all advanced a view of utility measurement according to which measuring utility consists of assigning numbers to objects by following a definite set of operations. From this perspective, the way of assigning utility numbers to objects is largely arbitrary and conventional, but the assigned numbers should allow the economist to predict the choice behavior of individuals.

This conventionalist and prediction-oriented view of utility measurement became standard among mainstream utility theorists, and its success goes far toward explaining the peaceful cohabitation of cardinal and ordinal utility within utility analysis that began in the mid-1950s and has lasted until the present day. This third phase of the debate on EUT is covered in chapter 12.

10.1. APPLYING EXPECTED UTILITY THEORY: FRIEDMAN AND SAVAGE

One of the early articles in support of the von Neumann–Morgenstern version of the expected utility hypothesis was published in 1948 by Friedman and Savage, who were both based at the University of Chicago.

10.1.1. Meeting at SRG, Collaborating in Chicago

As noted in chapter 7, section 7.6.2, Friedman studied at Chicago, where he formed a lifelong friendship with W. Allen Wallis, and began his career as a consumption theorist and an applied statistician. As we have seen, in 1942, Wallis and he published an extended critique of Louis Leon Thurstone's experimental attempt to elicit indifference curves. After holding positions at the National Bureau of Economic Research, the University of Wisconsin, and the Treasury Department, in March 1943, Friedman joined the Statistical Research Group (SRG), a wartime think tank providing statistical analysis for the US Army that was based at Columbia University and directed by Wallis.

Savage (1917–1971) also worked for the SRG. He studied mathematics at the University of Michigan (B.S. 1938, Ph.D. 1941), and spent the academic year 1941–1942 at the Institute for Advanced Study in Princeton as a postdoctoral student. There he became acquainted with von Neumann, at that time working on *Theory of Games* with Morgenstern, and Frederick Mosteller, a Ph.D. student in mathematics at Princeton University with whom Savage ended up teaching a course in algebra and trigonometry. In 1942, Savage left Princeton for Cornell University, and eventually, in March 1944, he ended up at SRG, where he met Friedman. At SRG, Friedman and Savage worked together on various statistical projects (Friedman and Savage 1947; Freeman, Friedman, Mosteller, and Wallis 1948). Savage also collaborated with Mosteller, who had interrupted his Ph.D. studies to join SRG (Girshick, Mosteller, and Savage 1946).

In 1946, after SRG had been dismantled, Friedman and Savage joined the University of Chicago. Friedman entered the department of economics, where he began teaching a course in price theory that revived his interest in utility analysis. Savage was appointed first at the Institute of Radiobiology and Biophysics and then, from 1949, at the newly created department of statistics chaired by Wallis. In 1947, Friedman and Savage began collaborating on a paper on EUT that was eventually published in the August 1948 issue of the *Journal of Political Economy* under the title "The Utility Analysis of Choices Involving Risk."[2]

10.1.2. S-Shaped Utility Curves and As-If Maximization

Based on data from the US Bureau of Labor Statistics, the National Bureau of Economic Research, books about the history of lotteries in different countries, and casual observation, Friedman and Savage (1948) identified three basic facts that a satisfactory theory of choice under risk should be able to explain: (1) individuals of all income levels buy insurance; (2) individuals of all income levels purchase lottery tickets or engage in similar forms of gambling; and (3) most individuals both purchase insurance and gamble. Friedman and Savage (297) claimed that if the utility curve of money is assumed to be S-shaped, that is, first concave, then convex, and then concave again, EUT can rationalize these three facts.

In showing how this can be done, Friedman and Savage introduced concepts such as risk aversion and risk seeking that quickly became central to the theory of risky decisions. An individual is risk-averse if he prefers a sure amount of money $I to a lottery whose expected payoff is $I and is risk-seeking if that preference goes in the opposite direction. They also showed that risk aversion and risk seeking are associated, respectively, with the concavity and the convexity of the utility curve of money, and they enriched their discussion of attitudes toward risk with a graphical illustration that is still used in microeconomics textbooks and is reproduced here in figure 10.1.

Finally, Friedman and Savage put forward an "as-if interpretation" of EUT, according to which EUT does not assert that individuals consciously calculate expected utilities but only that "individuals behave *as if* they calculated and compared expected utility" (298). In effect, and as shown by Daniel Hammond (2009), at more or less the same time as he completed his paper with Savage, Friedman also completed the first draft of a methodological essay titled "Descriptive Validity vs. Analytical Relevance in Economic Theory" (Friedman papers, box 43). In this essay, Friedman employed the as-if argument to claim that the validity of a scientific theory should be judged not on the descriptive realism of its assumptions but on

2. See more on Friedman, Savage, and their collaboration in Hammond 2010; Wallis 1980; Wallis 1981; Mosteller 1981.

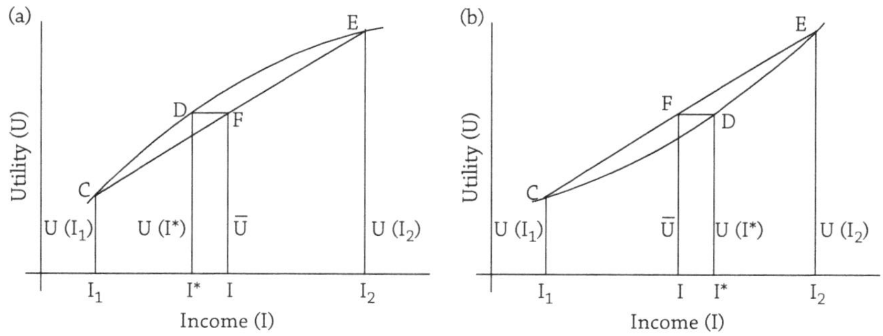

Figure 10.1. Friedman and Savage's utility curves and risk attitudes
Risk aversion is associated with a concave utility curve and is represented in diagram *a*. Risk seeking is associated with a convex utility curve and is represented in diagram *b*.
Source: Friedman and Savage 1948, 290. Reproduced with permission of the University of Chicago Press.

the validity of its implications. Chapter 12 follows the evolution of Friedman's methodological essay, which was eventually published as "The Methodology of Positive Economics" (1953b).

With respect to utility measurement issues, the Friedman–Savage article is important in two respects.

10.1.3. The Bernoullian Interpretation of the Utility Curves

Friedman and Savage identified the utility function u featured in the expected utility formula—and pictured in their graphical illustration of the theory—with the riskless utility function U of traditional utility theory. In other words, they followed the interpretation of the utility function u that in chapter 9 I have attributed to Morgenstern. Moreover, the explanatory structure of their EUT was that of Bernoulli's EUT rather than von Neumann and Morgenstern's EUT. Friedman and Savage explained the preferences regarding lotteries as causally derived from the utility of money (and the probabilities of various payoffs). Accordingly, they explained risk seeking as a consequence of the convexity of the utility function for riskless money, that is, as a consequence of the fact that the marginal utility of money is increasing: an individual prefers the lottery *because* for him, the utility of the sum that may be gained is larger than the utility of the sum that may be lost. Symmetrically, they explained risk aversion as deriving from the diminishing marginal utility of money. As we will see, over the course of the debate on EUT, Friedman and Savage retreated from this interpretation.

10.1.4. Measuring Utility and Testing EUT

Elaborating on a suggestion already present in von Neumann and Morgenstern's *Theory of Games*, Friedman and Savage explained how the numerical values of the utility function u, which they interpreted as the utility of money, can be inferred from indifference regarding monetary prospects and how the measures of u so obtained can be used to test the validity of EUT.

They imagined an individual who is found to be indifferent between a gamble yielding \$500 with probability 0.4 and \$1,000 with probability 0.6—such a gamble can be written as [\$500, 0.4; \$1,000, 0.6]—and \$600 for sure. If this individual is an expected utility maximizer, then for him, u(\$600) is equal to u(\$500) × 0.4 + u(\$1,000) × 0.6. But the function u is unique up to linear increasing transformations, that is, transformations of the form $F(u) = \alpha u + \beta$, with $\alpha > 0$. Since α and β are arbitrary, the two points of u are also arbitrary. Thus, we can state that u(\$500) = 0 and u(\$1,000) = 1 and establish that for this individual, u(\$600) = 0 × 0.4 + 1 × 0.6 = 0.6.

Such utility measures, Friedman and Savage pointed out, can be used to test the empirical validity of EUT. If, to continue the previous numerical example, in a further experiment, the individual is found to be indifferent between gamble [\$10,000, 0.2; \$500, 0.8] and \$1,000 for sure, then he should also be indifferent between gamble [\$10,000, 0.12; \$500, 0.88] and \$600 for sure.[3] If this is not the case, Friedman and Savage noted (304), "the supposition that individuals seek to maximize expected utility would be contradicted."

As we will see in chapter 13, the strategy suggested by Friedman and Savage to test EUT was promptly implemented by Mosteller, their associate at SRG.

10.2. MARSCHAK'S AXIOMS

The second main protagonist in the discussion on EUT was Marschak. While Friedman and Savage focused in their 1948 article on the possible applications of EUT, Marschak was more interested in the axiomatic foundations of the theory and the justification of the axioms.

10.2.1. Marschak at the Cowles Commission

Marschak (1898–1977) was a creative and energetic scholar who made multifaceted contributions in many areas of economics. A Russian Jew, he began studying engineering in Kiev in the mid-1910s, then participated in the Russian Revolution, but in 1919, he left Russia for Germany for political reasons. He studied economics and statistics first in Berlin and then in Heidelberg, where he graduated in 1922. In the mid-1920s, he worked as an economics journalist; in 1928, he joined the faculty of Kiel University; and in 1930, he moved to Heidelberg. When the Nazis rose to power in 1933, he and his family left Germany for Britain, where he found a job as a lecturer in statistics at Oxford University. Before the outbreak of the war, Marschak emigrated again, this time to the United States. Initially, he

3. If the individual is indifferent between [\$10,000, 0.2; \$500, 0.8] and \$1,000 for sure, then u(\$1,000) = u(\$10,000) × 0.2 + u(\$500) × 0.8; but u(\$1,000) = 1, and u(\$500) = 0, and therefore u(\$10,000) = 1/0.2 = 5. The expected utility of [\$10,000, 0.12; \$500, 0.88] is 5 × 0.12 + 0 × 0.88 = 0.6, which is equal to u(\$600).

worked at the New School for Social Research, and in 1943, he joined the University of Chicago as professor of economics and director of the Cowles Commission for Research in Economics, a research institute founded by businessman and economist Alfred Cowles.[4]

Since 1939, the commission had been located at the University of Chicago in the same building as the department of economics, but the two institutions were independent and pursued different research agenda.[5] At Cowles, ideas were disseminated through discussion papers, which were mimeographed, circulated within and outside the commission, and discussed in seminars and special staff meetings. Marschak always acknowledged that his contributions to the axiomatization of EUT benefited significantly from the comments of other Cowles researchers, such as Arrow, Herman Chernoff, Herman Rubin, Israel Herstein, and Edmond Malinvaud (who visited Cowles during the academic year 1950–1951).[6] In some papers, Marschak also thanked Savage, who was not a Cowles associate but often participated in the commission's seminars and research activities. Marschak served as director of the commission until 1948, when Tjalling Koopmans stepped in.

10.2.2. A Novel Axiomatization for EUT

As mentioned in chapter 9, in the 1930s, Marschak had criticized EUT in the Bernoulli version because he judged it implausible that individuals take into account only the average of utilities in evaluating risky alternatives (Marschak 1938). The axiomatization of EUT put forward by von Neumann and Morgenstern, however, prompted him to reconsider EUT.

In chapter 9, section 9.4.3, we also saw that von Neumann and Morgenstern's axioms are about preferences between indifference classes of lotteries rather than single lotteries, and this makes their exact meaning opaque. In a series of Cowles Commission discussion papers published from July 1948 to June 1949, Marschak (1948a; 1948b; 1949) put forward

4. See more on Marschak, his adventurous life, and his multifaceted scientific contributions in Arrow 1991; Hagemann 1997; Cherrier 2010. Between the mid-1940s and 1955, the Cowles Commission established itself as a pivotal center for economic research. Cowles affiliates included a number of brilliant young economists, such as Kenneth Arrow, Gerard Debreu, Trygve Haavelmo, Leonid Hurwicz, Lawrence Klein, Tjalling Koopmans, Harry Markowitz, Franco Modigliani, and Herbert Simon. See more on the Cowles Commission in Hildreth 1986; Düppe and Weintraub 2014; Herfeld 2018.

5. See more on the tense relationship between the Cowles Commission and Chicago's Department of Economics, especially after Friedman's return to Chicago in 1946, in Boumans 2016; Arrow 2016.

6. Arrow (1921–2017) studied mathematics and social sciences at the City College of New York (B.S. 1940) and mathematics at Columbia University (M.A. 1941). In 1941, he began a Ph.D. in economics at Columbia under Harold Hotelling (on whom, see chapter 7). After serving in the US Army during the war, in 1946, Arrow returned to his graduate studies at Columbia, and in April 1947, he joined the Cowles Commission. In the summer of 1948, he began collaborating with the RAND Corporation in Santa Monica. While at RAND, he initiated the study that later became his Ph.D. dissertation at Columbia and one of the most influential books of twentieth-century economics, *Social Choice and Individual Values* (1951b). In 1949, he left Cowles for Stanford, where he spent most of his academic career, but he maintained strong connections with the commission until at least the mid-1950s. See more on Arrow's early career in Kelly 1987; Arrow 2016. See more on Chernoff, Rubin, Herstein, and Malinvaud in, respectively, Bather 1996; Bock 2004; Cohn 1989; Krueger 2003. On Malinvaud, see also chapter 11, sections 11.7.1 and 11.8.

and progressively refined a novel axiomatization of EUT in which the postulates are about preferences between *single lotteries* rather than *indifference classes of lotteries*. Marschak's axiomatization found its final form in an article titled "Rational Behavior, Uncertain Prospects, and Measurable Utility," published in the April 1950 issue of *Econometrica*, the journal of the Econometric Society then directed by Ragnar Frisch, which in the 1950s became one of the most important economics journals.

Marschak's axiomatic system includes a postulate that he initially called Axiom B (1948a; 1948b), then Postulate IV_b (1949), and, finally, Postulate IV_2 (1950). The postulate states that given any three lotteries L_1, L_2, and L_3, if lotteries L_1 and L_2 are indifferent, then the two compound lotteries $[L_1, p; L_3, 1 - p]$ and $[L_2, p; L_3, 1 - p]$ should also be indifferent, and this holds for any probability p between 0 and 1.[7] To illustrate the postulate and highlight its compelling character, Marschak (1950, 120) used the following example: "Suppose a $1,000 bill and a car are equivalent. Compare two lottery tickets, one promising a $1,000 bill or a house with probabilities .9 and .1, the other promising a car or a house, also with probabilities .9 and .1. Then there is no reason to prefer one of the two lottery tickets to the other."

10.2.3. The Descriptive and Normative Dimensions of EUT

Marschak defined "rational behavior" under uncertainty as the behavior of an individual who follows the postulates of his axiomatization of EUT. For Marschak, rational behavior has a "descriptive" as well as a "recommendatory," that is, normative, dimension (1950, 112). Accordingly, rational behavior can be conceived of as an "approximate description of actual behavior" and, in this sense, is "susceptible of empirical tests"; but it can also be regarded as defining a set of "rules of behavior to be followed" (112). In Marschak's 1950 article, the descriptive and normative dimensions of the behavior implied by Postulates I–IV appear equally important. However, in a subsequent publication (Marschak [1951] 1974) and in correspondence with other economists (see chapter 11), Marschak emphasized the normative force of his postulates.

10.2.4. Measurable and Manageable Utility

With respect to measurement issues, Marschak identified the measurability of utility with the uniqueness of the utility numbers up to linear transformations: "From this [set of assumptions], the 'measurability' of utility is derived . . . in the sense that utility is unique up to a linear transformation" (135). To clarify the sense in which utility is measurable, he

7. Independently of Marschak, Norman Dalkey (1949), a researcher at the RAND Corporation in Santa Monica, California, and John Nash (1950), then still a Ph.D. student in mathematics at Princeton, also put forward axiomatizations of EUT that were based on postulates about preferences regarding single lotteries (rather than indifference classes of lotteries) and included axioms analogous to Marschak's Postulate IV_2. For a discussion of the contributions of Dalkey and Nash to the axiomatization of EUT, see Fishburn and Wakker 1995; Bleichrodt, Li, Moscati, and Wakker 2016.

compared it to altitude rather than, as was by then customary, to temperature. Both utility and altitude are unique up to the unit and zero point of measurement: "The altitude of a point on the earth's surface is unique up to two constants . . . depending on the origin, such as the sea level, and the unit, such as the meter. . . . In this sense, altitudes expressed in meters, and linear utility indices, are equally strictly measurable" (1950, 131).

Marschak then asked why this form of measurability has a special role in utility theory, while in other fields, other forms of measurability, such as ratio-scale measurability, are prominent. For Marschak, the form of measurability depends on the most important or frequent operations carried out in a given field. The most appropriate form of measurability for the objects in any one field is that which makes the important or frequent operations carried out in the field as simple as possible. Marschak called this property of a certain measurement form "manageability" (131). To illustrate his point, he used a counterexample. An ordinal measurability of altitude, that is, a measure allowing for the altitude numbers to be unique up to increasing transformations, would not be manageable when it came to carrying out the basic operations related to altitude, such as calculating the distance between two altitudes.

In the case of utility analysis, for Marschak, the most important operation is the calculation of the mathematical average of utilities. This is because the decision maker, if he abides by Postulates I–IV, will prefer the risky prospect with the highest mathematical average of the utilities: "In the case of utility indices of prospects, a particularly important kind of linear operations is . . . the forming of expected values . . . . For no other but linear utility indices is it true that the utility of a distribution (a prospect) is equal to the expected value of utilities of sure prospects" (132).

The measurability of utility in the linear sense, Marschak observed, could derive from a different set of postulates, such as Pareto's assumption 2. However, like Allen (1935, 155; see chapter 6, section 6.5.1 in this book) and von Neumann and Morgenstern ([1944] 1953, 24; see chapter 9, section 9.4.1 in this book), Marschak rejected this postulate because it is "neither immediately plausible nor is it amenable to easy observation" (1950, 134). When asked, a person can compare utility differences, but for Marschak, this comparison "does not show itself in any choice except in the choice to answer a certain question in a certain way" (134).

10.2.5. U and u

Concerning the interpretation of the relationship between the utility function u featured in the expected utility formula and the riskless utility function U of traditional utility theory, Marschak shared the view expressed by Friedman and Savage in 1948 that the two functions are equivalent, in the specific sense that one is a linear transformation of the other. Thus, in his 1950 *Econometrica* article, Marschak connected aversion and love for risk to, respectively, the diminishing and increasing marginal utility of money (120, 139). Similarly, in the abstract of a paper presented in September 1948 at a meeting of the Econometric Society and cited in the 1950 article, Marschak asserted that the uniqueness up to linear transformations of EUT's utility function u rehabilitates nonordinal concepts such as diminishing marginal utility and the traditional definition of complementarity in terms of cross-order derivatives: "Result (3) [concerning the cardinal measurability of u] makes the second and higher derivatives of utility (the first derivatives of marginal utility, including the Fisher–Pareto measure of complementarity as distinct from its Hicksian measure) determinate in sign, thus simplifying economic theory" (Marschak [1948] 1949, 64).

10.3. SAMUELSON VERSUS EXPECTED UTILITY THEORY

Like Marschak, Samuelson was initially critical of EUT. But while Marschak had revised his stance by the late 1940s, in 1950, Samuelson was still a staunch opponent of the theory. One of the main reasons for Samuelson's opposition to EUT was that he saw it as inconsistent with the ordinal approach to utility.

10.3.1. From Harvard to MIT

In chapter 6, section 6.8.3, we saw that in his Harvard Ph.D. dissertation of 1940, which was published in 1947 as *Foundations of Economic Analysis*, Samuelson downplayed the utility-free approach of his "Note" of 1938 and endorsed an ordinal utility approach substantially equivalent to that used by Hicks in *Value and Capital*. Accordingly, Samuelson dismissed cardinal utility as a special assumption by which, according to him, nothing at all is gained. He also rejected special assumptions implying cardinal utility, such as the additive separability of the utility function, because he judged them "not generally applicable," "arbitrary," "dubious," "highly unrealistic," "superfluous," or as leading to "really fantastic conclusions" (1947, 174–202).

Among the special assumptions implying cardinal utility discussed in *Foundations of Economic Analysis*, EUT is missing. The absence of EUT in its Bernoulli version can be explained by the widespread skepticism surrounding it in the 1930s and early 1940s, while the absence of EUT in von Neumann and Morgenstern's version appears to be simply due to the fact that Samuelson had completed *Foundations* before the publication of *Theory of Games* in 1944.

Since 1940, Samuelson had been based at MIT, where he was pivotal in building up the economics department and making it, by the late 1950s, one of the most prominent research departments of economics in the United States.[8] By 1947, at the age of thirty-two, he had already published more than thirty articles in major economics journals, and the appearance of *Foundations of Economic Analysis* consolidated his position as a leading American economist. In 1947, he was awarded the inaugural John Bates Clark Medal, the prestigious award of the American Economic Association for the economist under forty who had made the most significant contributions to the field. On top of all this, in 1948, he published an introductory economics textbook (Samuelson 1948) that was widely adopted in American universities. Thus, when in 1949–1950 Samuelson entered the discussion of EUT and

8. See more on Samuelson's role in the rise of MIT's economics department in Weintraub 2014.

vehemently attacked it, he was already an intensely bright star in the firmament of American economics.

10.3.2. Prologue: The Exchange with Baumol

From 1947 to 1949, Samuelson did not publish anything about EUT. But an exchange of November 1949 with Baumol, then a young assistant professor at Princeton with strong ordinalist views, reveals that Samuelson was already by this point airing his objections to EUT.[9]

In a letter dated November 18, 1949, Baumol asked Samuelson if he had already written or had "plans to write up your objections to the Neumann–Morgenstern Measurability of Utility argument," as "rumors of the thing have been spreading" (Samuelson papers, box 15). If not, Baumol continued, he himself would show how Samuelson's "*foundation* argument applied to this particular case," that is, how the ordinalist criticisms Samuelson had put forward in *Foundations* against the special assumptions generating cardinal utility also apply to the particular case of EUT's assumptions. On November 25, 1949, Samuelson replied that it was not likely that he would "get around to writing up my thoughts on the subject for a long time" and encouraged Baumol to write down his own criticisms of von Neumann and Morgenstern's cardinal utility function (Samuelson papers, box 15). As we will see in section 10.4, Baumol did just that.

Samuelson's prediction that he would not contribute to the debate on EUT proved incorrect. In April 1950, he completed a short paper on the topic, "Probability and the Attempts to Measure Utility" (Samuelson 1950b). Since the paper was published in the July 1950 issue of the Japanese journal *Economic Review*, in his correspondence, Samuelson often referred to it as the "Japanese paper." In early May 1950 Samuelson (1950a; 1950c) completed two further short papers that developed some of his criticisms of EUT but are less relevant for our narrative.[10]

10.3.3. The Japanese Paper

In accord with the positions expressed in his *Foundations*, Samuelson (1950b, 167) opened his Japanese paper by endorsing the ordinal utility approach and claiming that "to the modern theorist cardinal utility is irrelevant." He observed that cardinal restrictions on ordinal utility can be obtained "by a variety of different tricks" (167), which, however, always involve some arbitrary assumptions. For him, EUT, whether in the Bernoulli–Marshall, the von Neumann–Morgenstern, or the Friedman–Savage version, was just the latest of these tricks. In a footnote, Samuelson (119 n. 4) made generic mention of Marschak's work on EUT, but he referred neither to Marschak's Cowles Commission papers of the years 1948

9. The correspondence between Baumol and Samuelson from November 1949 to May 1950 has been discussed already by Heukelom 2014, 36–40.

10. See more on Samuelson's two papers of May 1950 in Moscati 2016a.

and 1949 nor to the article of Marschak that was forthcoming, or had just been published, in the April 1950 issue of *Econometrica*. As we will see shortly, Samuelson became aware of Marschak's article only in early May 1950.

In his Japanese paper, Samuelson attacked the axioms of EUT as well as its empirical implications. For him, von Neumann and Morgenstern's axioms put an arbitrary "straight-jacket" (169 n. 4) on the individual's ordinal preferences for lotteries. These preferences should satisfy only two properties: (1) they should be complete, transitive, and continuous, just as the individual's ordinal preferences between riskless commodity bundles are; (2) they should comply with what today we call monotonicity with respect to first-order stochastic dominance. In the case of choices between lotteries with monetary payoffs, monotonicity means that raising a payoff without changing the other payoffs, or increasing the probability of a larger payoff at the expense of the probability of a smaller payoff, raises preferability.

Samuelson declared that he found the von Neumann–Morgenstern axioms for EUT opaque. On the one hand, he observed, they concern preference relations and seem therefore to be ordinal in nature; on the other hand, the axioms imply that the preference relations can be represented by the expected utility formula, which features a cardinal utility function. Samuelson was puzzled by this apparent contradiction and could not understand how von Neumann and Morgenstern's ordinal axioms imply EUT. "I am simply confused," he admitted (172).

Samuelson guessed that von Neumann and Morgenstern had "implicitly added a hidden and unacceptable premise to their axioms" (172), but in April 1950, he was unable to identify this hidden assumption. Nevertheless, Samuelson christened the hidden premise the "independence assumption" (170 n. 7), because he associated it with the assumption that the utilities of different commodities are independent or additively separable. As already mentioned, in his *Foundations*, Samuelson had extensively criticized additive separability as far-fetched and had shown that it implies the cardinal measurability of utility and several implausible features of the demand function for commodities.

Finally, Samuelson attacked the alleged capacity of EUT to explain empirical phenomena. As explained earlier, in section 10.1.2, in their 1948 article, Friedman and Savage claimed that EUT can rationalize the three basic facts of gambling and insurance behavior, namely that individuals of all income levels buy insurance, that individuals of all income levels purchase lottery tickets or engage in similar forms of gambling, and that most individuals both purchase insurance and gamble. Samuelson (168) contested this claim, noting that, for instance, EUT cannot explain "the perfectly possible case of a man who refuses fair small bets at all income levels and yet buys lottery tickets." More generally, Samuelson contended that the phenomena associated with gambling are "infinitely richer" than the expected utility hypothesis permits and that there is as much to be learned about gambling "from Dostoyevsky as from Pascal."[11]

11. Fyodor Dostoyevsky wrote the autobiographical novel *The Gambler* (1867), whose protagonist was addicted to roulette. In his *Pensées* (1670), Blaise Pascal made a famous argument for believing in God based on the wager that if you do not believe in a God that exists, you risk eternal punishment, but if you do believe in a God that does not exist, the costs are much less dire.

10.3.4. Samuelson on u and U

Part of Samuelson's criticism of EUT depended on the fact that, like Friedman, Savage, and Marschak, he tacitly identified the von Neumann–Morgenstern utility function u in the expected utility formula with the riskless utility function U of traditional utility theory. As we saw, Samuelson was an ordinalist about U, and since he identified U with u, he was suspicious about a theory like EUT that was apparently based on cardinal utility.

Samuelson's identification of u with U was reinforced by an element that we do not find in the papers on EUT of Friedman, Savage, and Marschak, namely the identification of the "independence assumption," which is related to the form of the function u, with the assumption of additive separability, which is related to the form of U. Initially, Samuelson identified the two assumptions, and thus, he also tended to identify u with U.

10.4. BAUMOL AND THE CURVATURE OF THE UTILITY FUNCTION

Baumol (1922–2017) studied economics at the City College of New York (B.S. 1942) and then moved to the London School of Economics for graduate studies. He became acquainted with Samuelson in 1948, when the latter was visiting LSE, and in 1949, he published in *Economica* an appreciative review of Samuelson's *Foundations* (Baumol 1949). In 1949, Baumol also completed his doctoral studies at LSE with a dissertation on welfare economics written under Lionel Robbins and was then appointed assistant professor at Princeton's department of economics, whose faculty included Morgenstern.[12] As mentioned earlier in section 10.3.2, in November 1949, Baumol wrote to Samuelson that he planned to write a paper criticizing EUT from the ordinalist viewpoint expounded by Samuelson in *Foundations*. Baumol completed the paper in April 1950 and titled it "The Neumann–Morgenstern Utility Index—An Ordinalist View." The paper was later published in the *Journal of Political Economy* (Baumol 1951).

Some of the points made by Baumol are similar to those made by Samuelson in his Japanese paper. For instance, Baumol (1951, 64) also argued that von Neumann and Morgenstern's axioms put an arbitrary straightjacket on the individual's ordinal preferences, and he put forward an alternative set of axioms that, he argued, was purely ordinal.

For our purposes, however, the relevant part of the paper is its criticism of Friedman and Savage's explanation of risk attitudes in terms of the curvature of the utility function U, that is, in terms of diminishing or increasing marginal utility for riskless money. In fact, Baumol stressed, if the utility function U is ordinal, its curvature is not invariant to monotonic increasing transformations. Therefore, the individual's attitude toward risk can be changed simply by substituting one utility function U with a monotonic increasing transformation of it. This would make the parts of the Friedman–Savage analysis based on the curvature of the utility function meaningless: "If we then accept the view that any [utility] index obtained from a valid index by a monotone transformation is also valid, those of the

12. See more on Baumol in Krueger 2001.

Friedman–Savage results . . . which refer to the shape of the income marginal utility curve, lose all their meaning" (65). Clearly, Baumol's criticism is based on his identification of the utility function U for riskless money with the utility function u featured in EUT.

10.5. END OF THE FIRST PHASE OF THE DEBATE ON EUT

From 1947 to May 1950, Friedman and Savage, Samuelson and Baumol, and Marschak and his colleagues at the Cowles Commission wrote papers in which they took stances on the validity of EUT and the nature of the von Neumann–Morgenstern utility function u. Each subgroup of scholars reached conclusions about these issues without much interaction with the other subgroups.

Friedman and Savage supported EUT and argued that it can explain some important facts about choice behavior under risk. With respect to the nature of the utility function u, they identified it with the utility function U of traditional utility theory. Marschak supported EUT because its axioms appeared to him normatively compelling but also descriptively valid. His interpretation of the nature of the function u was like that of Friedman and Savage: the utility functions u and U are equivalent, in the specific sense that one is a linear transformation of the other. Samuelson and Baumol opposed EUT on both normative and descriptive grounds. However, they shared with Friedman, Savage, and Marschak the idea that the functions u and U are equivalent.

An intense exchange of letters on EUT among Samuelson, Savage, Marschak, Friedman, and Baumol began in May 1950. This correspondence, to which we now move, significantly changed the stances of these five economists, not only on EUT but also on the nature of the von Neumann–Morgenstern utility function u and its relation to the traditional utility function U.

CHAPTER 11

From Chicago to Paris

The Debate Continues, 1950–1952

After completing his Japanese paper in April 1950, Paul Samuelson circulated it among colleagues, asking for comments and criticisms. On April 20, 1950, he sent the essay to Jacob Marschak, on April 28 to William Baumol, and on May 1, it was Milton Friedman's turn. Samuelson asked Friedman to forward a second copy to Leonard J. Savage, whose address at the University of Chicago Samuelson did not have. Friedman did so in early May, including with Samuelson's paper a perplexed comment to Savage: "Dear Jimmie: . . . Can you figure out what it is about? I must confess I cannot" (Friedman papers, box 99)

Meanwhile, Baumol circulated his own paper, "The Neumann–Morgenstern Utility Index—An Ordinalist View". On May 2, 1950, he sent it to Samuelson, who was enthusiastic (Samuelson papers, box 15). Later that month, Baumol submitted the work for publication in the *Journal of Political Economy*, and editor Earl Hamilton asked Friedman to review it. After the summer of 1950, Baumol sent the paper also to Marschak.

The circulation of Samuelson's and Baumol's papers set in motion an exchange of letters on EUT among Friedman, Savage, Samuelson, Marschak, and Baumol, during which these five economists addressed four main topics concerning EUT: (1) the identification of the assumption that Samuelson called the Independence Axiom and Marschak called Postulate IV_2 as the key assumption underlying EUT; (2) the normative appeal of the Independence Axiom or, equivalently, Postulate IV_2 as a compelling requisite for rational behavior under risk; (3) the descriptive validity and simplicity of EUT as compared with the alternative theory of risky choices advocated by Samuelson in his Japanese paper; (4) the nature of the von Neumann–Morgenstern utility function u and the relationship between the Independence Axiom and the idea that the utilities of different commodities are independent. Elsewhere (Moscati 2016a), I have reconstructed the discussions on the first three topics; here I focus on the fourth issue. With respect to that, the most important exchange is between Friedman and Baumol, in which Friedman advanced an interpretation of the nature of the von Neumann–Morgenstern function u that later became standard in economics.

After their epistolary exchange of 1950–1951, the American supporters of EUT went public. In a prominent conference in Paris in May 1952, Friedman, Savage, Marschak, and also Samuelson, who in August 1950 had accepted EUT, advocated the theory and defended it against the attacks of Maurice Allais and other critics. Allais argued that the relationship between the utility of riskless monetary outcomes and the utility of risky lotteries is much more complex that the linear one hypothesized by EUT. Among other things, his viewpoint allowed Allais to conjecture that different methods of measuring the utility of money, which according to EUT should produce the same outcome, in fact generate different measures. As we will see in chapter 16, a number of experiments performed in the 1970s and 1980s proved that Allais's conjecture was correct.

Despite Allais's efforts, the arguments in Paris did not modify the positions of Friedman, Savage, Marschak, Samuelson, and the other supporters of EUT, in part because Allais's own theory of decision under risk appeared to them too vague and awkward to constitute a viable alternative. In October 1952, *Econometrica* published a symposium on EUT featuring articles by, among others, Samuelson and Savage. Some of the symposium articles, and especially Samuelson's paper, contributed to the stabilization of EUT as the dominant economic model of choice under risk.

11.1. MARSCHAK AND SAMUELSON ON INDEPENDENCE AND ADDITIVITY

As mentioned in chapter 10, section 10.3.3, in his Japanese paper, Samuelson (1950b, 170 n. 7) conjectured that von Neumann and Morgenstern had included a hidden "independence assumption" within their axioms, but in April 1950, he was still unable to identify it. On May 5, 1950, he completed a second paper on EUT, which was later published as a memorandum of the RAND Corporation, with which Samuelson had begun collaborating in 1949.[1] In this paper, Samuelson (1950a, 6–7) made explicit the hidden premise of the von Neumann–Morgenstern axioms, naming it the "Special Independence Assumption": "If two situations A and B are indifferent, so that V(A) = V(B) [the utility V(A) of A is equal to the utility V(B) of B], then . . . V(A,C) = V(B,C) [the utility of the probability mixture of situation A and situation C is equal to the utility of the probability mixture of situation B and situation C] *for all* C's." As already mentioned, Samuelson used the word *independence* because he associated this axiom with the assumption that the utilities of different commodities are independent or additively separable. The adjective *special* was intended in a pejorative sense, emphasizing the dubiously restrictive character of the assumption. Samuelson, in fact, considered it "generally untenable" (6) and the restriction it imposes on the individual's ordinal preferences between lotteries "unreasonable" (10).

On May 5, 1950, Samuelson was still unaware that Marschak, in his article in the April 1950 issue of *Econometrica*, had axiomatized EUT using Postulate IV_2, which is analogous

1. The RAND Corporation is a private think tank, originally funded by the US Army Air Force in 1946 through the Douglas Aircraft Company, with the goal of bringing together civil scientists from different backgrounds to work on interdisciplinary research projects with possible military applications. RAND became an independent nonprofit corporation in 1948. On the importance of RAND for post-WWII economics, see Leonard 2010; Erikson et al. 2013.

to his Independence Assumption. In an oral communication that evidently occurred in early May, however, Marschak called Samuelson's attention to Postulate IV_2, and in a further paper, Samuelson (1950c, 2) acknowledged the similarity between the two axioms. Samuelson's disbelief in the Independence Assumption extended to Postulate IV_2.

On May 11, 1950, Marschak wrote a letter to Samuelson in which he defended Postulate IV_2 or, equivalently, the Independence Axiom, on various grounds (Samuelson papers, box 66). His main argument was normative: he claimed that the assumptions underlying EUT, including Postulate IV_2, define rational behavior in conditions of risk. Samuelson, however, was not convinced by Marschak's normative argument (see more details in Moscati 2016a).

In his defense of Postulate IV_2, Marschak also distinguished it from the discredited hypothesis that the utilities of different commodities are additively separable. He stressed that while the latter has to do with the joint consumption of different goods, for example, beer *and* pretzels, Postulate IV_2 relates to the consumption of different goods in mutually exclusive situations where a choice is being made between outcomes, that is, *either* beer *or* pretzels. Thus, a man who is indifferent between beer and tea might well prefer the commodity bundle beer-and-pretzels to the commodity bundle tea-and-pretzels and at the same time be indifferent between a lottery consisting of "either beer or pretzels" and another lottery consisting of "either tea or pretzels." Marschak wrote: "I should not expect . . . [the] man to tell me that the mere co-presence in the same lottery bag of tickets inscribed 'pretzels' with tickets inscribed 'tea' will contaminate (or enhance) the enjoyment of either the liquid or the solid that will be the subject's lot."

In his rejoinder, dated May 15, 1950 (Samuelson papers, box 66), Samuelson accepted that different lottery prizes are mutually exclusive in a probability sense. But he then returned to his earlier concern about the additive separability of utilities and stated that he could not understand how this "*ex ante* preference pattern" toward lotteries could generate, as is the case in EUT, a utility indicator that "impute[s] an *independent* numerical score to each possible prize." The expected utility of a "beer or pretzels" lottery is in fact expressed by $u(\text{beer}) \times p + u(\text{pretzels}) \times (1 - p)$. But the expressions u(beer) and u(pretzels) seem to suggest that the utilities of beer and pretzels are independent of each other. For Samuelson, this was "a pun on words." A clarification on this issue would arise out of Friedman's correspondence with Baumol, which, together with others, was forwarded to Samuelson (see section 11.3).

11.2. SAMUELSON AND SAVAGE ON THE INDEPENDENCE AXIOM

On May 19, 1950, Savage sent a long letter to Samuelson containing extensive comments on the latter's Japanese paper; the letter was carbon-copied to Friedman (Samuelson papers, box 67). This letter marked the beginning of an intense exchange between Savage and Samuelson that focused on the normative plausibility of the Independence Axiom, or Postulate IV_2. Eventually, Savage succeeded where Marschak had failed: he convinced Samuelson that the Independence Axiom should be included among the assumptions defining rational behavior in conditions of risk. This happened when, in a letter dated August

12, 1950 (Samuelson papers, box 67), Savage presented the Independence Axiom as a special case of what, in *The Foundations of Statistics* ([1954] 1972, 21–24), he later called the Sure-Thing Principle.

11.2.1. The Sure-Thing Principle

In his letter, Savage considered three incomes A, B, C; two mutually exclusive events E and not-E; and two contracts I and II between which an individual named Jimmie (like himself) has to choose. In contract I, Jimmie's income is A in the event E and C in the event not-E. In contract II, Jimmie's income is B in the event E and C in the event not-E.[2] Savage argued that if he (as Jimmie) prefers income B to income A, he would certainly prefer contract II to contract I. The reason is that by choosing contract II, "I guarantee that whichever of the [two] events occurs I will have nothing to reproach myself for." If one accepts the argument as compelling, Savage continued, one should also accept the Independence Axiom, because "if E and not-E are disjoint random events of probabilities p and (1 – p)," the Independence Axiom "is a special case" (see more details in Moscati 2016a).

11.2.2. The Ordinal Nature of the EUT Axioms

In their correspondence of May–August 1950, Samuelson and Savage did not in general discuss issues concerning utility measurement. An exception was Savage's vindication of the ordinal character of the EUT axioms. As mentioned in chapter 10, section 10.3.3, in his Japanese paper, Samuelson had argued that the axioms concerning preferences between lotteries should be purely ordinal in nature. In his letter of May 19, 1950, Savage wrote that he shared Samuelson's ordinalist approach and agreed that the axioms underlying a theory of decision under risk should be ordinal in nature. But he then argued that the von Neumann–Morgenstern axioms have precisely this nature, as they concern only preference or indifference relations between lotteries: "The axioms of von Neumann–Morgenstern are as they stand, purely ordinal. Their empirical content can indeed be expressed in terms of ordinal utility and has indeed been expressed in no other terms."

In his reply of May 31, 1950, carbon-copied to Friedman and Marschak (Savage papers, box 29), Samuelson objected not to the ordinal nature of the axioms but to their plausibility and more specifically to the plausibility of the Independence Axiom.[3]

2. I have slightly modified the symbols Savage used to make his notation more consistent with that used in the rest of this book.

3. As Montesano (1982; 1985) has aptly stressed, given the ordinal character of the EUT axioms, the cardinal character of the von Neumann–Morgenstern utility function u depends on the circumstance that the theory is expressed in terms of the arithmetic mean of u. If the theory were expressed using some other mean, such as the geometric or the harmonic mean, a monotonic but not necessarily linear transformation of u (such as $v = e^u$) should be used. More concretely, if we use the arithmetic mean, the EUT axioms state that there exists a function u such that lottery L_1 is

11.3. FRIEDMAN'S NEW INTERPRETATION OF THE RELATIONS BETWEEN u AND U

For the purposes of our narrative, the most important exchange in all this correspondence is probably that between Friedman and Baumol. As we saw in chapter 10, section 10.1.3, in his 1948 article with Savage, Friedman had interpreted the utility function u featured in EUT in a Bernoullian way, that is, as if the function u were a linear transformation of the riskless utility function U of traditional utility theory. The criticisms contained in Baumol's paper prompted Friedman to change his interpretation of the nature of u and, eventually, to advance an instrumentalist conception of measurement.

11.3.1. Measurability of Utility as a Red Herring

As mentioned at the beginning of this chapter, Friedman was asked by the editor of the *Journal of Political Economy* to serve as a referee for Baumol's paper. In a letter to Baumol dated June 3, 1950, and carbon-copied to Savage and Samuelson, Friedman disclosed his role as reviewer and briefly commented on the paper (Baumol papers, box W1). Among other things, in his letter, Friedman argued that the question of the measurability of utility is a "red herring." For Friedman, EUT enables the making of predictions about some parts of choice behavior from the observation of other parts of choice behavior, and these predictions are made in terms of the expected value of "some function with assigned property and belonging to some class," namely the class of functions that are linear transformations of each other. For Friedman, calling the functions belonging to this class "measurable" is only a handy way of characterizing the class they belong to and has no further realistic meaning: " 'Measurability' is used to refer to the narrowness of the class. This is only a convenient way of speaking; it is a collection of rules for prediction; and denotes nothing about 'reality' in any other sense."

11.3.2. Two Functions

In his report on Baumol's paper, written from June to August 1950 and forwarded to Savage and Samuelson, Friedman elaborated on these considerations (Baumol papers, box W1). The function u, whose expected value is used to make predictions about future choice behavior, is traditionally called a utility function, but Friedman now argued that this name is misleading because it suggests that u coincides with the traditional utility function U expressing

preferred to lottery L_2 if and only if $\sum_{L_1} u(x_i)p_i > \sum_{L_2} u(x_j)p_j$. If we use the geometric mean, the same result can be stated by saying that the EUT axioms imply the existence of a function v such that lottery L_1 is preferred to lottery L_2 if and only $\prod_{L_1}[v(x_i)]^{p_i} > \prod_{L_2}[v(x_i)]^{p_j}$, whereby $u = e^u$. However, since all economists considered in our narrative refer to EUT expressed in terms of the arithmetic mean of u, I focus here on the linear increasing transformations of this function.

preferences between riskless alternatives. In order to avoid confusion, Friedman suggested calling the function u "the choice-generating function" and the function U "the utility function of certain incomes." The two functions u and U order alternatives in the same way, and therefore one is a monotonic transformation of the other. However, U need not belong to the class of linear transformations of u, and thus the expected value of U cannot be used to make predictions about choice behavior under risk.

This distinction between u and U allowed Friedman to argue that Baumol's criticism of the Friedman–Savage analysis of choices involving risk was "a non sequitur." As we saw, Baumol had argued that the results obtained by Friedman and Savage in their 1948 article are meaningless because they are based on the curvature of the utility function of money, while this curvature is not invariant to monotonic transformations of the function. Based on the distinction between the choice-generating function u and the utility function U of certain money, Friedman could now claim that his and Savage's analysis of choices involving risk was based on the curvature of u, not the curvature of U. And since u is unique only up to linear increasing transformation, its curvature has a well-defined meaning. For Friedman, therefore, Baumol's criticism relied on "a failure to distinguish sharply between two different mathematical functions," namely u and U. Accordingly, for Friedman, the results obtained in his paper with Savage are valid but should be reframed to make clear that they are based on the curvature of the choice-generating function u rather than the curvature of U: "Our results by no means lose all meaning; they simply have to be reworded to refer to the properties of the choice-generating function rather than the utility function of certain incomes." This is just what Friedman and Savage would do in an article published in the *Journal of Political Economy* in 1952. Baumol's correspondence of late 1950 and 1951 (see section 11.5) shows that he accepted Friedman's argument.

11.4. FRIEDMAN AND SAMUELSON ON ADDITIVITY AND THE DESCRIPTIVE POWER OF EUT

As mentioned in section 11.3.2, Friedman forwarded to Samuelson both his letter to Baumol and his report on Baumol's paper. Apparently, Friedman's distinction between the functions u and U helped Samuelson to overcome his initial belief that EUT entails a return to additively separable utility.

In his letter to Marschak of May 15, 1950 (see section 11.1), Samuelson had noticed that expressions such as u(beer) and u(pretzels) in the expected utility formula suggest that the riskless utilities of beer and pretzels are independent of each other. In the light of Friedman's distinction between the functions u and U, this inference appears unwarranted. First, since u and U are different functions, the form of the function u featured in the expected utility formula carries no implications for the complementarity or substitutability of beer and pretzels in riskless situations. Second, even if the utilities of beer and pretzels were independent and could be represented by an additively separable utility function U, this function would still differ from the von Neumann–Morgenstern, or choice-generating, function u, in the specific sense that u need not be a positive linear transformation of U. As we will see in section 11.7, Samuelson stressed this point in both papers on EUT that he completed in 1952 ([1952] 1966; 1952).

One last element of the Friedman–Samuelson correspondence is worth mentioning. On August 25, 1950, after Savage had convinced him of the compelling normative character of the Independence Axiom and thus the normative value of EUT, Samuelson admitted his capitulation to Friedman:

> Dear Milton: . . . [L]et me make an important surrender. Savage's patient letters and the induced cogitation have convinced me that he is right on the only important difference between us. . . . I called the [Independence] assumption gratuitous, arbitrary, etc. . . . etc. (You know how I can lay it on when I get going.) But now I must eat my words. As you know I hate to change my mind, but I hate worse to hold wrong views, and so I have no choice. (Samuelson papers, box 31)

Friedman replied a couple of weeks later. In a letter dated September 13, 1950, he welcomed Samuelson's conclusions about the plausibility of the Independence Axiom and thus of EUT but confessed that for him, the axioms underlying EUT and their normative appeal were less important than other qualities of the theory: "Dear Paul: . . . I must confess to never having myself really been deeply concerned with the axiomatic basis of the Ber.–Mar. [Bernoulli–Marshall] hypothesis" (Samuelson papers, box 31). For Friedman, it was the simplicity and empirical content of EUT that were really important. Friedman, in fact, judged EUT "the simplest and most direct way to extend the usual utility analysis to choices involving risk." Furthermore, EUT's empirical implications were far from obvious but not inconsistent with much common experience: "It has never seemed to me obviously true or necessary that individuals' reactions to complicated gambles should be completely predictable from their reactions to two-side ones—which has always seemed to me the fundamental empirical content of the B–M [Bernoulli–Marshall] hypothesis—and it still does not." Notably, Friedman explicitly admitted that certain phenomena related to gambling cannot really be explained by EUT and predicted that "to handle some experience," the theory would "need complication."

11.5. BAUMOL ENDORSES EUT

In the fall of 1950, Baumol sent his paper to Marschak. Stimulated by it, Marschak wrote a seven-page "Note on 'Measurable Utility'" which he forwarded to Baumol on December 5, 1950 (Baumol papers, box W1). In this note, Marschak basically expanded on the "manageability" argument he had made in his *Econometrica* article (see chapter 10, section 10.2.4). He claimed that the cardinal measurability of utility has a special role in utility theory because it allows calculation of the mathematical average of utilities which, in turn, *if* the axioms underlying EUT hold, allows predication of choices in conditions of risk.

In his reply of December 14, 1950, Baumol focused on the *if* clause of Marschak's argument, which, unlike Samuelson, he still could not accept (Baumol papers, box W1). In effect, Baumol believed that Samuelson had surrendered to EUT too easily. On January 9, 1951, he wrote to his former ally: "Dear Paul: I still suspect that you may have retreated a bit too much" (Baumol papers, box W1).

From January to July 1951, Baumol continued to exchange letters with Marschak and Samuelson in which he attempted to formulate decision rules that appeared fully reasonable but violated EUT. Samuelson and Marschak replied, either by arguing that Baumol's decision rules were in fact consistent with EUT or by claiming that those decision rules were less reasonable than they appeared.[4] Baumol, too, capitulated, writing to Marschak on July 16, 1951: "Dear Jack: . . . Since I last wrote to you in March I have had protracted discussions . . . with many people, in particular Paul Samuelson . . ., and have in many respects modified my opinions on the subject. . . . I am now willing to accept your axioms as attributes of rationality as we ordinarily use the term" (Baumol papers, box W1).

Thus, like Samuelson, Baumol accepted EUT on normative grounds. Concerning the measurability of utility, Baumol agreed with Marschak that the uniqueness of the utility function u up to linear increasing transformations is convenient, because it allows calculation of the mathematical average of utilities and thus prediction of the choice of a rational decision maker in conditions of risk. However, in accord with Friedman, Baumol stressed that the von Neumann–Morgenstern utility function u should not be identified with the riskless utility function U of early utility analysis: "While the utility index may be most convenient to have I do not at all believe that it is the classical utility function. Thus . . . there can be no meaning attached to classical propositions like diminishing marginal utility of income" (Baumol papers, box W1).

11.6. TAKING STOCK

The circulation of Samuelson's and Baumol's papers in late April and early May 1950 set in motion an intense correspondence among Samuelson, Savage, Marschak, Friedman, and Baumol during which all the major controversial aspects of EUT were addressed. Regarding measurability issues, from May 1950 to July 1951, the following four main points emerged from the discussion: (1) the Independence Axiom should not be confused with the hypothesis that utilities are additively separable; (2) the axioms underlying EUT concern preference and indifference rankings between lotteries and are therefore ordinal in nature; (3) although the utility function u featured in the EUT formula and the traditional utility function U order alternatives in the same way, they need not be linear transformations of each other; (4) accordingly, the curvature of u should not be interpreted in terms of the increasing or diminishing marginal utility of money or some other commodity. As we will see in chapter 12, from 1952 to 1954, these four ideas, originally presented in letters among a restricted number of economists, went public in the form of articles and books and quickly became mainstream among economists.

Clarification of the measurability issues associated with EUT certainly eliminated some of the objections that opponents such as Samuelson and Baumol had initially raised. However, it did not offer Samuelson and Baumol any positive reason to endorse EUT. Possibly, confidence in the descriptive power of the theory could have helped, but neither Samuelson

4. See, e.g., Samuelson to Baumol, February 7, 1951; Marschak to Baumol, February 21, 1951 (Baumol papers, box W1).

nor Baumol, and not even Marschak, shared Friedman's confidence. Initially, Savage shared Friedman's views, but over the course of his correspondence with Samuelson, his trust in the descriptive validity of EUT largely evaporated (see more on this in Moscati 2016a). Therefore, from 1950 to 1951, first Marschak and Savage and eventually also Samuelson and Baumol came to accept EUT because they came to see the axioms underlying the theory as requisites for rational behavior in conditions of risk and thus as normatively compelling.

After their epistolary exchanges of 1950–1951, the American advocates of EUT, new and old, made public their endorsement of the theory. The first main occasion on which this occurred was the Paris conference of May 1952 on the theory of decisions under uncertainty. Before turning to that conference, however, a brief overview of the main publications on EUT that appeared in 1951 is in order.

In 1951, four major articles on EUT were published. The first was Baumol's "The Neumann–Morgenstern Utility Index—An Ordinalist View," which appeared in the February 1951 issue of the *Journal of Political Economy*. The next appeared in the proceedings volume of a conference held at the University of California, Berkeley, in August 1950, which included Marschak's "Why 'Should' Statisticians and Businessmen Maximize 'Moral Expectation'?" ([1951] 1974). Marschak here emphasized the normative character of EUT. Then, in the October 1951 issue of *Econometrica*, Arrow (1951a) published the comprehensive review article on alternative approaches to the theory of decision-making under risk mentioned at the beginning of chapter 10.

Finally, in the October 1951 issue of the *Journal of Political Economy*, Frederick Mosteller and Philip Nogee published the findings of their experimental study on EUT. Mosteller and Nogee's experiment is discussed in detail here in chapter 13; for now, suffice it to say that the experiment grew directly out of Mosteller's discussions with Friedman and Savage and had two intertwined goals, which can be labeled the *measurement goal* and the *theory-testing goal*. The measurement goal was to verify whether EUT made it possible to elicit the von Neumann–Morgenstern utility function u. The theory-testing goal consisted of using the utility measures obtained through EUT to test the descriptive validity of the theory. Mosteller and Nogee argued that EUT performed relatively well on both scores, and in summarizing their findings, they claimed that "it is feasible to measure utility experimentally" (1951, 403), adding that "the notion that people behave in such a way as to maximize their expected utility is not unreasonable" (399). In the early 1950s, advocates of EUT such as Friedman and Savage (1952) and Alchian (1953) referred to Mosteller and Nogee's experiment as providing appreciable although far from definitive empirical support for the theory.

Samuelson and Savage did not publish on EUT in 1951. However, in the summer of that year, Savage completed a first draft of *The Foundations of Statistics* ([1954] 1972), and on July 2, 1951, he sent it to Samuelson (Savage papers, box 29). In the letter accompanying the manuscript, Savage stressed the importance of his discussions with Samuelson the previous summer: "Dear Samuelson: Attached is some dittoed material which I hope soon to complete and redraft as a book.... This work owes much to the written and oral discussions you and I had last summer." In September 1951, Savage moved to Paris, where he spent the academic year 1951–1952 working on *The Foundations of Statistics* on a fellowship from the John Simon Guggenheim Memorial Foundation. Thus, when the Paris conference took place, he was already in the vicinity.

11.7. UTILITY MEASUREMENT AT THE PARIS CONFERENCE

11.7.1. The Paris Conference: Overview

The Paris conference was held from May 12 to 17, 1952. It was organized by Allais (1911–2010), an economist with a background in engineering who had published an important treatise on general equilibrium and economic efficiency (Allais 1943), and mathematician Georges Darmois.[5] The participants from the United States were Arrow, Friedman, Marschak, Samuelson (who in 1952 was also the president of the Econometric Society), and Savage.[6] Besides Allais and Darmois, the most prominent French hosts were Pierre Massé and Georges Morlat, two other economists with a background in engineering; mathematicians Georges Guilbaud and Jean Ville; and economist Edmond Malinvaud, a student of Allais who, in the academic year 1950–1951, had visited the Cowles Commission in Chicago.[7] Ragnar Frisch (on whom see chapter 7, sections 7.1 and 7.2), Italian probability theorist Bruno de Finetti, English economist George Shackle, and Swedish statistician Herman Wold were also in attendance. The proceedings of the conference were published in 1953 in French (CNRS 1953) and are particularly interesting because they contain full reports of the discussions following the presentations.[8]

The central theme of the conference debates was the validity of EUT. Marschak, Friedman, Savage, Samuelson, Arrow, and also de Finetti voiced support and fired off one or another of the arguments that had emerged out of previous discussions, such as the normative force of the axioms implying the maximization of expected utility, the theory's capacity to describe and explain important economic phenomena such as gambling and insurance behavior, or the simplicity of the expected utility hypothesis. Primarily Allais, but also Massé and Morlat, fired back, arguing that they did not see any normatively compelling character in the Independence Axiom, contesting the capacity of EUT to explain the behavior of actual people, and contending that the key virtue of a scientific theory is truthfulness, not simplicity.

5. See more on Allais and the French tradition of economist-engineers in Munier 1991; Jallais and Pradier 2005.

6. Savage ([1952] 1953) presented an axiomatization of the subjective version of EUT that he would fully develop in his *Foundations of Statistics* ([1954] 1972). Arrow ([1952] 1953) showed how certain results in the theory of the optimal allocation of resources under conditions of certainty can be extended to conditions of uncertainty using EUT. Based on EUT, Friedman ([1952] 1953) explored the influence of different risk attitudes over the distribution of wealth in a society. Marschak ([1952] 1953) put forward a model for team decisions under uncertainty based on EUT. The papers by Friedman and Arrow were later published in English as Friedman 1953a and Arrow 1964, respectively. Marschak's contribution was essentially identical to Marschak and Waterman 1952. On Samuelson's paper at the Paris conference, see section 11.7.3.

7. Malinvaud (1923–2015) studied at the École Polytechnique and the Institut National de la Statistique et des Études Économiques (INSEE) in Paris. After visiting the Cowles Commission in 1950–1951, he returned to Paris and entered INSEE, where he spent most of his academic career. See more on Malinvaud in Krueger 2003.

8. See more on the Paris conference in Jallais and Pradier 2005; Mongin 2009; Mongin 2014.

11.7.2. The Allais Paradox

To make their case against EUT, Allais, Massé, and Morlat imagined a number of choice situations between pairs of lotteries for which a reasonable pattern of choice violates EUT (CNRS 1953, 156–157, 178–180, 314–317). The choice situation that Allais presented to Savage during a conference break later became known as the "Allais paradox" (Allais and Hagen 1979). Although the Allais paradox does not involve any utility measurement, a brief illustration is in order, since it will play some role in a later stage of our narrative.[9]

Allais imagined two pairs of lotteries: the first pair consists of lottery L_1, which pays 100 million francs with probability 1, that is, [100 million francs, 1], and lottery L_2 [500 million francs, 0.10; 100 million francs, 0.89; 0 francs, 0.01]. The second pair consists of lottery L_3 [100 million francs, 0.11; 0 francs, 0.89] and lottery L_4 [500 million francs, 0.10; 0 francs, 0.90]. Allais contended that most prudent people would prefer L_1 to L_2 and L_4 to L_3, so that pair of preferences should be considered as normatively valid. Even Savage preferred L_1 to L_2 and L_4 to L_3.[10] However, this pair of preferences violates EUT, because there exists no utility function u capable of rationalizing them by using the expected utility formula.[11]

After this general overview of the Paris conference, we can turn to the two most interesting papers that were presented on issues concerning utility measurement, those by Samuelson and Allais.

11.7.3. Samuelson on u and U, Revised Version

In his contribution, Samuelson (1952 [1966]) set out the main conclusions that had emerged from his 1950–1951 exchange with Friedman, Savage, Marschak, and Baumol. He insisted on the ordinal nature of the Independence Axiom and the other assumptions underlying EUT (128). Moreover, he pointed out that EUT is about mutually exclusive outcomes rather than joint consumption of different goods, so that the Independence Axiom is unrelated to the hypothesis that utilities are additively separable (130). Accordingly, the utility function u obtained from choices between lotteries and the traditional utility function U expressing preferences between riskless outcomes can differ, in the specific sense that one need not be a linear increasing transformation of the other. This is the point originally made by Friedman in his correspondence with Baumol (see section 11.3). Thus, in his conference paper, Samuelson argued: "If, for 100-per-cent-certain situations referring to, say, food and

9. See more on the circumstances in which Allais presented his "paradox" to Savage in Jallais and Pradier 2005. Allais discussed his paradox in a seventy-five-page essay that was appended to the proceedings of the Paris conference and in which he expounded his theory of decision under risk (Allais [1953] 1979, 88–90). The paradox appears also in the abridged version of the essay published in French in *Econometrica* (Allais 1953, 525–528).

10. See more on the normative dimension of the Allais paradox in Guala 2000; Mongin 2014.

11. To see why, note that according to EUT, preferring L_1 to L_2 implies that $u(100) > 0.10u(500) + 0.89u(100) + 0.01u(0)$. On the other hand, preferring L_4 to L_3 implies that $0.10u(500) + 0.90u(0) > 0.11u(100) + 0.89u(0)$. But there exists no utility function u satisfying both inequalities, which implies that this pair of preferences violates EUT. In his *Foundations of Statistics*, Savage ([1954] 1972, 101–103) famously discussed and revised the preferences stated in Paris.

clothing and shelter, there should happen to exist an additive utility indicator of the form $U = F(\text{food}) + G(\text{clothing}) + H(\text{shelter})$, such a utility scale could differ completely from the utility scale defined by probability" (136).

11.7.4. Allais's Cardinal Utility

In the paper he presented, as well as in his interventions in the discussions following other presentations, Allais ([1952] 1953) energetically advocated a cardinal conception of utility that was utterly at odds with the ordinal attitude that had dominated utility analysis in the first half of the twentieth century. For Allais, a cardinal utility function U over riskless alternatives can be defined directly, either by considering utility differences, as suggested in the discussions of the 1930s (see chapter 6), or by using the just-perceivable increments of sensation, as proposed by Francis Ysidro Edgeworth in the 1880s (see chapter 3, section 3.2.1). Allais believed that the utility function U can be determined in a direct way by introspective observation, which he deemed a perfectly legitimate source of evidence.

Although he was critical of Bernoulli, for Allais, the cardinal utility function U over riskless alternatives was also the primitive concept in the analysis of decision-making under risk. But while Bernoulli believed that the mathematical expectation of U would suffice to explain choices in conditions of risk, Allais argued that a much more complex function of U was needed. For him, this function of U should possess two main features. First, rather than being based on the objective probabilities p of the different events, it should be based on the subjective distortions d(p) of these objective probabilities. Allais held in fact that individuals tend to distort objective probabilities. Moreover, the distortion function d(p) is not uniform: "The subjective distortion of objective probabilities appears to depend, in general, on whether the probability of a gain or the probability of a loss is at issue, and on the amount of the gain and the loss" (130). Second, not only the mathematical expectation but also the variance and possibly other elements of the subjective-probability distribution of U should be taken into account.

In the animated discussion that followed Allais's presentation (CNRS 1953, 150–164), Savage objected that Allais's very general approach to risk did not provide any manageable formula to replace the handy expected utility formula (154). In similar vein, Marschak argued that "the principle of the maximization of the moral expectation [i.e., EUT] is too natural and simple to be abandoned at the current stage of research, also because the mathematics implied by other aspects of the problems (stocks, games, organizations) are sufficiently difficult" (152). Allais replied that employing "a simple, but apparently inexact formula" like that of EUT is not scientific and that proper science requires using "a more general formula, which however is consistent with the facts" (154).

11.7.5. Allais's Conjecture

As just mentioned, the primitive concept in Allais's analysis of decision-making under risk is the utility function U over riskless alternatives. But what is the relationship between Allais's function

U and the von Neumann–Morgenstern utility function u, whose existence is warranted by the EUT axioms? For Allais, when u exists, it is an increasing transformation of U. Since the axioms of EUT are often violated, however, the von Neumann–Morgenstern function u often does not exist. In the Allais paradox, for instance, the violation of EUT manifests itself in the fact that there exists no utility function u capable of rationalizing the preference pattern L_1 preferred to L_2 and L_4 preferred L_3 via the expected utility formula.

In a remark made at the end of the Paris conference, Allais went further and advanced a conjecture that a number of experiments performed in the 1970s and 1980s eventually proved correct (see chapter 16). Allais (CNRS 1953, 247) argued that even if the utility function u exists, it may be not unique. By this, he meant that different yet according to EUT equivalent methods of measuring the utility function u could in fact generate different measures of u: "The two methods allow building the index B(x) [i.e., u(x)]. If the Bernoulli theory [EUT] is valid, for a rational individual it should produce the same function B(x) in the two cases. In fact, I think it does not need to be so, at least in general" (CNRS 1953, 247). As discussed in chapter 13, the two methods Allais referred to in this passage would come to be called the certainty equivalence method and the probability equivalence method. For Allais, the potential inconsistency between different methods of measuring u ultimately depends on the fact that the actual relationship between the utility of riskless money and preferences between risky lotteries is not the simple, linear relationship hypothesized by EUT but much more complex. Therefore, different measurement methods may interact in different ways with the nonlinear relationship between the utility of money and preferences between risky lotteries and thus produce different utility measures.

However, Allais's point does not appear to have had any impact on either the theoretical or the experimental research on utility measurement conducted from the 1950s to the 1970s. This is probably due to the cursory character of Allais's remark and the fact that it was translated into English only in 1979 (Allais and Hagen 1979, 612–613).

11.8. END OF THE SECOND PHASE OF THE DEBATE ON EUT

The Paris discussions of May 1952 did not modify the positions of Friedman, Savage, Marschak, Samuelson, and the other supporters of EUT. In October 1952, *Econometrica* published a symposium on EUT. In this symposium, Malinvaud (1952) clarified how the Independence Axiom is hidden in von Neumann and Morgenstern's axiomatization of EUT. Specifically, he showed that the Independence Axiom is implied by the very fact that von Neumann and Morgenstern's assumptions concern preferences between indifference classes of lotteries rather than preferences between single lotteries.[12] Savage explained why an argument against the Independence Axiom put forward by Wold was a "non sequitur" (Wold, Shackle, and Savage 1952). Samuelson's article, "Probability, Utility, and the Independence Axiom" (1952) was basically a restatement of the paper he had presented a few months earlier at the Paris conference.

12. Malinvaud had in fact made his discovery when visiting the Cowles Commission in 1950–1951 and had already shared it with Marschak; see Marschak (1951, 8).

Concerning measurability issues, Samuelson repeated that the Independence Axiom and the other assumptions underlying EUT have an ordinal nature, that the expected utility hypothesis is about mutually exclusive outcomes rather than joint consumption of different goods, and that "independence in probability situations puts no restriction whatsoever upon the dependence or independence that holds in the nonstochastic situation" (1952, 673).

The Paris conference and the *Econometrica* symposium of 1952 marked the emergence of EUT as the mainstream model for risky choices in economics. The years 1947 to 1952 had seen the clarification, first through private correspondence and then in conferences and journal articles, of the axiomatic foundations of the theory, the ordinal nature of its assumptions, and the relationships between EUT and the traditional theory of riskless utility. After an initial period characterized by various changes of mind about the validity of EUT, the parties in favor and against stabilized, and the supporters turned out to be significantly both more numerous and more academically prominent than the opponents.

However, its advocates came to accept EUT for different reasons. A first group of economists accepted the theory on normative grounds. Samuelson accepted EUT only when, through the lens of Savage's Sure-Thing Principle, he came to view the Independence Axiom as a requisite for rational behavior in conditions of risk and thus as normatively compelling. Yet he always remained skeptical about the descriptive power of EUT. Baumol also accepted EUT only after he came to see the axioms underlying it as attributes of rationality. Savage initially advocated EUT by appealing to its simplicity, empirical validity, and normative plausibility, but his controversy with Samuelson induced him to focus on the normative defense of the theory, which he perfected by formulating the Sure-Thing Principle.

Others, such as Marschak, held a fluctuating position. Until 1950, Marschak argued that both the descriptive and the normative dimensions of EUT were important, but in subsequent publications, as well as in correspondence and at conferences in 1950 and 1951, he emphasized the normative validity of EUT as a theory of rational behavior under risk. However, as we will see in chapter 14, beginning in 1952, Marschak became increasingly attentive to deviations of actual from rational behavior, and in the early 1960s, he ran some experiments to test the empirical validity of EUT.

Friedman accepted EUT because he considered it a simple theory whose implications are not only far from obvious but also consistent with much common experience. As we will see in the next chapters, other economists, such as Robert Strotz and Armen Alchian, as well as the scholars who tested EUT experimentally in the 1950s, accepted EUT because they believed it was descriptively valid.

After 1952 and at least until the early 1960s, the main antagonist of EUT remained Allais, who rejected EUT on both the normative and descriptive levels. In an article published in French in *Econometrica*, Allais (1953) elaborated and refined the theory of decision-making under uncertainty that he had presented at the Paris conference. However, his very general and barely manageable approach did not find many followers. Even Morlat (1956; 1957) came to endorse the subjective version of EUT expounded by Savage in his *Foundations of Statistics*. Like Samuelson before him, Morlat came to see Savage's axioms, and especially the Sure-Thing Principle, as normatively compelling.

After October 1952, some further articles addressing the nature of the utility function featured in EUT were published. They differ from those discussed in this chapter and chapter 10, however, because they shifted the discussion from the question "What does the utility function u featured in EUT measure?" to the question "What does it mean, in general, to measure utility?" I consider these articles as belonging to the third and final phase of the debate on EUT, to which I now turn.

CHAPTER 12

Conventions, Operations, Predictions

Redefining Utility Measurement, 1952–1955

In chapter 6, we saw how in the debates of the 1930s that led to the definition of cardinal utility, economists such as Oskar Lange, Roy Allen, and Franz Alt abandoned the idea that utility is measurable only when a unit of utility is available and utility ratios can be assessed. For these economists, cardinal utility, that is, utility determinable on the interval scale, is also measurable. However, they did not discuss whether their idea that cardinal utility is measurable required a more general reconceptualization of the notion of measurement.

John von Neumann and Oskar Morgenstern also considered cardinal utility—or, as they called it, "numerical utility"—as measurable utility (see chapter 9, section 9.3.4). Moreover, and unlike Lange, Allen, and Alt, they explicitly discussed what it means, in general, to measure a thing. One important feature of their measurement theory was the association of measurability with the possibility of adding the objects to be measured. Nevertheless, in the late 1940s and early 1950s, von Neumann and Morgenstern's measurement theory had little impact on utility theorists, arguably because the authors of *Theory of Games* had presented it using illustrations taken from physics and mathematics rather than economics.

Chapters 10 and 11 discussed the first two phases of the debate on expected utility theory (EUT). In the first phase, ranging from 1947 to 1950, Milton Friedman, Leonard J. Savage, Jacob Marschak, Paul Samuelson, and William Baumol took largely independent stances on the validity of EUT and the nature of the von Neumann–Morgenstern cardinal utility function u featured in EUT. In the second phase, ranging from 1950 to 1952, these five economists reached a shared view about the nature of the function u and agreed that u should not be confused with the riskless, cardinal utility function U of earlier utility analysis. In the third phase of the debate, which is reconstructed in this chapter and which lasted from 1952 to 1955, Friedman and Savage, as well as three other utility theorists, namely Robert Strotz, Armen Alchian, and Daniel Ellsberg, came to elaborate a novel conception of utility measurement that definitively liberated utility measurement from its remaining bonds with units, ratios, and additivity.

Despite some differences in tone and accent, Friedman, Savage, Strotz, Alchian, and Ellsberg advocated fundamentally the same view of utility measurement. According to them, measuring utility consists of assigning numbers to objects—be they riskless commodity bundles, lotteries, or the uncertain payoffs of lotteries—by following a definite set of operations. While the particular way of assigning utility numbers to objects is largely arbitrary and conventional, the assigned numbers should allow the economist to predict the choice behavior of individuals. The optimistic methodological corollary was that if the predictions are contradicted by observed behavior, then the model and the utility measures obtained through it should be replaced by another model and by other utility measures. Notably, this conception of utility measurement refers to the predictive or descriptive power of utility analysis and is independent of the normative considerations that were so important for the initial success of EUT.

In the final part of this chapter, I argue that this novel view of utility measurement is responsible, together with the acceptance of Friedman's as-if methodology, for the happy cohabitation of cardinal and ordinal utility that began in utility analysis in the mid-1950s and endures to this day.

12.1. FRIEDMAN AND SAVAGE ON MEASUREMENT, CONVENTIONS, AND PREDICTIONS

As we saw in chapters 10 and 11, Baumol (1951) criticized the explanation of risk attitudes in terms of the utility function of money that Friedman and Savage had put forward in their 1948 paper. Although in the correspondence of 1950–1951, many of the differences between them were cleared up, after the publication of Baumol's article, the two Chicago scholars began writing a public reply to their Princeton correspondent. They worked on this reply from 1951 to 1952 but only in a sporadic manner, because Savage was spending that academic year on leave in Paris.

On April 14, 1952, a month before the Paris conference, Friedman sent Baumol an early draft of the paper, asking him for comments (Baumol papers, box W1). Friedman, Savage, and Baumol exchanged some letters on the draft, which was eventually published in the December 1952 issue of the *Journal of Political Economy* under the title "The Expected-Utility Hypothesis and the Measurability of Utility." In the published paper, Friedman and Savage thanked not only Baumol but also Marschak for helpful comments.

12.1.1. Savage Goes Normative, Friedman Goes Descriptive

The drafts of the article (Friedman papers, box 43), as well as its final version, testify to different reasons Savage and Friedman supported EUT after the discussions of 1950. Some parts of the article, attributable mainly to Savage, offer normative arguments in support of the theory. In particular, the article contains the first published version of Savage's axiomatization of EUT based on the Sure-Thing Principle, which, as we have seen in chapter 11, sections 11.2.1 and 11.4, played a crucial role in persuading Samuelson to accept

EUT (Friedman and Savage 1952, 467–469).[1] Other parts of the article, ascribable mainly to Friedman, defend the descriptive validity of EUT. In particular, the article elaborates on the as-if argument in support of EUT already presented in the 1948 paper: EUT hypothesizes that individuals behave *as if* they maximized expected utility, and based on this hypothesis, EUT allows us to predict their choice behavior in situations involving risk. What should count for the scientific validity of the theory is not whether individuals really maximize expected utility but whether EUT's predictions are not contradicted by their choice behavior (465–467).[2]

12.1.2. Baumol's Non Sequitur

Friedman and Savage acknowledged that the terminology they had used in their 1948 article was insufficiently clear and had promoted confusion between the riskless utility function U of traditional utility theory and the von Neumann–Morgenstern utility function u. They were now cautious in even calling the function u a utility function, and argued that perhaps "a new name for this measure rather than the name 'utility'" should have been used (464). In any case, to avoid further terminological confusion, Friedman and Savage refrained from indicating u with the name Friedman had suggested in his 1950 report on Baumol's paper, namely the "choice-generating function" (see chapter 11, section 11.3.2). For the rest, Friedman and Savage's 1952 reply to Baumol is chiefly an elaboration of the argument already made by Friedman in his 1950 report on Baumol's paper: because the Friedman–Savage analysis of choices involving risk is based on the curvature of the cardinally measurable function u rather than the ordinal function U, Baumol's criticism that such analysis is not invariant to monotonic transformations of the utility function "is a non sequitur" (471).

12.1.3. Measurement Is Convention

More generally, Friedman and Savage discussed the sense in which EUT "'makes' utility 'measurable'" (465) and thus the sense in which the values of the von Neumann–Morgenstern function u can be interpreted as measures of utility. They began quoting a passage from Baumol's article that argued: "In a sense any scale of measurement is arbitrary. Thus, aside from inconvenience, need anything be wrong with the use of a measure

1. As mentioned in chapter 11, Savage had already presented this axiomatization at the Paris conference of May 1952, but the proceedings of the conference were published only in 1953. See more on the normative parts of Friedman and Savage's 1952 article in Zappia 2016.

2. In the fall of 1952, a few months after completing his second paper with Savage, Friedman also completed the second draft of his essay on "The Methodology of Positive Economics" (as mentioned in chapter 10, the first draft was written in 1948; see Hammond 2009). The second draft bore the title "The Relevance of Economic Analysis to Prediction and Policy" (Friedman papers, box 43) and is quite close to the published version of the essay (Friedman 1953b). On similarities and differences between the Friedman–Savage 1952 article and Friedman's 1953 essay, see Starmer 2009.

of distance which varies as the square . . . of the metric scale?" (Baumol 1951, 65; quoted in Friedman and Savage 1952, 471).

Friedman and Savage agreed with Baumol that any scale of measurement is arbitrary, but, echoing the argument for "manageability" previously made by Marschak (1950; see chapter 10, section 10.2.4), they stressed that convenience is a powerful and scientifically legitimate reason for adopting one scale of measurement rather than another. Convenience also determines the limits of applicability of a measurement scale, in the sense that a measurement scale loses its relevance beyond the range of phenomena for which it is convenient (Friedman and Savage 1952, 474). To illustrate their point, Friedman and Savage considered the possibility of measuring length with a convention different from the usual one, namely taking the square of length as the measure of length. Although in principle possible, this alternative measure would make it inconvenient to perform most of the typical operations we carry out with lengths.[3]

Friedman and Savage then applied to utility the argument from convenience made for length. They argued that if EUT is accepted, taking the numerical values of the von Neumann–Morgenstern function u as measures of utility is as conventional and convenient as taking the numbers ordinarily associated with lengths as measures of length: "If the expected-utility hypothesis is accepted, there is the same justification for calling 'utility' 'measurable,' and u its 'measure,' as there is for calling length . . . 'measurable' " (472).[4]

12.1.4. Measurement for Prediction

In particular, the u measure of utility is convenient if it permits the prediction of behavior. As Friedman and Savage had already suggested in their 1948 article (see chapter 10, section 10.1.4), knowledge of an individual's choices among simple lotteries with only one or two outcomes allows calculating in a convenient way some numerical values of the function u. In turn, these u values can be used to calculate the expected utility of more complex lotteries and thus to predict that the individual will choose the lottery associated with the highest expected value of u. This approach, Friedman and Savage noted in 1952, had already been pursued experimentally by Mosteller and Nogee (1951), with results that justified some "mild optimism" (Friedman and Savage 1952, 466).

Friedman and Savage stressed that the convenience of the u measure of utility relies on the validity of EUT. If this hypothesis is rejected because a better alternative is found, then "convenience may lead to the acceptance of a radically different 'measure' of utility, or whatever new concept may replace it" (472).

3. For example, in order to determine the total length of two rigid rods placed side by side, rather than adding lengths, we should first compute the square roots of the lengths, sum them, and then take the square of the sum. That is, instead of simply calculating x + y, we should compute the much more awkward $(\sqrt{x} + \sqrt{y})^2$.

4. Here, and in some of the following quotations from Friedman and Savage's article, I slightly modify their notation in order to make it consistent with the notation used in the rest of this book.

12.1.5. Two Realms, Ordinal and Cardinal

With respect to the range of applicability of the u measures of utility, Friedman and Savage argued that measure does not extend, at least in its specifically cardinal part, to the analysis of riskless choices. Thus, as already noted in their reply to Baumol, the second derivative of the von Neumann–Morgenstern function u cannot be interpreted as indicating the diminishing or increasing marginal utility of certain money. For the analysis of riskless choices, Friedman and Savage argued, the most convenient convention of utility measurement is still the ordinal convention.

In the first place, Vilfredo Pareto and later writers had shown that in fact, "numerical utility is not necessary for analyzing riskless choices" (Friedman and Savage 1952, 464). Moreover, the various hypotheses implying the cardinal measurability of riskless utility that traditionally had been used in utility theory, such as that the utilities of different good are additively separable or that the marginal utility of money is constant, had been "contradicted by a great deal of evidence" (473).

This does not mean, however, that riskless utility is intrinsically ordinal. Rather, Friedman and Savage explicitly admitted the possibility that future empirical evidence could make it convenient to adopt a cardinal measure of riskless utility: "The failure of these experiments [i.e., those aimed at making riskless utility cardinally measurable] should be interpreted neither as a consequence of the nonmeasurability of utility in some absolute sense nor as showing that utility is not measurable.... It may be that future experiments along the same general lines will be more successful" (473).

Friedman and Savage's 1952 article already contain all the key elements of the novel conception of utility measurement that emerged from the discussions on the nature of the von Neumann–Morgenstern function u. The articles that Strotz, Alchian, and Ellsberg published in 1953 and 1954 enriched and completed the picture. After 1952, Friedman and Savage also independently reiterated and refined the positions on utility measurement expressed in their joint article.

12.2. STROTZ AND MEASUREMENT AS AN INVENTED CONVENTION

12.2.1. Introducing Strotz

Many of the protagonists of our story, including Marschak, Friedman, Savage, and Baumol, gathered at the meeting of the Econometric Society held in Chicago from December 27 to 29, 1952, in conjunction with the meetings of other social science organizations.[5] On the morning of December 28, a session on "Recent Developments in Mathematical Economics and Econometrics" was jointly organized by the Econometric Society and the American

5. In the history of economics, the 1952 Chicago meeting is usually remembered because Kenneth Arrow, Gerard Debreu, and Lionel McKenzie read their papers on the existence of general equilibrium there; see Düppe and Weintraub 2014.

Economic Association, with papers by Cowles Commission director Tjalling Koopmans, the commission's research affiliates Leonid Hurwicz and Strotz, and discussion by Baumol.

Strotz (1922–1994) had begun studying economics at Duke University but had moved to the University of Chicago, from which he graduated with a B.S. in 1942. After serving in the Army during the war, he returned to Chicago for his Ph.D. and there became involved in the research activities of the Cowles Commission. After completing his Ph.D. with a dissertation on welfare economics, Strotz continued his academic career at Northwestern University. From Northwestern, he maintained close connections with the Cowles group in nearby Chicago. In 1954, he replaced Ragnar Frisch as the managing editor of *Econometrica*.[6]

At the Chicago meeting, Strotz presented a paper titled "Cardinal Utility," in which he took stock of debate on the topic since the publication of *Theory of Games* in 1944. The paper was published in May 1953 in *American Economic Review, Papers and Proceedings*.

12.2.2. Measurement Is Invented

Like Friedman and Savage (1952), Strotz (1953, 386) stressed the conventional character of any method of measurement and argued that the choice of a specific method depends on its convenience with respect to certain purposes: "One method of measurement may be more convenient than another for some purposes and less convenient for other purposes. . . . Our choice of a measure is largely a matter of convenience or manageability."

Also for Strotz, in utility analysis, the relevant purpose is the prediction of behavior, and therefore what economists are looking for is an arbitrary measure of utility that allows them to "predict consumer behavior by use of a simple formula" (387). By adopting this perspective, Strotz claimed, the major misunderstanding that had hampered discussions between cardinalists and ordinalists can be cleared aside: "We now realize that [the] philosophical question of whether utility is intrinsically measurable is a spurious one and that measurement has meaning, not as a property of things, but as a predictive procedure. Crucial to an understanding of this entire subject is the realization that measurement is always invented and never discovered" (385).

Yet not all invented measures of utility are acceptable. If an invented measure generates predictions that are contradicted by economic behavior, it should be rejected. As an example of the latter, Strotz examined a measure of utility that makes the marginal utility of income constant with respect to changes in commodity prices. This measure had been implicitly adopted by Alfred Marshall and greatly simplifies the analysis of consumer behavior but must be rejected because it has implications that do not "square with the facts" (388).[7]

By contrast, for Strotz, the specific measure of utility invented by von Neumann and Morgenstern not only is highly manageable but also works sufficiently well in predicting choice behavior among risky alternatives. This, however, does not mean that the von

6. See more on Strotz in Coen 2008.

7. The constancy of the marginal utility of income with respect to price changes implies that the income elasticity of demand for each commodity is unitary, that is, that a given percentage increase in the consumer's income is reflected in an equal percentage increase in the consumer's demand for each commodity. However, consumers typically do not react to income increases in this way.

Neumann–Morgenstern measure is convenient for all classes of problems relevant to utility analysis: "Nothing rules out the usefulness of another measure for another purpose" (397). In particular, for Strotz, the Pareto–Hicks ordinal measure of utility is perfectly adequate for predicting behavior under certainty.

12.2.3. Baumol Goes Public

In his discussion at the December 28 session, Baumol (1953) applauded Strotz's approach to utility measurement and made public that he had abandoned the critical stance on EUT expressed in his 1951 article: "Under the patient tutorship of Professors Friedman, Marschak, and Savage, as well as others, I have seen the light" (415). Notably, Baumol now fully subscribed to the idea that the von Neumann–Morgenstern utility index u is "not the utility [U] the neoclassicist spoke of and whose second partial derivatives he introspected to be negative (diminishing marginal utility)" (415).

12.3. ALCHIAN'S UTILITY NUMBERS AS CHOICE INDICATORS

12.3.1. EUT and Cardinal Utility at RAND

The third contribution adopting an explicitly measurement-theoretic viewpoint on utility measurement was authored by Alchian (1914–2013). He studied economics at Fresno State College, California, and then at Stanford University. At Stanford, he studied under Allen Wallis before the latter moved to New York to direct the Statistical Research Group (see chapters 7, section 7.6.2, and 10, section 10.1.1). In 1946, after military duty, Alchian joined the University of California at Los Angeles. More or less at the same time and on Wallis's recommendation, Alchian became a regular consultant to the RAND Corporation in Santa Monica.[8]

Among Alchian's colleagues at RAND were Norman C. Dalkey, a philosopher by training who in the late 1940s was working on the axiomatization of expected utility theory (Dalkey 1949);[9] Kenneth Arrow, who began his association with RAND in 1948; and Samuelson, who started his collaboration with RAND as a visitor to its Santa Monica headquarters from January to April 1948.[10] Through his interactions with Dalkey, Arrow, and Samuelson, by 1950, Alchian was well informed about the early discussions on EUT and in fact was very puzzled by them. In a letter to Samuelson dated June 27, 1950 (Samuelson papers, box 62), Alchian wrote:

> Dear Paul: . . . For a decade or so economists have been told to abandon cardinality. Some times it appeared that cardinality in a linear sense was impossible and at other times it

8. See more on Alchian's early career in Alchian 1996; Levallois 2009; Leonard 2010.
9. Dalkey (1915–2004) had studied philosophy first at Chicago and then at UCLA. After military service during the war and some teaching at UCLA, in 1948, Dalkey joined RAND and began working on utility analysis, aggregation of preferences, and game theory, before moving to issues related to information processing and prediction. See more on Dalkey in Rescher 2005.
10. On RAND and Arrow's and Samuelson's collaboration with it, see, respectively, chapters 10, footnote 6, and 11, section 11.1.

> seemed that some were saying it was unnecessary. Now, we have Neumann telling us it is not impossible under certain reasonable axioms. Samuelson, however, seems to be saying that his [von Neumann's] axioms are not so reasonable. Dalkey and Arrow, if I understand them, say that the axioms are reasonable.

Given this confusion, Alchian urged Samuelson to draft an expository article "written for economists at the American Economic Review level" and added that otherwise, he was tempted to work on such an expository piece and publish it "for the run-of-the-mill economist."

At the annual meeting of the American Economic Association and other social science societies held in Chicago in December 1950, Alchian served as a discussant of the experimental study in which Mosteller and Nogee had attempted to measure the utility of money on the basis of EUT. As we will see in chapter 13, Alchian in effect not only discussed but also presented the Mosteller–Nogee paper. In the early 1950s, Alchian remained interested in issues concerning utility measurement and ended up writing the expository piece for the "run-of-the-mill economist" he had envisaged in his letter to Samuelson. The article was titled "The Meaning of Utility Measurement" and was published in the March 1953 issue of the *American Economic Review*.

12.3.2. Four Types of Measurement

Alchian (1953, 26) did not cite Stanley Smith Stevens (1946) yet nevertheless opened his article with a definition of measurement analogous to the one given by the Harvard psychologist: "*Measurement* in its broadest sense is the assignment of numbers to entities" (on Stevens, see chapter 8). For Alchian, such an assignment of numbers to entities has two main dimensions. The first concerns the purpose of measurement: why are we interested in assigning numerical values to certain entities or some of their aspects? The second is the uniqueness of measurement: which is the set of numerical values that is consistent with the measurement purpose at hand?

In the specific case of utility, for Alchian, as for Friedman, Savage, and Strotz, the fundamental purpose of measurement is to predict choice: "Can we assign a set of numbers (measures) to the various entities and predict that the entity with the largest assigned number (measure) will be chosen?" (Alchian 1953, 31). If this is the case, we can consider those numbers as good choice indicators and call them, following a long-standing tradition in economics, "utilities": "One christens the assigned numbers 'utilities.' . . . Utility measures are essentially nothing but choice indicators" (29, 44).

The second main dimension of utility measurement concerns the type of transformations that utility numbers can be subjected to without losing their status as good choice predictors. Alchian focused on four types of transformations: (1) the "monotone transformations" $F[u(x)]$, whereby F is a monotonically increasing function; (2) the "linear transformations" $\alpha u(x) + \beta$, with $\alpha > 0$; (3) the "additive transformations" $u(x) + \beta$; and (4) the "multiplicative transformations" $\alpha u(x)$, with $\alpha > 0$. Alchian (27–29) illustrated the different types of transformations using a numerical table and a series of numerical examples.

12.3.3. Back to Ordinal and Cardinal Utility

Alchian stated that the transformations relevant for utility analysis at the time he was writing were the monotonic transformations, associated with the notion of ordinal utility, and the linear transformations, associated with cardinal utility.[11]

For Alchian, the utility numbers assigned to riskless alternatives are unique up to monotone transformations, that is, they are ordinal, because these transformations do not spoil the numbers' predictive power as indicators of choice among riskless alternatives. With respect to choice among risky alternatives, such as lotteries, EUT suggests a simple method to assign numbers to lottery outcomes. If the numbers so assigned allow us to predict correctly the individual's choices among lotteries, then, argued Alchian, "we have successfully measured utility and have done it with [a] convenient computational formula" (39). He invoked the outcomes of the Mosteller–Nogee experiment to argue that EUT in fact yields "a sufficiently large majority of correct predictions" (43). However, if we want to use the simple expected utility formula, then we have to accept that the utility numbers featured in it are unique up to linear transformations.

Alchian summarized his discussion of utility measurement by stressing the instrumental and situation-related nature of measurement:

> A moral of our survey is that to say simply that something is, or is not, measurable is to say nothing. The relevant problems are: (1) can numerical values be associated with entities and then be combined according to some rules so as to predict choices in stipulated types of situations, and (2) what are the transformations that can be made upon the initially assigned set of numerical values without losing their predictive powers (validity)? (47)

In 1954, two important works that addressed issues concerning EUT in conjunction with more general issues concerning the nature of utility measurement were published. The first was Savage's magnum opus, *The Foundations of Statistics*; the second was an article published by a twenty-three-year-old graduate student at Harvard University named Daniel Ellsberg.[12]

11. In chapters 2 and 3, I argued that the early marginalists conceived of utility in a way that is consistent with the uniqueness of utility numbers up to what Alchian called "multiplicative transformations."

12. In 1954, Oxford economist Charles Kennedy also published an article dealing with utility from a measurement-theoretic viewpoint. However, his article is not relevant for our narrative, because Kennedy (1954, 12) focused his discussion on differences between riskless utilities and explicitly ignored the debate on EUT and the utility function featured in it. Also in 1954, Nicholas Georgescu-Roegen (see chapter 7, section 7.6.1) published "Choice, Expectations and Measurability," which, despite its title, is also irrelevant for our narrative. Georgescu-Roegen (1954, 520) referred to the case of lexicographic preferences to argue that the very project of summarizing individual tastes in a single number, be it ordinal or cardinal, is fundamentally mistaken. For a review of the literature on lexicographic preferences, see Fishburn 1974.

12.4. THE NOTION OF UTILITY IN SAVAGE'S *FOUNDATIONS OF STATISTICS*

As we saw in chapter 11, Savage completed a first draft of his manuscript in July 1951 and sent it to Samuelson. Then, at the Paris conference of May 1952, Savage ([1952] 1953) presented an outline of his version of EUT. *The Foundations of Statistics* was published two years after this, in the summer of 1954.[13]

12.4.1. Subjective EUT

In *The Foundations* ([1954] 1972), Savage expounded a version of EUT based on a "subjective" (or "personalistic" or "Bayesian") understanding of probability. As mentioned in passing in chapter 9, one of the controversial issues raised by von Neumann and Morgenstern's EUT concerns the fact that in their theory, the probabilities of uncertain events are objectively given, which is, however, rarely the case in practice. Beginning in the late 1940s, Savage ([1949] 1950) attempted to extend decision analysis to situations where objective probabilities are not available and decision makers only have subjective beliefs about the likelihood of uncertain events. This subjective approach to probability had been already developed by Cambridge mathematician, economist, and philosopher Frank Ramsey ([1926] 1950), although in a paper that attracted little attention before 1950, and by Bruno de Finetti (1937), the Italian probability theorist whom we have met as one of the participants in the Paris conference of 1952.

In Savage's framework, the risky alternatives are no longer lotteries of the form "outcome x with (objective) probability p; outcome y with (objective) probability (1 − p)." Rather, the alternatives are gambles (in Savage's terminology, "acts") of the form "outcome x if event E occurs; outcome y if event E does not occur," in which the decision maker has his personal beliefs about the likelihood of event E. Savage showed that if the decision maker's preferences between gambles satisfy the Sure-Thing Principle and other postulates, then (1) there exists a (subjective) probability function π that expresses the decision maker's beliefs about the likelihood of the different events;[14] (2) there exists a cardinal function u defined over the set of outcomes; (3) gamble G_1 is not preferred to gamble G_2 if and only if the expected value of G_1 is not larger than the expected value of G_2, whereby expected values are calculated using the functions π and u. This substantially means that if Savage's axioms are satisfied, EUT can be applied also to analyze decision-making in situations that involve risk and for which decision makers only have subjective beliefs about the likelihood

13. For more on the origins of Savage's *Foundations*, see Giocoli 2013.

14. Following the axiomatization of probability theory introduced by Russian mathematician Andrey Kolmogorov (1933) and accepted by Savage, a probability function must display three features, independently of whether probability is interpreted in a subjective or objective way: (1) the probability number π assigned to any event must fall in the range [0, 1]: $0 \leq \pi \leq 1$; (2) the probability number π assigned to the certain event Ω is 1: $\pi(\Omega) = 1$; (3) if E and R are mutually exclusive events, the probability of the event obtained by their union is equal to the sum of the probabilities of E and R: $\pi(E \cup R) = \pi(E) + \pi(R)$.

of the uncertain events.[15] By extending EUT to situations where the probabilities of uncertain events are subjective, Savage reinforced the supremacy of EUT in the economic theory of decision-making. However, as we will see in chapter 13, the introduction of subjective probabilities into the picture makes the experimental measurement of utility based on EUT trickier.

12.4.2. Utility Measurement in *The Foundations*

Regarding issues concerning utility measurement, in *The Foundations*, Savage elaborated on the conventionalist approach to measurement that he and Friedman had advocated in their joint 1952 article. As discussed earlier here in section 12.1.2, in that article, Friedman and Savage only very reluctantly called the von Neumann–Morgenstern function u a utility function, pointing out that such a utilitarian label was just a convention. In *The Foundations*, Savage ([1954] 1972, 73) made this conventional dimension even more explicit by *defining* utility as a function whose expected values reflect the preferences between gambles: "A *utility* is a function u associating real numbers with consequences in such a way that . . . $G_1 \preccurlyeq G_2$ [gamble G_1 is not preferred to gamble G_2] if and only if $\sum_{G_1} \pi(x_i)u(x_i) \leq \sum_{G_2} \pi(x_j)u(x_j)$ [the mathematical expectation of u over G_1's outcomes is not greater than the mathematical expectation of u over G_2's outcomes]."[16]

Savage thus returned to an idea that in chapter 9 we attributed to von Neumann, namely that utility is that thing for which the calculus of mathematical expectations is legitimate. Savage also contrasted the utility function u so defined to the traditional utility function U defined for riskless situations, defining the latter as "the now almost obsolete economic notion of utility," which is sometimes still "confused with the one [u] under discussion" (91).

12.5. ELLSBERG'S OPERATIONAL UTILITY MEASUREMENT

The second important work published in 1954 that addressed issues concerning the nature of utility measurement was "Classic and Current Notions of 'Measurable Utility,'" and it was published in the September 1954 issue of the *Economic Journal*. Its author, Ellsberg (born 1931), had completed his B.A. in economics at Harvard in 1952 with a dissertation on "Theories of Rational Choice under Uncertainty," written under the supervision of John Chipman, a Harvard assistant professor and a research associate at the Cowles Commission. In the academic year 1952–1953, Ellsberg studied for a year at Cambridge University in England, on a Woodrow Wilson Fellowship.

15. For an introductory presentation of Savage's theory, see Kreps 1988; Gilboa 2009. The Sure-Thing Principle substantially corresponds to Postulate 2 of Savage's axiomatic system ([1954] 1972, 21–26).
16. I have slightly modified Savage's notation in order to maintain consistency with the notation used in the rest of this book.

At Cambridge, Ellsberg familiarized himself with the interpretation of the relationship between the functions u and U dominant there, namely that of Dennis Robertson (1890–1963), the successor of Marshall and Arthur Pigou in the chair of political economy. As mentioned in the introduction of chapter 10, in a series of writings, Robertson (1950; 1951; 1952) had argued that the von Neumann–Morgenstern cardinal utility function u and the traditional cardinal utility function U are fully interchangeable and that, therefore, EUT warrants a return to cardinal utility after the purges imposed by strict ordinalism.

On returning to Harvard, Ellsberg revised the first chapter of his undergraduate dissertation, transforming it into what became his *Economic Journal* article. The revision profited from discussions with Samuelson, Morgenstern, and Mosteller and from unpublished papers by, among others, Maurice Allais (Ellsberg 1954, 529). Ellsberg's interpretation of the relationships between the utility functions u and U is totally opposed to that of Robertson.[17]

12.5.1. Different Operations, Different Utilities

Although he did not mention Stevens, in his article, Ellsberg offered an explicitly operationalist restatement of the issues concerning the measurement of utility. Like Stevens, Ellsberg followed Percy Williams Bridgman and argued that a scientific concept is defined by the set of operations through which the concept is measured: "A 'thing' is 'what is measured by a particular operation' " (Ellsberg 1954, 548). Accordingly, as Bridgman had pointed out, two different sets of operations are presumed to identify and measure two different "things": "If we have more than one set of operations we have more than one concept" (Bridgman 1927, 10; quoted in Ellsberg 1954, 547).

To avoid confusion, Ellsberg continued, it is preferable to use different names for "things" measured by different operations. We may assume that two different operations measure the "same thing" and, accordingly, use a single name for it only if we have good reasons to assume that the two sets of operations yield numerical results that are equal or at least not significantly divergent.

12.5.2. Two Utility Indices

Ellsberg applied this operational approach to utility analysis. He stressed that the operations through which utility theorists had defined the cardinal utility function U before 1944 are different from the operations through which von Neumann and Morgenstern defined their cardinal utility function u. The cardinal index U—which Ellsberg called the "Jevons–Marshall index"—is based on the individual's capacity to introspectively rank utility differences. From a historical viewpoint, the label "Jevons–Marshall index" is unfortunate, because, as argued in chapters 2 and 3, neither Jevons nor Marshall focused on the ranking of

17. See more on Ellsberg in Zappia 2016. Outside the economics profession, Ellsberg is mainly known for his 1971 leak of the Pentagon Papers, secret documents related to the Vietnam War. On Ellsberg's life, career, and political activity outside academia, see Wells 2001; Ellsberg 2002.

utility differences. As we saw in chapter 6, the ranking of utility differences became relevant only later, with Pareto, Lange, Alt, and the other economists involved in the 1930s debate on the determinateness of the utility function. A historically more appropriate name for this utility index would have been the "Lange–Alt index."

The cardinal index u—called by Ellsberg the "von Neumann–Morgenstern" index—relies on the individual's capacity to determine the probability p that makes him indifferent between a given amount \$M of money for sure and lottery [$\$M_1$, p; $\$M_2$, 1 – p], where the monetary payoffs $\$M_1$ and $\$M_2$ are given. For instance, an individual is asked to determine the probability p that makes him indifferent between \$500 for sure and lottery [\$1,000, p; \$0, 1 – p]. If the individual states that for him, this probability is p = 0.8, then by construction, the individual is indifferent between lottery [\$1,000, 0.8; \$0, 0.2] and \$500 for sure. Since the utility function u is cardinal, two points of it are arbitrary, and therefore we can assume, without loss of generality, that u(\$1,000) = 1 and u(\$0) = 0. The von Neumann–Morgenstern index associated with \$500 is the value u that satisfies the EUT equation u(\$500) = u(\$1,000) × 0.8 + u(\$0) × 0.2, that is, u(\$500) = 0.8.[18]

As will become clear in chapter 13, there are various methods to elicit the utility function u within the EUT framework. Since it is based on the identification of a probability value, the method considered by Ellsberg is today usually called the probability equivalence method.

To illustrate the difference between the two indices, Ellsberg considered the following scenario. Imagine that the same individual who is indifferent between lottery [\$1,000, 0.8; \$0, 0.2] and \$500 for sure and for whom, therefore, u(\$500) = 0.8, is also able to compare by introspection the utility differences of riskless utilities. In particular, Ellsberg imagined that for this individual U(\$1,000) – U(\$500) is equal to U(\$500) – U(\$0). If we assume, again without loss of generality, that U(\$1,000) = 1 and U(\$0) = 0, we can state that for this individual, the Jevons–Marshall index U associated with \$500 is 0.5: U(\$500) = 0.5.[19]

Summing up, in the situation imagined by Ellsberg, we have U(\$500) = 0.5, and at the same time, u(\$500) = 0.8. Ellsberg saw no conflict in this type of result because it draws from two independent set of operations: "The two sets of results are independent, hence do not conflict" (547).

12.5.3. The Relationships between the Two Indices

The von Neumann–Morgenstern index and the Jevons–Marshall index are linked by the fact that they rank the alternatives in the same way. Therefore, one index can be obtained by an increasing transformation of the other. Thus, in Ellsberg's numerical example, u(\$1,000) > u(\$500) > u(\$0) and U(\$1,000) > U(\$500) > U(\$0).

However, the increasing transformation linking the two indices does not need to be linear (533). Accordingly, it may well happen that the second derivatives of the two indices do

18. In fact, u(\$500) = u(\$1,000) × 0.8 + u(\$0) × 0.2 = 1 × 0.8 + 0 × 0.2 = 0.8.
19. In fact, from U(\$1,000) = 1, U(\$0) = 0, and U(\$1,000) – U(\$500) = U(\$500) – U(\$0), we obtain 1 – U(\$500) = U(\$500) – 0, that is, 2 × U(\$500) = 1, or U(\$500) = 0.5.

not have the same sign. In Ellsberg's example, the second derivative of the Jevons–Marshall index U, which may be interpreted in terms of the marginal utility of money, is constant, while the second derivative of the von Neumann–Morgenstern index u, which can be associated with attitude toward risk, is diminishing. Ellsberg's hypothetical individual is thus risk-averse even if for him, the marginal utility of money is constant. For Ellsberg, this example makes clear that it is not possible to explain the risk attitude of an individual in risky situations as a consequence of the trend of his marginal utility for riskless money.

But as Ellsberg observed, there is more to be said: it may well happen that one index exists while the other does not. For instance, an individual may be able to identify the probability p that makes a lottery indifferent to a given amount of money, while being incapable of ranking the utility differences between different amounts of money. In this case, the von Neumann–Morgenstern index exists, while the Jevons–Marshall index does not. In reverse, an individual may well be able to rank the utility differences between different amounts of money but, in choosing among lotteries, may violate EUT (554–555). In this latter case, the von Neumann–Morgenstern index u does not exist, while the Jevons–Marshall index does. As discussed in chapter 11, section 11.7.5, this is the type of situation Allais called attention to, and, as mentioned in the introduction to section 12.5, Ellsberg had read an unpublished paper by Allais.[20]

12.6. FRIEDMAN, FROM AS-IF TO HUMPTY DUMPTY

Friedman published his renowned essay on "The Methodology of Positive Economics" in 1953. Here he elaborated on the as-if methodological view that he had already outlined in his 1948 and 1952 articles with Savage.[21] Although Friedman did not address in the essay issues concerning utility measurement, the methodology of economics he advocated reinforces the conception of utility measurement advanced in the 1952 article with Savage, according to which utility measures are valuable insofar as they allow the prediction of economic behavior. For Friedman (1953b, 15) now made his famous argument that the relevant parameter to judge the scientific value of an economic theory is not the realism of its assumptions but its capacity of yielding accurate predictions: "The relevant question to ask about the 'assumptions' of a theory is not whether they are descriptively 'realistic,' for they never are, but whether they are sufficiently good approximations for the purpose in hand. And this question can be answered only by seeing whether the theory works, which means whether it yields sufficiently accurate predictions." If, despite the patent unrealism of its assumptions, a theory yields accurate predictions for a certain class of economic phenomena, one can say that those phenomena work *as if* the assumptions of the theory were realistic.

While Friedman's as-if methodology has been criticized from many quarters,[22] from the mid-1950s on, it has been very influential among mainstream economists. One important

20. The paper, "Notes théoriques sur l'incertitude de l'avenir et le risque," was presented by Allais at the European Congress of the Econometric Society held in Louvain, Belgium, in September 1951; see Ellsberg 1954, 545 n. 2; Allais and Hagen 1979, 144.

21. The literature generated by Friedman's 1953 essay is immense. For general discussions, see Hausman 1992; Hands 2001. For more recent assessments, see Mäki 2009.

22. See e.g. Caldwell 1980; Musgrave 1981; more recently, Thaler 2016.

reason for this enduring success is that Friedman's as-if approach offered a suitable methodological justification for typical research practices.[23] As I will argue at the end of this chapter, the widespread acceptance of Friedman's methodological views has played an important role in fostering the peaceful cohabitation of cardinal and ordinal utility that utility analysis has witnessed since the mid-1950s. Before concluding the chapter, however, I turn briefly to another paper in which Friedman discussed the nature of utility measurement.

In the December 1954 issue of the *Economic Journal*, Robertson published an article in which he restated his claim that the von Neumann–Morgenstern function u and the traditional cardinal utility function U are fully interchangeable. Among other things, Robertson (1954, 675) ironically reproached Friedman and Savage for excessive caution in naming the function u a utility function in their 1952 article: "*They* [Friedman and Savage], having as they believe produced the baby, are inclined to treat him as a little illegitimate of no account in the world, and even to apologise for calling him by his true and honourable name Utility."

In his reply to Robertson, Friedman (1955) reiterated his claim that the functions u and U identify two different concepts that should not be conflated. To make the point, Friedman now adopted the operational argument used by Ellsberg in his 1954 article and even alluded to the operationalist definition of intelligence used by psychologist E. G. Boring (see chapter 8, section 8.3.1):

> A concept . . . has no meaning independently of the operations specified for measuring it. For example, "length" is that property of a thing to which a number is assigned by the operation of laying a rule alongside the thing. "Intelligence" is that property of a person to which a number is assigned by the operation of scoring an "intelligence test." "Utility" is that property of a thing for a person to which a number is assigned by one or another set of operations. (Friedman 1955, 406)

Since the functions u and U are defined by two different sets of operations, they identify two different concepts. To reinforce his point, Friedman quoted a passage from Lewis Carroll's *Through the Looking Glass*, in which Humpty Dumpty declares: "When *I* use a word . . . it means just what I choose it to mean" (quoted in Friedman 1955, 405). Friedman argued that the same holds for utility measures: according to the operational definition of utility measure one chooses to adopt, utility can be ordinal, cardinal, or even measurable on a unit-based scale:

> The question "Is utility measurable?" is, strictly interpreted, a meaningless question. If, in Humpty Dumpty's words, I "choose" utility "to mean" that property of a person's position in life which is measured by the product of the number of hairs on his head and the number of books on his shelves, then utility is measurable by a scale that is unique with respect even to origin and unit of measure. (407)

Whether utility is measurable, Friedman contended, is not a relevant question. What are relevant questions are whether a particular definition of utility is useful for predicting the

23. For a discussion of this point, see Hands 2013b.

choices of individuals and what are the properties of the set of numbers a particular definition of utility is associated with.

12.7. SUMMING UP

12.7.1. Measurement, Conventions, Predictions

After the publication of the *Econometrica* symposium on EUT in October 1952, Friedman, Savage, Strotz, Alchian, and Ellsberg all published further articles addressing the nature of the von Neumann–Morgenstern utility function. These later articles, however, differed from those that had appeared before October 1952 in that they shifted the discussion from the question "What does the von Neumann–Morgenstern utility function u measure?" to the question "What does it mean, in general, to measure utility?" In addressing this second question, these economists came to elaborate a novel view of utility measurement.

According to this view, measuring utility consists of assigning numbers to objects by following a definite set of operations. These numbers are called utility numbers or, more briefly, utilities. The way of assigning numbers to objects is largely arbitrary and conventional. The essential restriction is that the assigned utility numbers should allow the economist to predict the choice behavior of individuals.

I contend that from the mid-1950s, this conventionalist and prediction-oriented view of utility measurement became the standard view among mainstream utility theorists. Besides Friedman, Savage, Strotz, Alchian, and Ellsberg, also Koopmans (1957, essay II), Arrow (1958), and Baumol (1958; 1961, chap. 7) fundamentally adhered to it. Marschak, in his *Econometrica* article of April 1950 (see chapter 10, section 10.2.4) and in his correspondence with Baumol of December 1950 (see chapter 11, section 11.5), had already associated utility measurement with "manageability," that is, convenience, and the capacity to predict choice behavior.

12.7.2. Friedman and Stevens, Economics and Psychology

The notion of measurement advocated by Friedman, Savage, Strotz, Alchian, and Ellsberg for the measurement of utility is similar to the notion of measurement advocated by Stevens for the measurement of sensations and intellectual abilities (see chapter 8). More generally, the processes that led to the definition of these two notions of measurement in, respectively, economics and psychology display a number of analogies.

In both cases, the process was ignited by a specific disciplinary issue rather than some abstract methodological motivation. In psychology, the issue was the psychologists' concern to give full scientific legitimacy to their quantification practices in their controversy with the physicists of the 1930s. In economics, the problem was to clarify the nature of the von Neumann–Morgenstern utility function u and its relationship with the utility function U of traditional utility analysis. In both cases, the specific disciplinary problem eventually turned into the more general question of what it means to measure a thing. And, as already observed, the answers given to that question by Stevens in psychology and by Friedman and other utility theorists in economics were similar. Scholars in both disciplines arrived at a broad definition of measurement that stressed its conventional and operational nature and made it independent of the availability of units, the possibility of assessing ratios, and the capacity to add objects. For utility theorists, the debate on EUT thus played the same role that the controversy of the 1930s on the measurability of sensations had played for experimental psychologists.[24]

The main difference between Stevens's conception of measurement and that advocated by Friedman and the other utility theorists is that only the latter connected valid measurement with correct prediction of choice behavior. This difference reflects a more general difference of scientific goals: at least since Irving Fisher and Pareto, for economists, the explanation or prediction of behavior is more important than it has been for psychologists (see chapters 3 and 5).

12.7.3. The Happy Cohabitation of Cardinal and Ordinal Utility

Beginning in the mid-1950s, various models of individual behavior based on cardinal utility were put forward by economists such as Gerard Debreu (1958), Koopmans (1960), and Marschak ([1960] 1974), as well as by decision theorists with a noneconomics background, such as Patrick Suppes (Suppes and Winet 1955) and Duncan Luce (1956; 1958; 1959). None of these cardinal utility models was criticized for its use of cardinal utility in the way EUT had been criticized a decade earlier. Rather, these cardinal utility models quietly found their place on the economists' shelf near EUT and the ordinal utility models.

This happy cohabitation of cardinal and ordinal utility continued through the second half of the twentieth century and is well documented by many advanced textbooks in microeconomics. Consider, for instance, the standard textbook that, despite being more than twenty years old, is used in most Ph.D. programs in economics, namely *Microeconomic Theory* by Andreu Mas-Colell, Michael Whinston, and Jerry Green (1995). In the Mas-Colell, as it is usually called, the chapters on preference and choice (chaps. 1–2), demand (chap. 3), and general equilibrium (chaps. 15–17) are based on ordinal utility only. Cardinal utility is employed to analyze choice under uncertainty (chap. 6), strategic interaction (chaps. 7–9), and intertemporal decisions (chap. 20). And this is without any substantial discussion by Mas-Colell and his coauthors of the possible tension between ordinal and cardinal approaches to utility. Such peaceful cohabitation stands in sharp contrast to the animated quarrels on

24. Despite these analogies, the processes that led to the novel notions of measurement in psychology and economics occurred independently of each other. As discussed in chapter 8, although Stevens published his landmark article on measurement in 1946, two years after the publication of the first edition of *Theory of Games and Economic Behavior*, he had elaborated his conception of measurement in the early 1940s independently of von Neumann and Morgenstern. On the other hand, neither von Neumann and Morgenstern nor Friedman, Savage, Strotz, Alchian, and Ellsberg referred in their works to Stevens and his approach to measurement. The only solid connection between the two processes is Bridgman's operational philosophy, which helped both Stevens and Ellsberg to articulate their broad, unit-free understanding of measurement. As we have seen, Ellsberg's operationalism was later adopted by Friedman in his 1955 reply to Robertson.

the measurability of utility that, as we have seen in the first eleven chapters of this book, characterized utility theory from the marginal revolution of the 1870s through the debates on EUT of the late 1940s and early 1950s.

My explanation for this change of attitude, and for the fact that the change took place around the mid-1950s, refers to two main factors: the wide acceptance among utility theorists of the view of utility measurement put forward by Friedman, Savage, and others in the early 1950s and the contemporaneous success of Friedman's as-if methodology among economists at large.

Concerning the first factor, within the conventionalist and prediction-oriented view of utility measurement advocated by Friedman & Co., the contrast between ordinal and cardinal utility fades away. From this perspective, it is no longer the case that utility is intrinsically cardinal or intrinsically (just) ordinal. Rather, ordinal and cardinal utility indicate two equally legitimate ways of assigning numbers to the objects of choice. Accordingly, in areas of economic analysis where ordinal utility suffices to obtain valuable results, such as demand analysis and general equilibrium theory, the principle of Occam's razor imposes using ordinal utility only. In other areas of economic analysis, such as the theory of choice under uncertainty or the theory of intertemporal decisions, where manageable models and valuable results need cardinal utility, cardinal utility can be legitimately adopted.

The second major factor capable of explaining the cohabitation of cardinal and ordinal utility in microeconomics after the mid-1950 is, in my view, the acceptance of Friedman's as-if methodology by mainstream economists. If the relevant parameter to judge the scientific value of an economic model is not the realism of its assumptions but its capacity to yield accurate predictions, it makes little sense to question whether the model is based on cardinal or ordinal utility or whether utility is intrinsically cardinal or ordinal. What counts, rather, is whether the model allows predicting choice behavior correctly, irrespective of its cardinal or ordinal underpinnings. Accordingly, if a model based on cardinal utility yields accurate predictions for a certain class of individual choices, such as intertemporal choices, one can say that the individual choses what to do at various points in time as if he maximized an intertemporal cardinal utility function.

12.8. EPISTEMOLOGICAL ANALYSIS

The final sections of parts I and II of this book have reviewed the debates of the period covered in those parts with respect to the five epistemological dimensions of the problem of utility measurement set out in the prologue. Accordingly, in this final section of part III, I review the debates of the period 1945–1955.

12.8.1. The Understanding of Measurement

Given the extended discussion in section 12.7, this topic can be passed over rapidly here. In this chapter, I have argued that the debate on EUT played for utility theory the same role that the controversy of the 1930s between psychologists and physicists on the measurability of sensations and intellectual abilities played for psychology.

As already pointed out, Friedman, Savage, Strotz, Alchian, and Ellsberg all elaborated a view of utility measurement as consisting of the assignment of numbers to objects according to a definite set of operations. Such utility measures are largely conventional, but they should allow the prediction of the choice behavior of individuals.

The open issue is whether utility measures based on models such as EUT do, in fact, provide good predictions of choice behavior. In part IV, I discuss a series of laboratory experiments that addressed this issue.

12.8.2. The Scope of the Utility Concept

In the period 1945–1955, no fundamental rediscussion of the scope of preferences and utility took place. Preferences and utility remained preferences and utility "all things considered" (see chapter 3, section 3.5.2), thereby encompassing all possible psychological motivations that may induce an individual to prefer option x to option y.

This all-encompassing notion of preference is particularly important for the non-Bernoullian version of EUT advanced by von Neumann and Morgenstern and perfected by Marschak (1950), Samuelson (1952), Savage ([1954] 1972), and others. As illustrated in chapters 9 and 10, in modern, non-Bernoullian EUT, the preference and indifference relations defined by the axioms concern lotteries or gambles. This means that an individual may prefer lottery L_1 to lottery L_2 for very different psychological reasons: his desire for money ("I prefer L_1 because, on average, L_1 yields more money than L_2"), his attitude toward risk ("Although, on average, L_2 yields more money than L_1, L_2 is too risky for me"), his pleasure in the very act of gambling ("Although on average, L_2 yields more money than L_1, and is also less risky than L_1, L_1 is a multistage lottery that gives me more fun"), and other possible psychological factors. Among the psychological reasons for preferring one lottery over another, the EUT axioms accommodate well desire for money and attitude toward risk but rule out pleasure for gambling and other psychological factors that, as the post-1970 research will point out (see chapter 16), may influence an individual's preferences between lotteries.

This feature of EUT is important for understanding the scope of the von Neumann–Morgenstern utility function u. As the debate between Friedman and Baumol made clear, the function u is a black box that combines all psychological factors that may influence the individual's preferences between lotteries and are not ruled out by the EUT axioms. In particular, the function u combines different and independent psychological factors, such as the individual's desire for money and his attitude toward risk. The compounded nature of u explains why it cannot be identified with the traditional concept of diminishing (or increasing) marginal utility of money. Since this latter concept is defined in a risk-free framework, the marginal utility of money may be related to the individual's desire for money but is disconnected from other psychological factors that may influence the individual's preferences between lotteries and are specifically related to his or her attitude toward risk.

12.8.3. The Status of Utility

According to what I called the instrumentalist view, utility is a purely theoretical construct that can be useful for explaining or predicting certain economic phenomena but does not necessarily have any real correlate in the mind of the economic agent. Before the 1940s, the only utility theorist who advanced such an interpretation of utility was Léon Walras (see chapter 2, section 2.3.4). For him, concepts such as utility in economics and mass and force in physics should be considered "hypothetical causes which should be . . . introduced into the calculations with a view to linking them to their effects" (Walras [1909] 1990, 213). But discussions about the nature of the von Neumann–Morgenstern utility function u and the rise of Friedman's as-if methodology made the instrumentalist interpretation of the status of utility popular among economists.

An instrumentalist interpretation of the utility function u can be found already in certain passages of *Theory of Games*, such as the one in which von Neumann and Morgenstern ([1944] 1953, 28) argue that they have defined the function u as "that thing for which the calculus of mathematical expectations is legitimate." Similarly, in *The Foundations of Statistics*, Savage ([1954] 1972, 73) defines u as the function associating numbers with the outcomes of gambles in such a way that for the preferred gamble, the mathematical expectation of u is maximal. In both cases, the function u is presented as merely a mathematical construct that is useful for explaining choices between lotteries or gambles but does not necessarily have any psychological interpretation.

In his 1950 report on Baumol's paper and in later articles, Friedman stressed that the von Neumann–Morgenstern function u and its mathematical average should only be used to predict choice behavior. Friedman even suggested that to avoid possible psychological misinterpretations of u, it should be called the "choice-generating function" (Baumol papers, box W1). Likewise, for Alchian (1953, 44), the values of the function u were "essentially nothing but choice indicator[s]." Friedman's and Alchian's statements express an instrumentalist interpretation of utility, which they saw as a tool to predict choices that does not necessarily have any psychological correlate in the mind of the economic agent.

This emerging instrumentalist interpretation of utility was reinforced by the rise of Friedman's as-if methodology. As discussed, according to the as-if approach, what is relevant in judging the validity of a scientific theory is not whether the assumptions or the concepts on which the theory is built are realistic but whether its predictions are correct. Accordingly, insofar as EUT "works," that is, insofar as "it yields sufficiently accurate predictions" (Friedman 1953b, 15), the status of the utility function u featured in EUT is not relevant, and it may well be the case that u does not have any existing correlate in the decision maker's mind.

As we will see in part IV, although this instrumentalist interpretation of the status of the utility function u became quite popular among economists working with EUT, it was generally rejected by psychologists, philosophers, and other noneconomists who engaged with the theory.

12.8.4. The Data for Utility Measurement

As will become clearer in chapters 13 and 14, within the EUT framework, the measurement of the utility function u of an individual is based on the recording of his *preference* (or indifference) *judgments* between pairs of lotteries (or between a lottery and a given amount of money for sure) or, alternatively, on the observation of his pairwise *choices* between the same types of objects. As in the period 1900–1945 (see chapter 7, section 7.7.4), the distinction between preference judgments obtained by introspection and observed choices was immaterial.

In the simple scenario considered by Ellsberg in his discussion of utility measurement (see section 12.5), the elicitation of the von Neumann–Morgenstern utility function u works as follows. If an individual is indifferent or is unable to choose between lottery [$1,000, 0.8; $0, 0.2] and $500 for sure, then EUT implies that for him, u($500) = u($1,000) × 0.8 + u($0) × 0.2. Since two points of the function u are arbitrary, we can assume that u($1,000) = 1 and u($0) = 0, and thus we obtain that for this individual, u($500) = 0.8.

In this example, we have assumed that the individual is already indifferent between a given lottery and a given amount of money for sure. As we will see in chapter 13, in many experiments aimed at measuring utility, the problem was in effect to identify this indifference situation.

12.8.5. The Aims of Utility Theory

EUT has both descriptive and normative aims, and accordingly, the utility measurements based on EUT have both descriptive and normative implications. On the descriptive side, EUT aims at explaining certain facts about the behavior of individuals in conditions involving risk. For such explanations, eliciting the shape of the von Neumann–Morgenstern function u is often important, since in EUT, the concavity of the curve is associated with risk aversion, while a convex utility curve is associated with risk seeking. For instance, in their 1948 article (see chapter 10, section 10.1.2), Friedman and Savage argued that EUT explains why most individuals buy insurance and, at the same time, purchase lottery tickets or engage in similar forms of gambling. Their explanation of this phenomenon relied on the hypothesis that the function u is first concave, then convex, and then concave again.

With respect to the predictive aims of EUT, in the experiments performed in the 1950s and 1960s and to be discussed in chapters 13 and 14, the measures of the utility function u obtained from an individual's choices regarding a first set of lotteries were used to predict, via the EUT formula, the individual's choices regarding a second set of lotteries. If these predictions were correct, EUT was deemed validated.

Moving to the normative dimension, EUT has normative implications for both individual behavior and social welfare. At the individual level, if an individual deems that the EUT axioms identify rational behavior in conditions of risk, he can use EUT to guide his choices between complex risky options. That is, the individual can choose between simple risky options he understands well and obtain from these choices, via the EUT formula, some measures of his utility function u. He can then use these utility measures to calculate the expected utility of more complex risky options and choose the option with the highest expected utility.

EUT can also be used to revise certain choices. As we saw in chapter 11, section 11.7.2, during the Paris conference of 1952, Allais presented Savage with the choice situation later associated with the "Allais paradox." On questioning by Allais, Savage stated that he preferred lottery L_1 to lottery L_2 and lottery L_4 to lottery L_3, thus violating EUT. In *The Foundations of Statistics*, Savage ([1954] 1972, 101–103) famously discussed the preferences he had expressed in Paris. He argued that these preferences conflict with the Sure-Thing Principle and are therefore erroneous. Accordingly, he corrected himself and claimed that upon reflection, he preferred L_3 to L_4.[25]

In social welfare analysis, the so-called Impossibility Theorem demonstrated by Arrow in his *Social Choice and Individual Welfare* (1951b) exposed the limits of the theories of social welfare based on ordinal utility and the ban on interpersonal comparisons of utilities. One possible way out of this impasse was suggested by John Harsanyi (1953; 1955), and is outlined here because it represents an important normative application of EUT to social welfare issues.

In Harsanyi's approach, each member of a society has to identify the social optimum without knowing what his or her actual position in that society will be. Therefore, each society member faces a problem of choice under risk. By assuming that all individuals are expected utility maximizers and that their von Neumann–Morgenstern utility functions u can be used to evaluate social distributions, and by admitting interpersonal comparisons of utilities, Harsanyi showed that social welfare is measured by a linear weighted sum of individual utilities.

Harsanyi's approach to social welfare theory generated a significant debate, which we do not need to address here.[26] Rather, we now move to the experimental attempts to measure the utility of money on the basis of EUT that were performed by Mosteller, Suppes, and other researchers in the 1950s and 1960s.

25. Some historians of decision theory, such as Jallais and Pradier (2005), have interpreted Savage's self-correction as a retreat to a normative defense of EUT after the Allais paradox had convinced him that EUT is descriptively invalid. The exchange of letters between Savage and Samuelson in summer 1950 (see chapter 11) contradicts this "normative retreat story" and shows that for Savage, the normative force of the Sure-Thing Principle was a crucial motivation for endorsing EUT well before the Paris conference and independently of the Allais paradox. If there was one person responsible for Savage's normative turn, it was Samuelson, not Allais. See more on this point in Mongin 2014; Moscati 2016a.

26. For a useful assessment, see Weymark 2005.

PART FOUR

Expected Utility Theory and Experimental Utility Measurement, 1950–1985

CHAPTER 13

Experimental Utility Measurement

The Age of Confidence I, 1950–1960

As explained in part III, expected utility theory (EUT) suggests a handy way to measure the von Neumann–Morgenstern cardinal utility function u of an individual on the basis of his or her preferences or choices between risky options. Beginning in the late 1940s, a number of researchers attempted to implement that suggestion in controlled laboratory experiments. In particular, these researchers focused on lotteries and other gambles with monetary payoffs, and from the subjects' choices regarding these monetary risky options, they inferred the utility function u, which they typically interpreted as the utility of riskless money. The first of these experiments was performed at Harvard University in 1948 and 1949, that is, not only before the Paris conference of 1952 but also before the exchange of letters of 1950 among Milton Friedman, Leonard J. Savage, Jacob Marschak, Paul Samuelson, and William Baumol that modified the views these five economists held on EUT and the nature of the utility function u (see chapter 11). The experiment was conducted by Frederick Mosteller, a statistician who had worked at the Statistical Research Group with Friedman and Savage during the war (see chapter 10, section 10.1.1), and Philip Nogee, then a Harvard Ph.D. student in psychology. Other experiments followed in the 1950s and after, often conducted by important figures in economics and neighboring disciplines, such as Marschak, philosophers Patrick Suppes and Donald Davidson, and psychologist Sidney Siegel.

In this chapter, I reconstruct the history of the EUT-based attempts to measure the cardinal utility of money in laboratory experiments from 1950 to 1960, from Mosteller and Nogee's pioneering study, which was published in 1951, to the experiment conducted by Suppes and his student Karol Valpreda Walsh, whose results were published in 1959. In the next chapter, I discuss two experiments on utility measurement performed at Yale University in the early 1960s to which Marschak contributed, either directly or indirectly

As anticipated in chapter 11, the lab experiments conducted from the late 1940s to the early 1960s had two intertwined goals. The first, which can be called the measurement goal, was to verify whether EUT made it actually possible to measure the von Neumann–Morgenstern utility function u. In the terms introduced in chapter 2, the measurement at issue is a form of indirect measurement. The measurand u, which is not directly observable, is supposed to be connected with an observable variable y, namely the observed preference or choice regarding lotteries, by a certain functional relationship F so that y = F(u). As will become clear, in the case of EUT-based utility measurement, the function F was the expected utility formula or some "stochastic" modification of it. In particular, Mosteller, Suppes, and the other experimenters considered in this chapter were interested in checking the shape of the utility function u, since in EUT, the concavity of the curve u is associated with an averse attitude toward risk, while a convex utility curve is associated with risk seeking (see chapter 10, section 10.1.2). The measurement goal characterizes the lab experiments considered in here and in chapter 14 and distinguishes them from other thought, field, or lab experiments on EUT performed in the period 1950–1965.

The second goal can be called the theory-testing goal: in various ways, the utility measures obtained through EUT were used to test the descriptive validity of the theory. In most experiments conducted in 1950–1965, the utility measures inferred from an individual's choices regarding a first set of lotteries were used to predict, via the EUT formula, the individual's choices regarding a second set of lotteries. The theory was deemed validated if the predictions were correct.

Beginning with the informal experiment that Maurice Allais conducted at the Paris conference of 1952, which gave rise to the so-called Allais paradox, some other experiments aimed at testing EUT were performed in the period 1950–1965 but did not involve utility measurement. They typically adopted Allais's testing format, which, as discussed in chapter 11, section 11.7.2, is based on the direct comparison of choices between two pairs of lotteries and therefore does not require measuring the utility of the lottery payoffs.

The whole period 1950–1965 can be characterized as an "age of confidence" in experimental research on EUT-based utility measurement. In the 1950s, in fact, the experimenters were confident about both EUT and the possibility of measuring utility through it. They designed their experiments so as to neutralize some psychological factors that could jeopardize the validity of the theory and spoil the significance of the experimental measurements of utility, and they tended to conclude that their experimental findings supported both the experimental measurability of utility based on EUT and the descriptive validity of the theory. In the early 1960s, the experimenters focused on the goal of testing EUT, while the measurement goal became less important. However, they continued to interpret their experimental findings as validating EUT and the possibility of measuring utility through it.

As we will see in chapter 16, beginning in the late 1960s, that confidence faded, and a general skepticism toward EUT and EUT-based utility measurements materialized.

13.1. MOSTELLER AND NOGEE'S EXPERIMENT

13.1.1. The Context: Friedman, Savage, and Alchian

Mosteller (1916–2006) initially studied mathematics and statistics at the Carnegie Institute of Technology and in 1939 began his Ph.D. at Princeton's department of mathematics. In 1944, he interrupted his studies and moved to New York to work at the Statistical Research Group (SRG), the US Army think tank directed by Allen Wallis (see chapters 7, section

7.6.2, and 10, section 10.1.1). At SRG, Mosteller found Savage, with whom he had become acquainted in 1941–1942 when Savage was a postdoctoral student in Princeton, and he met Friedman. In 1944 and 1945, Mosteller, Savage, and Friedman worked together on various statistical projects, and in particular, Mosteller and Savage coauthored a paper on sequential statistical estimators (Girshick, Mosteller, and Savage 1946).

When the war ended, Mosteller returned to Princeton and completed his Ph.D. with a dissertation in statistics. In 1946, he joined the faculty of Harvard's department of social relations, then chaired by sociologist Talcott Parsons. The department hosted disciplines as diverse as psychology, sociology, and anthropology and was endowed with a laboratory for psychological experiments. In this interdisciplinary environment, Mosteller became increasingly involved in psychology, and beginning in 1947–1948, he coauthored with some Harvard colleagues various papers measuring visual stimuli, perspective illusions, and pain sensations (Bruner, Postman, and Mosteller 1950; Keats, Beecher, and Mosteller 1950). In 1948–1949, Mosteller also taught a course on psychometric methods. Given this background, it is not surprising to find that in late 1947 or early 1948, he conceived of an experiment to measure utility. In his intellectual autobiography, Mosteller (2010, 196) recalls: "Von Neumann and Morgenstern's book, *Theory of Games and Economic Behavior*, led to much research on ideas of utility, and I thought it would be worth actually trying to measure utility in real people to see what would happen."

In February 1948, Mosteller began to discuss the experiment's design in letters to Friedman and Savage, who had just completed their joint article on "The Utility Analysis of Choices Involving Risk" (Friedman and Savage 1948; see chapter 10, section 10.1). Wallis also contributed to the discussion, albeit in a minor way (Friedman papers, box 39). In a letter dated February 27, 1948, and addressed to both Friedman and Savage, Mosteller discussed which payoffs and winning probabilities the gambles in the experiment should have ("I have thought over Jimmie's idea that we should maintain true odds at 1:1 . . . but I don't see where it gets me") and how to phrase the instructions to the experimental subjects ("One phrase I have considered is 'Try to make as much money as you can.' But this has drawbacks"). Generally speaking, Friedman and Savage gave prompt feedback to Mosteller and supported his experimental project. In the published version of their paper, Mosteller and Nogee (1951, 372) presented their study as in effect an outgrowth of Friedman and Savage's 1948 article.

In late February and early March 1948, Mosteller conducted a couple of pilot studies for the experiment, and it was at this point that he co-opted into the project Nogee (1916–1980), then a Harvard Ph.D. student in clinical psychology whom Mosteller was supervising. Mosteller and Nogee conducted the actual experiment a year after the pilot study, that is, from February through May 1949, and devoted the second part of 1949 and the early months of 1950 to analyzing the experimental data. From time to time, Friedman and Savage asked Mosteller about the progress of the project.[1]

Since it involves a number of the protagonists in our story, a small accident concerning the presentation of the Mosteller–Nogee paper at the 1950 annual meeting of the social

1. See, in particular, Friedman to Mosteller, March 3, 1948; Savage to Mosteller, March 28, 1948. Friedman papers, box 39.

science societies is worth mentioning. The meeting was held in Chicago, and Mosteller's session, which was jointly sponsored by the American Economic Association, the American Statistical Association, and the Econometric Society, was scheduled for four p.m. on December 27. The session was chaired by Marschak, who had recently published his *Econometrica* article on EUT (Marschak 1950), and included Kenneth Arrow's paper on the alternative approaches to the analysis of choices involving risk (Arrow 1951a; see the introduction to chapter 10). The two discussants were Franco Modigliani, then at the University of Illinois, and Armen Alchian (Econometric Society 1951). Because of a heavy snowfall, Mosteller's train from Boston was late, and his paper was delivered by Alchian: "The train finally arrived in Chicago somewhat after 4 P.M. . . . I rushed to the auditorium and arrived just before the close of my session . . . . One of the discussants, Armen Alchian, an economist, had kindly delivered my talk, some said better than I could have done" (Mosteller 2010, 198).

The article was eventually published in October 1951 in the *Journal of Political Economy* under the title "An Experimental Measurement of Utility." By that time, Nogee had left Harvard to become an assistant professor at Boston University.

13.1.2. Measuring Utility

The Mosteller–Nogee experiment involved two parts, which correspond, respectively, to what I have called the measurement goal and the theory-testing goal of the experiment. In the first part, Mosteller and Nogee elicited the von Neumann–Morgenstern utility functions u of ten Harvard undergraduates and five Massachusetts National Guardsmen.

They confronted each subject with a series of gambles yielding $\$M_1 = -5$¢ with a known probability p, e.g., $p = 2/3$, and yielding a given amount of money $\$M_2$ with the residual probability $(1 - p)$. Then they modified the amount $\$M_2$ until the point where the subject was "indifferent" (in a probabilistic sense that will be clarified in section 13.1.3) between participating in the gamble [–5¢, p; $\$M_2$, (1 – p)] or not participating, that is, between the gamble and the sure amount of money corresponding to the status quo. If the subject obeys the axioms of EUT, this indifference indicates that for him $u(-5¢) \times p + u(\$M_2) \times (1 - p) = u(\$0)$, whereby u($0) is the utility of the status quo. In particular, Mosteller and Nogee assumed (without loss of generality) that $u(-5¢) = -1$ and $u(\$0) = 0$, and thus obtained that $u(\$M_2) = p/(1 - p)$. For instance, if $p = 2/3$, $u(\$M_2) = 2$. The amount of money $\$M_2$ used by Mosteller and Nogee ranged between 2.5 cents and $5.07.

This outline of Mosteller and Nogee's approach makes clear that they measured utility indirectly: the unobservable measurand is the von Neumann–Morgenstern utility function u, the observable variable y is the indifference relation between a gamble and a sure amount of money, and the functional relationship F connecting u with y has the general form $y = F(u, p)$, where p are the probabilities of the payoffs and F is the expected utility formula. Given the probabilities p, the observation of y allows inference of the value of u that satisfies the equation $y = F(u, p)$.

Using this approach, Mosteller and Nogee identified seven points of the von Neumann–Morgenstern utility function u of each subject. By connecting these seven points with straight lines, they drew an approximate graph of the utility curves u of the subjects. For instance,

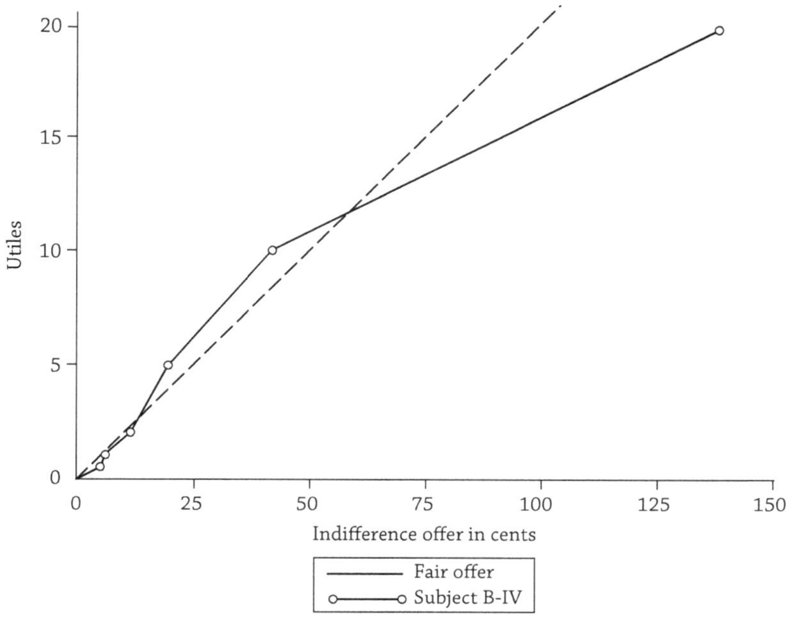

Figure 13.1. Utility curve elicited by Mosteller and Nogee
The continuous broken line shows the experimental utility curve u of subject B-IV. The utility level 101 is not shown. The dotted straight line is the hypothetical utility function of an individual neutral to risk.
Source: Mosteller and Nogee 1951, 387. Reproduced with permission of the University of Chicago Press.

figure 3b of their article, which is reproduced here in figure 13.1, shows the estimated utility curve u of experimental subject B-IV.

Mosteller and Nogee found that the utility curves u did not present a uniform shape. In particular, while the Harvard students tended to have concave utility curves for money, that is, to be risk-averse, the Massachusetts National Guardsmen tended to have convex utility curves for money, that is, to be risk-seeking.

It is important to stress that Mosteller and Nogee interpreted the von Neumann–Morgenstern utility functions u that they had elicited as if they measured the utility of riskless money for each subject. That is, they identified the von Neumann–Morgenstern utility function u inferred from choices between risky alternatives with the traditional utility function U expressing preferences between riskless alternatives. Accordingly, they associated risk aversion with diminishing marginal utility of riskless money and risk seeking with increasing marginal utility (399).

This interpretation of the function u should not be surprising. As pointed out in chapter 10, this was also the interpretation of u endorsed by Friedman and Savage in their 1948 article. As discussed in chapters 11 and 12, it was only later on, in the early 1950s, that Friedman and the other utility theorists modified their interpretation of the nature of u and began to conceive of it as an indicator of choice under risk that is correlated ordinally, but not cardinally, with the traditional utility function U.

Before moving to the theory-testing part of the Mosteller–Nogee study, it is important to discuss in some detail the design of the utility-measuring part of their experiment. This design exhibits a tension between the economic image of human agency associated with EUT and a sensitivity to psychological factors that EUT neglects or explicitly rules out. I begin by discussing the elements of the experimental design that mirror more directly the EUT assumptions (items 1–4) and then move to the elements that were shaped by psychological considerations (items 5–6).

13.1.3. Design

1. *Real money.* In the psychometric experiments to measure visual stimuli and other sensations that Mosteller had conducted with his colleagues at Harvard's department of social relations, subjects had to respond to stimuli, for example, by saying which light they perceived as brighter, but did not receive any reward or penalty depending on their responses. In contrast, Mosteller and Nogee introduced actual monetary rewards into the experiment and devoted part of their article to arguing that these rewards represented nontrivial incentives for their subjects (1951, 376, 402–403).

As discussed in chapter 7, section 7.6.2, in 1942 Friedman and Wallis had criticized Louis Leon Thurstone's 1931 experimental attempt to measure the indifference curves of an individual, because his experimental subject had to choose from fictional rather than actual commodities. "For a satisfactory experiment," they wrote, "it is essential that the subject give actual reactions to actual stimuli" (Wallis and Friedman 1942, 179). Neither in the correspondence among Mosteller, Friedman, Savage, and Wallis that I perused nor in the Mosteller and Nogee article is there any reference to Friedman and Wallis's critique of Thurstone's experiment. However, Mosteller and Nogee's commitment to real and nontrivial monetary incentives implicitly agrees with Friedman and Wallis's claim that experiments in which subjects give conjectural responses to hypothetical stimuli are of little interest for economists.

2. *Objective probabilities.* Mosteller and Nogee informed their experimental subjects about the objective probabilities of winning and losing. Around the same time, empirical studies on betting behavior carried out by psychologists Malcolm Preston and Philip Baratta (1948) and Richard Griffith (1949) suggested that bettors harbor "psychological probabilities" that do not coincide with the corresponding mathematical probabilities. In particular, these studies indicated that bettors overvalue low mathematical probabilities and underestimate high ones. The rediscovery of Frank Ramsey's 1926 essay "Truth and Probability" promoted the idea of a subjective approach to probability, which was developed in the following years by Savage (see chapter 12, section 12.4.1).

The possibility that individuals may harbor subjective (or psychological) probabilities that differ from objective (or mathematical) probabilities is problematic for EUT-based utility measurement. In fact, and as would be stressed by Ward Edwards (1953; see section 13.2), if subjective and objective probabilities are different and the experimenter has no clue about the former, the expected utility formula presents two unknowns—the values of the utility function u and the subjective probabilities π—so that it becomes useless for measuring u in terms of probabilities.

Although Mosteller and Nogee cited Ramsey a number of times and discussed at length whether subjective and objective probabilities coincide, their experimental design is based on objective probabilities only and, therefore, on the implicit assumption that experimental subjects do not distort objective probabilities.[2]

3. *Complicated probabilities*. Mosteller and Nogee presented their experimental subjects with gambles that had quite complicated odds. The winning probabilities p corresponding to the seven points of the utility function u elicited by Mosteller and Nogee were, in fact, 66.67, 49.75, 33.22, 16.67, 8.95, 4.71, and 0.98. Although for an EUT decision maker, all probability figures are equally comprehensible, from a psychological viewpoint, it is natural to argue that subjects may find it hard to understand probability figures such as those used by Mosteller and Nogee.

4. *Gamble versus sure outcome*. In the Mosteller–Nogee experiment, subjects had to choose between a proper gamble, in which they could win $\$M_2$ or lose 5 cents, and the sure outcome associated with the refusal to gamble. In the EUT framework, there is no difference between gamble-versus-gamble choices and gamble-versus-sure-outcome choices, because EUT rules out the existence of a specific utility or disutility deriving from the very act of gambling. However, if such specific utility for gambling exists, it would distort utility measures such as those obtained by Mosteller and Nogee. A positive utility for gambling would in fact lead to overestimation of the utility of sure amounts of money, while a negative utility for gambling would have the opposite effect.

Although these elements of the Mosteller–Nogee experimental design rely on the image of human agency associated with EUT, other elements suggest a sensitivity to psychological considerations that EUT rules out.

5. *Money versus probability*. To discuss this feature of the Mosteller–Nogee experimental design, I take a roundabout route, because this allows me to introduce some general concepts that will prove useful for the rest of the narrative. If we already know that a subject is indifferent between a lottery $[\$M_1, p; \$M_2, (1-p)]$ and an amount of money for sure $M, where $\$M_1$, $\$M_2$, $M, and p are given, we can fix two values of his utility function u and use the expected utility formula to identify a new numerical value of the function u; that is, we can measure u. For instance, as in Daniel Ellsberg's example discussed in chapter 12, section 12.5.2, if we know that the subject is indifferent between lottery [$1,000, 0.8; $0, 0.2] and $500 for sure, the expected utility formula tells us that for him, $u(\$1{,}000) \times 0.8 + u(\$0) \times 0.2 = u(\$500)$. If, without loss of generality, we assume that $u(\$1{,}000) = 1$ and $u(\$0) = 0$, we obtain $u(\$500) = 0.8$.

In the Mosteller–Nogee experiment, as well as in other experiments we will discuss, the problem was in effect that of identifying the indifference situation. Generally speaking, this can be done by adjusting one of the parameters p, $M, $\$M_1$, or $\$M_2$ until the point where the lottery $[\$M_1, p; \$M_2, (1-p)]$ becomes indifferent to the amount of money for sure $M. According to which parameter is adjusted, we obtain a specific method to measure utility.

2. To be precise, one should distinguish between the subjective probabilities featuring in the Ramsey–Savage model as commonly used in economics today, and the subjective probabilities originally pinpointed by Preston and Baratta and resulting from distortions of objective probabilities. The Ramsey–Savage subjective probabilities are fully compatible with EUT, and in fact allow extending EUT to situations where objective probabilities are not available. In contrast, the Preston–Baratta subjective probabilities emerge where objective probabilities are available and get transformed, leading to deviations from EUT. The subjective probabilities discussed by Mosteller and Nogee are the distorted probabilities à la Preston–Baratta.

If, given $M_1, $M_2, and $M, we adjust the probability p, we adopt what is currently called the *probability equivalence method* to measure utility. If, given p, $M_1, and $M_2, we adjust the amount of money for sure $M until the indifference point is reached, we apply the so-called *certainty equivalence method*. Finally, if, given p, $M, and one of the lottery payoffs, say $M_1, we adjust the other payoff $M_2 until indifference is obtained, we adopt the *money equivalence method*.

In their experiment, Mosteller and Nogee adopted the money equivalence method: they modified $M_2 until the point where the subject was indifferent between participating in the gamble [−5¢, p; $M_2, (1 − p)], where p was given, and the sure amount of money $0 corresponding to the status quo.

According to EUT, the probability equivalence method, the certainty equivalence method, and the money equivalence method should deliver consistent results and thus lead to the same utility measures. Therefore, using one method rather than another should not make any difference. However, for Mosteller and Nogee, it did make a difference. In their article, Friedman and Savage (1948, 292) had suggested using the probability equivalence method to reach the indifference point. By contrast, Mosteller and Nogee preferred the money equivalence procedure, because, they argued, "most people are more familiar with amounts of money than with probabilities" (1951, 373).

6. *Probabilistic versus deterministic indifference*. In each of the three measurement methods discussed in the previous section, the measurement of utility is based on the identification of indifferent alternatives. However, it is difficult to observe indifference in an actual experimental setting. Experimental subjects typically prefer one alternative to another, for example, they prefer participating in the gamble or, alternatively, they prefer the status quo. However, it is not clear what the behavioral correlate of indifference would be. Dithering? That the subject dithers for some sufficiently long time?

To circumvent the problem, Mosteller and Nogee resorted to the method of comparative judgment that Thurstone had put forward in 1927 to measure sensations. As explained in chapter 4, section 4.2.2, in Thurstone's approach each experimental subject is confronted with the same pair of stimuli more than once. Because of judgment errors, distraction, or variation in sensibility, the subject's comparative judgment between the two stimuli fluctuates. One stimulus is taken to be stronger than the other if the former is perceived as stronger more than 50 percent of the time.

Mosteller and Nogee adapted Thurstone's psychometric idea to the economic notion of indifference. They defined a subject as indifferent between participating in a gamble of the form [−5¢, p; $M_2, (1 − p)] and the status quo if, when confronted with the same choice more than once, he accepted and rejected participating in the gamble equally often: "When . . . B and D are chosen equally often, i.e., each chosen in half of their simultaneous presentations, the individual is said to be indifferent between B and D" (1951, 374).

Mosteller and Nogee accompanied this definition of indifference with an explicit criticism of the deterministic, that is, nonprobabilistic, approach to preference built into the EUT axioms. They argued that "subjects are not so consistent about preference and indifference as Von Neumann and Morgenstern postulated" (404). Rather, gradation of preference is the rule, as "the experience of psychologists with psychological tests has shown" (374).

13.1.4. Testing EUT

In the second part of their experiment, Mosteller and Nogee used the utility measures elicited in the first part to predict, via the EUT formula, whether the subjects would accept or reject other gambles. Notably, the testing part of the experiment is independent of the interpretation given to the von Neumann–Morgenstern utility function u. Whether u is interpreted as the traditional utility function U for riskless money, as Mosteller and Nogee interpreted it, or as "the choice-generating function," as Friedman and most utility theorists came to interpret it in the early 1950s, it is scientifically legitimate to use the numerical values of u elicited in the measuring part of the experiment to check the validity of EUT in the testing part of the study.

The gambles used in the second part of the experiment, which Mosteller and Nogee called "doublet hands," were much more complex than the gambles used in the first part. From the economic viewpoint, this is perfectly legitimate because an EUT decision maker displays well-defined preferences regarding all gambles, independently of whether these gambles are simple or complex. From a psychological standpoint, however, using utility measures elicited from simple gambles to predict choices regarding complex gambles may appear questionable.

13.1.5. Findings

Mosteller and Nogee presented the findings of their experimental study as supporting both the experimental measurability of utility based on EUT and the descriptive validity of the theory. Concerning the first part of the experiment, Mosteller and Nogee were able to elicit the utility curves u of all but one of the experimental subjects and thus concluded that "it is feasible to measure utility experimentally" (403). As mentioned in section 13.1.2, the utility curves did not present a uniform shape: the Harvard students tended to have concave utility curves, that is, to be risk-averse, while the Massachusetts National Guardsmen tended to have convex utility curves, that is, to be risk-seeking.

The findings of the second part of the experiment were more problematic, but nevertheless, Mosteller and Nogee assessed them favorably, arguing that "the notion that people behave in such a way as to maximize their expected utility is not unreasonable" (399).

13.1.6. Summing Up

The experimental design through which Mosteller and Nogee measured utility exhibits a tension between elements that mirror the EUT assumptions and elements that take into account psychological factors neglected or explicitly ruled out by EUT. Thus, on the one hand, Mosteller and Nogee ruled out the possibility that actual individuals may distort objective probabilities, misunderstand complicated odds, derive utility from the very act of gambling, or behave differently when faced with different types of gambles. On the other hand, other elements of their design—such as having experimental subjects adjust amounts of money rather than probabilities, or the probabilistic approach to indifference—rely on psychological insights at odds with EUT.

Notably, Mosteller and Nogee did not use their understanding of the psychology of decision-making to construct choice situations in which the experimental subjects tend to violate EUT—as Allais would do a couple of years later at the Paris conference. Rather, they used their psychological considerations to simplify the decision tasks faced by the experimental subjects and thereby neutralize some psychological factors that could jeopardize the validity of EUT and thus spoil the significance of the experimental measurements of utility based on it. Finally, Mosteller and Nogee appraised their experimental findings as supporting both the measurability of utility and the validity of EUT. As we will see in the remainder of this chapter and in chapter 14, Mosteller and Nogee's confident approach was shared by the other experimenters who engaged with the EUT-based measurement of utility in the 1950s and early 1960s.

13.2. INTERLUDE: 1952–1954

The Mosteller–Nogee article was published in the context of the buoyant debate on EUT studied in chapters 10 through 12 and played some role in the rise of the theory. From 1952 to 1954, advocates of EUT such as Friedman and Savage (1952, 466), Robert Strotz (1953, 397), and Alchian (1953, 43) argued that the Mosteller–Nogee experiment provided appreciable, although far from definitive, empirical support for EUT. At the Paris conference, Marschak suggested that Mosteller and Nogee's probabilistic notion of indifference could be extended into a more general "stochastic" approach to choice and that such a stochastic approach could accommodate possible deviations of actual human behavior from rational behavior as defined by EUT: "A natural weakening [of the EUT model] consists of making the model stochastic. In the experiences . . . of the psychologists who, like Thurstone, study choice phenomena, the results are described in terms of relative frequencies of preferences for A or B. Mosteller's observations . . . have the same nature" (CNRS 1953, 25–26).

By contrast, critics of EUT such as Alan Manne (1952, 667–668) claimed that Mosteller and Nogee's interpretation of their own experimental findings was exceedingly optimistic. Allais (1953, 541) argued that the Mosteller–Nogee results were inconclusive because the choice situations considered are not ones where EUT is typically violated.

At any rate, the Mosteller–Nogee experiment showed that EUT has clear empirical implications, can be used to make predictions, and can therefore be falsified by experimental findings. This was not the case for other theories of decision under risk such as that of Allais. More important, even if inconclusive, the results of the Mosteller–Nogee experiment did not contradict EUT. Therefore, supporters of the theory such as Friedman and Savage (1952, 466) could claim that the experiment justified some "mild optimism" about the validity of EUT.

As argued in chapter 11, by the end of 1952, EUT stabilized as the dominant economic model of choice under risk. This explains why Davidson, Suppes, and Siegel, when they entered the economics of decision-making from their home disciplines, focused on EUT rather than other theories of choice under risk. But before I turn to their experiment and outline how they embarked on the measurement of utility, a further contextual element should be brought into the picture.

As discussed in section 13.1.3, Mosteller and Nogee had discussed the possibility that subjective and objective probabilities may not coincide. Edwards, another of Mosteller's Ph.D. students in psychology at Harvard, investigated this issue further.[3] In his doctoral dissertation and a series of papers derived from it, Edwards (1953; 1954a; 1954b; 1954c) presented experimental results confirming that bettors harbor subjective probabilities that are at odds with objective probabilities. In particular, Edwards (1953, 363) pointed out that this fact "has serious implications for the utility curves of Mosteller and Nogee and indeed for the whole method of utility measurement proposed by von Neumann and Morgenstern." In fact, if subjective and objective probabilities are different and the experimenter has no clue about the former, the expected utility formula cannot be used to elicit the utility function u:

> Choices among bets can be used to measure utility only if it is legitimate to assume that the probabilities which enter the equations from which the utilities are calculated are the same as the probabilities which determine the choices of Ss [the experimental subjects]. If Ss prefer some probabilities to others, such an assumption is untenable, and any utility measurement based on it is invalid. (Edwards 1953, 363)

The problem highlighted by Edwards is a problem of indirect measurement. As observed in section 13.1.2, Mosteller and Nogee's indirect measurement of utility is based on the supposition that there exists a functional relationship $y = F(u,p)$ connecting the measurand u with the observable variable y and the known probabilities p. If, because of subjective distortions or some other reasons, the probabilities p are unknown, the functional relationship $y = F(u,p)$ can no longer be used to infer the values of u from the values of y. In the next section, we will see how Davidson, Suppes, and Siegel took account of this problem and contrived a cunning device to overcome it.

13.3. THE DAVIDSON-SUPPES-SIEGEL EXPERIMENT

The second experiment to measure the von Neumann–Morgenstern utility function of an individual within the EUT framework was carried out at Stanford University in the spring of 1954 by philosophers Davidson and Suppes with the collaboration of psychologist Siegel. In addition to being the second experiment to measure utility, the Davidson–Suppes–Siegel study is relevant for our wider narrative because it played an important role in shaping Suppes's theory of measurement, which will be discussed in chapter 15.

3. See more on Edwards in Shanteau, Mellers, and Schum 1999. On Edwards and the so-called Michigan School, see chapter 16.

13.3.1. Introducing Suppes

Suppes (1922–2014) studied physics and meteorology at the University of Chicago (B.S. 1943), and in 1947, having served in the Army Air Force during the war, he entered Columbia University as a graduate student in philosophy (Suppes 1979). At Columbia, he came under the influence of Ernest Nagel, the philosopher whose views on measurement were discussed in chapter 4, section 4.1.4, and also took courses in advanced mathematical topics. Around 1948, he was one of a group of Columbia Ph.D. students who organized an informal seminar on von Neumann and Morgenstern's *Theory of Games*. He graduated in June 1950 under Nagel's supervision and in September of the same year joined the department of philosophy at Stanford University, where he remained for the rest of his working life.

Suppes's early publications had little, if anything, to do with economics, psychology, or the behavioral sciences in general. Rather, he worked on the theory of measurement and the foundations of physics using an axiomatic approach. Thus, in his first article, Suppes (1951) put forward an axiomatization of unit-based measurement that built on the axiomatizations proposed by Otto Hölder ([1901] 1996) and Nagel (1931; see chapters 1, section 1.4.1, and 4, section 4.1.4).[4] In other early publications, Suppes and his coauthors advanced a set-theoretical axiomatic foundation of particle mechanics (McKinsey, Sugar, and Suppes 1953; McKinsey and Suppes 1953a; McKinsey and Suppes 1953b). Regarding measurement issues, these articles remained within the orbit of the unit-based conception of measurement.

In the early 1950s, two main factors contributed to a shift in Suppes's research interests toward economics, psychology, and the behavioral sciences in general. The first was the influence of J. C. C. "Chen" McKinsey, Suppes's postdoctoral tutor at Stanford. McKinsey (1908–1953) was a logician who had worked intensively on game theory at the RAND Corporation.[5] In 1951, having been forced to leave RAND because his homosexuality was considered a security risk (Nasar 1998), McKinsey joined Stanford's philosophy department. At the time, he was completing his *Introduction to the Theory of Games* (McKinsey 1952), which would become the first textbook in game theory.

From McKinsey, Suppes learned not only game theory but also the set-theoretical methods that would play a crucial role in his subsequent work. McKinsey also encouraged Suppes to attend the seminar conducted by eminent logician Alfred Tarski at the University of California at Berkeley. According to Suppes (1979, 8), "it was from McKinsey and Tarski

4. Suppes considered a set of objects, a binary relation between these objects interpretable as the inequality relation ≤, and a binary function interpretable as the operation of addition +. He put forward seven axioms concerning the set of objects, the relation ≤, and the operation + and proved that, although less restrictive than Hölder's, his axioms were nonetheless sufficient to warrant the measurability of the elements of the set in the unit-based, or ratio, sense. Suppes's seven axioms (1951, 164–165) are as follows: (1) ≤ is transitive; (2) + is closed in the set of objects K; (3) + satisfies the associative law; (4) if x, y, and z are in K, and $x \leq y$, then $(x + z) \leq (y + z)$, that is, "adding" the same element does not alter order; (5) if x and y are in K, and not $(x \leq y)$, then there is a z in K such that $x \leq y + z$ and $y + z \leq x$, that is, any element x may be obtained by "summing" two other elements y and z; (6) if x and y are in K, then not $(x + y \leq x)$, that is, the "sum" is greater than the "summands"; (7) if x and y are in K and $x \leq y$, then there is a number n such that $y \leq nx$ (Archimedean property).

5. On RAND, see Leonard 2010; Erikson et al. 2013. On Alchian and RAND, see chapter 12, section 12.3.1.

that I learned about the axiomatic method and what it means to give a set-theoretical analysis of a subject."[6]

The second and possibly more powerful factor that contributed to shift Suppes's research interests toward the behavioral sciences was funding.

13.3.2. The Stanford Value Theory Project

In 1953, McKinsey and Suppes obtained significant grants from the Ford Foundation and two military agencies, the Office of Naval Research and the Office of Ordnance Research of the US Army, for work on the theory of decisions involving risk. The project was named the Stanford Value Theory Project (Isaac 2013; Suppes 1979).[7] McKinsey and Suppes co-opted Davidson into the enterprise. Davidson (1917–2003), another philosopher, had joined Stanford's philosophy department in 1951 and by this point had not yet published the work on the philosophy of mind and action for which he is known today. In the 1950s, he was still busy with teaching and did not yet have a clear philosophical project. As he explained in a later interview: "Suppes and McKinsey took me under their wing . . . because they thought this guy [i.e., Davidson] really ought to get some stuff out" (Lepore 2004, 252).

Most of the research connected with the Stanford Value Theory Project was conducted from 1953 to 1955 and appeared in print from 1955 to 1957. However, McKinsey contributed only to the first part of the project; in October 1953, he committed suicide. The final output consisted of three articles, all of a theoretical character (Davidson, McKinsey, and Suppes, 1955; Suppes and Winet 1955; Davidson and Suppes 1956), and the experimental study in which we are interested here.

Davidson and Suppes began thinking about the experiment in November 1953. However, as neither had any previous experience in experimental investigation, they therefore brought Siegel into the project. Siegel (1916–1961), then completing his Ph.D. in psychology at Stanford, had begun his doctoral studies in 1951 at the age of thirty-five, after having taken a rather singular educational path (Engvall Siegel 1964). In the doctoral dissertation he completed in fall 1953, Siegel (1954) presented a possible measure of authoritarianism based on experimental techniques.

Davidson, Suppes, and Siegel conducted their experiment in spring 1954. They presented their experimental results in a Stanford Value Theory Project report published in August 1955 and then, two years later, in the book *Decision Making: An Experimental Approach* (1957). On the book's cover, the work is presented as coauthored by Davidson and Suppes "in collaboration with Sidney Siegel," who meanwhile had moved to Pennsylvania State University. In practice, it is difficult to disentangle the individual contributions to the experiment, and therefore, in the following, I treat it as a joint product.

6. See more on McKinsey's scientific contributions and personality in Davidson, Goheen, and Suppes 1954; Lepore 2004; Burdman Feferman and Feferman 2004. This last book is also a good reference for Tarski's work in logic.

7. On why in the 1950s the Ford Foundation and military agencies such as the Office of Naval Research were interested in funding research on decision-making, see Pooley and Solovey 2010; Erikson et al. 2013; Herfeld 2017.

13.3.3. Measuring Utility

The primary aim of Davidson, Suppes, and Siegel was "to develop a psychometric technique for measuring utility" in an interval scale, that is, in a cardinal way, within the EUT framework (1957, 25). In particular, they were "originally inspired by the desire to see whether it was possible to improve on Mosteller and Nogee's results" (20).

The general structure of the Mosteller–Nogee and Davidson–Suppes–Siegel experiments is analogous. In the measuring part of their experiment, Davidson, Suppes, and Siegel attempted to elicit the von Neumann–Morgenstern utility function u of nineteen male Stanford students on the basis of their preferences in gambles where small amounts of money were at stake. Like Mosteller and Nogee, they interpreted the elicited utility function u as if it measured the utility of riskless money for each subject.

However, they modified a number of the elements of the Mosteller–Nogee design in order to make the decision tasks faced by their experimental subjects more psychologically friendly than those faced by the Mosteller–Nogee subjects. In this way, they attempted to avoid confusions or biases in their subjects, thereby generating utility measures as similar as possible to those that would have been obtained if the choices had been made by consistent EUT decision makers. To understand how they managed to do this, we must enter into the technical details of their experimental design, which we will discuss by way of the six elements considered in relation to the Mosteller–Nogee design (section 13.1.3).

13.3.4. Design

1. *Real money*. Like Mosteller and Nogee, Davidson, Suppes, and Siegel used real monetary payoffs. In particular, the gambles' payoffs ranged from –35 cents to +50 cents. The use of real money was motivated by philosophical preoccupations very much in accord with those expressed by Friedman and Wallis in their critique of Thurstone's experiment. Davidson, Suppes, and Siegel (1957, 7), in fact, followed the behaviorist approach to human agency advocated by Bertrand Russell (1921) and Ramsey ([1926] 1950), downplaying the relevance of introspection for decision analysis and arguing that "it is with actual decision-making behavior that decision theory is concerned."

2. *Subjective probabilities*. While the Mosteller–Nogee experiment was based on objective probabilities, Davidson, Suppes, and Siegel explicitly advocated a subjective approach to probability and followed the Ramsey–Savage subjective version of EUT. Accordingly, they considered gambles of the form "x cents of dollar if event E occurs, –y cents of dollars if event E does not occur"—for brevity, [x¢, E; –y¢, not-E]—whereby each subject was supposed to assign his subjective probabilities $\pi(E)$ and $\pi(\text{not-E})$ to the two events. However, and as explained in section 13.2, if subjective probabilities are unknown, the expected utility formula cannot be used to elicit the utility function u.

Davidson, Suppes, and Siegel cited the articles by Preston and Baratta (1948) and Edwards (1954a) showing that individuals often distort objective probabilities and therefore were well aware that the problem could not be solved by choosing events with apparently straightforward objective probabilities, such as heads or tails in tossing a coin. Moreover, in the pilots of their experiment (1957, 51), they found that their subjects often preferred gamble [x¢, heads; –x¢, tails] to gamble [–x¢, heads; x¢, tails], showing that they considered heads more probable than tails. They eventually solved the problem by constructing a special die with a nonsense syllable, ZOJ, on three faces and another nonsense syllable, ZEJ, on the other three.[8] In a pilot experiment, they verified that subjects treated the event "the syllable ZOJ comes up when tossing a die" and the event "the syllable ZEJ comes up when tossing a die" as equally likely.

3. *Simple probabilities.* In using the ZEJ and ZOJ events, Davidson, Suppes, and Siegel not only solved the problem associated with the identification of subjective probabilities but also avoided the psychologically tricky odds that the Mosteller–Nogee subjects were presented with. If experimental subjects understand fifty-fifty gambles better than gambles with more complex odds, then the utility measures obtained from their choices between ZOJ–ZEJ gambles are more reliable than the measures obtained from their choices between complicated lotteries such as those used by Mosteller and Nogee.

4. *Gamble versus gamble.* In order to address the problem represented by the possibility that gambling itself may have a positive or negative utility, Davidson, Suppes, and Siegel presented the experimental subjects with two proper gambles rather than, as Mosteller and Nogee had done, a proper gamble and a sure amount of money corresponding to the status quo. In fact, they observed (1957, 23), if gambling has a positive or negative utility, the utility measures obtained in the gamble-versus-sure-outcome situation would be distorted, respectively, downward or upward. In contrast, in the gamble-versus-gamble situations, the utilities for gambling associated with the two bets should cancel out, leading to more precise utility measures.

5. *Money versus probability.* In the Davidson–Suppes–Siegel experiment, the payoffs of all gambles had the same probability, namely 0.5. Accordingly, the identification of indifferent gambles was necessarily based on modification of the monetary payoff at stake in the gambles. In this respect, the experiment was similar to the Mosteller–Nogee one, and both employed the money equivalence method to measure utility.

6. *Approximate indifference.* Like Mosteller and Nogee, Davidson, Suppes, and Siegel faced the problem of identifying an empirical correlate of the notion of indifference. They could not follow Mosteller and Nogee and use Thurstone's probabilistic definition of indifference, because their subjects did not change their minds when confronted more than once with the same pair of gambles. For them, this outcome was chiefly due to the fact that their gambles were simpler than those used by Mosteller and Nogee.

They thus adopted a definition of indifference according to which two gambles G_1 and G_2 are indifferent if G_1 is preferred to G_2, but, by adding one single cent to one of G_2's payoffs, the new gamble G_2^* is preferred to G_1. For instance, if a subject prefers

8. According to Alberta Engvall Siegel (1964, 9), Siegel's second wife, it was Siegel who came up with the idea of the ZOJ–ZEJ die: "A central problem [in the experiment] was identifying an event which had subjective probability .50 for the subject, and Sid devised a zero-association nonsense-syllable die to serve as this event." I have found no evidence confirming or disproving this claim. In their autobiographies, Davidson (1999) and Suppes (1979) tend to downplay Siegel's role in the experiment (Davidson does not even mention Siegel), but they do not discuss the paternity of the ZOJ–ZEJ die.

G_1 = [15¢, ZOJ; −12¢, ZEJ] to G_2 = [11¢, ZOJ; −9¢, ZEJ] but prefers G_2^* = [12¢, ZOJ; −9¢, ZEJ] to G_1, then G_1 and G_2 are said to be indifferent. This is an approximate definition of indifference in the sense that it only allows the statement that there exists some amount of money z included between 11¢ and 12¢ such that [z¢, ZOJ; −9¢, ZEJ] is indifferent to G_1. Because of this approximate definition of indifference, Davidson, Suppes, and Siegel elicited the bounds of the subjects' utility curves u rather than the utility curves themselves.

13.3.5. Findings

In the measuring part of their experiment, Davidson, Suppes, and Siegel managed to elicit the bounds of the utility curves u of fifteen of their nineteen experimental subjects. The subjects' utility curves were presented in graphs like the one reproduced here in figure 13.2, which refers to subject 1.

Like Mosteller and Nogee, they did not find a uniform shape of the utility curves: the curves of ten subjects were convex for wins (risk seeking) and concave for losses (risk aversion), the curves of two subjects displayed the opposite trend, while the utility curves of the remaining three subjects were fundamentally linear (risk neutrality).

In the second part of the experiment, they reelicited the utility curves of ten of the original fifteen experimental subjects from their choices regarding the same set of lotteries used in the first part and found that for nine subjects, the utility curves elicited in the two parts were in fact very similar. Thus, like Mosteller and Nogee, they arrived at an optimistic conclusion to their experimental study, arguing that measuring cardinal utility experimentally appears feasible: "The chief experimental result may be interpreted as showing that for some individuals and under appropriate circumstances it is possible to measure utility in an interval scale" (19).

This result, in turn, supported the thesis that "an individual makes choices among alternatives involving risk as if he were trying to maximize expected utility" (26).[9]

9. In 1955, and without Siegel's collaboration, Davidson and Suppes performed another experiment, this time aimed at measuring the utility of nonmonetary objects, namely LP records, rather than the utility of money (published as chap. 3 of Davidson, Suppes, and Siegel 1957, 84–103). The significance of the experiment, however, was marred by the high number of intransitive choices observed by Davidson and Suppes, which were probably due to the fact that most students perceived the LPs as too similar. Independently of Davidson and Suppes, Siegel also conducted some further experiments aimed at measuring the utility of nonmonetary objects, such as books and cigarettes (Siegel 1956; Hurst and Siegel 1956). These experiments aimed at measuring utility according to the so-called "higher-ordered metric scale," which is weaker than the interval measurement scale associated with cardinal utility. In particular, Hurst and Siegel (1956) used EUT and the higher-ordered metric measurement of utility to predict the decisions of their experimental subjects between pairs of gambles. They found that these predictions were fairly accurate, so that, they argued, EUT was confirmed.

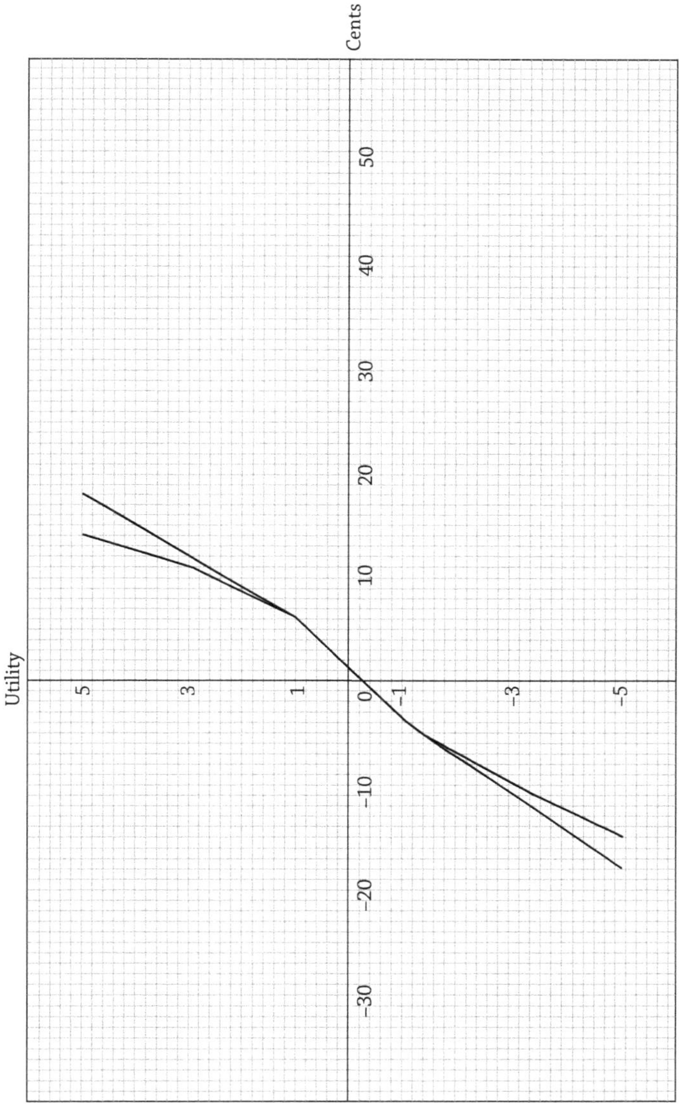

Figure 13.2. Utility curve elicited by Davidson, Suppes, and Siegel
Bounds for the utility curve u of experimental subject 1. The two continuous lines are the bounds within which the "true" utility curve lies. The bounds are drawn for the utility values −5, −3, −1, +1, +3, +5, which are connected by straight lines.
Source: Davidson, Suppes, and Siegel 1957, 63. Reproduced with permission of Stanford University Press.

13.3.6. Comment

In designing their experiment, Davidson, Suppes, and Siegel took into account a number of psychological phenomena that Mosteller and Nogee had neglected, such as the fact that actual individuals may distort objective probabilities or get confused when facing gambles with complicated odds. If considered from the viewpoint of EUT, these phenomena may be seen as disturbing factors that jeopardize the validity of the theory and spoil the significance of the experimental measurements of utility. However, Davidson, Suppes, and Siegel took those aspects of the psychology of decision-making into account mostly in order to neutralize them. One may say that they took into consideration the psychology of decision only so as to induce their experimental subjects to behave like brave EUT decision makers. It is not therefore very surprising that they concluded that utility is measurable and EUT validated.

In terms of the problem of indirect measurement, they considered that the functional relationship connecting the measurand u with the observable variable y may not be the expected utility relationship y = F(u, p) but can have a more complex functional form y = G(u, p, w, k, z, . . .), where w is the subjective distortion of objective probabilities, k is the pleasure of gambling, z is a factor reflecting the fact that people understand money better then probability, and so on. Davidson, Suppes, and Siegel attempted to neutralize the disturbing factors w, k, z, . . . so as to anchor their indirect measurement of u to the "original," well-defined, and much simpler expected utility relationship y = F(u, p).

With respect to the interpretation of the measured utility function u, Davidson, Suppes, and Siegel, like Mosteller and Nogee, interpreted it as the traditional utility function U. Accordingly, they held that they had measured the utility of money (on an interval scale). While Mosteller and Nogee's interpretation was in line with the dominant interpretation of the function u when their experiment was conducted, in the case of Davidson, Suppes, and Siegel, this was no longer the case. As discussed in chapters 11 and 12, by the mid-1950s, the majority of utility theorists working on EUT accepted the view that the cardinal properties of u, such as its concavity, cannot be interpreted as if they expressed cardinal concepts associated with the traditional utility function U, such as diminishing marginal utility. As Friedman, Savage, and others had made clear, this is due to the fact that the von Neumann–Morgenstern function u is elicited from the individual's preferences between risky alternatives and therefore conflates all possible factors that may influence these preferences, not only the individual's desire for money captured by the function U but also his attitude toward risk, the way he may subjectively distort the objective probabilities of the payoffs, the pleasure or displeasure he may associate with the very act of gambling, and possibly other factors. Why, then, did Davidson, Suppes, and Siegel maintain the pre-1950 interpretation of the nature of u?

I surmise that this was because they were not economists and did not share the instrumentalist interpretation of utility that, also thanks to the rise of Friedman's as-if methodology, became dominant among economists dealing with utility in the 1950s (see chapter 12). To give a quantitative determination to a hypothetical object, which does not have any clear psychological interpretation and is only useful for predicting choices, may be appealing for economists interested in, say, the demand for insurance but is not very interesting to a philosopher or a psychologist who wants to understand how human agency works. These noneconomists were interested in measuring a "thing" with a clear psychological correlate in the individual's mind and, lacking any better psychological interpretation, identified that "thing" with the utility of riskless money.

Also of relevance for our narrative is that the mentalist interpretation Davidson, Suppes, and Siegel gave to the function u shaped the design of their experiment. It is because they wanted to measure the utility of money that they attempted to neutralize other factors that may affect the shape of the utility function u—such as the subjective distortion of objective probabilities or the pleasure in gambling—and so spoil the significance of the utility measures obtained.

13.3.7. Reception

The Davidson–Suppes–Siegel experiment was discussed in the economics literature of the late 1950s, often in connection with the Mosteller–Nogee experiment, but it made less impact. In *Games and Decisions*, which quickly became a key reference point for economists working in decision analysis, Duncan Luce and Howard Raiffa (1957) summarized the methods used by Mosteller–Nogee and Davidson–Suppes–Siegel to measure utility, praised the latter experiment as "the most elegant in the area," but they pointed out that the two experiments' utility measures do not appear replicable or applicable outside the laboratory. Despite this limitation, which today we would call an external validity problem, Luce and Raiffa argued that laboratory attempts to measure utility are worth undertaking in order to see "if under any conditions, however limited, the postulates of the model can be confirmed" (37).

In the *American Economic Review*, Ellsberg (1958) criticized the armchair method typically used in the economic theory of decision-making and praised Davidson, Suppes, and Siegel for their effort to turn the utility notion into a genuine empirical variable and actually measure it: "Without an attempt to fit numbers into propositions, without the vital interaction of hypotheses with data, decision theory must remain largely without content: advice that does not advise, predictions that do not predict. The authors of this volume . . . take the radical step of dirtying their hands with actual experimental data" (1009).

Ellsberg, however, made an external-validity point similar to Luce and Raiffa's: he doubted that the utility measures that Davidson, Suppes, and Siegel had obtained for monetary amounts ranging from –35 cents to +50 cents could be extrapolated to the larger monetary amounts "that would really be interesting to an economist" (1010). Ellsberg also argued that although the subjective version of EUT adopted by Davidson, Suppes, and Siegel can explain choice behavior in some uncertain situations, "there are important classes of uncertain situations in which normal people will systematically *violate* [it]" (1010). Ellsberg did not illustrate which uncertain situations he had in mind, but with hindsight, one cannot avoid thinking of the kinds of situations he presented in his celebrated 1961 article on "Risk, Ambiguity, and the Savage Axioms" (see chapter 16).

In a review article titled "Utilities, Attitudes, Choices," published in *Econometrica*, Arrow (1958, 12) praised "the revival of interest in the measurability of utility" based on experimental techniques and argued that the results of the Mosteller–Nogee and Davidson–Suppes–Siegel experiments were "generally consistent" with EUT. Like Luce, Raiffa, and Ellsberg, however, Arrow noted that the two experiments' results appear hardly generalizable to situations different from the very specific ones designed in them.

13.4. SUPPES AND WALSH'S INEQUALITIES

Around 1958, Suppes conducted another experiment in which he and his student Karol Valpreda Walsh measured the utility of money using an elicitation method different from those adopted by Mosteller–Nogee and Davidson–Suppes–Siegel. Suppes and Walsh did not ask the experimental subjects—eight sailors from a US Navy airbase in the San Francisco Bay area—to identify the monetary amount that made two gambles indifferent. Rather, they asked the sailors to choose one of two gambles. This method is usually called the preference comparison method. Based on their choices and using linear programming techniques, Suppes and Walsh elicited the sailors' von Neumann–Morgenstern utility functions, which they interpreted as the sailors' utility functions for riskless money. The experiment benefited from comments by Marschak and was published in the July 1959 issue of *Behavioral Science*, a journal established in 1956 by Marschak and other eminent scholars as an outlet for interdisciplinary contributions to the theory of behavior (Suppes and Walsh 1959).

The basic idea behind the Suppes–Walsh linear programming technique can be illustrated as follows. Consider four amounts of money $\$M_1$, $\$M_2$, $\$M_3$, $\$M_4$, such that $\$M_1 > \$M_2 > \$M_3 > \$M_4$. If people like money, it is reasonable to assume that $u(\$M_1) > u(\$M_2) > u(\$M_3) > u(\$M_4)$. Consider now two fifty-fifty lotteries [$\$M_1$, 0.5; $\$M_4$, 0.5] and [$\$M_2$, 0.5; $\$M_3$, 0.5]. According to EUT, if we observe a subject choosing the former lottery over the second, we can infer that for him, $u(\$M_1) \times 0.5 + u(\$M_4) \times 0.5 > u(\$M_2) \times 0.5 + u(\$M_3) \times 0.5$, that is, $u(\$M_1) - u(\$M_2) > u(\$M_3) - u(\$M_4)$. This inequality provides information about the subject's utility function u. The key idea of the linear programming method is that by observing a sufficiently large number of choices, and thus by obtaining a sufficiently large number of inequalities of this type, we can estimate the subject's utility curve u with satisfactory precision.

In the first part of the experiment, Suppes and Walsh asked each of the eight sailors to choose his preferred lottery in a series of pairs of fifty-fifty, ZOJ–ZEJ gambles. Based on their choices, Suppes and Walsh measured the utility of seven amounts of real money ranging from −39¢ to +42¢ and constructed the utility curves u of each sailor. Unlike Mosteller–Nogee and Davidson–Suppes–Siegel, they did not discuss the shape of the elicited utility curves but noted only that their curvature "varied considerably from subject to subject" (205 n. 3).

In the second part of the experiment, they used these utility curves to predict the sailors' choices between ZOJ–ZEJ lotteries with payoffs different from those considered in the first part. They tested these predictions not only in terms of absolute goodness of fit with choice data but also in comparison with the goodness of fit of a choice model alternative to EUT, namely the actuarial model. According to this latter model, individuals prefer the lottery with the highest expected value rather than the highest expected utility.

Suppes and Walsh argued that EUT performed well in terms of both absolute and comparative goodness of fit. Concerning the former, out of 560 predictions based on EUT, "only 53 [were] wrong" (1959, 209). With respect to comparative goodness of fit, they concluded that the statistical tests they considered "indicate clear predictive superiority for the utility model" over the actuarial model (210).

As we will see in next chapter, a number of aspects of the Suppes–Walsh experimental design were adopted a few years later by Trenery Dolbear. Apart from Dolbear and Marschak, however, the Suppes–Walsh experiment does not seem to have been much noticed by economists.

13.5. THE AGE OF CONFIDENCE I: SUMMING UP

The three groups of scholars engaged in the EUT-based experimental measurement of the utility of money in the 1950s, namely Mosteller–Nogee, Davidson–Suppes–Siegel, and Suppes–Walsh, concluded that their findings supported the experimental measurability of cardinal utility, as well as the descriptive validity of EUT. Commentators such as Luce, Raiffa, Arrow, and Ellsberg were less optimistic and considered the results of the experiments hardly extendable to more realistic situations. But even under their pessimistic interpretation, the findings of the three experiments did not contradict EUT, and in this sense they "corroborated" it.

This corroborating outcome was in part due to the design strategy adopted by the experimenters. Mosteller and Nogee used their psychological insights, for example, that people understand amounts of money better than probabilities, to simplify the decision tasks faced by their experimental subjects and thus eliminate factors that could confuse them and lead to anomalous choices. Davidson, Suppes, and Siegel pushed this strategy further, presenting their experimental subjects only with easily comprehensible fifty-fifty gambles, ruling out subjective distortions of objective probabilities, and neutralizing the effects of the utility of gambling. Suppes and Walsh also focused on fifty-fifty gambles for which subjective distortions of probabilities were ruled out.

The design strategies these three experiments adopted may be seen as too favorable to EUT. However, following Kenneth Binmore (1999), one may argue that the empirical implications of a scientific theory should be tested, in the first place, under "ideal" conditions, that is, conditions that are as similar as possible to the theoretical assumptions from which the implications are deduced. This approach to theory testing should be applied especially to new scientific theories, as EUT was at the time, in order to give them a "best shot." Only at a later stage should one check what happens when ideal conditions are departed from, possibly not so much to reject the theory but to identify the boundaries within which it is valid. According to this methodological stance, the testing strategy adopted by Mosteller–Nogee, Davidson–Suppes–Siegel, and Suppes–Walsh was not excessively favorable to EUT but was rather a sound one.[10] As we will see in chapter 16, however, from the late 1960s, experimenters adopted a different, if not opposite, testing strategy.

Concerning the shape of the utility curves of the experimental subjects, that is, their attitude toward risk, the experiments of the 1950s were inconclusive: they only showed that the curvature and thus the risk attitude vary significantly from subject to subject. A different and more clear-cut finding—for example, that the large majority of subjects are risk-averse—would have been more fruitful for possible applications of EUT. Probably because of this inconclusive finding, the goal of checking the shape of the subjects' utility curves lost importance in the experiments performed after 1960.

10. I owe this observation to Francesco Guala.

CHAPTER 14

Marschak and Utility Measurement at Yale

The Age of Confidence II, 1960–1965

This chapter continues the history of the experimental attempts to measure the von Neumann–Morgenstern utility function initiated in chapter 13 by discussing two laboratory experiments performed at Yale University in the early 1960s. Jacob Marschak, whom we have already encountered at many points in our narrative, contributed directly or indirectly to both.

14.1. MARSCHAK AND THE THEORY OF STOCHASTIC CHOICE

As we saw in chapters 10 and 11, from 1943, Marschak worked at the Cowles Commission, then located at the University of Chicago. Around 1950, he accepted expected utility theory (EUT), mainly because he saw in it a compelling normative theory of rational behavior. In the early 1950s, however, he became increasingly attentive to deviations of actual behavior from rational behavior, not only in risky situations but also in the absence of uncertainty. As mentioned in chapter 13, section 13.2, at the 1952 Paris conference he even suggested that adopting a stochastic approach to choice that built on Mosteller and Nogee's probabilistic notion of indifference could accommodate deviations of actual behavior from rational behavior.

According to the stochastic approach, when a subject chooses between the same pair of alternatives x and y more than once, because of judgment errors, distraction, or other factors, sometimes he ranks x over y and sometimes y over x. The subject is said to prefer x to y if the probability p_{xy} that he chooses x over y is at least 0.5, that is, if $p_{xy} \geq 0.5$, and to be indifferent between x and y if $p_{xy} = 0.5$. A number of behaviors incompatible with a nonprobabilistic theory of decision-making, such as that the individual first chooses x over y and then y over x, can be accommodated by the stochastic element of the model. Marschak's first publications on stochastic choice theory appeared in the mid-1950s ([1954] 1974; [1955] 1974).[1]

Mainly because of tensions with Milton Friedman and other members of Chicago's economics department, in 1955, the Cowles Commission moved from Chicago to Yale University, where it also changed its name to the Cowles Foundation for Research in Economics.[2] Marschak followed the commission to Yale, but in 1960, he left for the Western Management Science Institute at UCLA.

From 1955 to 1960, the stochastic theory of choice was one of Marschak's main research themes (another was the economic theory of teams), and he investigated it on both the theoretical and the experimental level (Marschak [1960] 1974, Block and Marschak [1960] 1974). In particular, he coauthored one experimental article on stochastic choice with Donald Davidson, whom Marschak had met in 1955–1956 during a sabbatical year spent at the Center for Advanced Study in the Behavioral Sciences at Stanford (Davidson and Marschak [1959] 1974).[3]

14.2. DOLBEAR'S STOCHASTIC EUT

The first of the two Yale experiments on utility measurement was performed by Trenery Dolbear as part of his Ph.D. dissertation. Dolbear (born 1935) entered Yale as a graduate student in the fall of 1957, and Marschak helped arouse his interest in choice behavior: "Marschak's presence and his interest in choices by individuals, often involving aspects of expected utility . . . and experiments were clearly an important exposure for many of us" (email to the author, July 13, 2016).

14.2.1. Background

Dolbear's idea of conducting an experimental study on EUT arose out of an initial interaction with Alan Manne, an associate professor of economics at Yale from 1956 to 1961, who in 1952 had criticized Mosteller and Nogee's interpretation of their own experimental findings as overly optimistic (see chapter 13, section 13.1.5). Manne was also interested in the Davidson–Suppes–Siegel experiments, and in 1960, he hired Dolbear to develop some offshoots from them. During the summer of 1960, Dolbear and Manne, along with William Brainard, another graduate student, and psychologist Gordon Maurice Becker, who was then visiting the Cowles Foundation, conducted a pilot experiment that built on the Davidson–Suppes–Siegel study but was never published. After this first joint experiment,

1. In the second half of the 1950s, the stochastic approach to choice became a hot research topic drawing contributions from economists such as Quandt (1956) and Debreu (1958) and mathematical psychologists such as Luce (1957; 1958; 1959). See more on the history of stochastic choice theory in Lenfant 2018. On Luce, see chapter 15.

2. See more on the tensions between the Cowles Commission and Chicago's department of economics in Boumans 2016.

3. See more on Marschak and the evolution of his research interests in Cherrier 2010.

Dolbear began conceiving of his own experimental study, and an important input in this phase came from Marschak, who suggested that he employ a "stochastic model of choice" (Dolbear 1963, 428).

As supervisor for his dissertation, Dolbear chose William Fellner, a macroeconomist who in the late 1950s and early 1960s had become interested in the theory of choice under uncertainty and had conducted some experiments with Yale students to analyze their attitudes toward uncertain events with unknown probabilities (Fellner 1961). Dolbear carried out his experiment in June and July 1962 and published his findings in the fall 1963 issue of *Yale Economic Essays*.

14.2.2. Design

Dolbear extended the stochastic approach, which Marschak and others had usually applied to choices between riskless alternatives, to choices between lotteries. In particular, Dolbear assumed that (1) when an individual is confronted with a pair of lotteries A and B, he will choose more frequently the lottery with the higher expected utility; (2) the probability p_{AB} of choosing lottery A over lottery B is an increasing function Φ of the difference between the expected utility of A, indicated as EU_A, and the expected utility of B, indicated as EU_B: $p_{AB} = \Phi[EU_A - EU_B]$.[4]

Dolbear's stochastic version of EUT allows measurement of the von Neumann–Morgenstern utility u of the lotteries' payoffs through a maximum-likelihood estimation approach. The basic idea is that given the model $p_{AB} = \Phi[EU_A - EU_B]$, by observing a sufficient number of a subject's choices between lotteries, and thus by recording the frequencies p_{AB} with which the subject chooses one lottery over the other, it is possible to identify the utilities u of the payoffs that make the recorded frequencies p_{AB} the most likely ones.

Evidently, in Dolbear's design, the functional relationship between the measurand u and the observable variable y, that is, the subject's choices between lotteries, is much more complex than it is in the Mosteller–Nogee and Davidson–Suppes–Siegel designs. Probably for this reason, Dolbear avoided identifying the elicited utilities u with the utilities U of riskless money and consistently called the estimated values of u "Neumann–Morgenstern utilities."

Ten subjects participated in Dolbear's experiment. Five were students at Yale, and five were prospective pilots studying at Yale's Air Force Language School. Like Suppes and Walsh, Dolbear did not ask the experimental subjects to identify an amount of money making two lotteries indifferent (money equivalence method) but had them choose the preferred lottery in pairs of two-payoff lotteries (preference comparison method). The lotteries had monetary payoffs ranging from –\$1 to \$9.75. The money at stake in the lotteries was

4. In particular, Dolbear used the exponential function $\Phi[EU_A - EU_B] = 1 - \frac{1}{2}e^{-[EU_A - EU_B]}$ and justified this choice by arguing that such a function is computationally convenient and satisfies a number of reasonable properties. For instance, if two lotteries have the same expected utility, then $p_{AB} = \Phi[EU_A - EU_B] = 0.5$, that is, they have the same probability of being selected.

real, and the monetary amounts were much more significant than those used by Mosteller–Nogee, Davidson–Suppes–Siegel, and Suppes–Walsh.

14.2.3. Findings

In the first part of the experiment, Dolbear used only fifty-fifty lotteries and measured the utility of the payoffs using the maximum-likelihood estimation procedure just outlined. As in previous experiments, the elicited utility curves did not display any clearly dominant shape: the curves of four subjects were fundamentally concave, the curve of one subject was convex for most of its extension, one curve was almost linear, and the utility curves of the remaining four subjects displayed mixed shapes, being partly concave and partly convex.

In the second part of the experiment, Dolbear used the obtained measures to predict further choices between non-fifty-fifty lotteries and thus test the descriptive validity of his stochastic version of EUT. Like Suppes and Walsh, Dolbear tested EUT not only in terms of its absolute goodness of fit with choice data but also in comparison with the goodness of fit of other choice models: the actuarial model, already considered by Suppes and Walsh, and the maximin model, according to which individuals prefer the lottery with the highest minimum payoff. Dolbear found that for most subjects, the probabilistic version of EUT led to satisfactory predictions in terms of absolute goodness of fit and that those predictions were "statistically superior to actuarial maximization for 7 of the 10 subjects" and to maximin choice "for 8 of the 10 subjects" (Dolbear 1963, 418).

14.3. THE EXPERIMENT AND ELICITATION MECHANISM OF BECKER, DEGROOT, AND MARSCHAK

The second Yale experiment to measure utility was carried out by Marschak in association with Becker and Morris DeGroot.

14.3.1. The Trio

Becker (born in 1924) completed his Ph.D. in psychology at the University of Pittsburgh in 1956, and, as mentioned, in 1960, he visited the Cowles Foundation at Yale. He and Marschak there conducted some pilot experiments on the capacity of individuals to solve simple operations research problems. When Marschak moved to UCLA, he invited Becker to visit for the academic year 1960–1961.

DeGroot (1931–1989) was a statistician who graduated from the University of Chicago under Leonard J. Savage's supervision in 1957 and then moved to the Carnegie Institute of Technology. Marschak, who was a visitor at Carnegie in the academic year 1958–1959, introduced DeGroot to problems of utility and decision-making. He also invited DeGroot to spend the academic year 1960–1961 at UCLA. In that year, Becker, DeGroot, and

Marschak completed three articles on stochastic choice (1963a; 1963b; 1963c), in addition to writing up their experimental study on EUT-based utility measurement (1964). Their joint discussions also led DeGroot (1963) to write a paper pointing out a series of flaws in the statistical methods used by Suppes and Walsh in their experiment. All five articles were published in *Behavioral Science*.

Although the Becker–DeGroot–Marschak article on the experimental measurement of utility was published in 1964, the actual experiment appears to have been carried out at Yale in 1960. As they explain (1964, 230), the experimental subjects were "two male students obtained through the Yale Student Placement Office," and the experiment was conducted at the "Cowles Foundation for Economic Research, Yale University." However, according to the Cowles reports of research activities (Cowles Foundation 1961; 1964), from 1961 to 1964, the three did not visit Yale. Therefore, the experiment appears to have been carried out at some point in the first part of 1960, when Becker was visiting the Cowles Foundation and before Marschak left for UCLA at the end of June.

14.3.2. The Becker–DeGroot–Marschak Mechanism

Becker, DeGroot, and Marschak presented the two Yale students with two-payoff lotteries, where the payoffs consisted of real amounts of money ranging from 0¢ to 100¢. The only probabilities they used in the lotteries were 0.25, 0.50, and 0.75, because, they argued, "it did not seem unreasonable to assume that the simple probabilities ½ and (to a lesser extent) ¾ were 'understood' by the subject[s]" (1964, 227). By assuming (without loss of generality) that u(0¢) = 0 and u(100¢) = 1, the experimenters were able to calculate the expected utility of various lotteries. For instance, the expected utility of lottery [0¢, 0.5; 100¢, 0.5] is $0 \times 0.5 + 1 \times 0.5 = 0.5$.

To elicit the von Neumann–Morgenstern utility function u, they employed the certainty equivalence method; that is, they asked each student to determine the certainty equivalent of a given lottery, which is the amount $M of money for sure that made him indifferent to that lottery. Since, by construction, the certainty equivalent of a lottery has the same utility of the lottery, if the student's certainty equivalent of lottery [0¢, 0.5; 100¢, 0.5] is, say, 40¢, then u(40¢) = 0.5. In order to induce the subjects to reveal their true certainty equivalent, Becker, DeGroot, and Marschak introduced a cunning procedure.

They asked each subject to declare his certainty equivalent for a given lottery and told him that thereafter they would draw a number between 1 and 100 at random. If this number was equal to or higher than the declared certainty equivalent, the subject would receive an amount of cents equal to that number. If the drawn number was less, the subject would play the lottery and receive the payoff associated with the realized alternative.[5]

5. To continue the example used in the text, imagine that a subject states that, for him, the certainty equivalent of lottery [0¢, 0.5; 100¢, 0.5] is 40¢. Then the random number is drawn. If this number is equal to or higher than 40, say 82, the subject receives 82¢. If the drawn number is less than 40, say 17, the subject plays the lottery and gets either 0¢ or 100¢, each with probability 0.5.

Becker, DeGroot and Marschak showed that for a subject facing this situation, it is always optimal to declare his true certainty equivalent for the lottery. Under the name "BDM mechanism," this procedure quickly became a standard tool of experimental economics, not only to induce individuals to declare the true certain equivalent of a lottery but, more generally, to induce them to state the true price at which they are willing to sell any given object.[6]

14.3.3. Findings

Returning to the experiment, BDM presented each student with three series of twenty-four lotteries, for a total of seventy-two lotteries, and asked him to identify in a sequential manner the certainty equivalent for each lottery. BDM constructed each series of lotteries in such a way that several lotteries had the same expected utility.[7] If the student was an expected-utility maximizer, for him these lotteries should also have the same certainty equivalent. If this was not the case, EUT was violated.

Regarding the interpretation of the elicited utility values, BDM adopted the (by then) standard view among economists, also shared by Dolbear: the estimated utility values are not to be confused with the cardinal utility of riskless money, but are "numerical *constants*" (226) that can be used to predict the subject's choices between lotteries.

Becker, DeGroot, and Marschak found that the certainty equivalents of the lotteries with the same expected utility were often different, but also that the discrepancy between them decreased from session to session of the experiment. They interpreted these findings in a way favorable to EUT: they argued that as the subjects became more familiar with the experimental task, their behavior became "more consistent with an expected utility model," so that EUT could be admitted as an "approximate" model of observed behavior (230–232). Concerning the shape of the utility curves of the two subjects, they found that the curve of one student was almost linear, thus indicating his risk neutrality, while the curve of the other student was more convex, thus indicating attraction to risk.

14.4. THE AGE OF CONFIDENCE II: COMMENTS

If we compare the experimental studies of the 1950s with those of the 1960s, we see a modification in the relative weight given to the two goals of the experiments, namely the measurement goal and the theory-testing goal. In the studies of the 1950s, and especially in those of Mosteller–Nogee and Davidson–Suppes–Siegel, the goal of checking whether it is possible to measure the utility function u and assessing its curvature was important per se. In the

6. As became clear only later, if the subject's preferences do not satisfy the Independence Axiom or other assumptions of EUT, the use of the BDM mechanism as an elicitation device becomes problematic; see Karni and Safra 1987; Segal 1988.

7. For example, if 40¢ is the certainty equivalent of lottery [0¢, 0.5; 100¢, 0.5], then lottery [40¢, 0.5; 100¢, 0.5] and lottery [0¢, 0.25; 100¢, 0.75] have the same expected utility. In fact, u(40¢) = 0.5. Therefore, the expected utility of lottery [40¢, 0.5; 100¢, 0.5] is $0.5 \times 0.5 + 1 \times 0.5 = 0.75$. Also the expected utility of lottery [0¢, 0.25; 100¢, 0.75] is $0 \times 0.25 + 1 \times 0.75 = 0.75$.

experiments of the 1960s, by contrast, the measurement goal tended to become purely instrumental to the objective of testing the empirical validity of EUT.

Three factors would seem to have been at play in this modification. First, the early experiments had suggested that measuring the utility function u is indeed possible, thus making the "possibility question" less pressing. Moreover, the "shape question" also lost importance, because the experiments did not identify any dominant shape of the utility curve and only suggested that risk attitudes vary considerably from subject to subject. Finally, unlike the experiments of the 1950s, the experiments of the 1960s were performed by economists, namely Dolbear and Marschak, who accepted the by then standard economic interpretation of u. According to this interpretation, the estimated values of u do not measure the utility of riskless money but are "numerical constants" that can be used to predict individual choice behavior under risk.

With respect to the goal of theory testing, there was no discontinuity between the experimental studies of the 1950s and those of the 1960s. Mosteller–Nogee, Suppes–Walsh, Dolbear, and Becker–DeGroot–Marschak tested EUT using a similar approach: in the first part of their experiments, they obtained measures of the utility function u from the individual's choices regarding a first set of lotteries; in the second part, they used those measures and the EUT formula to predict the individual's choices regarding a second set of lotteries; finally, they checked whether the predictions were correct, in which case EUT was validated. Only Davidson–Suppes–Siegel adopted a different approach: in the second part of their experiment, they reelicited the utility functions of the experimental subjects from their choices between the same set of lotteries used in the first part, and, employing the same elicitation method, they then checked whether the utility functions elicited in the two sessions were sufficiently similar, in which case EUT was validated.

Even with respect to the interpretation of the experimental outcomes, there is no discontinuity between the experimental studies of the 1950s and those of the 1960s. Like Mosteller, Suppes, and their coauthors, Dolbear and Becker–DeGroot–Marschak also assessed their experimental findings as validating EUT: the theory was not 100 percent correct, but in a stochastic or approximate sense, it still appeared to be an acceptable descriptive theory of decision-making under risk. Also in terms of comparative goodness of fit, EUT performed better than alternative decision models such as the actuarial and the maximin models.

A final comment on the five experiments of the 1950s and 1960s is that overall, three different procedures to measure utility were used: Mosteller–Nogee and Davidson–Suppes–Siegel employed the money equivalence method, Becker–DeGroot–Marschak adopted the certainty equivalence method, while Suppes–Walsh and Dolbear utilized the preference comparison method. However, none of the five groups of experimenters investigated the question of whether these different but theoretically equivalent methods to measure utility in fact generated the same utility measures.[8]

8. In the 1960s, a number of management scientists and applied economists performed field experiments to measure the utility of money of real economic operators, such as oil and gas operators (Grayson 1960), managers of a chemical firm (Green 1963), executives in engineering companies (Swalm 1966), or beef-cattle farmers (Officer and Halter 1968). The design and goals of these field experiments, however, were significantly different from the laboratory experiments considered in this chapter and chapter 13. For instance, the economic operators had to express their preferences between conjectural gambles that were described as investment options for the

In the decade following Becker, DeGroot, and Marschak's 1964 article, apparently no further experimental studies on utility measurement were published. Nevertheless, the conceptual background of the experimental measurement of utility through EUT changed significantly. I discuss these developments in chapter 16. But before doing so, in chapter 15, I briefly reconstruct how Suppes's involvement with utility analysis stimulated him to elaborate the "representational theory of measurement" that later became the dominant view of measurement within measurement theory.

companies the operators worked for. Therefore, it was unclear whether the elicited utility functions were the personal utility functions of the operators or the utility functions that the operators attributed to their companies. Because of these differences, these field experiments have little relevance for our story here and therefore are not discussed. For a review of the main findings of this literature, see Fishburn and Kochenberger 1979.

CHAPTER 15

From Utility Measurement to the Representational Theory of Measurement

The Case of Suppes, 1950–1970

This chapter offers a conclusion to the history of measurement theory begun in chapter 1 and continued through chapters 4, 8, 9, and 12. In chapter 1, we saw that before and beyond the rise of marginal utility theory during the last decades of the nineteenth century, the unit-based conception of measurement dominated all fields of inquiry from their earliest origins, and the early marginalists (not unnaturally) adhered to that conception. In chapter 4, I examined the controversy over the notion of psychological measurement that engaged British physicists and psychologists in the 1930s. I remarked that despite the similarity between the debate on sensation differences in psychology and the almost contemporary debate on utility differences in utility theory, the two remained unconnected. As discussed in chapter 8, in psychology, the impasse was broken in the early 1940s, when Stanley Smith Stevens proposed a new definition of measurement as the assignment of numbers to objects according to a certain set of rules. Since there are various sets of rules for assigning numbers to objects, there are various forms, or scales, of measurement. Stevens's definition of measurement was broad enough to include the psychologists' quantification practices as measurement.

In the early 1940s, John von Neumann and Oskar Morgenstern put forward a theory of measurement that, while independent of Stevens's theory, presents a number of analogies with it. As I remarked in chapter 9, however, there are two major differences between the measurement theories of von Neumann–Morgenstern and Stevens. First, von Neumann and Morgenstern bound the possibility of proper measurement with the possibility of adding objects, and in this sense, their theory was less liberal than that of Stevens. Second, von Neumann and Morgenstern adopted an axiomatic approach and provided an explicit representation theorem connecting their axioms with the numerical measures of utility.

By contrast, axioms and representation theorems are absent from Stevens's approach to measurement.

In the late 1940s and early 1950s, von Neumann and Morgenstern's measurement theory had little impact on utility theorists. As I argued in chapter 12, the debate on expected utility theory (EUT) of the early and mid-1950s played for utility theory the same role that the controversy of the 1930s between psychologists and physicists had played for psychology. Utility theorists such as Milton Friedman, Leonard J. Savage, Robert Strotz, Armen Alchian, and Daniel Ellsberg came to conceive of utility measurement as the assignment of numbers to objects according to a definite set of operations. Utility measures so conceived are largely conventional, but they should allow prediction of the choice behavior of individuals. Despite the similarity between this conception of measurement and Stevens's, Friedman, Savage, and the other utility theorists mentioned here did not cite Stevens and apparently elaborated their conception of measurement independently of him.

To summarize, between the marginal revolution and the 1950s, there were few intersections between the history of the theory of measurement elaborated in physics, psychology, and other disciplines and the history of utility theory. The main exception was Louis Leon Thurstone, who played an important role in both the theory of sensation measurement and the experimental implementation of utility theory (see chapters 4 and 7). In this chapter, I show how in the 1950s and 1960s, the histories of measurement theory and utility theory intersected in an important way. In particular, I argue that the so-called representational theory of measurement—which was elaborated by Patrick Suppes and his coauthors, found its full-fledged expression in the book *Foundations of Measurement* (Krantz, Luce, Suppes, and Tversky 1971), and quickly became the dominant theory of measurement—has its origins in Suppes's research in utility theory within the Stanford Value Theory Project.

An initial remark on terminology is in order. In this work, I use the expression *representational theory of measurement* only to refer to the axiomatic version of the representational approach to measurement elaborated by Suppes and his coauthors. By contrast, Joel Michell (1999) and other historians of measurement theory (including myself in previous works, e.g., Moscati 2013b; 2016b) have used the label in a broader way, that is, to indicate any approach that defines measurement as the process of assigning numbers to represent properties. According to this broad use, not only Suppes but also Norman Robert Campbell, Ernest Nagel, and Stevens (see chapters 4 and 8) conceived of measurement in a representational way. I have come to believe, however, that this use of the label *representational theory of measurement* is misleading, because it conflates measurement theories, such as Campbell's and Stevens's, that are significantly different from each other. Accordingly, by representational theory of measurement here, I mean only the approach elaborated by Suppes and his coauthors.[1]

1. To avoid the same kind of confusion, Boumans (2015) chose a different strategy of terminology and labeled the theory of measurement elaborated by Suppes and his coauthors the "axiomatic theory of measurement."

15.1. FROM UNITS TO UTILITY DIFFERENCES

As discussed in chapter 13, section 13.3.1, Suppes had a background in physics and mathematics and before the early 1950s was not very familiar with economics, psychology, or the behavioral sciences in general. Unsurprisingly, therefore, he initially adhered to the unit-based conception of measurement that was dominant in physics and mathematics, and in his first article, he provided a set-theoretic axiomatization of unit-based measurement that built on the axiomatizations proposed by Otto Hölder ([1901] 1996) and Ernest Nagel (1931). Notably, in this article, Suppes (1951) did not cite Stevens (1946) or mention the latter's theory of measurement. As explained in chapter 13, sections 13.3.1 and 13.3.2, in the early 1950s, two main factors contributed to a shift in Suppes's research interests toward the behavioral sciences: interaction with McKinsey, Suppes's postdoctoral advisor at Stanford, and a substantial grant awarded in 1953 for work on the theory of decisions involving risk in what was named the Stanford Value Theory Project.

In October 1953, Suppes and his doctoral student Muriel Winet completed a first version of a Stanford Value Theory Project paper titled "An Axiomatization of Utility Based on the Notion of Utility Differences" (Suppes and Winet [1953] 1954). The paper was presented in November 1953 at a meeting of the American Mathematical Society and was later published in the April–July 1955 issue of the first volume of *Management Science*, a newly founded journal open to studies in decision theory from different disciplines.[2]

Suppes and Winet's work returns us to the debates of the 1930s on cardinal utility and utility differences within a riskless framework (see chapter 6). They advanced a set-theoretic axiomatization of cardinal utility based on the assumption that individuals not only are able to rank the utility of different alternatives, as is assumed in the ordinal approach to utility, but also are capable of ranking the differences between the utilities of those alternatives.

Suppes and Winet (1955, 259) noted that the notion of utility differences had been already discussed in economics and cited Oskar Lange's 1934a article on the topic. They also took a stance against the economists' opposition to introspection that since the mid-1930s had played a crucial role in the marginalization of utility differences in economic analysis. In particular, Suppes and Winet (1955, 261) claimed that in many areas of economic theory, "there is little reason to be ashamed of direct appeals to introspection" and that there are sound arguments for justifying "the determination of utility differences by introspective methods." They then pointed out that despite the importance and legitimacy of utility differences, an axiomatic treatment of them in the rigorous axiomatic style of von Neumann and Morgenstern was still missing:

> In the literature of economics . . . the notion of utility differences has been much discussed in connection with the theory of measurement of utility. However, to the best of our knowledge, no adequate axiomatization for this difference notion has yet been given at a level of

2. In 1957, Winet completed her Ph.D. at Stanford under Suppes with a dissertation on "Interval Measurement of Subjective Magnitudes with Subliminal Differences" (Wood Winet Gerlach 1957), a topic strictly related to that of the article coauthored with her adviser.

generality and precision comparable to the von Neumann and Morgenstern construction of a probabilistic scheme for measuring utility. (259)

Evidently, Suppes and Winet were ignorant of the fact that almost twenty years earlier, Franz Alt ([1936] 1971) had provided a rigorous axiomatization of cardinal utility anticipating their axiomatization in significant respects (see chapter 6, section 6.6.2).

Like Alt, Suppes and Winet considered two preference relations, which they labeled Q and R. Q is a standard, binary preference relation: xQy means that x is not preferred to y. R is a quaternary relation concerning "differences" or "intervals" between alternatives: (x,y) R(z,w) means that the interval between x and y is not greater than the interval between z and w. Suppes and Winet imposed eleven axioms on the relations Q and R and proved what they explicitly called a "representation theorem" (265): the axioms imply the existence of a function U that can be interpreted as a utility function, is unique up to linear increasing transformations, and is such that the interval between x and y is smaller than the interval between z and w if and only if the absolute utility difference between x and y is smaller than the absolute utility difference between z and w (265–270).[3] More formally, xQy if and only if $U(x) \leq U(y)$, and (x,y)R(z,w) if and only if $|U(x) - U(y)| \leq |U(z) - U(w)|$.[4]

Concerning the relationship between the cardinal utility function U they had obtained and the function u featured in EUT, Suppes and Winet adopted the same view as that of other noneconomists dealing with utility analysis in the 1950s, namely that the two functions are interchangeable (see chapter 13, sections 13.1.2 and 13.3.6). Accordingly, they argued that an individual should prefer lottery [x, 0.5; w, 0.5] to lottery [z, 0.5; y, 0.5], "if and only if the utility difference between x and y is less than that between z and w" (259).

Suppes and Winet referred to two articles Stevens had published before 1946 (Stevens 1936b; Stevens and Volkmann 1940) but did not mention Stevens's measurement theory, did not use his scale-of-measurement terminology, and, accordingly, did not label the cardinal utility U as utility measurable on an interval scale. Nevertheless, by identifying conditions that warrant the interval-scale measurement of an object, Suppes overcame the unit-based conception that confines measurement to ratio measurement. Suppes's superseding of the

3. Suppes and Winet's axioms are as follows. Axioms 1–4 require that both Q and R are complete and transitive. Axiom 5 imposes that only the "extension" of the interval between two elements x and y matters and not the relative order of x and y; thus, interval (x,y) is equivalent to interval (y,x). Axiom 6 states that any interval (x,y) can be bisected, that is, that for any two elements x and y, there exists a midpoint element t such that interval (x,t) is equivalent to interval (t,y). Axiom 7 states that if two elements x and y are indifferent, then one can be substituted for the other without modifying the order relationships among intervals: if xQy, yQx, and (x,z)R(u,v), then (y,z)R(u,v). Axiom 8 requires that if y is between x and z, then the interval between x and y is smaller than the interval between x and z. Axiom 9 is an additivity assumption on R: if interval (x,y) is smaller than interval (u,w) and interval (y,z) is smaller than interval (w,v), then the "sum" (x,z) of the two smaller intervals is smaller than the "sum" (u,v) of the two larger intervals. Axiom 10 imposes a continuity property: if interval (x,y) is strictly smaller than interval (u,v), then there is an element t between u and v such that interval (x,y) is still not greater than interval (u,t). Axiom 11 is an Archimedean assumption; it fundamentally states that each interval can be expressed as the sum of a finite sequence of smaller, equivalent intervals.

4. Baccelli and Mongin (2016) discuss the problems associated with Suppes and Winet's focus on absolute rather than simple (i.e., algebraic) utility differences.

unit-based view of measurement became more explicit in a paper he read at the annual meeting of the Pacific Division of the American Philosophical Association held at Stanford University in December 1953.

15.2. FROM ONE MEASUREMENT TO MANY MEASUREMENTS

This paper, which does not belong to those funded by the Stanford Value Theory Project, bore the title "Some Remarks on Problems and Methods in the Philosophy of Science" and was published the following year in *Philosophy of Science*. In this article, Suppes (1954) made various programmatic proposals for the advancement of the philosophy of science, some of which concerned the theory of measurement.

Suppes argued that the most urgent task facing the philosophy of science was "axiomatizing the theory of all developed branches of empirical science" (244). For Suppes, the axiomatization task could be divided into four steps: (1) listing the primitive notions of a given theory and characterizing them in set-theoretical terms; (2) indicating the axioms that the notions must satisfy; (3) investigating the deductive consequences of the axioms; (4) providing an empirical interpretation of the axiomatized theory. Suppes claimed that measurement theory relates to the fourth step and should show us how "we may legitimately pass from the rough and ready region of qualitative, common-sense observations to the precise and metrical realm of systematic science" (246).

At this point, Suppes explicitly asserted that there are "various types of measurement" and noted that in the literature, there are "several sets of axioms for measurement of different sorts" (246). As examples, he listed the measurement axioms put forward by Hölder ([1901] 1996), Nagel (1931), von Neumann and Morgenstern ([1944] 1953), Suppes (1951), and Suppes and Winet ([1953] 1954). In a footnote, he further noted that from a mathematical viewpoint, the task of axiomatizing a given type of measurement is equivalent to "the search for a representation theorem in the domain of real numbers, with the representation unique up to the appropriate transformations" (246 n. 9).

These last quoted passages show that by the end of 1953, Suppes had abandoned the unit-based understanding of measurement that had informed his 1951 article and now endorsed a new conception of measurement that combined elements of Stevens's and von Neumann and Morgenstern's views of measurement. Like Stevens, Suppes now conceived of measurement in a broad way and acknowledged that unit-based measurement is only one among many possible different types of measurement. Unlike Stevens but like von Neumann and Morgenstern, Suppes advocated an axiomatic approach, or, more specifically, a set-theoretical axiomatic approach, to measurement theory.

15.3. A COHERENT THEORY OF MEASUREMENT

A further step toward the elaboration of the representational theory of measurement can be found in the second installment of the Stanford Value Theory Project. This is the paper titled "Outlines of a Formal Theory of Value, I," which Suppes coauthored with Davidson and

McKinsey. McKinsey had read an earlier and much shorter version of the paper in May 1953 at a seminar at the UCLA. After his death in October 1953, Davidson and Suppes expanded and revised this paper, which was eventually published in the April 1955 issue of *Philosophy of Science.*

In their article, Davidson, McKinsey, and Suppes (1955, 141) put forward different sets of axioms identifying normative conditions for a "rational preference pattern" in choice behavior. In particular, they claimed that a rational preference pattern must satisfy transitivity, and in support of this claim, they advanced the argument for which their article is usually cited in the economics literature, namely the "money pump argument." Basically, Davidson, McKinsey, and Suppes showed that an individual with intransitive preferences—a hypothetical university professor they called Mr. S.—can be induced to pay money for nothing (145–146).[5] For our purposes, however, the most important part of their article is the aside on measurement theory contained in section 3.

In this section, the authors explicitly adopted the scale-of-measurement terminology and, without citing Stevens, introduced a classification of measurement scales that closely resembles the one introduced by the Harvard psychologist in 1946. They identified, in order of increasing strength, the "ordinal," "interval," and "ratio" scales, already discussed by Stevens, as well as an "absolute scale," which does not admit any arbitrary element and can be transformed only by the identity function $F(x) = x$. An example of a magnitude measurable according to the absolute scale is probability.

Furthermore, just as Stevens had done, Davidson, McKinsey, and Suppes criticized the traditional identification of measurement with ratio measurement as well as the association of measurability with the possibility of adding the objects to be measured. They argued that "this ratio requirement is too rigid" and that the erroneous identification of measurement with ratio measurement "lies in the assumption that the only things which are measurable in a strong sense are . . . magnitudes for which there exists a natural operation corresponding closely to the addition of numbers" (151). This error also "led to the erroneous view that no kind of measurement appropriate to physics is applicable to psychological phenomena" (151 n. 8).

Moving to the measurement of preferences, the authors agreed that preferences "cannot be measured in the sense of a ratio scale" but added that this circumstance does not exclude "the possibility . . . that preferences can be measured in the sense of an interval scale" (151), that is, by using a cardinal utility function, which latter view was the one they supported.

The aside on measurement concludes with a passage that defined the concept of "coherent theory of measurement." This definition expresses, succinctly but with great precision, the representational conception of measurement that Suppes was going to articulate in his subsequent works: "A coherent theory of measurement is given by specifying axiomatically conditions imposed on a structure of empirically realizable operations and relations. The theory is formally complete if it can be proved that any structure satisfying the axioms is isomorphic to a numerical structure of a given kind" (151).

5. For an introduction to the money pump argument, see Anand 1993.

15.4. EXPERIMENTS AND MEASUREMENT THEORY

Part of the Stanford Value Theory Project centered on the EUT-based experimental measurement of utility that I extensively discussed in chapter 13, sections 13.3.3, 13.3.4, and 13.3.5. Here I merely recall the measurement-theoretic view that underlay the measurement of utility performed by Davidson, Suppes, and Siegel. At the beginning of their book *Decision Making: An Experimental Approach*, the authors presented the role of the EUT axioms in representational terms: "We require that the axioms . . . permit us to prove (a) that it is possible to assign numbers to the elements of any set . . . in such a way as to preserve the structure imposed on such sets by the axioms, and (b) any two assignments of numbers . . . are related by some specified group of transformations" (Davidson, Suppes, and Siegel 1957, 5–6). In particular, they specified that the EUT axioms "yield interval measurement of utility" (6) and presented the findings of their experiment by using the scale-of-measurement terminology introduced by Stevens: "The chief experimental result may be interpreted as showing that for some individuals and under appropriate circumstances it is possible to measure utility in an interval scale" (19).

The book was the last research item of the Stanford Value Theory Project to be published. As we have seen, between the beginning of the project in 1953 and the publication of this last item in 1957, Suppes's views on measurement changed significantly. He moved beyond the unit-based understanding of measurement that he initially reckoned on, definitively embraced a broad notion of measurement similar to that of Stevens, and envisaged, under the label "a coherent theory of measurement," the project of a thoroughgoing axiomatization of that broad notion. His first decisive step toward the realization of this project was a paper he coauthored with Dana Scott.

15.5. THE CONCEPTUAL FRAMEWORK FOR THE REPRESENTATIONAL THEORY OF MEASUREMENT

Dana S. Scott (born 1932) studied mathematics and logic at the University of California at Berkeley, where he became a pupil of Alfred Tarski (Burdman Feferman and Feferman 2004). Suppes had met Scott in 1952, when the latter was an undergraduate student in a course on the philosophy of science that he taught at Berkeley (Suppes 1979). After graduating from Berkeley in 1954, Scott moved to Princeton University for doctoral studies under Alonzo Church, another prominent logician, and received his Ph.D. in 1958. Scott and Suppes completed a first version of their joint paper, "Foundational Aspects of Theories of Measurement," in April 1957; the paper was later published in the June 1958 issue of the *Journal of Symbolic Logic*.[6] In the article, Scott and Suppes did not work out a systematic

6. In April 1957, Suppes also completed an introductory textbook on logic, which he dedicated to the memory of J. C. C. McKinsey (Suppes 1957, v). The last chapter of the book is devoted to the set-theoretical foundations of the axiomatic method, while elsewhere in it, Suppes briefly discusses measurement theory (265–266). This discussion, however, does not add any new elements to the picture drawn so far.

treatment of the representational theory of measurement but rather delineated the conceptual framework in which such a treatment would later be developed.

Scott and Suppes (1958) grounded their approach in the notion of a relational system recently introduced by Tarski (1954–1955). A relational system $\mathfrak{A} = \langle A, R_1, \ldots, R_n \rangle$ is a set-theoretical structure in which A is a nonempty set of elements called the *domain* of $\mathfrak{A}$, and $R_1, \ldots, R_n$ are relations between one, two, or more elements of A (functions connecting elements of A can be conceived of as relations). For instance, A can be a set of sounds and R_1 the binary relation *louder than* expressing the acoustic judgment of a given subject; then $\mathfrak{A}_1 = \langle A, R_1 \rangle$ is a relational system. Using the notion of relational system, the intuitive idea of isomorphism can be made precise. Two relational system $\mathfrak{A} = \langle A, R_1, \ldots, R_n \rangle$ and $\mathfrak{B} = \langle B, S_1, \ldots, S_n \rangle$ are said to be isomorphic when there exists a one-to-one function f from A onto B such that for each relation R_i and for each sequence $\langle a_1, \ldots, a_m \rangle$ of elements of A, the relation R_i holds on these elements if and only if a relation S_i holds for the image of $\langle a_1, \ldots, a_m \rangle$ in B through f. More compactly, $R_i(a_1, \ldots, a_m)$ if and only if $S_i(f(a_1), \ldots, f(a_m))$.

A numerical relational system $\mathfrak{N} = \langle \mathbb{R}, N_1, \ldots, N_n \rangle$ is a system whose domain of elements is the set $\mathbb{R}$ of real numbers. A numerical assignment for a relation system $\mathfrak{A}$ with respect to a numerical relational system $\mathfrak{N}$ is a function f from $\mathfrak{A}$ onto $\mathfrak{N}$ such that $R_i(a_1, \ldots, a_m)$ if and only if $N_i(f(a_1), \ldots, f(a_m))$. The function f does not need to be one-to-one, for in many cases, we may want to assign the same number to two distinct objects. If such a numerical function f exists, Scott and Suppes call the relation system $\mathfrak{A}$ *imbeddable* in $\mathfrak{N}$. Using a less esoteric terminology, we may say that the relation system $\mathfrak{A}$ is represented by the numerical relational system $\mathfrak{N}$.

By the end of the first section of their paper and following all these preliminaries, Scott and Suppes (115) could finally define "a theory of measurement" as a class K of isomorphic relational systems for which there exists "a numerical relational system $\mathfrak{N}$ . . . such that all relational systems in K are . . . imbeddable in $\mathfrak{N}$."

In their second section, Scott and Suppes investigated the conditions under which a theory of measurement for a given class of relational systems exists. The third section turned to the issue of axiomatizability. They called a theory of measurement axiomatizable if there exists "a set of sentences of first-order logic (the axioms of the theory)," such that "a relational system is in the theory if and only if the system satisfies all the sentences in the set" (123).[7] Without entering here into technical details, we can say that Scott and Suppes showed that the existence and axiomatizability of a theory of measurement depends, among other things, on whether the domain of the relational system is finite or infinite and on which type of numerical relations N_i are considered.

For our purposes, what is particularly important is that Scott and Suppes illustrated their new conceptual framework for measurement theory with examples drawn from utility analysis. In these examples, the domain A of a relational system is constituted by a set of choice objects, and the relations $\langle R_1, \ldots, R_n \rangle$ on A are preference relations over these objects satisfying certain axioms. In particular, Scott and Suppes (118–122) considered preference

7. First-order logic allows for quantification regarding objects. In particular, it admits the universal quantifier ∀ ("for every object") and the existential quantifier ∃ ("there exists an object"). However, first-order logic does not permit quantification regarding sets of objects ("for every set of objects"), for which second-order logic is required.

axioms analogous to those used by Suppes and Winet (1955) in their utility-difference model and also the axioms introduced by Duncan Luce (1956) in his model of semiordered preferences.[8]

Given that Scott's background was in mathematics and logic, it seems fair to assume that these examples taken from utility analysis are due to Suppes. This reinforces the conclusion that Suppes's early work in measurement theory was crucially influenced by his contemporaneous engagement with utility analysis.

15.6. SUPPES, ZINNES, AND STEVENS

In their 1958 article, Scott and Suppes explained how certain traditional problems of measurement theory, namely those related to the assignment of numbers to objects, could be restated and clarified within the new conceptual framework they put forward. However, they barely discussed problems related to the class of transformations to which the assigned numbers can be legitimately subjected and did not explain how these problems could be expressed within their new framework. Moreover, although Scott and Suppes illustrated their framework with examples taken from utility analysis, these illustrations were far from systematic. In particular, they did not explain what the theory for each of the four scales typically discussed in measurement analysis would look like in the new framework. In the following years, Suppes undertook this work of clarification and systematization with a number of coauthors.

His first important contribution in this direction was a seventy-page essay on "Basic Measurement Theory" coauthored with psychologist Joseph L. Zinnes (Suppes and Zinnes 1963).[9] The essay was published as the first chapter of the first volume of the three-volume *Handbook of Mathematical Psychology* edited by Luce (see section 15.7), Robert Bush, a physicist turned psychologist and a research associate of Frederick Mosteller,[10] and Eugene Galanter, a psychologist who had collaborated with Stevens at Harvard (Stevens and Galanter 1957).[11]

8. In order to account for situations in which an individual cannot discriminate between similar objects, Luce (1956) considered a generalization of standard utility theory in which the relation of strict preference between objects is transitive while the indifference relation is not. Such a preference structure is called a semiorder, and Luce showed how to construct a utility function that assigns numbers to semiordered objects.

9. Zinnes (born 1930) studied psychology at the University of Michigan. After graduating in 1959 with a dissertation on "A Probabilistic Theory of Preferential Choice," he settled at Indiana University. Already in 1961, he and Suppes had published a first joint work, this one on stochastic learning theories (Suppes and Zinnes 1961).

10. On Bush, see Mosteller 1974.

11. In an outgrowth of his 1957 article with Stevens, Galanter attempted to experimentally measure the utility of riskless money by asking subjects questions such as "Suppose I were to give you . . . $10.00. . . . I want you to think about how much money you would want in order to feel twice as happy as the $10.00 would make you feel" (Galanter 1962, 211). The subjects did not receive any reward or penalty depending on their answers to these questions. Based on the subjects' answers and the assumption that the utility function for riskless money U($M) is a power function, Galanter estimated that $U(\$M) = 3.71(\$M)^{0.43}$. Galanter's experiment did not have any influence in utility analysis. This lack of impact can be explained by two circumstances: first, since

Building on the conceptual framework defined by Scott and Suppes (1958), Suppes and Zinnes argued that there are two fundamental problems in measurement theory: the "representational problem" and the "uniqueness problem." The representational problem is solved by establishing the axiomatic characterization of "the formal properties of the empirical operations and relations used in the [measurement] procedure" and in showing that "they are isomorphic to appropriately chosen numerical operations and relations" (1963, 4). The uniqueness problem is solved by "the specification of the degree to which this assignment [i.e., the assignments of numbers to objects] is unique" (4). In practice, the solution of the uniqueness problem takes the form of specifying "the scale type of measurements arising from a given system of empirical relations" (10).

Based on this definition of the fundamental problems of measurement theory, Suppes and Zinnes took issue with Stevens's nonaxiomatic approach to measurement and his idea that the scales of measurement could be defined in terms of empirical operations rather than in terms of a mathematical problem of uniqueness. Without explicitly naming Stevens yet clearly referring to him, Suppes and Zinnes wrote:

> Some writers of measurement theory appear to define scales in terms of the existence of certain empirical operations. Thus interval scales are described in terms of the existence of an empirical operation which permits the subject . . . to compare intervals and to indicate in some way whether or not they are equal. In the present formulation of scale type, no mention is made of . . . empirical relations. . . . Scale type is defined entirely in terms of the class of numerical assignments which map a given empirical system homomorphically onto . . . the . . . numerical system. (15)

Some years later, Stevens (1968, 854) replied to Suppes and Zinnes's criticism by dismissing the axiomatic approach to measurement as an empty formalism that took no account of the empirical dimension of measurement. In particular, Stevens argued that advocates of the axiomatic approach to measurement such as Suppes and Zinnes and also Luce and Tukey (1964) "downgrade the empirical in favor of the formal" and "drift off into the vacuum of abstraction." For Stevens, "a full theory of measurement cannot detach itself from the empirical substrate that gives it meaning" (854).[12]

15.7. COLLABORATION WITH LUCE AND THE GENESIS OF *FOUNDATIONS OF MEASUREMENT*

The idea of a systematic treatise on measurement originated from Suppes's interaction with Luce. After studying aeronautical engineering and mathematics at MIT (B.S. 1945, Ph.D.

the 1930s utility theorists had rejected introspective judgments attempting to assess utility ratios (see chapter 6 of this book); second, in the 1950s, utility theorists had become skeptical about experiments based on non-incentivized tasks (see chapter 13 of this book).

12. Similar criticisms of the axiomatic approach to measurement have been made in recent years by Frigerio, Giordani, and Mari (2010); Boumans (2015); and others.

1950), Luce (1925–2012) moved to Columbia University, where he became interested in the applications of mathematics to behavioral science.[13] A colleague of Luce at Columbia was Howard Raiffa, who had studied mathematics and statistics at the University of Michigan and was familiar with game theory and mathematical psychology.[14] In 1954, Luce and Raiffa agreed to write together a short exposition of game theory that grew into a five-hundred-page book. Eventually published in 1957 and dedicated to the memory of von Neumann, who had died earlier that year, this book was titled *Games and Decisions* (Luce and Raiffa 1957). As mentioned in chapter 13, section 13.3.7, *Games and Decisions* quickly became a key reference for all scholars working in game and decision theory.

While writing *Games and Decisions*, Luce became interested in the stochastic theory of choice, and in the second half of the 1950s, he elaborated his own axiomatic version of this theory (Luce 1957; 1958; 1959). In summer 1957, a controversy over the key axiom of Luce's approach to stochastic choice, the so-called Choice Axiom, saw Luce and Suppes on opposing sides. The argument ended with Suppes accepting the Choice Axiom, and marked the beginning of a scientific collaboration and friendship between the two (Luce 1989; Suppes 1979).

In the early 1960s, Luce's research interests shifted again, this time toward the theory of measurement. In this period, he coauthored two important articles on the topic, one with mathematician John W. Tukey (Luce and Tukey 1964), the other with Suppes (Luce and Suppes 1965). By this point, as Luce (1989, 261) recalled in an autobiographical essay, he and Suppes "increasingly felt the need for a systematic presentation and integration of the materials on measurement." When they began working on such a book project, however, Luce and Suppes realized that they needed help in areas where they were not especially expert, and so they invited two young mathematical psychologists based at the University of Michigan to join them, namely David Krantz and Amos Tversky.[15] Originally intended as a single-volume project, the book expanded into first two and eventually three volumes. It is the first volume of *Foundations of Measurement*, published in 1971, that interests us here (volumes 2 and 3 appeared much later, in 1989 and 1990, respectively).

13. This reconstruction of Luce's early career is based on Luce 1989.

14. Raiffa (1924–2016) received a B.S. in mathematics (1946), an M.Sc. in statistics (1947), and a Ph.D. in mathematics (1951), all from the University of Michigan. As a graduate student, he became interested in game theory, which became the topic of his doctoral dissertation. In the academic year 1951–1952, Raiffa stayed at the University of Michigan as a postdoctoral student under psychologist Clyde Coombs, with whom he collaborated on research projects related to mathematical psychology and the theory of psychological measurement (Coombs, Raiffa, and Thrall 1954). In 1952, Raiffa joined Columbia University as an assistant professor, and in 1957, he moved to Harvard University, where he remained for the rest of his career. See more on Raiffa in Fienberg 2008.

15. Krantz (born 1938) studied mathematics at Yale University (B.A. 1960) and mathematical psychology at the University of Pennsylvania. After receiving his Ph.D. in 1964, Krantz moved to the University of Michigan, where he remained until 1985. Tversky (1937–1996) studied philosophy and psychology at the Hebrew University of Jerusalem (B.A. 1961) and mathematical psychology at the University of Michigan, earning his Ph.D. in 1965, where he remained until he returned to Israel in 1967. See more on Krantz and Tversky in Heukelom 2014; on Tversky, see also chapter 16.

15.8. TAKING STOCK

The first volume of *Foundations* articulated the representational conception of measurement outlined by Suppes in the articles coauthored with Scott (Scott and Suppes 1958) and Zinnes (Suppes and Zinnes 1963). The basic ingredients of the representational approach are the axioms, which define the relations and operations between the objects to be measured; the representation theorems, which connect the properties of these relations and operations to numerical operations and relations; and the uniqueness theorems, which specify the scale type of measurement permitted by the assumptions characterizing each measurement system. In this volume, Krantz, Luce, Suppes, and Tversky (1971) apply their representational approach to analyze, clarify, and systematize measurements belonging to fields as diverse as mechanics, thermodynamics, electrical theory, geometry, mathematics, statistics, probability theory, psychology, and, last but not least, utility theory.

As shown in this chapter, utility analysis and, more specifically, issues related to utility measurement played a fundamental role in the emergence of the representational theory of measurement. In particular, I have argued that Suppes's superseding of the unit-based understanding of measurement he had embraced in the early 1950s, his endorsement of a liberal definition of measurement à la Stevens in the mid-1950s, his conceiving of the project of an axiomatic underpinning of this notion of measurement in the late 1950s, and the realization of this project during the 1960s all have their origins in the utility analysis research he conducted within the Stanford Value Theory Project. As mentioned in section 15.7, the other senior author of *Foundations of Measurement*, Luce, also arrived at measurement theory from utility analysis.

The direct impact of *Foundations of Measurement* in economics was significant but not huge. In the journals and books collected in the JSTOR database, the book is cited sixty-four times from 1971 to 1985.[16] However, the axiomatic and representational approach to measurement that Suppes and his coauthors had been elaborating since the late 1950s entered into utility analysis also in an indirect way, through the works of Peter C. Fishburn. From his first monograph on *Decision and Value Theory* (1964), then in *Utility Theory for Decision Making* (1970), and more than three hundred articles published since 1965, Fishburn advanced an axiomatic, measurement-theoretic-oriented treatment of utility analysis, which was deeply influenced by the representational theory of measurement of Suppes, Luce, and their coauthors and which, in turn, has been quite influential among utility theorists.[17]

16. I limited my search to the following sections of JSTOR: finance, business, management, and organizational behavior. The sixty-four citations are concentrated in three journals: *Management Science* (sixteen), *Operations Research* (nine), and *Econometrica* (seven). Data were retrieved on May 12, 2018.

17. Fishburn (born 1936) studied industrial engineering at Pennsylvania State University (B.S. 1958) and then operations research under Russell L. Ackoff at the Case Institute of Technology in Cleveland (M.S. 1961, Ph.D. 1962). In 1964, he entered the Research Analysis Corporation, a center of operations research funded by the US Army, where he remained until 1970. After a year spent at the Institute for Advanced Study in Princeton, Fishburn moved to Pennsylvania State, where he remained until 1978. In that year, he joined the Bell Laboratories at Murray Hill, New Jersey, where he spent the rest of his working life. Unfortunately, a good reconstruction of Fishburn's work and career is still lacking.

This chapter has been devoted to the origins of the representational theory of measurement. As such, it has brought closure to the history of the theory of measurement begun in chapter 1 and continued through chapters 4, 8, 9, and 12. With this closure, we can now return to the experiments to measure utility based on EUT. As we will see in chapter 16, the experiments performed after 1970 reflected an increasing skepticism toward the theory.

CHAPTER 16

Measuring Utility, Destabilizing EUT

Behavioral Economics Begins, 1965–1985

In the decade following the publication of the Becker–DeGroot–Marschak article in 1964 (see chapter 14), apparently no further experimental study on utility measurement based on expected utility theory (EUT) was published. In this period, however, the conceptual background to the experimental measurement of utility through EUT changed significantly. This was because the validity of EUT was increasingly called into question, and this was independent of any measurement issues. The choice patterns violating EUT originally conceived of by Maurice Allais (1953) and Daniel Ellsberg (1961) began to be investigated and were confirmed in actual laboratory experiments. From the late 1960s to the early 1970s, other decision patterns violating EUT were highlighted by a group of young psychologists based at the University of Michigan, namely Sarah Lichtenstein, Paul Slovic, and Amos Tversky. Their findings were published in a series of works that are considered seminal in the field that from the late 1980s began to be called behavioral economics.

The increasing doubts about the validity of EUT from the mid-1960s affected the general approach of the new experimenters who engaged with the EUT-based measurement of utility from the mid-1970s. Basically, they were skeptical about the theory and, in order to prove it false, showed that different elicitation methods to measure utility, which according to EUT should produce the same outcome, in fact generate different measures. These experimental findings undermined the earlier confidence that EUT makes it possible to measure utility. More generally, these findings contributed to destabilizing EUT as the dominant economic model of decision-making under risk and helped foster the blossoming of non-EUT models that began in the mid-1970s and has continued to the present.

The history recounted in this final chapter, and thus in the book, ends in 1985, the year in which John Hershey and Paul Schoemaker published an article that definitively put the problem of the inconsistency between different EUT-based utility measures on the map of decision theorists. The year 1985 marks a suitable terminus for our story. After this date, a number of new research programs related to utility measurement began, such as the attempts to measure utility experimentally within non-EUT frameworks or, more recently, by using neuroscientific techniques. Dealing appropriately with the post-1985 developments in the history of utility measurement would probably require another book. Moreover, these research programs are still ongoing and therefore do not yet lend themselves to proper historiographical study. In the epilogue to this book, however, I briefly review some of the main research programs that since 1985 have continued the struggle of decision theorists with the issue of utility measurement.

16.1. A CHANGING LANDSCAPE, 1964–1974

16.1.1. From the Allais Paradox to the Ellsberg Paradox

As discussed in chapter 11, section 11.7.2, first at the Paris conference of 1952 and then in an article published in *Econometrica* in 1953, Allais imagined a decision problem in which, he argued, EUT is often violated and for good reasons. This decision problem later became known as the Allais paradox. As I stressed, Allais's approach to testing EUT did not involve any utility measurement; he considered two pairs of lotteries, argued that a majority of perfectly reasonable people would prefer lottery L_1 over lottery L_2 and lottery L_4 over lottery L_3, and showed that this pair of preferences violates EUT because there exists no von Neumann–Morgenstern utility function u capable of rationalizing them by using the expected utility formula.

During the 1950s and until the mid-1960s, the Allais paradox had a negligible impact on the evolution of decision theory. One reason for this lack of impact was that during this period, the Allais paradox remained a thought experiment without any laboratory confirmation. Furthermore, and as discussed in chapter 12, section 12.8.5, in *The Foundations of Statistics*, Leonard J. Savage ([1954] 1972, 101–103) put forward a normative argument against the paradox that was quite influential among economists: when the decision maker reflects on the Allais preference pattern, he understands that it conflicts with the Sure-Thing Principle and therefore wants to avoid or revise that pattern.[1] Finally, Allais's own theory of decision under risk was too general and awkward to constitute a viable alternative to EUT.

In 1961, another "paradox" entered the landscape of decision theory, namely the so-called Ellsberg paradox. As mentioned in chapter 13, section 13.3.7, in reviewing the Davidson–Suppes–Siegel experiment, Ellsberg (1958) suggested that there are important classes of choice situations in which normal people systematically violate EUT, yet he did not state which uncertain situations he had in mind. Elaboration came in an article Ellsberg published in the November 1961 issue of the *Quarterly Journal of Economics* titled "Risk, Ambiguity, and the Savage Axioms." While the target of Allais's paradox was von John Neumann and Oskar Morgenstern's version of EUT with objective probabilities, Ellsberg's target, as the title of his article makes clear, was Savage's version of EUT with subjective probabilities. Apart from this difference, the structure of the two paradoxes is very similar.

Ellsberg (1961, 653–656) imagined an urn containing thirty red balls and sixty black or yellow balls in unknown proportions. One ball is to be drawn at random from the urn, and the decision maker has to express his preferences between two pairs of gambles. In the first pair, gamble G_1 yields \$100 if a red ball is drawn and \$0 otherwise; gamble G_2 yields \$100

1. On the limitations of Savage's argument, see Mongin 2014.

if a black ball is drawn and $0 otherwise. In the second pair, gamble G_3 yields $100 if a red ball or a yellow ball is drawn and $0 otherwise; gamble G_4 yields $100 if a black ball or a yellow ball is drawn and $0 otherwise. Like Allais's, Ellsberg's was a thought experiment and, being based on the direct comparison of two pairs of gambles, did not involve any utility measurement.

Ellsberg argued that because most people dislike gambles that, like G_2 and G_3, are "ambiguous," in the sense that they contain unknown or vague probabilities, a frequent preference pattern is G_1 preferred to G_2 and G_4 preferred to G_3. This preference pattern, however, violates EUT even in Savage's subjective version of the theory.[2] Ellsberg argued that the preference pattern G_1 preferred to G_2 and G_4 preferred to G_3 is not only frequent but also normatively defendable. What is more, Ellsberg claimed, on being presented with these imagined choice situations, respectable decision theorists such as Norman Dalkey (see chapter 12, section 12.3.1) and Jacob Marschak had violated EUT "cheerfully, even with gusto" (655), and were not willing, even upon reflection, to revise their choices.

Ellsberg's article was followed by a comment by Howard Raiffa, the author, with Duncan Luce, of *Games and Decisions* and a colleague of Ellsberg at Harvard University (see chapter 15, section 15.7). Ellsberg had also presented Raiffa with his ambiguous urn decision problem, and according to Ellsberg (1961, 656), Raiffa tended, "intuitively, to violate the axioms" but felt "guilty about it" and went into further analysis to correct his initial choice. In his comment on Ellsberg's article, Raiffa (1961) basically claimed that if people are presented with an opportunely reframed version of Ellsberg's decision problem, they avoid, and want to avoid, the Ellsbergian preference pattern.[3]

To summarize the situation, it is fair to say that until the mid-1960s, most decision theorists tended to dismiss violations of EUT à la Allais or Ellsberg either as errors that upon reflection decision makers would want to correct or as related to fictional choice situations that rarely occur in reality. In the mid-1960s, however, things began to change.

16.1.2. Allais and Ellsberg Reloaded

Beginning in the mid-1960s, actual laboratory experiments were commenced that studied the choice patterns imagined by Allais and Ellsberg, while the psychological phenomena that could explain these patterns began to be investigated in a systematic way. To begin with, Selwyn W. Becker, a psychologist who had worked with Sidney Siegel, and Fred O. Brownson

2. If we apply Savage's rules to infer probabilities from preferences between gambles, the decision maker's preference of G_1 over G_2 indicates that he considers the probability of red larger than the probability of black: p(red) > p(black). The decision maker's preference of G_4 over G_3 indicates that he considers the probability of black or yellow larger than the probability of red or yellow: p(black) + p(yellow) > p(red) + p(yellow). The latter inequality implies p(black) > p(red), which, however, is the opposite of p(red) > p(black). Since it is impossible, Ellsberg argued (655), even to infer qualitative probabilities for the events involved in gambles G_1, G_2, G_3, and G_4, it is also impossible "to find probability numbers in terms of which these choices [G_1 preferred to G_2, G_4 preferred to G_3] could be described . . . as maximizing the mathematical expectation of utility." See more on Ellsberg's paradox and its history in Zappia 2016.

3. Roberts (1963) offered another normative reply to the Ellsberg paradox.

(1964) published in the *Journal of Political Economy* an experimental study showing that fifteen of thirty-four students at the Graduate School of Business at the University of Chicago displayed an Ellsberg-like pattern of choice.

In his book *Probability and Profit* (1965), William Fellner, whom we have already met as Trenery Dolbear's supervisor at Yale (chapter 14, section 14.2.1), suggested accommodating Ellsbergian choice patterns by considering probabilities not adding up to one. In opposition to this probabilistic solution, experimental economist Vernon Smith (1969) put forward a utility interpretation of the Ellsberg paradox according to which the utility of money in situations where probabilities are unknown, as in the Ellsberg case, is different from the utility of money when probabilities are known.

Kenneth MacCrimmon, a student of Marschak at UCLA, conducted a series of experiments on EUT for his Ph.D. dissertation. Among other things, MacCrimmon (1965) found that fourteen of thirty-six business executives who participated in his experiments displayed an Allais-like pattern of choice, while twenty-one showed at least one Ellsberg-like violation of EUT. MacCrimmon's dissertation and a subsequent paper summarizing its main results (1968) were widely discussed in the decision theory literature of the period.

In 1967, Donald G. Morrison, then an assistant professor of business at Columbia University, published in *Behavioral Science* an article on "The Consistency of Preference in Allais's paradox." Morrison proposed accommodating Allais-like choice patterns within the EUT framework by taking into account the decision maker's asset position.

16.1.3. The Michigan School

Under the leadership of psychologists Donald Marquis, George Katona, Clyde Coombs, and Ward Edwards, during the 1950s and early 1960s, the psychology department at the University of Michigan had become one of top departments in the United States. The department was organized into different research units. Coombs, who had studied with Louis Leon Thurstone at Chicago, directed the Mathematical Psychology Program, which focused on the theory and practice of psychological measurement. Edwards, who had studied with Frederick Mosteller at Harvard, directed the Engineering Psychology Laboratory, which concentrated on the experimental investigation of human decision-making (Heukelom 2010).[4]

Among the psychologists who graduated from the University of Michigan under Coombs and Edwards in the early and mid-1960s were Lichtenstein, Slovic, and Tversky, whom we have already met in chapter 15, section 15.7, as one of the authors of *Foundations of Measurement*. In effect, since his doctoral dissertation, Tversky's research interests had combined the mathematical theory of measurement with the experimental study of individual decision-making.[5] Some experimental studies performed by Lichtenstein, Slovic, and

4. See more on Edwards in chapter 13 and more on Coombs in Tversky 1992. As noted in chapter 15, footnotes 9 and 14, Zinnes and Raiffa also studied at the University of Michigan.

5. On Tversky's early career and research interests, see Colman and Shafir 2008; Heukelom 2014.

Tversky in the late 1960s and early 1970s also contributed to the change in the landscape of decision analysis that took place in the mid-1960s and the mid-1970s.

In a first experiment, Slovic and Lichtenstein (1968) noted that experimental subjects rate as more attractive lotteries with higher winning probabilities. However, the same subjects are willing to pay more for lotteries with higher winning payoffs. In a follow-up experiment, Lichtenstein and Slovic (1971) showed that this attitude easily generates a reversal of preference—that is, lottery L_1 is chosen over lottery L_2, but lottery L_2 is prized more than lottery L_1—that is incompatible with EUT.

Tversky (1969) highlighted a different type of anomaly. Based on the psychological insight that people pay attention to probability differences only when they exceed certain thresholds, Tversky showed that it is easy to induce individuals to choose in an intransitive way—that is, to choose lottery L_1 over lottery L_2, lottery L_2 over lottery L_3, and lottery L_3 over lottery L_1—by suitably modifying the monetary payoffs and winning probabilities of a series of lotteries. Intransitivity of choices is incompatible with EUT.

The experimental findings on choice patterns violating EUT were reviewed and discussed in a series of introductory publications in decision theory that appeared in the early 1970s, such as *Mathematical Psychology: An Elementary Introduction* by Coombs, Robyn M. Dawes, and Tversky (1970); *Decision Theory and Human Behavior* by psychologist Wayne Lee (1971); and the extended review essay on "Individual Decision Behavior" by psychologists Amnon Rapoport and Thomas S. Wallsten (1972).

16.1.4. Classifying Measurement Methods

A final novelty of the post-1965 period is that some researchers, such as Peter Fishburn (1967), Raiffa (1968), and John Hull, Peter Moore, and Howard Thomas (1973), explicitly discussed the different methods to measure utility within the EUT framework. For instance, Fishburn (1967) identified twenty-four measurement methods and classified them according to whether they use probabilities, whether they are based on preference judgments or indifference judgments, and whether they apply to continuous or discrete factors. These works, however, did not investigate the issue of the mutual consistency of the different measurement methods and had little impact on the experimental research on utility measurement of the 1970s and early 1980s.

16.1.5. Comment

The strategy for testing EUT adopted by Lichtenstein, Slovic, and Tversky was significantly different from, if not opposite to, the strategy adopted by Mosteller–Nogee and Davidson–Suppes–Siegel. While the latter used their psychological insights to simplify the decision tasks faced by the experimental subjects and thus eliminate the factors that could lead the subjects to violate EUT, Tversky and his associates at the University of Michigan exploited their psychological insights, for example, that people tend to ignore probability differences below certain thresholds, to design choice situations in which the experimental subjects tend to violate EUT. This approach to experimental design and testing aimed at showing, as Tversky (1969, 40, 45) explicitly stated, that the violations of EUT could not be "attributed to momentary fluctuations or random variability" but were "systematic, consistent, and predictable." These violations appeared therefore to be due to fundamental psychological causes that need to be investigated, rather than to random factors to be removed as disturbing elements. The Michigan approach to experimental design and testing became the blueprint for future behavioral economists.

As argued in chapter 13, section 13.5, the testing strategy favorable to EUT adopted by Mosteller–Nogee and Davidson–Suppes–Siegel can be judged a sound one for a new scientific theory, as EUT was in the 1950s. By the mid-1960s, however, EUT was no longer a new theory deserving a "best shot" but an established theory to be tested under conditions departing from the ideal ones implemented in the experimental designs of the 1950s. Considered from this viewpoint, the Michigan testing strategy does not constitute a methodological U-turn with respect to the Mosteller–Nogee and Davidson–Suppes–Siegel strategy but represents rather a timely development of the latter.

The testing experiments on EUT mentioned in this section adopted a measurement-free approach à la Allais–Ellsberg, rather than the measurement-based approach à la Mosteller–Nogee or Davidson–Suppes–Siegel. For the purpose of testing EUT, the measurement-free approach may be judged preferable, because by ruling out the intermediate step involving the measurement of utility, it also rules out the possibility that violations of EUT are imputed to some failure in the measurement procedure rather than to EUT itself (Mongin 2009). However, and as we will see in the next section, the measurement-based approach provides useful insights about the possible causes of EUT violations and in this sense fruitfully complements the measurement-free approach.

16.2. DISTORTED PROBABILITIES 1: KARMARKAR'S EXPERIMENT

This section and the two that follow focus on the experiments on EUT conducted in the mid-1970s and the mid-1980s that entailed utility measurement. These experiments were part of the uprising against EUT described in section 16.1. More specifically, they destabilized EUT by showing that different methods of measuring utility, which according to EUT should deliver the same result, in fact generate different utility measures. The experimenters of this period tended to apply the Michigan approach: they used their psychological insights to construct choice situations that produced mutually inconsistent utility measures. The first two experiments were conducted by MIT scholars not based in the economics department.

16.2.1. Background and Motivations

In 1970, Uday S. Karmarkar (born 1947) began a Ph.D. in management science at MIT's Sloan School of Management. Serving as teaching assistant for a course on decision theory held by Gordon Kaufman, Karmarkar began "to feel that it was not easy to answer questions about lotteries and certainty equivalents" and wondered "if it would be even harder if the gambles were not 50:50" (email to the author, August 1, 2016). Around 1974, he conducted an exploratory experiment on the topic with two MIT students and two friends; the results were published in a Sloan School working paper (Karmarkar 1974).

The motivations Karmarkar gives in this paper for his experimental study reflect the doubts about the descriptive power of EUT that had grown from the mid-1960s. He argued that "a survey of recent work in decision modelling in the behavioral science area, makes it abundantly clear that for the most part [expected] utility theory is not deemed rich enough to be a descriptive tool in the general sense" (1974, 4). In support of this claim, Karmarkar referred to the books of Coombs, Dawes, and Tversky (1970) and Lee (1971) mentioned in section 16.1. As main counterexamples to EUT, Karmarkar cited the Ellsberg and Allais paradoxes and conjectured that choice patterns à la Allais–Ellsberg had to do with subjective distortions of objective probabilities.

16.2.2. Design and Findings

To test his hypothesis, Karmarkar considered two-outcome lotteries with payoffs ranging between \$0 and \$100. Unlike the experiments on utility measurement of the 1950s and 1960s, in Karmarkar's experiment, the payoffs were fictional. He elicited the von Neumann–Morgenstern utility curves u of each experimental subject using the certainty equivalence method; that is, he identified the amount of money for sure \$M that the subject considered indifferent to a lottery of the form [$\$M_1$, p; $\$M_2$, 1 – p], where the values of p, $\$M_1$, and $\$M_2$ were given and $\$M_1$ and $\$M_2$ ranged between \$0 and \$100.[6] He performed this elicitation exercise three times, with lotteries where the probability p was equal, respectively, to p = 0.5, p = 0.75, and p = 0.90.

In this way, Karmarkar obtained three utility curves u for each subject. According to EUT, the three curves should coincide. In fact, Karmarkar (1974, 10) found, for all subjects, "separate and distinct utility curves for each different value of the odds used." In particular, the concavity of the utility curves increased with the odds: "The general tendency is toward an increase in risk aversion with increasing odds" (17). For instance, for experimental subject A, Karmarkar identified the three utility curves u represented here in figure 16.1, where the most concave utility curve u was obtained using p = 0.90 and the least concave, and almost linear, utility curve was obtained for p = 0.5.

As preliminary and informal as it was, Karmarkar's study appears to have been the first experiment to provide persuasive evidence of the inconsistency between different EUT-based utility measures. Notably, the inconsistency documented by Karmarkar was not between, say, the certainty equivalence method and the money equivalence method but between different ways of implementing the same (certainty equivalence) method.

6. In effect, Karmarkar (1974, 31) used an approximate version of the certainty equivalence method. He identified two amounts of money for sure $\$M^+$ and $\$M^-$ that were, respectively, more preferred and less preferred to the lottery [$\$M_1$, p; $\$M_2$, 1 – p]. He then defined the certainty equivalent \$M of lottery [$\$M_1$, p; $\$M_2$, 1 – p] as the average between $\$M^+$ and $\$M^-$. However, this additional aspect of Karmarkar's design is not relevant for the issues discussed here.

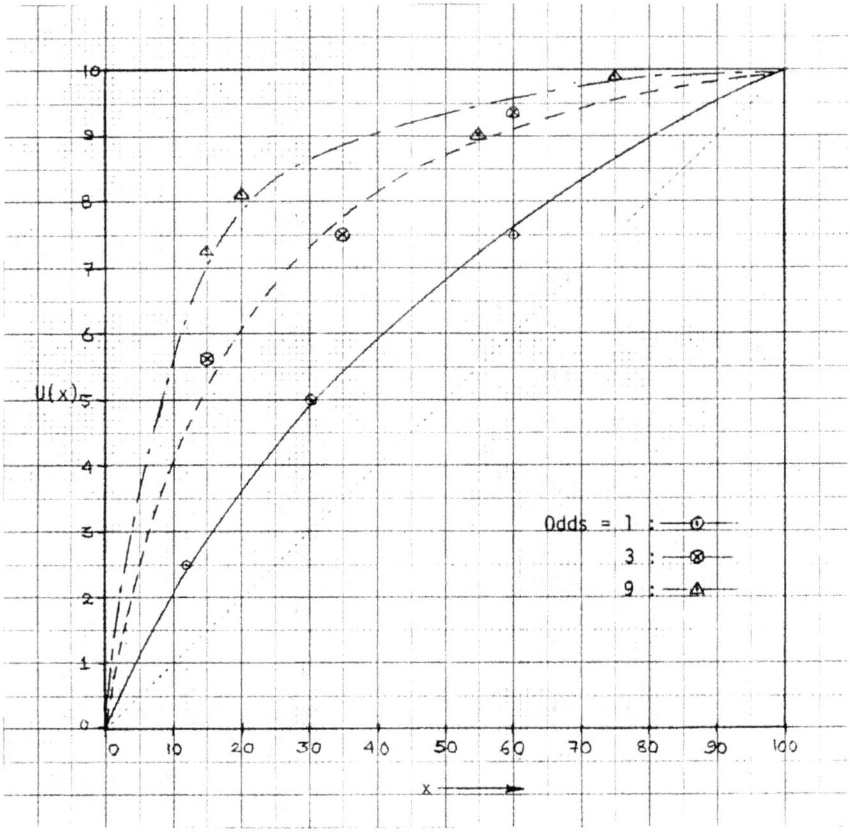

Figure 16.1. Utility curves elicited by Karmarkar
The utility curves u of experimental subject A. The most concave curve u is obtained for p = 0.90, the intermediate curve for p = 0.75, and the least concave utility curve for p = 0.5.
Source: Karmarkar 1974, 12. Reproduced with permission of Uday Karmarkar.

16.2.3. The SWU Model

While at the Sloan School, Karmarkar did not pursue his experimental research and instead wrote his dissertation on multilocation inventory theory. In 1975, he moved to the Graduate School of Business at the University of Chicago and was encouraged there by Hillel J. Einhorn to return to the topics of his 1974 working paper from a theoretical perspective. Einhorn was a brilliant behavioral scientist who in 1977 played a major role in creating the Center for Decision Research at Chicago's Graduate School of Business (Hogarth and Klayman 1990). Karmarkar (1978) followed Einhorn's suggestion and elaborated a formal model—the Subjectively Weighted Utility (SWU) model—which extends EUT by introducing a weighting function that captures subjective distortions of objective probabilities.[7] Among

7. While in EUT the decision maker maximizes the expression $\sum u(x_i)p(x_i)$, with $i = 1, \ldots, n$, where x_i are the lottery's payoffs, $u(x_i)$ the von Neumann–Morgenstern utilities of the payoffs,

other things, the SWU model accounts for the fact that utility measures elicited from lotteries with different odds can be different. In the SWU article, Karmarkar summarized the main results of his 1974 experiment and thereby made them available to a broader public.

In the late 1970s and early 1980s, Karmarkar's SWU model was widely debated in the decision theory literature along with two other modifications of EUT that had appeared in the same period and incorporated a similar subjective weighting function of probabilities: Jagdish Handa's Certainty Equivalence model (1977) and Daniel Kahneman and Amos Tversky's Prospect Theory (1979). The articles by Handa and Kahneman–Tversky, however, do not focus on utility measurement and therefore will not be discussed here.

16.3. DISTORTED PROBABILITIES 2: MCCORD AND DE NEUFVILLE'S EXPERIMENT

16.3.1. The Evolving Context, 1978–1982

In the late 1970s and early 1980s, a number of extensions or modifications of EUT were put forward, while new, measurement-free experimental tests of the descriptive and normative validity of EUT were conducted (MacCrimmon and Larsson 1979; Kahneman and Tversky 1979; Grether and Plott 1979; Schoemaker 1980). Notably, non-EUT models and experiments concerning the validity of EUT gained economists' attention and were published in top economics journals, such as the *American Economic Review* (Grether and Plott 1979), *Econometrica* (Kahneman and Tversky 1979; Machina 1982), the *Journal of Political Economy* (Handa 1977), the *Economic Journal* (Loomes and Sugden 1982), and the *Journal of Economic Behavior and Organization* (Quiggin 1982).

In 1979, Allais and Ole Hagen, a Norwegian behavioral scientist who endorsed Allais's critical stance on EUT, edited a book titled *Expected Utility Hypotheses and the Allais Paradox*. Among other things, the book popularized the expression *Allais paradox* and contained an English translation of the seventy-five-page essay in which Allais had originally expounded his theory of decision under risk in 1953 (Allais [1953] 1979; Allais's *Econometrica* article of 1953, written in French, was an abridged version of this essay). The book also contained an English translation of the remark that Allais had made in 1952 at the end of the Paris conference in which he had conjectured that different methods of measuring the von Neumann–Morgenstern function u may generate different measures of it (Allais and Hagen 1979, 612–613).

In 1982, the *Journal of Economic Literature* published a first review article on the limitations of EUT and the empirical evidence for and against it (Schoemaker 1982). In the same year, Allais and Hagen organized at Oslo the first of a series of international conferences on the "Foundations of Utility and Risk" (FUR). Several papers critical of EUT were presented

and $p(x_i)$ their objective probabilities, in the SWU model, the decision maker maximizes the expression $\Sigma u(x_i)w[p(x_i)]/\Sigma w[p(x_i)]$, where the weighting function $w[p(x_i)]$ is defined as $w[p(x_i)] = \frac{(Odds_i)^\alpha}{1+(Odds_i)^\alpha}$ and $Odds_i = \frac{p(x_i)}{1-p(x_i)}$; see Karmarkar 1978, 62–64.

here, one of which was an experimental study on utility measurement conducted by Richard de Neufville (born 1939), an MIT professor of engineering systems, and Mark McCord (born 1955), then a Ph.D. candidate in engineering at MIT supervised by de Neufville.

16.3.2. Engineering and Utility Measurement

De Neufville's interest in utility measurement derived from his engineering practice. He understood engineering as "making choices between technical alternatives based on their perceived value," that is, their utility. Therefore, "as an engineer," he wanted to know "to what extent we can be comfortable with measurements of utility" (email to the author, August 21, 2016).

During the 1970s, de Neufville became increasingly skeptical about the practical usefulness of the certainty equivalence method and the other procedures used to assess utility functions expounded by Ralph L. Keeney—another MIT engineer with whom de Neufville had collaborated on a project for an airport in Mexico City—and Raiffa in their textbook *Decisions with Multiple Objectives* (1976).

In a series of papers coauthored with McCord, de Neufville showed the deficiencies of the standard assessment procedures and suggested a number of ways to ameliorate them (McCord and de Neufville 1983; 1985; 1986). I focus here on the experimental study McCord and de Neufville presented at the Oslo conference, which was published in the conference volume (McCord and de Neufville 1983) and as part of McCord's Ph.D. dissertation (McCord 1983).

16.3.3. Design and Findings

Building on Karmarkar's 1974 experiment, McCord and de Neufville attempted to show that the EUT-based experimental measures of utility depend on the lotteries' probabilities in a way that violates EUT. Their experimental subjects were twenty-three professors, graduate students, and undergraduates in engineering or sciences at MIT who had to state their preferences between two-outcome lotteries with payoffs ranging between \$0 and \$10,000. The payoffs were hypothetical. Based on these preferences, they elicited the subjects' utility functions using three variants of the certainty equivalence method.

In the first variant, the subject had to indicate the certainty equivalent of an initial fifty-fifty lottery. This certainty equivalent then replaced one of the two payoffs in the initial lottery so as to obtain a second fifty-fifty lottery. The subject now had to indicate the certainty equivalent of the second lottery. This second certainty equivalent replaced one of the two payoffs in the second lottery, and the procedure was iterated until a sufficient number of points of the subject's utility curve were determined. The second elicitation method was similar, but instead of using fifty-fifty lotteries, McCord and de Neufville employed lotteries with different probabilities, such as $p = 0.75$ or $p = 0.625$. In the third procedure, the payoffs of the lotteries were fixed at \$10,000 and \$0, and the probabilities varied. That is, the subjects were asked to identify the certainty equivalents of a series of lotteries of the form [$10,000, p; $0, 1 – p] for different values of p.

According to EUT, these three assessment methods should produce the same utility function of money. However, like Karmarkar, McCord and de Neufville (1983, 188) found that this was not the case and that "large descriptive differences exist between the function resulting from the various methods of assessment." Moreover, these differences were systematic rather than random and indicated that "individuals preferred to deviate in a fairly consistent fashion from the behavior presumed by the [EUT] axioms" (189).

16.3.4. Consequences for the Validity of EUT

One important feature that distinguishes the McCord and de Neufville paper from Karmarkar's is that the former explicitly discussed the consequences of the inconsistency between the different measures of the utility function u for the descriptive and normative validity of EUT. At the descriptive level, if "the assessed utility function depends on the probabilistic situation used in the elicitation" (183), it is not clear whether and how this utility function can be applied to predict the individual's choices in other probabilistic settings.

At the normative level, as discussed in chapter 12, section 12.8.5, in the EUT framework the utility measures obtained from the decision maker's choices between simple lotteries can be employed to calculate the expected utility of more complex risky options and thus advise the decision maker about how to choose between them. This decision maker may be an engineer who has to choose between complex alternative options, such as preserving clear air or employing cheap coal power. However, if several diverging utility measures are obtained, it is unclear which one should be employed to advise the decision maker or the engineer. McCord and de Neufville concluded by arguing that the inconsistency between different EUT-based utility measures undermines the practical applications of EUT: "The conclusion is that the justification of the practical use of expected utility decision analysis . . . is weak. Specifically, the whole computational side of the method, which seeks to prescribe a normatively best choice by means of a calculus based on a description of a person's utility, does not appear valid" (196).

16.4. CERTAINTY EQUIVALENCE VERSUS PROBABILITY EQUIVALENCE: THE EXPERIMENTS OF SCHOEMAKER AND HIS COAUTHORS

Two experimental articles published in *Management Science* in the first half of the 1980s put the problem of the inconsistency between different EUT-based utility measures even more firmly on the map of decision theorists. The first, "Sources of Bias in Assessment Procedures for Utility Functions," was authored by John C. Hershey, Howard Kunreuther, and Paul Schoemaker (1982). The second, "Probability versus Certainty Equivalence Methods in

Utility Measurement: Are They Equivalent?" was written by Hershey and Schoemaker (1985).[8]

As discussed in the previous two sections, the experiments of Karmarkar and McCord–de Neufville showed that the same EUT-based measurement method, namely the certainty equivalence method, generates mutually inconsistent utility measures when implemented in different probability settings. Schoemaker and his coauthors now exposed another problem of EUT-based utility measurement. They showed that two different measurement methods, namely the certainty equivalence method and the probability equivalence method, which according to EUT should produce the same outcome, in fact generate two different and incompatible measures of utility.

As discussed in chapter 11 and mentioned in section 16.3.1, in a remark made at the end of the Paris conference of 1952, Allais had already conjectured that the certainty equivalence method and the probability equivalence method may produce inconsistent utility measures. Although Schoemaker and his coauthors did not refer to Allais's 1952 conjecture, with hindsight their experiments may be seen as vindicating his early intuition.

16.4.1. Backgrounds

Schoemaker (born 1949) studied physics, first in the Netherlands and then at the University of Notre Dame in Indiana, and became interested in issues related to risk through studying the debate between deterministic and probabilistic views of the universe. When he moved to graduate studies in economics and finance at the University of Pennsylvania's Wharton School, his interest shifted to "the role of risk and uncertainty in the social, rather than physical, realities" (Schoemaker 1980, xviii). In the course of his Ph.D. studies at Wharton's newly created department of decision sciences, Schoemaker became dissatisfied with the economic theory of risk, and he wrote his dissertation on EUT, its limits, and the experiments on decisions under risk. The dissertation, completed in 1977, soon became a book (Schoemaker 1980). Meanwhile, in 1979, Schoemaker moved to the Center for Decision Research at Chicago's graduate business school.[9]

Kunreuther (born 1938), who had received his Ph.D. in economics from MIT in 1965, was Schoemaker's Ph.D. adviser. A professor of decision sciences at Wharton, from 1977 to 1980 he also served as the chairman of the decision sciences department. Since the early 1970s, his research had focused on the theory and management of risk, not only in economic contexts but also in relation to natural events such as weather or earthquakes.

Hershey (born 1943) had received his Ph.D. in 1970 from Stanford University and was also at Wharton's decision sciences department, then as an associate professor. Before

8. If we use Google Scholar citations as a measure of impact, the picture is as follows: Karmarkar (1974): 34 citations; Karmarkar (1978): 375; McCord and de Neufville (1983): 78; Hershey, Kunreuther, and Schoemaker (1982): 487; Hershey and Schoemaker (1985): 365. Data retrieved on May 12, 2018.

9. Schoemaker did not overlap with Karmarkar, who left Chicago for the University of Rochester in 1979.

collaborating with Schoemaker and Kunreuther, his research had focused on healthcare and insurance decision-making.

16.4.2. CE versus PE, Act I

In their 1982 article, Hershey, Kunreuther, and Schoemaker investigated various factors that could influence the elicitation of risk preferences, that is, the curvature of the elicited utility function u, in a way EUT does not account for. The first factor they identified was the very elicitation method that is adopted and, in particular, they compared the certainty equivalence (CE) method with the probability equivalence (PE) method.

In a first experiment, Hershey, Kunreuther, and Schoemaker elicited the utility curves of thirty-two Wharton students through the CE procedure. They asked the students to answer ten questions of the form "You face a situation where you have a 50% chance of losing $200. Would you be willing to pay $100 to avoid this situation?" (1982, 940). If the students were not indifferent between the lottery and $100, they had to adjust the $100 amount of money so as to reach their indifference point.

The utility curves of thirty-two other Wharton students were elicited through the PE method, that is, through ten questions of the form "You can pay $100 to avoid a situation where you may lose $200. Would you pay if there were a 50% chance of losing?" If the answer was no, the students had to adjust the 0.5 probability to reach their indifference point. As in the Karmarkar and McCord–de Neufville experiments, the payoffs in these lotteries were hypothetical.

16.4.3. Findings

Hershey, Kunreuther, and Schoemaker found that the CE method generally yielded greater risk seeking, that is, more convex utility curves, than the PE method: "In the CE group 29 of the 32 subjects gave risk seeking responses for a majority of the questions, as compared with only 16 in the PE group" (942).

As shown by Karmarkar's experiment, which these experimenters mentioned, the elicitation of risk preferences can also be influenced by the probabilities used in the lotteries. In particular, in a second experiment based on the CE method, involving eighty-two Wharton students, and with lotteries of the form [$10,000, p; $0, 1 – p], they found that the proportion of risk-averse individuals increased as p increased from 0.01 to 0.999. They summarized their results: "the emerging picture is that basic preferences under uncertainty exhibit serious incompatibilities with traditional expected utility theory" (936).

16.4.4. CE versus PE, Act II

In their 1985 article, Hershey and Schoemaker investigated in more detail the inconsistency between the utility measures obtained thorough the CE and the PE methods. Their starting point was the two major limitations of the experiment devoted to this topic and presented in the 1982 article; it compared the two elicitation methods over two different groups of individuals rather than over the same individuals, and it considered only lotteries involving losses. The experiments Hershey and Schoemaker presented in their 1985 article attempted to overcome these limitations.

They considered two two-stage measurement procedures. In the first stage of the first procedure—labeled the CE–PE method—each subject was asked to identify the CE of a given lottery, for example, of lottery [$200, 0.5; $0, 0.5]. In the second stage, which took place one week later, the same subjects were asked to identify the probability p making a lottery with equal payoffs indifferent to the CE identified in the first stage. Thus, if in the first stage the subject stated that the certainty equivalent of lottery [$200, 0.5; $0, 0.5] was $70, in the second stage he was asked to determine the probability p that made him indifferent between the lottery [$200, p; $0, 1 – p] and $70 for sure. If the subject obeyed the EUT axioms, such probability p should be 0.5. In the second procedure—called the PE–CE method—the order between CE and PE methods was reversed.

The experimental subjects were 147 undergraduate students in a business course at the University of Pennsylvania who were divided into four groups. The subjects in the first group faced lotteries with gains, and their utility functions were elicited through the CE–PE procedure. Subjects in the second group faced lotteries with gains, but their utility functions were elicited through the PE–CE procedure. The subjects in the third and fourth groups faced lotteries with losses, and their utility functions were elicited through, respectively, the CE–PE and the PE–CE procedure. In the gain lotteries, the payoffs ranged between $0 and $10,000, while in the loss lotteries, they ranged between $0 and –$10,000. As in the Hershey–Kunreuther–Schoemaker article, all payoffs were purely hypothetical.

16.4.5. Findings

The Hershey–Schoemaker experiment confirmed the findings of the earlier experiment by Hershey, Kunreuther, and Schoemaker: the elicited utility measures, and thus the elicited risk propensities, depended significantly on whether the CE or the PE method was adopted. This was true for approximately two-thirds of the 147 experimental subjects.

Moreover, the deviations from EUT were not random but displayed patterns of bias. In particular, for both gains and losses, "the CE–PE subjects were relatively more risk-averse in the PE mode," and "the PE–CE subjects were relatively less risk-averse in the CE mode" (1985, 1221–1222). That is, the major finding of the Hershey–Kunreuther–Schoemaker experiment, namely that the PE method yields greater risk aversion (i.e., more concave utility curves) than the CE method was reinforced.

16.4.6. Explanations

Hershey and Schoemaker noted that the inconsistency between the two methods, and more specifically the higher risk aversion induced by the PE method, cannot be explained by subjective distortions of objective probabilities like those suggested by Karmarkar, McCord, and de Neufville. In the Hershey–Schoemaker setting, in fact, the two methods deliver mutually consistent utility measures even if subjects distort objective probabilities (1217). Accordingly, Hershey and Schoemaker explored several alternative explanations, such as differences in salience between the probability and payoff dimensions, regret or rejoice influences, endowment effects, and the "PE mode reframing" explanation, the last of which was the one they preferred.

Based on Kahneman and Tversky's Prospect Theory and the latter's work on framing effects (Kahneman and Tversky 1979; Kahneman and Tversky 1984; Tversky and Kahneman 1981), Hershey and Schoemaker argued that in PE situations, subjects tend to reframe the initial choice between \$100 for sure and a fifty-fifty chance of winning \$200 or \$0 as a choice between \$100 for sure and a fifty-fifty chance of winning \$100 or losing \$100. But, they continued (1985, 1224), if the utility function is steeper for losses than for gains, as proposed in Prospect Theory, then the PE mode makes the subjects more risk-averse. They concluded their article: "From a psychological perspective utility measurement seems to be plagued by a variety of biases, as identified in this paper. Their relative influence and possible interactions merit further study as part of a larger research program to examine possible biases in utility measurements" (1229).

16.5. SUMMARY AND CLOSE: FROM CONFIDENCE TO SKEPTICISM

The experimental research on EUT-based utility measurement performed during the period 1950–1985 had two intertwined goals: measuring utility and testing EUT. With respect to both goals, this line of research displayed a distinct trajectory that may be characterized as "from confidence to skepticism."

Mosteller, Suppes, and the other experimenters of the 1950s were confident about both EUT and the possibility of measuring utility through it. They designed their experiments so as to neutralize some psychological factors that could jeopardize the validity of the theory and spoil the significance of the experimental measurements of utility and tended to conclude that their experimental findings supported both the experimental measurability of utility based on EUT and the descriptive validity of the theory. Dolbear, Marschak, and the other experimenters of the 1960s focused on the goal of testing EUT but continued to interpret their experimental findings as validating both the theory and the possibility of measuring utility through it.

From the mid-1960s to the mid-1970s, apparently no further EUT-based experimental study on utility measurement was published. In this period, however, the validity of EUT was increasingly called into question, and this was independent of any measurement issues. A series of laboratory experiments confirmed the existence of decision patterns violating EUT, such as those originally imagined by Allais and Ellsberg or those later identified by Lichtenstein, Slovic, and Tversky. Moreover, from the mid-1970s, a number of alternative theories to EUT, such as Handa's Certainty Equivalence model (1977), Karmarkar's SWU model (1978), and Kahneman and Tversky's Prospect Theory (1979), were put forward to explain such decision patterns. The new decision theories, in turn, suggested further decision patterns violating EUT and led to new experiments to test these possible violations.

Karmarkar, de Neufville, Schoemaker, and the other experimenters who engaged with the EUT-based measurement of utility from the mid-1970s were skeptical about EUT. Rather than designing their experiments to neutralize disturbing psychological factors, they used their psychological insights to show that different utility measures obtained within the EUT framework are often mutually inconsistent. In particular, Karmarkar and McCord–de Neufville showed that the same measurement method, namely the certainty equivalence method, generates mutually inconsistent utility measures when implemented in different probability settings. Schoemaker and his coauthors completed the picture by showing that the certainty equivalence method and the probability equivalence method, which according to EUT should produce the same outcome, in fact generate two different utility measures. Furthermore, the recorded inconsistencies appear to be systematic rather than at random, suggesting that they are due to some fundamental flaw of EUT rather than to occasional disturbing factors.

The inconsistency between different EUT-based utility measures undermines EUT at both the descriptive and the normative level. At the descriptive level, it makes it problematic to use the EUT-based utility measures obtained in a certain situation to predict the decision maker's choices in another situation. At the normative level, it calls into question the use of the utility measures obtained from the decision maker's choices between simple lotteries to advise him about how to choose between more complicated lotteries.

In sum, the experiments on utility measurement of the period 1974–1985 undermined the earlier confidence that EUT makes it possible to measure utility in an experimental way. More generally, these experiments provided evidence that added to other, measurement-free, experimental evidence against the validity of EUT that had accumulated since the mid-1960s. In this way, the experimental findings of Karmarkar, McCord, de Neufville, Hershey, Kunreuther, and Schoemaker contributed to destabilizing EUT as the dominant economic model of decision-making under risk and provided a favorable climate for the blossoming of non-EUT models that began in the mid-1970s. In this sense, these experimental findings are a significant component of the early phase of behavioral economics.

This from-confidence-to-skepticism story, however, does not have a Popperian happy ending consisting of the definitive dismissal of a now falsified EUT. Even after 1985, and still today, EUT remains the primary model in numerous areas of economics dealing with risky decisions, such as finance, the theory of asymmetric information, and game theory. Although an exhaustive epistemological analysis of the scientific endurance of EUT is still lacking, EUT's resilience seems very much due to its simplicity and adaptability, as well as the circumstance that none of the alternative theories has yet achieved the level of consensus that EUT once enjoyed. As Itzhak Gilboa and Massimo Marinacci (2013, 232) have argued in a recent survey of the decision-theoretic literature, it is not clear that a single theory of decision-making under uncertainty will replace EUT, and "even if a single paradigm will eventually emerge, it is probably too soon to tell which one it will be."

The flaws of EUT-based utility measurement do not undermine the possibility of utility measurement in general. Thus, even after 1985, the economists' struggle to measure utility continued. I point to some post-1985 episodes in the history of utility measurement in the epilogue to this book. Here, however, I move to discussing utility measurement in the period 1950–1985 along the five epistemological axes set out in the prologue and considered at the ends of the previous three parts of this work.

16.6. EPISTEMOLOGICAL ANALYSIS
16.6.1. The Understanding of Measurement

As discussed in chapter 12, in the early and mid-1950s, Friedman, Savage, Strotz, Alchian, and Ellsberg all advocated a view of utility measurement according to which it consists of the assignment of numbers to objects according to a definite set of operations. In this conception, the way of assigning utility numbers to objects is largely conventional, with the key restriction that the assigned numbers must allow the economist to predict the choice behavior of individuals.

The experiments to measure utility performed in the 1950s and 1960s may be seen as a successful application of this view of utility measurement. The experimenters were able to assign utility numbers to amounts of money according to a definite set of operations—such as the certainty equivalence method, the probability equivalence method, the money equivalence method, and the preference comparison method (see chapter 13). In turn, these utility numbers proved useful in predicting individual behavior under risk.

The experiments of the 1970s and early 1980s exposed the limits of this operational approach to utility measurement. They showed that supposedly irrelevant modifications in the measurement method, such as using lotteries with winning probabilities $p = 0.75$ rather than $p = 0.9$, can significantly change the utility measures obtained. But if there exist multiple utility measures, it is not clear which one the economist should use to predict the choice behavior of individuals.

16.6.2. The Scope of the Utility Concept

Mosteller, Suppes, and the other experimenters who attempted to measure the utility function u in the 1950s interpreted it as the traditional utility function U expressing the individual's preferences regarding riskless money. In contrast, Dolbear, Marschak, and the other experimenters of the 1960s accepted the interpretation of the utility function u that had been introduced by Friedman in 1950 and had by then become standard among utility theorists (see chapters 11 and 12). According to this view, the function u combines all psychological factors that may influence the individual's preferences between monetary lotteries and are not ruled out by the EUT axioms. In particular, the function u combines two different and independent psychological factors, namely the individual's desire for money and his or her attitude toward risk.

The experimenters who engaged with the EUT-based measurement of utility from the mid-1970s did not contest this standard interpretation of the von Neumann–Morgenstern function u.[10] Rather, these scholars showed that the values of the von Neumann–Morgenstern u depend on factors that EUT rules out, such as the subjective distortion of objective probabilities (Karmarkar, McCord, and de Neufville) or the framing effects induced by the probability equivalence method (Hershey, Kunreuther, and Schoemaker).

10. Schoemaker (1982, 533–535) explicitly advocated this interpretation.

16.6.3. The Status of Utility

The interpretation of the scope of the utility function u is strictly related to the interpretation of its status. Thus, Mosteller, Suppes, and the other experimenters of the 1950s were "mentalists" about utility: they believed that the utility measures they had obtained quantified, on an interval scale, an existing psychological object, namely the desire for money. In contrast, Dolbear, Marschak, and the other experimenters of the 1960s were "instrumentalists" and interpreted the measures of the von Neumann–Morgenstern utility function u as numerical parameters that can be used to predict individual choice behavior under risk but do not have any specific psychological correlate in the decision maker's mind.

The experimenters of the 1970s and early 1980s were also instrumentalist about the status of the von Neumann–Morgenstern function u and refrained from giving a psychological interpretation of its numerical values. Their experiments in effect showed that for the same subject, multiple and diverging von Neumann–Morgenstern utility values can be identified; and it is difficult to conceive of a psychological variable, be it desire for money or aversion to risk, that is measured at the same time and for the same person by different numbers, say 2, 7, and 10.

16.6.4. The Data for Utility Measurement

As we saw in chapters 13, 14, and 15, the EUT-based experimental measurement of the von Neumann–Morgenstern utility function u is a form of indirect measurement relying on the expected utility formula. This formula states that if L is a lottery yielding $\$M_1$ with probability p and $\$M_2$ with probability $(1 - p)$, then $u(L) = u(\$M_1) \times p + u(\$M_2) \times (1 - p)$. This mathematical expression permits the construction of equations or inequalities containing an unknown variable that is determined by some observable "activity" of the experimental subject, such as a choice, a preference judgment, an indifference judgment, or the identification of a monetary amount or a probability value. The variable so determined permits the assignment of a numerical value to u.

More concretely, in most of the experiments discussed in part IV, the relevant equation was $u(\$M) = u(\$M_1) \times p + u(\$M_2) \times (1 - p)$, where $M is the lottery L yielding $M for sure. In the certainty equivalence method of measuring utility, $\$M_1$, $\$M_2$, $u(\$M_1)$, $u(\$M_2)$, and p are given, and the subject is asked to identify the monetary amount $M that makes him indifferent between $M for sure and lottery $[\$M_1, p; \$M_2, 1 - p]$. Based on this monetary identification, we can assign a numerical value to u($M). In the probability equivalence method, $\$M_1$, $\$M_2$, $u(\$M_1)$, $u(\$M_2)$, and $M are given, and the subject is asked to identify the probability p that makes him indifferent between $M for sure and lottery $[\$M_1, p; \$M_2, 1 - p]$. Based on this probability identification, we can assign a numerical value to u($M). In some other experiments, such as that of Suppes and Walsh, the expected utility formula was used to construct inequalities of the form $u(\$M_1) \times p + u(\$M_2) \times (1 - p) > u(\$M_3) \times \dot{p} + u(\$M_4) \times (1 - \dot{p})$. The subject is here asked to choose or express his preference between lottery $[\$M_1, p; \$M_2, 1 - p]$ and lottery $[\$M_3, \dot{p}; \$M_4, 1 - \dot{p}]$, where $\$M_1$, $\$M_2$, $\$M_3$, $\$M_4$, and probabilities p and $\dot{p}$ are given. Based on a series of these observed choices, or observed preference judgments, we can assign numerical values to u($\$M_1$), u($\$M_2$), u($\$M_3$), and u($\$M_4$).

Some comments on this measurement procedure are in order. A first point concerns the observable activity the experimental subjects should perform. On the one hand, the authors of the experiments considered in part IV did not distinguish sharply between choice and preference judgment and treated these two activities, which in principle are different, as equivalent. On the other hand, some of these experimenters, and notably Mosteller–Nogee and Davidson–Suppes–Siegel, clearly distinguished between the identification of monetary amounts and the identification of probability values. Mosteller–Nogee and Davidson–Suppes–Siegel believed that people are more familiar with money than with probability and, accordingly, judged the task of identifying probabilities more difficult than the task of identifying monetary amounts.

Second, like Thurstone (see chapter 7, section 7.5) and other scholars who attempted to test utility analysis in the lab, the experimenters considered in part IV also faced the problem that the notion of indifference lacks a clear observational correlate. They overcame this problem either by resorting to a probabilistic definition of preference (the solution adopted by Mosteller and Nogee), or by adopting an approximate definition of preference (the solution of Davidson, Suppes, and Siegel), or by avoiding indifference judgments altogether and asking the subjects to state which lottery they preferred (the solution of Suppes–Walsh and Dolbear).

Third, while the experimenters of the 1950s and 1960s considered the use of real monetary rewards essential for the scientific validity of their measurements, the experimenters who measured utility in the 1970s and early 1980s had no problems in using fictional payoffs. The issue of whether real monetary incentives are actually necessary to motivate experimental subjects remains a subject of controversy between mainstream economists, who typically argue that monetary incentives are indeed necessary, and behavioral economists, who generally do not think so.[11] Here I remark only that in this respect, the methodological stance of Karmarkar, McCord–de Neufville, and Hershey–Kunreuther–Schoemaker was very much in line with that of current behavioral economists.

16.6.5. The Aims of Utility Theory

The experiments to measure von Neumann–Morgenstern utility performed in the period 1950–1985 focused on the descriptive aims of EUT but had implications also for its normative goals.

As discussed in chapter 13, the experimenters of the 1950s were confident about the validity of EUT and related their utility measurements to the explanatory and predictive power of the theory. At the explanatory level, Mosteller, Suppes, and the other experimenters of the 1950s were interested in eliciting the shape of the utility curves of their experimental

11. See Camerer and Hogarth 1999; Hertwig and Ortmann 2001; Guala 2005; and Fréchette and Schotter 2015.

subjects. As suggested by Friedman and Savage (1948), that shape could be used to explain phenomena related to gambling and insurance behavior in terms of attitudes toward risk. The idea of using utility measurement for such explanatory goals, however, was quickly abandoned. For the experiments of the 1950s showed that curvature and thus risk attitude varies significantly, and in an unpredictable way, from subject to subject. With respect to the predictive power of EUT, we saw that in the experiments of the 1950s, the utility measures inferred from an individual's choices regarding a first set of lotteries were used to predict, via the EUT formula, his choices regarding a second set of lotteries. The experimenters of the 1950s thus interpreted their findings as validating the predictive power of EUT.

In chapter 14, we saw that for the experimenters of the 1960s, the goal of eliciting the shape of the utility curves of the experimental subjects lost importance and that utility measurement was mainly associated with the goal of checking the predictive power of EUT. Dolbear, Marschak, and coauthors—like Mosteller, Suppes, and coauthors—also interpreted their experimental findings in an optimistic way: EUT is not 100 percent correct, but in a stochastic or approximate sense, it still displays an acceptable predictive power.

The findings of the experiments of the 1970s and early 1980s undermined the meaning of utility measurement, not only for predictive but also for normative aims. With respect to predictive goals, if several diverging utility measures can be inferred from the choices of an individual regarding a first set of lotteries, it is unclear which utility measure should be used to predict his choices regarding a second set of lotteries. Regarding normative goals, the problem is similar: the multiplicity of utility measures makes it unclear which utility measure should be used to advise the decision maker about how to choose between complicated lotteries.

Epilogue

In this book, I have reconstructed the history of economists' ideas about the measurability of utility from 1870 to 1985 and investigated how these ideas influenced the development of utility theory during those 115 years. In particular, I have brought into focus an element that tacitly shaped the interplay between the economists' ideas about utility measurement and the evolution of utility analysis, namely the economists' understanding of what measurement means in general. In part I of the book, I investigated the relationships between the unit-based understanding of measurement of the early utility theorists and their utility theories. In part II, I explored the connection between the discussions that led to the definition of ordinal and cardinal utility and the emergence of a non-unit-based notion of utility measurement in the 1930s. In part III, I showed how the 1945–1955 debate on the nature of the von Neumann–Morgenstern utility function eventually led economists to elaborate a conception of utility measurement that definitely liberated it from any association with units. Finally, in part IV, I examined a series of experimental attempts to measure utility on the basis of expected utility theory (EUT) and reconstructed how between 1950 and 1985, utility theorists became increasingly skeptical about EUT and the significance of the utility measurements obtained through it.

Over the course of the book, I have also explored the relationships and intersections between the history of utility measurement in economics and the history of sensation measurement in psychology. These two histories share a similar starting point, namely the unit-based conception of measurement that around 1870 dominated both disciplines; a similar initial problem, namely that of measuring, in a unit-based sense, an elusive psychological variable; and a similar evolution, that is, the gradual superseding of the unit-based understanding of measurement and eventually also the elaboration, around 1950, of a notion of measurement that was broad enough to include the psychologists' and utility theorists' quantification practices as measurement.

Finally, I have explored the epistemological dimension of utility measurement along five main axes: (1) the already-mentioned interaction between the utility theorists' general understanding of measurement, their utility theories, and the development of utility analysis; (2) the connection between the broadening of the scope of the utility concept and the shift from direct to indirect forms of utility measurement; (3) the relation between the mentalist and instrumentalist interpretations of the epistemological status of utility and the interpretation of the utility numbers; (4) the evolution of the ideas about which kinds of data can be legitimately used to measure utility; (5) the relationships between the approach to utility measurement and the descriptive or normative aims for which the utility measures are used. After 1985 and until today, economists' research on utility measurement has continued vigorously. Here I point to some main research trends in the post-1985 period.

As already mentioned, around the mid-1980s, utility theorists acknowledged the flaws of experimental utility measurements based on EUT. These flaws, however, do not undermine the possibility of measuring utility experimentally on the basis of some nonexpected utility model. The basic idea underlying such measurements can be illustrated as follows. Within EUT, the utility of lottery [$\$M_1$, p; $\$M_2$, 1 – p], with $\$M_1 \geq \$M_2 \geq 0$, is given by $u(\$M_1) \times p + u(\$M_2) \times (1 - p)$, where u is the von Neumann–Morgenstern utility function. In the so-called rank-dependent utility models (see, e.g., Quiggin 1982; Yaari 1987; Tversky and Kahneman 1992), the utility of lottery [$\$M_1$, p; $\$M_2$, 1 – p] is given by $v(\$M_1) \times w(p) + v(\$M_2) \times [1 - w(p)]$, where the cardinal function v is interpreted as a function capturing the utility of the monetary payoffs $\$M_1$ and $\$M_2$, and w is a weighting function that captures the subjective distortions of objective probability p. If we can define the functional form of w, either on theoretical grounds or on the basis of some other, independent experiment, then it becomes possible to elicit v using the certainty equivalence method or some other elicitation method. Since the subjective distortions of objective probabilities are captured by the weighting function w, these distortions should no longer interfere with the process of utility measurement; accordingly, the inconsistencies between different elicitation methods of utility observed under EUT should disappear. To illustrate how utility measurement works within rank-dependent utility models, let us reconsider the numerical example Friedman and Savage used in their 1948 article (see chapter 10, section 10.1.4) to illustrate how utility measurement works within EUT. Imagine that the individual is found to be indifferent between lottery [\$1,000, 0.6; \$500, 0.4] and \$600 for sure. Since the function v is cardinal, we can state that $v(\$500) = 0$ and $v(\$1{,}000) = 1$. If we assume that $w(p) = p^2$, by solving the equation $v(\$600) = v(\$1{,}000) \times (0.6)^2 + v(\$500) \times [1 - (0.6)^2]$, we find that $v(\$600) = 0.36$.[1]

Proponents of rank-dependent utility models have often interpreted the cardinal function v as expressing the riskless utility of the payoffs, that is, as equivalent (up to linear transformations) to the cardinal utility function U defined in the debates on transition ranking and utility differences that took place in the 1930s. The experimental measurement of utility within nonexpected utility models began in the late 1980s (Krzysztofowicz and Kock 1989) and has since flourished, especially in the 2000s.[2]

1. If the individual is indifferent between [\$1,000, 0.6; \$500, 0.4] and \$600 for sure, then $v(\$600) = v(\$1{,}000) \times (0.6)^2 + v(\$500) \times [1 - (0.6)^2]$. Since $v(\$1{,}000) = 1$ and $v(\$500) = 0$, then $v(\$600) = 1 \times 0.36 + 0 \times [1 - 0.36] = 0.36$. In chapter 10, we saw that for an expected utility maximizer who is indifferent between [\$1,000, 0.6; \$500, 0.4] and \$600 for sure, $u(\$600) = 0.6$.

2. See, among others, Wakker and Deneffe 1996; Abdellaoui, Barrios, and Wakker 2007; Abdellaoui, Bleichrodt, and l'Haridon 2008. More recently, researchers have focused on the comparison between the cardinal utility function v, which is elicited from choices between risky options within rank-dependent utility models, and the cardinal utility function elicited from intertemporal choices. The main finding of this literature is that utility under risk and utility over time differ, in

A second post-1985 research trend in utility measurement has been concerned with the measurement of utility-related concepts. Beginning in the mid-1990s, Daniel Kahneman and coauthors (see in particular Kahneman 1994; Kahneman, Wakker, and Sarin 1997) have stressed the distinction between the traditional, choice-related notion of utility, now labeled "decision utility," and other utility-related concepts such as "experienced utility," which refers to the individual's instantaneous subjective feeling of pleasure or pain associated with his current experiences rather than choices; "remembered utility," which refers to the subjective feeling of pleasure or pain that the individual associates with past experiences when he remembers them; or "happiness," which should capture the global life satisfaction of an individual as affected by his health, marital and employment status, or civic trust. Moreover, Kahneman and other behavioral economists have argued that experienced utility, remembered utility, happiness, and possibly other forms of nondecision utility can be measured on a cardinal scale, or even on a ratio scale, through questionnaires, reports of current subjective experience, or physiological indices. This research trend in utility measurement has generated a significant amount of debate concerning the reliability of the methods for measuring these utility-related concepts, the mutual relationships between these concepts, and the exact relationship between these concepts and the traditional concept of utility.[3]

A third and more recent research trend in utility measurement is based on neuroscientific techniques. A number of neuroscientists, such as Paul Glimcher (2011) and Camillo Padoa-Schioppa (2011), have argued that the economic concept of utility has a precise and measurable neural correlate. In particular, Glimcher identifies the neural correlate of utility with so-called subjective values (SVs). SVs are the mean firing rates of a specific population of neurons located in the prefrontal cortex and the ventral striatum of the brain. SVs have as measurement units action potentials per second, ranging from 0 to 1,500, which can be measured in monkeys using single-neuron measurement techniques. Because SVs are proportional to blood-oxygen-level dependence (BOLD) signals, they can also be inferred in human subjects using functional magnetic resonance imaging (fMRI). Therefore, according to Glimcher, SVs as measured by BOLD provide a ratio-scale measure of neural utility. This third post-1985 research approach to utility measurement has also generated significant discussions, and critics of neuroeconomics have questioned the reliability of the measurement methods proposed to measure neural utility, disputed the existence of an actual relationship between neural utility and the traditional concept of decision utility, and, at a more general level, attacked the tacit reductionist philosophy associated with neuroeconomics.[4]

These three post-1985 research trends in utility measurement differ not only in their specific theoretical content but also with respect to issues related to measurement. In the first place, they use different kinds of data to measure utility. The experimental measurement of utility within nonexpected utility models typically relies on choice data. In contrast, the measurement

the sense that they are not cardinally correlated. See Epper, Fehr-Duda and Bruhin 2011; Andreoni and Sprenger 2012; Abdellaoui, Bleichrodt, l'Haridon, and Paraschiv 2013; Epper and Fehr-Duda 2015; Andreoni and Sprenger 2015.

3. For reviews of this debate, see Kahneman and Krueger 2006; Kahneman and Thaler 2006; Angner 2013; Morewedge 2016.

4. See, e.g., Harrison 2008; Gul and Pesendorfer 2008; Ross 2011; Fumagalli 2013.

of experienced utility, happiness, and other forms of nondecision utility is usually based on questionnaires or reports of current subjective experience. Finally, the neuroeconomic measurement of utility depends on data produced through complex brain-imaging techniques.

Second, most utility theorists engaged in the experimental measurement of utility within non-EUT models attempt to characterize axiomatically the measurement-theoretic properties of the utility function they measure, that is, whether the function is ordinal, cardinal, or even measurable on a ratio scale. In contrast, the contributors to the second and third research trends described here are not interested in axiomatic characterizations of their measurement practices. If we contrast Patrick Suppes's axiomatic approach to measurement with the pragmatic and antiaxiomatic approach advocated by Stanley Smith Stevens (see chapters 8 and 15), we can say that the first group of researchers follow Suppes's approach to measurement, while those interested in the measurement of experienced utility, happiness, or neural utility are more in line with Stevens's views.[5]

What these three research trends do seem to share is a mentalistic interpretation of the status of utility. This is pretty obvious in the case of neuroeconomists, who pursue the measurement of "utility in the brain," and also for behavioral economists, who want to measure psychological states such as experienced utility or happiness. Yet it is valid also for the utility theorists engaged in the experimental measurement of utility within non-EUT models (see, e.g., Wakker 1994; Abdellaoui, Barrios, and Wakker 2007). These models have more free parameters than EUT and can therefore differentiate between various factors that influence the individual's preferences between lotteries. In contrast, and as discussed in chapter 12, in EUT, the individual's attitude toward risk, his desire for money, and possibly all other factors that affect his preferences between lotteries are packed into the von Neumann–Morgenstern utility function. Thus, it is difficult to give this function a plausible psychological interpretation. In contrast, in the rank-dependent utility model, the individual's attitude toward risk is captured by the weighting function w, and this makes it easier to interpret the elicited utility function v as expressing numerically the psychological desire for money.

This brief overview of some post-1985 research trends in utility measurement shows that the economists' struggle to measure utility, which began with the marginal revolution almost one hundred fifty years ago, is far from concluded. Perhaps at some point in the future, the utility notion will no longer be the cornerstone of so much economic theory, and economists will explain prices, consumer behavior, market equilibria, and other relevant economic phenomena without referring to utility. For instance, future economists might explain economic phenomena by using a sophisticated bounded-rationality model based on a series of simple and easily applicable heuristics. In this hypothetical scenario, the problems associated with utility measurement would disappear, and future economists might find the history of these problems as obscure and bizarre as today's astronomers find the history of the problems internal to the Ptolemaic system. Currently, however, this scenario is not in sight, and utility will probably stay with us for some while. Thus, the history of economists' unremitting struggle to measure utility is not the history of our past but remains the history of our present.

5. See more on the contrast between approaches to measurement à la Suppes and à la Stevens in recent research in behavioral economics in Angner 2011.

ACKNOWLEDGMENTS

This book originated in a paper I presented at the 2008 meeting of the History of Economics Society. The paper, "Changing the Yardstick," attempted to address the transformation of the notion of measurement that occurred in utility theory from the marginal revolution to the mid-1950s. Comments from colleagues helped me understand that the topic was far too rich and complex to be dealt with in a single paper. I therefore began working on a series of separate papers addressing more circumscribed episodes in the history of utility measurement. I did not think of these papers as potential parts of a book until around 2012, when Scott Parris of Oxford University Press asked me whether I had any ideas for a monograph related to the history of microeconomics. The discussion with Scott made me realize that the pieces I was writing could become the chapters of a book. My first thanks thus go to Scott, whose maieutic powers are at the very origin of this book and who has followed the development of the project with empathy and care even after his retirement from the publishing business.

During the long preparation of the book, I have been helped and supported by many friends and colleagues. Marco Dardi, Philippe Mongin, and Aldo Montesano have generously spent a lot of their time discussing with me the nuances of utility analysis that are relevant for issues related to utility measurement. I greatly benefited from their advice. In the early stages of the project, a number of discussions with Philippe also helped me to better define the goals and scope of the book. Francesco Guala read significant portions of the manuscript, and we discussed them in a number of amiable lunch conversations. Among other things, I owe to Francesco a better understanding of the epistemological issues associated with utility measurement and the realization that it was preferable to leave the most recent research in utility measurement out of the present narrative. Jean Baccelli also read significant parts of the manuscript, and his sharp comments and philosophical perceptiveness have greatly improved the work. Simon Cook supplied countless valuable suggestions on how to improve the language of the book and, more important, how to make the narrative more coherent and effective. Steve Medema has always been extremely supportive of the project, and his punctual comments led me to clarify my own thinking on a number of issues. I would like to thank Steve also for gently pushing me to bring the project to an end. Itzhak Gilboa, Nicola Giocoli, Massimo Marinacci, Peter Wakker, and Carlo Zappia have offered insightful and very helpful comments on the parts of the book dealing with expected utility theory. Peter also read the preproof version of the manuscript and provided a number of valuable last minute remarks. Richard de Neufville, Trenery Dolbear, and Uday Karmarkar graciously answered my questions concerning their experiments in utility measurement.

I also thank my colleagues at Insubria University Francesco Figari and Raffaello Seri and, at Bocconi University, Pierpaolo Battigalli for a number of helpful discussions on some specific aspects of the book's topic. Luca Congiu, a Ph.D. student of mine at Insubria, provided excellent research assistance.

Beyond Insubria and Bocconi, the project greatly benefited from conversations with colleagues from many other institutions. In particular, I am grateful to Wade Hands, Catherine Herfeld, Roger Backhouse, John Davis, Marcel Boumans, Jeff Biddle, Richard Bradley, Kevin Hoover, Jean-Sébastien Lenfant, Harro Maas, Mary Morgan, Michael Mandler, Joseph Persky, David Teira, Erik Angner, Annalisa Rosselli, James Wible, Pedro Duarte, Margaret Schabas, Floris Heukelom, Franco Donzelli, Mikaël Cozic, Dorian Jullien, and Roberto Fumagalli for their useful comments and insights on various parts of the book. I also thank the anonymous readers for Oxford University Press, whose constructive comments on the original book project and the first version of the manuscript led to substantial improvements to the work. Of course, none of the abovementioned friends and colleagues is responsible for whatever is flawed in my history of utility measurement.

Over the years, I have had the chance to present early versions of parts of the book at seminars at the London School of Economics, Duke University, the École Normale Supérieure in Paris, the Ludwig Maximilian University of Munich, the University of Turin, the University Paris 1 Panthéon-Sorbonne, the University of Lausanne, the University of Nice Sophia Antipolis, the Max Planck Institute of Economics in Jena, UNED Madrid, the University of Siena, Lumière University Lyon, and the Sant'Anna School of Advanced Studies in Pisa; at various academic conferences of the History of Economics Society (HES), the European Society for the History of Economic Thought (ESHET), the International Network for Economic Method (INEM), and the Associazione Italiana per la Storia dell'Economia Politica (STOREP); and in a couple of the D-TEA workshops. I thank the participants of all these events for their comments and suggestions.

I wrote significant parts of the book while visiting a number of European institutions. I thank the Centre for Philosophy of Natural and Social Science at the London School of Economics, the Friedrich Schiller University of Jena, the Institute for the History and Philosophy of Science and Technology in Paris, and the Munich Center for Mathematical Philosophy for their hospitality. Some of these academic visits were made possible by funds provided by Fondazione Cariplo, the European Society for the History of Economic Thought, and the Munich Center for Mathematical Philosophy; I gratefully acknowledge the financial assistance of these institutions. I also thank Matteo Rocca, the director of the economics department at Insubria, for his important support of the entire project and for helping me accommodate periods abroad with the life of our department.

I am grateful to the members of the staff at Yale University Library, the Hoover Institution Archives, and especially the David M. Rubenstein Rare Book and Manuscript Library at Duke University for their kind and helpful assistance when I was working in the archives of Baumol, Friedman, Morgenstern, Savage, and Samuelson. I also thank the staff at Bocconi University Library for promptly retrieving the publications I have used for the project and Antonio Ragona, the Bocconi doorman, for his warm welcomes on early Sunday mornings. Finally, I am grateful to David Pervin, Hayley Singer, and the editorial team at Oxford University Press for the care they have given to this project over the last two years.

Several portions of this book draw on work previously published elsewhere. Chapters 1, 2, 7, and 13 expand on three articles published in *History of Political Economy* (© Duke University Press): "Early Experiments in Consumer Demand Theory: 1930–1970," 39, no. 3 (2007): 359–401; "Were Jevons, Menger, and Walras Really Cardinalists? On the Notion of Measurement in Utility Theory, Psychology, Mathematics, and Other Disciplines, 1870–1910," 45, no. 3 (2013): 373-414; "Measuring the Economizing Mind in the 1940s and 1950s: The Mosteller–Nogee and Davidson–Suppes–Siegel Experiments to Measure the Utility of Money," 48 (annual supplement, 2017): 239–269. Chapters 3 and 5 draw in part on the chapter "Austrian Debates on Utility Measurement, from Menger to Hayek," in *Hayek: A Collaborative Biography*, Part IV: *England, the Ordinal Revolution and the Road to Serfdom, 1931–1950*, edited by R. Leeson, 137–179, New York: Palgrave Macmillan, 2015, reproduced with permission of Palgrave Macmillan. Chapter 6 is derived in part from an article published in the *European Journal of the History of Economic Thought* (© Taylor & Francis): "How Cardinal Utility Entered Economic Analysis, 1909–1944," 20, no. 6 (2013): 906–939, http://www.tandfonline.com/doi/full/10.1080/09672567.2013.825001. Chapters 10 and 11 draw on the article "How Economists Came to Accept Expected Utility Theory: The Case of Samuelson and Savage," *Journal of Economic Perspectives* 30, no. 2 2016): 219–236, © American Economic Association, reproduced with permission of the *Journal of Economic Perspectives*. Chapter 15 is derived in part from an article published in the *Journal of Economic Methodology* (© Taylor & Francis): "Measurement Theory and Utility Analysis in Suppes' Early Work, 1951–1958," 23, no. 3 (2016): 252–267, http://www.tandfonline.com/doi/full/10.1080/1350178X.2016.1189113. Finally, chapters 14 and 16 are derived in part from an article published in the *European Journal of the History of Economic Thought* (© Taylor & Francis): "Expected Utility Theory and Experimental Utility Measurement, 1950–1985: From Confidence to Scepticism," 24, no. 6 (2017): 1318–1354, http://www.tandfonline.com/doi/abs/10.1080/09672567.2017.1378692. Figure 7.1 is reproduced with permission of Taylor & Francis. Figures 10.1 and 13.1 are reproduced with permission of the University of Chicago Press. Figure 13.2 is reproduced with permission of Stanford University Press. Figure 16.1 is reproduced with permission of Uday Karmarkar.

REFERENCES

Abdellaoui, M., C. Barrios, and P. P. Wakker. 2007. "Reconciling Introspective Utility with Revealed Preference: Experimental Arguments Based on Prospect Theory." *Journal of Econometrics* 138: 336–378.

Abdellaoui, M., H. Bleichrodt, and O. l'Haridon. 2008. "A Tractable Method to Measure Utility and Loss Aversion under Prospect Theory." *Journal of Risk and Uncertainty* 36: 245–266.

Abdellaoui, M., H. Bleichrodt, O. l'Haridon, and C. Paraschiv. 2013. "Is There One Unifying Concept of Utility? An Experimental Comparison of Utility under Risk and Utility over Time." *Management Science* 59: 2153–2169.

Afriat, S. N. 1967. "The Construction of Utility Functions from Expenditure Data." *International Economic Review* 8: 67–77.

Alchian, A. 1953. "The Meaning of Utility Measurement." *American Economic Review* 43: 26–50.

Alchian, A. 1996. "Principles of Professional Advancement." *Economic Inquiry* 34: 520–526.

Aldrich, J. 1996. "The Course of Marshall's Theorizing about Demand." *History of Political Economy* 28: 171–217.

Allais, M. 1943. *À la recherche d'une discipline économique*. Paris: Ateliers Industria.

Allais, M. [1952] 1953. "Fondements d'une théorie positive des choix comportant un risque." In *Économétrie*, Actes du colloque "Fondements et applications de la théorie du risque en économétrie," 127–140. Paris: Centre National de la Recherche Scientifique.

Allais, M. 1953. "Le comportement de l'homme rationnel devant le risque: Critique des postulats et axiomes de l'école americaine." *Econometrica* 21: 503–546.

Allais, M. [1953] 1979. "The Foundations of a Positive Theory of Choice Involving Risk and a Criticism of the Postulates and Axioms of the American School." In *Expected Utility Hypotheses and the Allais Paradox*, edited by M. Allais and O. Hagen, 27–145. Dordrecht: Reidel.

Allais, M., and O. Hagen, eds. 1979. *Expected Utility Hypotheses and the Allais Paradox*. Dordrecht: Reidel.

Allen, R. G. D. 1933. "On the Marginal Utility of Money and Its Application." *Economica* 40: 186–209.

Allen, R. G. D. 1935. "A Note on the Determinateness of the Utility Function." *Review of Economic Studies* 2: 155–158.

Allen, R. G. D. 1936. "Professor Slutsky's Theory of Consumer's Choice." *Review of Economic Studies* 3: 120–129.

Allen, R. G. D. 1938. *Mathematical Analysis for Economists*. London: Macmillan.

Allen, R. L. 1993. *Irving Fisher: A Biography*. New York: Wiley.

Alt, F. 1936. "Über die Messbarkeit des Nutzens." *Zeitschrift für Nationalökonomie* 7: 161–169.

Alt, F. [1936] 1971. "On the Measurability of Utility." In *Preferences, Utility, and Demand*, edited by J. S. Chipman, L. Hurwicz, M. K. Richter, and H. F. Sonnenschein, 424–431. New York: Harcourt Brace Jovanovich.

Alt, F., and A. Akera. 2006. "Franz Alt Interview: 23 January and 2 February, 2006." *ACM Oral History Interviews* 1: 1–89.

Amoroso, L. 1921. *Lezioni di economia matematica*. Bologna: Zanichelli.

Anand, P. 1993. "The Philosophy of Intransitive Preference." *Economic Journal* 103: 337–346.

Andreoni, J., and C. Sprenger. 2012. "Risk Preferences Are Not Time Preferences." *American Economic Review* 102: 3357–3376.

Andreoni, J., and C. Sprenger. 2015. "Risk Preferences Are Not Time Preferences: Reply." *American Economic Review* 105: 2287–2293.

Angner, E. 2011. "Current Trends in Welfare Measurement." In *The Elgar Companion to Recent Economic Methodology*, edited by J. B. Davis and D. W. Hands, 121–154. Cheltenham: Elgar.

Angner, E. 2013. "Is It Possible to Measure Happiness? The Argument from Measurability." *European Journal for Philosophy of Science* 3: 221–240.

Arrow, K. J. 1951a. "Alternative Approaches to the Theory of Choice in Risk-Taking Situations." *Econometrica* 19: 404–437.

Arrow, K. J. 1951b. *Social Choice and Individual Values*. New York: Wiley.

Arrow, K. J. [1952] 1953. "Le rôle des valeurs boursières pour la répartition la meilleure des risques." In *Économétrie*, Actes du colloque "Fondements et applications de la théorie du risque en économétrie," 41–48. Paris: Centre National de la Recherche Scientifique.

Arrow, K. J. 1958. "Utilities, Attitudes, Choices: A Review Note." *Econometrica* 26: 1–23.

Arrow, K. J. 1960. "The Work of Ragnar Frisch, Econometrician." *Econometrica* 28: 175–192.

Arrow, K. J. 1964. "The Role of Securities in the Optimal Allocation of Risk-Bearing." *Review of Economic Studies* 31: 91–96.

Arrow, K. J. 1991. "Jacob Marschak." *Biographical Memoirs* 60: 127–156.

Arrow, K. J. 2016. *On Ethics and Economics: Conversations with Kenneth J. Arrow*, edited by K. R. Mondore and N. M. Lampros. New York: Routledge.

Auspitz, R., and R. Lieben. 1889. *Untersuchungen über die Theorie des Preises*. Leipzig: Duncker und Humblot.

Baccelli, J. 2016. "Essais d'analyse de la théorie axiomatique de la décision." Ph.D. dissertation, Ecole Normale Supérieure, Paris.

Baccelli, J., and P. Mongin. 2016. "Choice-Based Cardinal Utility: A Tribute to Patrick Suppes." *Journal of Economic Methodology* 23: 268–288.

Backhouse, R. E. 2014. "Paul A. Samuelson's Move to MIT." *History of Political Economy* 46, supp.: 60–77.

Backhouse, R. E. 2015. "Revisiting Samuelson's *Foundations of Economic Analysis*." *Journal of Economic Literature* 53: 326–350.

Backhouse, R. E. 2017. *Founder of Modern Economics: Paul A. Samuelson*, Vol. 1: *Becoming Samuelson, 1915–1948*. New York: Oxford University Press.

Barber, W. J. 2005. "Irving Fisher of Yale." *American Journal of Economics and Sociology* 64: 43–55.

Barone, E. 1894. "Sulla 'Consumers' Rent.'" *Giornale degli Economisti* 9: 211–224.

Bather, J. 1996. "A Conversation with Herman Chernoff." *Statistical Science* 11: 335–350.

Baumol, W. J. No date. Papers. David M. Rubenstein Rare Book and Manuscript Library, Duke University.

Baumol, W. J. 1949. "Relaying the Foundations." *Economica* 16: 159–168.

Baumol, W. J. 1951. "The Neumann–Morgenstern Utility Index—An Ordinalist View." *Journal of Political Economy* 59: 61–66.

Baumol, W. J. 1953. "Discussion." *American Economic Review, Papers and Proceedings* 43: 415–416.

Baumol, W. J. 1958. "The Cardinal Utility Which Is Ordinal." *Economic Journal* 68: 665–672.

Baumol, W. J. 1961. *Economic Theory and Operations Analysis*. Englewood Cliffs, N.J.: Prentice-Hall.

Becker, G. M., M. H. DeGroot, and J. Marschak. 1963a. "An Experimental Study of Some Stochastic Models for Wagers." *Behavioral Science* 8: 199–202.

Becker, G. M., M. H. DeGroot, and J. Marschak. 1963b. "Probabilities of Choices among Very Similar Objects." *Behavioral Science* 8: 306–311.

Becker, G. M., M. H. DeGroot, and J. Marschak. 1963c. "Stochastic Models of Choice Behavior." *Behavioral Science* 8: 41–55.

Becker, G. M., M. H. DeGroot, and J. Marschak. 1964. "Measuring Utility by a Single-Response Sequential Method." *Behavioral Science* 9: 226–232.

Becker, S. W., and F. O. Brownson. 1964. "What Price Ambiguity? Or the Role of Ambiguity in Decision-Making." *Journal of Political Economy* 72: 62–73.

Benham, F. C. 1934. "Notes on the Pure Theory of Public Finance." *Economica* 1: 436–458.

Bergson, A. 1938. "A Reformulation of Certain Aspects of Welfare Economics." *Quarterly Journal of Economics* 52: 310–334.

Bergson, H. [1889] 1960. *Time and Free Will*. New York: Harper.

Bernardelli, H. 1934. "Notes on the Determinateness of the Utility Function, II." *Review of Economic Studies* 2: 69–75.

Bernoulli, D. [1738] 1954. "Exposition of a New Theory on the Measurement of Risk." *Econometrica* 22: 23–36.

Binmore, K. 1999. "Why Experiment in Economics?" *Economic Journal* 109: F16–F24.

Bishop, R. L. 1943. "Consumer's Surplus and Cardinal Utility." *Quarterly Journal of Economics* 57: 421–449.

Bjerkholt, O. 1998. "Ragnar Frisch and the Foundation of the Econometric Society and Econometrica." In *Econometrics and Economic Theory in the 20th Century: The Ragnar Frisch Centennial Symposium*, edited by S. Strøm, 26–57. Cambridge: Cambridge University Press.

Bjerkholt, O., and A. Dupont. 2010. "Ragnar Frisch's Conception of Econometrics." *History of Political Economy* 42: 21–73.

Black, R. D. C., ed. 1972–1981. *Papers and Correspondence of William Stanley Jevons*, 7 vols. London: Macmillan.

Blaug, M. 1997. *Economic Theory in Retrospect*, 5th ed. Cambridge: Cambridge University Press.

Bleichrodt, H., C. Li, I. Moscati, and P. P. Wakker. 2016. "Nash Was a First to Axiomatize Expected Utility." *Theory and Decision* 81: 309–312.

Block, H. D., and J. Marschak. [1960] 1974. "Random Orderings and Stochastic Theories of Responses." In J. Marschak, *Economic Information, Decision, and Prediction: Selected Essays*, Vol. 1, 172–217. Dordrecht: Reidel.

Bock, M. E. 2004. "Conversations with Herman Rubin." In *A Festschrift for Herman Rubin*, edited by A. Dasgupta, 408–417. Beachwood, Ohio: Institute of Mathematical Statistics.

Boehm, S. 1992. Austrian Economics between the Wars. In *Austrian Economics: Tensions and New Directions*, edited by B. J. Caldwell and S. Boehm, 1–30. Boston: Kluwer.

Böhm-Bawerk, E. von. [1881] 1962. *Whether Legal Rights and Relationships Are Economic Goods*. In *Shorter Classics of Böhm-Bawerk*, 25–138. South Holland: Libertarian Press.

Böhm-Bawerk, E. von. [1884] 1890. *Capital and Interest: A Critical History of Economical Theory*. London: Macmillan.

Böhm-Bawerk, E. von. [1886] 1932. *Grundzüge der Theorie des wirtschaftlichen Güterwerts*. London: London School of Economics.

Böhm-Bawerk, E. von. [1889] 1891. *Capital and Interest: The Positive Theory of Capital*, Vol. 1. London: Macmillan.

Böhm-Bawerk, E. von. [1909–1912] 1959. *Capital and Interest: The Positive Theory of Capital*, Vols. 2 and 3. South Holland: Libertarian Press.

Boring, E. G. 1923. "Intelligence As the Tests Test It." *New Republic* 35: 34–37.

Boring, E. G. 1929. *A History of Experimental Psychology*. New York: Appleton.

Bostaph, S. 1978. "The Methodological Debate between Carl Menger and the German Historicists." *Atlantic Economic Journal* 6: 3–16.

Boumans, M. 2005. *How Economists Model the World into Numbers*. London: Routledge.

Boumans, M., ed. 2007. *Measurement in Economics: A Handbook*. London: Academic Press.

Boumans, M. 2015. *Science outside the Laboratory*. New York: Oxford University Press.

Boumans, M. 2016. "Friedman and the Cowles Commission." In *Milton Friedman: Contributions to Economics and Public Policy*, edited by R. A. Cord and J. D. Hammond, 585–604. New York: Oxford University Press.
Bourdeau, M. 2015. "Auguste Comte." In *Stanford Encyclopedia of Philosophy (Winter 2015)*, edited by E. N. Zalta. https://plato.stanford.edu/archives/win2015/entries/comte/.
Bowley, A. L. 1924. *The Mathematical Groundwork of Economics*. Oxford: Clarendon Press.
Bowley, A. L. 1932. "Review of *New Methods of Measuring Marginal Utility* by R. Frisch." *Economic Journal* 42: 252–256.
Bridgman, P. W. 1927. *The Logic of Modern Physics*. New York: Macmillan.
Brown, A., and A. Deaton. 1972. "Surveys in Applied Economics: Models of Consumer Behaviour." *Economic Journal* 82: 1145–1236.
Brown, W. 1911. *The Essentials of Mental Measurement*. Cambridge: Cambridge University Press.
Brown, W. 1913. "Are the Intensity Differences of Sensation Quantitative? IV." *British Journal of Psychology* 6: 184–189.
Brown, W., and G. H. Thomson. 1921. *The Essentials of Mental Measurement*. Cambridge: Cambridge University Press.
Bruner, J. S., L. Postman, and F. Mosteller. 1950. "A Note on the Measurement of Reversals of Perspective." *Psychometrika* 15: 63–72.
Bruni, L. 2002. *Vilfredo Pareto and the Birth of Modern Microeconomics*. Cheltenham: Elgar.
Bruni, L., and F. Guala. 2001. "Vilfredo Pareto and the Epistemological Foundations of Choice Theory." *History of Political Economy* 33: 21–49.
Bruni, L., and A. Montesano, eds. 2009. *New Essays on Pareto's Economic Theory*. London: Routledge.
Burdman Feferman, A., and S. Feferman. 2004. *Alfred Tarski: Life and Logic*. New York: Cambridge University Press.
Burk, A. 1936. "Real Income, Expenditure Proportionality, and Frisch's 'New Methods of Measuring Marginal Utility.'" *Review of Economic Studies* 4: 33–52.
Burnside, W. 1911. *Theory of Groups of Finite Order*. Cambridge: Cambridge University Press.
Busino, G., ed. 1989. *Vilfredo Pareto. Lettres et correspondances*. Geneva: Droz.
Cairnes, J. E. [1872] 1981. "New Theories in Political Economy." In *Papers and Correspondence of William Stanley Jevons*, 7 vols., edited by R. D. C. Black, 7: 146–152. London: Macmillan.
Caldwell, B. J. 1980. "A Critique of Friedman's Methodological Instrumentalism." *Southern Economic Journal* 47: 366–374.
Camerer, C. F., and R. M. Hogarth. 1999. "The Effects of Financial Incentives in Experiments." *Journal of Risk and Uncertainty* 19: 7–42.
Campbell, N. R. 1920. *Physics: The Elements*. Cambridge: Cambridge University Press.
Campbell, N. R. 1921. *What Is Science?* London: Methuen.
Campbell, N. R. 1928. *An Account of the Principles of Measurement and Calculation*. London: Longmans, Green, & Company.
Campbell, N. R. 1933. "The Measurement of Visual Sensations." *Proceedings of the Physical Society* 45: 565–590.
Cantor, G. [1887] 1932. "Mitteilungen zur Lehre vom Transfiniten." In *Gesammelte Abhandlungen*, edited by E. Zermelo, 378–439. Berlin: Springer.
Caplin, A. 2008. "Economic Theory and Psychological Data: Bridging the Divide." In *The Foundations of Positive and Normative Economics*, edited by A. Caplin and A. Schotter, 336–371. New York: Oxford University Press.
Caplin, A., and A. Schotter, eds. 2008. *The Foundations of Positive and Normative Economics*. New York: Oxford University Press.
Cassel, G. 1899. "Grundriss einer elementaren Preislehre." *Zeitschrift für die gesamte Staatswissenschaft* 55: 395–458.
Cattell, J. M. 1902. "Measurement." In *Dictionary of Philosophy and Psychology*, edited by J. M. Baldwin, Vol. 2, 57–58. London: Macmillan.

Chambers, P. C., and F. Echenique. 2016. *Revealed Preference Theory*. Cambridge: Cambridge University Press.

Chang, H. 1995. "Circularity and Reliability in Measurement." *Perspective on Science* 3: 153–172.

Chang, H. 2004. *Inventing Temperature*. Oxford: Oxford University Press.

Chang, H. 2009. "Operationalism." In *Stanford Encyclopedia of Philosophy (Fall 2009)*, edited by E. N. Zalta. http://plato.stanford.edu/archives/fall2009/entries/operationalism/.

Cherchye, L., I. Crawford, B. De Rock, and F. Vermeulen. 2009. "The Revealed Preference Approach to Demand." In *Quantifying Consumer Preferences*, edited by D. J. Slottje, 247–279. Bingley: Emerald.

Cherrier, B. 2010. "Rationalizing Human Organization in an Uncertain World: Jacob Marschak, from Ukrainian Prisons to Behavioral Science Laboratories." *History of Political Economy* 42: 443–467.

Chipman, J. S. 1971. "Introduction to Part II." In *Preferences, Utility, and Demand*, edited by J. S. Chipman, L. Hurwicz, M. K. Richter, and H. F. Sonnenschein, 321–331. New York: Harcourt Brace Jovanovich.

Chipman, J. S. 1976. "The Paretian Heritage." *Revue Européenne des Sciences Sociales* 14: 65–173.

Chipman, J. S., and J.-S. Lenfant. 2002. "Slutsky's 1915 Article: How It Came to Be Found and Interpreted." *History of Political Economy* 34: 553–597.

CNRS. 1953. *Économétrie*, Actes du colloque "Fondements et applications de la théorie du risque en économétrie." Paris: Centre National de la Recherche Scientifique.

Coen, R. M. 2008. "Strotz, Robert H." *The New Palgrave Dictionary of Economics*, edited by S. N. Durlauf and L. E. Blume. London: Palgrave Macmillan, http://www.dictionaryofeconomics.com.

Cohen, M. R., and E. Nagel. 1934. *An Introduction to Logic and Scientific Method*. New York: Harcourt Brace.

Cohn, P. M. 1989. "Israel Nathan Herstein." *Bulletin of the London Mathematical Society* 21: 594–600.

Colander, D. 2007. "Edgeworth's Hedonimeter and the Quest to Measure Utility." *Journal of Economic Perspectives* 21: 215–225.

Colman, A. M., and E. Shafir. 2008. "Tversky, Amos." In *New Dictionary of Scientific Biography*, edited by N. Koertge, 7: 91–97. New York: Scribner.

Coombs, C. H. 1950. "Psychological Scaling without a Unit of Measurement." *Psychological Review* 57: 145–158.

Coombs, C. H., R. M. Dawes, and A. Tversky. 1970. *Mathematical Psychology: An Elementary Introduction*. Englewood Cliffs, N.J.: Prentice-Hall.

Coombs, C. H., H. Raiffa, and R. M. Thrall. 1954. "Some Views on Mathematical Models and Measurement Theory." *Psychological Review* 61: 132–144.

Cournot, A. A. [1838] 1897. *Researches into the Mathematical Principles of the Theory of Wealth*. New York: Macmillan.

Cowles Foundation. 1961. "Report of Research Activities July 1, 1958–June 30, 1961." Cowles Foundation, Yale University.

Cowles Foundation. 1964. "Report of Research Activities July 1, 1961–June 30, 1964." Cowles Foundation, Yale University.

Čuhel, F. 1907. *Zur Lehre von den Bedürfnissen*. Innsbruck: Wagnerschen Universität Buchhandlung.

Čuhel, F. [1907] 1994. "On the Theory of Needs" (translation of chap. 6 of Čuhel 1907). In *Classics in Austrian Economics*, Vol. 1: *The Founding Era*, edited by I. M. Kirzner, 305–337. London: Pickering and Chatto.

Čuhel, F. [1907] 2007. "On the Theory of Needs." *New Perspectives on Political Economy* 3: 27–56.

Dalkey, N. C. 1949. "A Numerical Scale for Partially Ordered Utilities." RAND Corporation, Research Memorandum 296.

Dardi, M. 2008. "Utilitarianism without Utility: A Missed Opportunity in Alfred Marshall's Theory of Market Choice." *History of Political Economy* 40: 613–632.

Darrigol, O. 2003. "Number and Measure: Hermann von Helmholtz at the Crossroads of Mathematics, Physics, and Psychology." *Studies in the History and Philosophy of Science* 34: 515–573.

Davidson, D. 1999. "Intellectual Autobiography." In *The Philosophy of Donald Davidson*, edited by L. E. Hahn, 3–70. Chicago: Open Court.

Davidson, D., and J. Marschak. [1959] 1974. "Experimental Tests of a Stochastic Decision Theory." In J. Marschak, *Economic Information, Decision, and Prediction: Selected Essays*, Vol. 1, 133–171. Dordrecht: Reidel.

Davidson, D., and P. Suppes. 1956. "A Finitistic Axiomatization of Subjective Probability and Utility." *Econometrica* 24: 264–275.

Davidson, D., J. Goheen, and P. Suppes. 1954. "J. C. C. McKinsey." *Proceedings and Addresses of the American Philosophical Association* 27: 103–104.

Davidson, D., J. C. C. McKinsey, and P. Suppes. 1955. "Outlines of a Formal Theory of Value, I." *Philosophy of Science* 22: 140–160.

Davidson, D., P. Suppes, and S. Siegel. 1957. *Decision Making: An Experimental Approach*. Stanford: Stanford University Press.

Davis, H., and S. S. Stevens. 1938. *Hearing: Its Psychology and Physiology*. New York: Wiley.

Deaton, A. 1986. "Demand Analysis." In *Handbook of Econometrics*, edited by Z. Griliches and M. D. Intriligator, 3: 1767–1839. Amsterdam: North-Holland.

Deaton, A., and J. Muellbauer. 1980. *Economics and Consumer Behavior*. Cambridge: Cambridge University Press.

Debreu, G. 1954. "Representation of a Preference Ordering by a Numerical Function." In *Decision Processes*, edited by R. M. Thrall, C. H. Coombs, and R. L. Davis, 159–165. New York: Wiley.

Debreu, G. 1958. "Stochastic Choice and Cardinal Utility." *Econometrica* 26: 440–444.

Dedekind, R. [1888] 1999. *Was Sind und Was Sollen die Zahlen?* In *From Kant to Hilbert: A Source Book in the Foundations of Mathematics*, Vol. 2, edited by W. Ewald, 787–833. Oxford: Clarendon Press.

De Finetti, B. 1937. "La prévision: Ses lois logiques, ses sources subjectives." *Annales de l'Institut Henri Poincaré* 7: 1–68.

DeGroot, M. H. 1963. "Some Comments on the Experimental Measurement of Utility." *Behavioral Science* 8: 146–149.

Delboeuf, J. 1873. *Etude psychologique*. Brussels: Hayez.

Delboeuf, J. 1875. "La mesure des sensations." *Revue Scientifique* 46: 1014–1017.

Delboeuf, J. 1878. "La loi psychophysique et le nouveau livre de Fechner." *Revue Philosophique* 5: 34–63, 127–157.

Delboeuf, J. 1883. *Examen critique de la loi psychophysique*. Paris: Baillere.

De Pietri-Tonelli, A. 1927. *Traité d'économie rationnelle*. Paris: Giard.

De Rosa, G., ed. 1960. *Vilfredo Pareto. Lettere a Maffeo Pantaleoni 1890–1923*, 3 vols. Rome: Banca Nazionale del Lavoro.

Descartes, R. [1628] 1999. *Rules for the Direction of the Mind*. In *The Philosophical Writings of Descartes*, Vol. 1, 7–77. Cambridge: Cambridge University Press.

Dobb, M. H. 1966. "Oskar Lange." *Journal of the Royal Statistical Society*, series A 129: 616–617.

Dolbear, F. T. 1963. "Individual Choice under Uncertainty: An Experimental Study." *Yale Economic Essays* 3: 419–469.

Dominedò, V. 1933. "Considerazioni intorno alla teoria della Domanda." *Giornale degli Economisti e Rivista di Statistica* 73: 30–48, 765–807.

Dooley, P. C. 1983. "Consumer's Surplus: Marshall and His Critics." *Canadian Journal of Economics* 16: 26–38.

Du Bois-Reymond, P. 1882. *Die allgemeine Funktionentheorie*. Tübingen: Laupp.

Düppe, T., and E. R. Weintraub. 2014. *Finding Equilibrium*. Princeton: Princeton University Press.

Dupuit, J. [1844] 1952. "On the Measurement of the Utility of Public Works." *International Economic Papers* 2: 83–110.
Econometric Society. 1951. "Report of the Chicago Meeting, December 27–30, 1950." *Econometrica* 19: 321–350.
Edgeworth, F. Y. 1881. *Mathematical Psychics*. London: Kegan Paul.
Edgeworth, F. Y. 1884. "The Philosophy of Chance." *Mind* 9: 223–235.
Edgeworth, F. Y. 1887. *Metretike: or, The Method of Measuring Probability and Utility*. London: Temple.
Edgeworth, F. Y. 1894. "Professor J. S. Nicholson on 'Consumers' Rent.'" *Economic Journal* 4: 151–158.
Edgeworth, F. Y. 1900. "The Incidence of Urban Rates, I." *Economic Journal* 10: 172–193.
Edgeworth, F. Y. 1907. "Appreciations of Mathematical Theories." *Economic Journal* 17: 221–231.
Edgeworth, F. Y. 1915. "Recent Contributions to Mathematical Economics." *Economic Journal* 25: 36–63, 189–203.
Edwards, W. 1953. "Probability-Preferences in Gambling." *American Journal of Psychology* 66: 349–364.
Edwards, W. 1954a. "Probability-Preferences among Bets with Differing Expected Values." *American Journal of Psychology* 67: 56–67.
Edwards, W. 1954b. "The Reliability of Probability-Preferences." *American Journal of Psychology* 67: 68–95.
Edwards, W. 1954c. "The Theory of Decision Making." *Psychological Bulletin* 51: 380–417.
Ekelund, R. B., and R. F. Hébert. 1985. "Consumer Surplus: The First Hundred Years." *History of Political Economy* 17: 419–454.
Ekelund, R. B., and R. F. Hébert. 1990. *A History of Economic Theory and Method*, 3rd ed. New York: McGraw-Hill.
Ellsberg, D. 1954. "Classic and Current Notions of 'Measurable Utility.'" *Economic Journal* 64: 528–556.
Ellsberg, D. 1958. "Review of *Decision Making: An Experimental Approach* by D. Davidson, P. Suppes, and S. Siegel." *American Economic Review* 48: 1009–1011.
Ellsberg, D. 1961. "Risk, Ambiguity, and the Savage Axioms." *Quarterly Journal of Economics* 75: 643–669.
Ellsberg, D. 2002. *Secrets: A Memoir of Vietnam and the Pentagon Papers*. New York: Viking.
Engvall Siegel, A. 1964. "Sidney Siegel: A Memoir." In *Decision and Choice: Contributions of Sidney Siegel*, edited by S. Messick and A. H. Brayfield, 1–24. New York: McGraw-Hill.
Epper, T., and H. Fehr-Duda. 2015. "Risk Preferences Are Not Time Preferences: Balancing on a Budget Line: Comment." *American Economic Review* 105: 2261–2271.
Epper, T., H. Fehr-Duda H., and A. Bruhin, A. 2011. "Viewing the Future through a Warped Lens: Why Uncertainty Generates Hyperbolic Discounting." *Journal of Risk and Uncertainty* 43: 163–203.
Erikson, P., et al. 2013. *How Reason Almost Lost Its Mind*. Chicago: University of Chicago Press.
Farquhar, P. H. 1984. "Utility Assessment Methods." *Management Science* 30: 1283–1300.
Fechner, G. T. [1860] 1966. *Elements of Psychophysics*, Vol. 1. New York: Holt, Rinehart and Winston.
Feest, U. 2005. "Operationism in Psychology." *Journal of the History of the Behavioral Sciences* 41: 131–149.
Fellner, W. 1961. "Distortion of Subjective Probabilities As a Reaction to Uncertainty." *Quarterly Journal of Economics* 75: 670–689.
Fellner, W. 1965. *Probability and Profit*. Homewood, Ill.: Irwin.
Ferguson, A., et al. 1938. "Quantitative Estimates of Sensory Events, Interim Report." *British Association for the Advancement of Science* 108: 277–334.
Ferguson, A., et al. 1940. "Quantitative Estimates of Sensory Events, Final Report." *Advancement of Science* 2: 331–349.

Fernandez-Grela, M. 2006. "Disaggregating the Components of the Hicks-Allen Composite Commodity." *History of Political Economy* 38, supp.:32–47.

Fienberg, S. E. 2008. "The Early Statistical Years, 1947–1967: A Conversation with Howard Raiffa." *Statistical Science* 23: 136–149.

Fishburn, P. C. 1964. *Decision and Value Theory*. New York: Wiley.

Fishburn, P. C. 1967. "Methods of Estimating Additive Utilities." *Management Science* 13: 435–453.

Fishburn, P. C. 1970. *Utility Theory for Decision Making*. New York: Wiley.

Fishburn, P. C. 1974. "Lexicographic Orders, Utilities and Decision Rules: A Survey." *Management Science* 20: 1442–1471.

Fishburn, P. C. 1989. "Retrospective on the Utility Theory of von Neumann and Morgenstern." *Journal of Risk and Uncertainty* 2: 127–158.

Fishburn, P. C., and G. A. Kochenberger. 1979. "Two-Piece Von Neumann–Morgenstern Utility Functions." *Decision Sciences* 10: 503–518.

Fishburn, P. C., and P. P. Wakker. 1995. "The Invention of the Independence Condition for Preferences." *Management Science* 41: 1130–1144.

Fisher, I. 1892. *Mathematical Investigations in the Theory of Value and Prices*. New Haven: Yale University Press.

Fisher, I. 1918. "Is 'Utility' the Most Suitable Term for the Concept It Is Used to Denote?" *American Economic Review* 8: 335–337.

Fisher, I. 1927. "A Statistical Method for Measuring 'Marginal Utility' and Testing the Justice of a Progressive Income Tax." In *Economic Essays Contributed in Honor of John Bates Clark*, edited by J. B. Hollander, 157–193. New York: Macmillan.

Fréchette, G. R., and A. Schotter, eds. 2015. *Handbook of Experimental Economic Methodology*. New York: Oxford University Press.

Frederick, S., G. Loewenstein, and T. O'Donoghue. 2002. "Time Discounting and Time Preference: A Critical Review." *Journal of Economic Literature* 40: 351–401.

Freeman, H. A., M. Friedman, F. Mosteller, and W. A. Wallis, eds. 1948. *Sampling Inspection*. New York: McGraw-Hill.

Friedman, M. No date. Papers. Hoover Institution Archives, Hoover Institution, Stanford, Calif.

Friedman, M. [1952] 1953. "La théorie de l'incertitude et la distribution des revenus suivant leur grandeur." In *Économétrie*, Actes du colloque "Fondements et applications de la théorie du risque en économétrie," 65–78. Paris: Centre National de la Recherche Scientifique.

Friedman, M. 1953a. "Choice, Chance, and the Personal Distribution of Income." *Journal of Political Economy* 61: 277–290.

Friedman, M. 1953b. "The Methodology of Positive Economics." In M. Friedman, *Essays in Positive Economics*. Chicago: University of Chicago Press.

Friedman, M. 1955. "What All Is Utility?" *Economic Journal* 65: 405–409.

Friedman, M., and L. J. Savage. 1947. "Planning Experiments Seeking Maxima." In *Techniques of Statistical Analysis*, edited by C. Eisenhart, M. W. Hastay, and W. A. Wallis, 363–372. New York: McGraw-Hill.

Friedman, M., and L. J. Savage. 1948. "The Utility Analysis of Choices Involving Risk." *Journal of Political Economy* 56: 279–304.

Friedman, M., and L. J. Savage. 1952. "The Expected-Utility Hypothesis and the Measurability of Utility." *Journal of Political Economy* 60: 463–474.

Frigerio, A., A. Giordani, and L. Mari. 2010. "Outline of a General Model of Measurement." *Synthese* 175: 123–149.

Frisch, R. [1926] 1971. "On a Problem in Pure Economics." In *Preferences, Utility, and Demand*, edited by J. S. Chipman, L. Hurwicz, M. K. Richter, and H. F. Sonnenschein, 386–423. New York: Harcourt Brace Jovanovich.

Frisch, R. 1932. *New Methods of Measuring Marginal Utility*. Tübingen: Mohr.

Frisch, R. 1936. "Annual Survey of General Economic Theory: The Problem of Index Numbers." *Econometrica* 4: 1–38.

Fumagalli, R. 2013. "The Futile Search for True Utility." *Economics and Philosophy* 29: 325–347.

Galanter, E. 1962. "The Direct Measurement of Utility and Subjective Probability." *American Journal of Psychology* 75: 208–220.

Georgescu-Roegen, N. 1936. "The Pure Theory of Consumer's Behavior." *Quarterly Journal of Economics* 50: 545–593.

Georgescu-Roegen, N. 1954. "Choice, Expectations and Measurability." *Quarterly Journal of Economics* 68: 503–534.

Gilboa, I. 2009. *Theory of Decision under Uncertainty*. Cambridge: Cambridge University Press.

Gilboa, I., and M. Marinacci. 2013. "Ambiguity and the Bayesian Paradigm." In *Advances in Economics and Econometrics: Theory and Applications*, Vol. 1, edited by D. Acemoglu, M. Arellano, and E. Dekel, 179–242. New York: Cambridge University Press.

Giocoli, N. 1998. "The 'True' Hypothesis of Daniel Bernoulli: What Did the Marginalists Really Know?" *History of Economic Ideas* 6: 7–43.

Giocoli, N. 2003a. "Fixing the Point: The Contribution of Early Game Theory to the Tool-Box of Modern Economics." *Journal of Economic Methodology* 10: 1–39.

Giocoli, N. 2003b. *Modeling Rational Agents*. Cheltenham: Elgar.

Giocoli, N. 2013. "From Wald to Savage: *Homo Economicus* Becomes a Bayesian Statistician." *Journal of the History of the Behavioral Sciences* 49: 63–95.

Girshick, M. A., F. Mosteller, and L. J. Savage. 1946. "Unbiased Estimates for Certain Binomial Sampling Problems with Applications." *Annals of Mathematical Statistics* 17: 13–23.

Glimcher, P. W. 2011. *Foundations of Neuroeconomic Analysis*. Oxford: Oxford University Press.

Gossen, H. H. [1854] 1983. *The Laws of Human Relations*. Cambridge, Mass.: MIT Press.

Graaff, J. de V. 1957. *Theoretical Welfare Economics*. Cambridge: Cambridge University Press.

Grayson, C. J. 1960. *Decisions under Uncertainty*. Cambridge, Mass.: Harvard Business School, Division of Research.

Green, P. C. 1963. "Risk Attitudes and Chemical Investment Decisions." *Chemical Engineering Progress* 59: 35–40.

Grether, D. M., and C. R. Plott. 1979. "Economic Theory of Choice and the Preference Reversal Phenomenon." *American Economic Review* 69: 623–638.

Griffith, R. M. 1949. "Odds Adjustments by American Horse-Race Bettors." *American Journal of Psychology* 62: 290–294.

Guala, F. 2000. "The Logic of Normative Falsification: Rationality and Experiments in Decision Theory." *Journal of Economic Methodology* 7: 59–93.

Guala, F. 2005. *The Methodology of Experimental Economics*. Cambridge: Cambridge University Press.

Gul, F., and W. Pesendorfer. 2008. "The Case for Mindless Economics." In *The Foundations of Positive and Normative Economics*, edited by A. Caplin and A. Schotter, 3–39. New York: Oxford University Press.

Hagemann, H. 1997. "Jacob Marschak." In *Heidelberger Sozial- und Staatswissenschaften*, edited by R. Blomert, H. U. Esslinger, and N. Giovannini, 219–254. Marburg: Metropolis Verlag.

Halevy, E. 1901. *La formation du radicalisme philosophique*, Vol. 1: *La jeunesse de Bentham 1776–1789*. Paris: Alcan.

Hammond, D. 2006. "More Fiber Than Thread? Evidence on the Mirowski-Hands Yarn." *History of Political Economy* 38, supp.: 130–152.

Hammond, D. 2009. "Early Drafts of Friedman's Methodology Essay." In *The Methodology of Positive Economics: Reflections on the Milton Friedman Legacy*, edited by U. Mäki, 68–89. Cambridge: Cambridge University Press.

Hammond, D. 2010. "The Development of Post-War Chicago Price Theory." In *The Elgar Companion to the Chicago School of Economics*, edited by R. B. Emmett, 7–24. Cheltenham: Elgar.

Hancock, K., and J. E. Isaac. 1998. "Sir Henry Phelps Brown, 1906–1994." *Economic Journal* 108: 757–778.

Handa, J. 1977. "Risk, Probabilities, and a New Theory of Cardinal Utility." *Journal of Political Economy* 85: 97–122.

Hands, D. W. 2001. *Reflection without Rules*. Cambridge: Cambridge University Press.

Hands, D. W. 2010. "Economics, Psychology, and the History of Consumer Choice Theory." *Cambridge Journal of Economics* 34: 633–648.

Hands, D. W. 2011. "Back to the Ordinalist Revolution." *Metroeconomica* 62: 386–410.

Hands, D. W. 2013a. "Foundations of Contemporary Revealed Preference Theory." *Erkenntnis* 78: 1081–1108.

Hands, D. W. 2013b. "GP08 Is the New F53." In *Mark Blaug: Rebel with Many Causes*, edited by M. Boumans and M. Klaes, 245–266. Cheltenham: Elgar.

Hands, D. W. 2014. "Paul Samuelson and Revealed Preference Theory." *History of Political Economy* 46: 85–116.

Hands, D. W. 2017. "The Road to Rationalisation: A History of 'Where the Empirical Lives' (or Has Lived) in Consumer Choice Theory." *European Journal of the History of Economic Thought* 24: 555–588.

Hardcastle, G. L. 1995. "S. S. Stevens and the Origins of Operationism." *Philosophy of Science* 62: 404–424.

Harrison, G. W. 2008. "Neuroeconomics: A Critical Reconsideration." *Economics and Philosophy* 24: 303–344.

Harsanyi, J. C. 1953. "Cardinal Utility in Welfare Economics and in the Theory of Risk-Taking." *Journal of Political Economy* 61: 434–435.

Harsanyi, J. C. 1955. "Cardinal Welfare, Individualistic Ethics, and Interpersonal Comparisons of Utility." *Journal of Political Economy* 63: 309–321.

Hausman, D. M. 1992. *The Inexact and Separate Science of Economics*. Cambridge: Cambridge University Press.

Hausman, D. M. 2008. "Mindless or Mindful Economics: A Methodological Evaluation." In *The Foundations of Positive and Normative Economics*, edited by A. Caplin and A. Schotter, 125–151. New York: Oxford University Press.

Hausman, D. M. 2012. *Preference, Value, Choice, and Welfare*. Cambridge: Cambridge University Press.

Hayek, F. A. 1934. "Carl Menger." *Economica* 1: 393–420.

Hayek, F. A. [1963] 1995. "The Economics of the 1930s As Seen from London." In *Contra Keynes and Cambridge*, edited by B. Caldwell, 49–73. London: Routledge.

Hayek, F. A. [1968] 1992. "The Austrian School of Economics." In *The Fortunes of Liberalism*, edited by P. G. Klein, 42–52. London: Routledge.

Heidelberger, M. 2004. *Nature from Within*. Pittsburgh: Pittsburgh University Press.

Helmholtz, H. von. [1887] 1999. "Numbering and Measuring from an Epistemological Viewpoint." In *From Kant to Hilbert: A Source Book in the Foundations of Mathematics*, Vol. 2, edited by W. Ewald, 727–752. Oxford: Clarendon Press.

Herfeld, C. 2017. "Between Mathematical Formalism, Normative Choice Rules, and the Behavioural Sciences: The Emergence of Rational Choice Theories in the Late 1940s and Early 1950s." *European Journal of the History of Economic Thought* 24: 1277–1317.

Herfeld, C. 2018. "From Theories of Human Behavior to Rules of Rational Choice: Tracing a Normative Turn at the Cowles Commission, 1943–54." *History of Political Economy* 50: 1–48.

Hershey, J. C., and P. J. H. Schoemaker. 1985. "Probability versus Certainty Equivalence Methods in Utility Measurement: Are They Equivalent?" *Management Science* 31: 1213–1231.

Hershey, J. C., H. C. Kunreuther, and P. J. H. Schoemaker. 1982. "Sources of Bias in Assessment Procedures for Utility Functions." *Management Science* 28: 936–954.

Hertwig, R., and A. Ortmann. 2001 "Experimental Practices in Economics: A Challenge for Psychologists?" *Behavioral and Brain Sciences* 24: 383–403.

Heukelom, F. 2010. "Measurement and Decision Making at the University of Michigan in the 1950s and 1960s." *Journal of the History of the Behavioral Sciences* 46: 189–207.

Heukelom, F. 2014. *Behavioral Economics: A History*. New York: Cambridge University Press.

Hicks, J. R. 1931. "The Theory of Uncertainty and Profit." *Economica*, old series 32: 170–189.

Hicks, J. R. 1934. "The Application of Mathematical Methods to the Theory of Risk." *Econometrica* 2: 194–195.

Hicks, J. R. 1937. *Théorie mathématique de la valeur*. Paris: Hermann.

Hicks, J. R. 1939a. "The Foundations of Welfare Economics." *Economic Journal* 49: 696–712.

Hicks, J. R. 1939b. *Value and Capital*. Oxford: Clarendon Press.

Hicks, J. R. 1981. "Prefatory Note." In J. R. Hicks, *Wealth and Welfare: Collected Essays on Economic Theory*, Vol. 1, 3–5. Oxford: Blackwell.

Hicks, J. R., and R. G. D. Allen. 1934. "A Reconsideration of the Theory of Value." *Economica* 1: 52–76, 196–219.

High, J. A. von, and H. Bloch. 1989. "On the History of Ordinal Utility Theory: 1900–1932." *History of Political Economy* 21: 351–365.

Hilbert, D. 1899. *Grundlagen der Geometrie*. Leipzig: Teubner.

Hildreth, C. 1986. *The Cowles Commission in Chicago, 1935–1955*. Berlin: Springer.

Hogarth, R. M., and J. Klayman. 1990. "Hillel J. Einhorn (1941–1987)." In *Insights in Decision Making*, edited by R. M. Hogarth, xiii–xiv. Chicago: University of Chicago Press.

Hölder, O. [1901] 1996. "The Axioms of Quantity and the Theory of Measurement, Part I." *Journal of Mathematical Psychology* 40: 235–252.

Hotelling, H. 1932. "Review of *New Methods of Measuring Marginal Utility* by R. Frisch." *Journal of the American Statistical Association* 27: 451–452.

Hotelling, H. 1938. "The General Welfare in Relation to Problems of Taxation and of Railway and Utility Rates." *Econometrica* 6: 242–269.

Houthakker, H. S. 1950. "Revealed Preference and the Utility Function." *Economica* 17: 159–174.

Howey, R. S. 1960. *The Rise of the Marginal Utility School, 1870–1889*. Lawrence: University of Kansas Press.

Howson, S. 2011. *Lionel Robbins*. Cambridge: Cambridge University Press.

Hudik, M. 2007. "František Čuhel (1862–1914)." *New Perspectives on Political Economy* 3: 3–14.

Hull, J., P. G. Moore, and H. Thomas. 1973. "Utility and Its Measurement." *Journal of the Royal Statistical Society*, series A (general) 136: 226–247.

Hurst, P. M., and S. Siegel. 1956. "Prediction of Decisions from a Higher Ordered Metric Scale of Utility." *Journal of Experimental Psychology* 52: 138–144.

Ingram, J. K. 1888. *A History of Political Economy*. Edinburgh: Black.

Ingrao, B., and G. Israel. 1990. *The Invisible Hand*. Cambridge, Mass.: MIT Press.

Isaac, J. 2013. "Donald Davidson and the Analytic Revolution in American Philosophy, 1940–1970." *Historical Journal* 56: 757–779.

Israel, G., and A. M. Gasca. 2009. *The World As a Mathematical Game*. Basel: Birkäuser.

Jaffé, W., ed. 1965. *Correspondence of Léon Walras and Related Papers*, 3 vols. Amsterdam: North-Holland.

Jaffé, W. 1976. "Menger, Jevons and Walras De-Homogenized." *Economic Inquiry* 14: 511–524.

Jaffé, W. 1977. "The Walras-Poincaré Correspondence on the Cardinal Measurability of Utility." *Canadian Journal of Economics* 10: 300–307.

Jallais, S., and P.-C. Pradier. 2005. "The Allais Paradox and Its Immediate Consequences for Expected Utility Theory." In *The Experiment in the History of Economics*, edited by P. Fontaine and R. Leonard, 25–49. New York: Routledge.

"Jevons on the Theory of Political Economy." [1871] 1981. In *Papers and Correspondence of William Stanley Jevons*, 7 vols., edited by R. D. C. Black, 7: 152–157. London: Macmillan.

Jevons, W. S. 1871. *The Theory of Political Economy*. London: Macmillan.
Jevons, W. S. 1874. *The Principles of Science*. London: Macmillan.
Jevons, W. S. 1879. *The Theory of Political Economy*, 2nd ed. London: Macmillan.
Jones, L. V. 1998. "L. L. Thurstone's Vision of Psychology As a Quantitative Rational Science." In *Portraits of Pioneers in Psychology*, Vol. 3, edited by G. A. Kimble and M. Wertheimer, 85–102. Mahwah, N.J.: Erlbaum.
Jorland, G. 1987. "The Saint Petersburg Paradox 1713–1937." In *The Probabilistic Revolution*, Vol. 1, edited by L. Krüeger, L. J. Daston, and M. Heidelberger, 157–190. Cambridge, Mass.: MIT Press.
Kahneman, D. 1994. "New Challenges to the Rationality Assumption." *Journal of Institutional and Theoretical Economics* 150: 18–36.
Kahneman, D., and A. B. Krueger. 2006. "Developments in the Measurement of Subjective Well-Being." *Journal of Economic Perspectives* 20: 3–24.
Kahneman, D., and R. H. Thaler. 2006. "Utility Maximization and Experienced Utility." *Journal of Economic Perspectives* 20: 221–234.
Kahneman, D., and A. Tversky, A. 1979. "Prospect Theory: An Analysis of Decision under Risk." *Econometrica* 47: 263–292.
Kahneman, D., and A. Tversky. 1984. "Choices, Values, and Frames." *American Psychologist* 39: 341–350.
Kahneman, D., P. P. Wakker, and R. K. Sarin. 1997. "Back to Bentham? Explorations of Experienced Utility." *Quarterly Journal of Economics* 112: 375–405.
Kant, I. [1787] 1997. *Critique of Pure Reason*. Cambridge: Cambridge University Press.
Karmarkar, U. S. 1974. "The Effect of Probabilities on the Subjective Evaluation of Lotteries." Working Paper 698–74, Sloan School of Management, MIT.
Karmarkar, U. S. 1978. "Subjectively Weighted Utility: A Descriptive Extension of the Expected Utility Model." *Organizational Behavior and Human Performance* 21: 61–72.
Karni, E., and Z. Safra. 1987. "'Preference Reversal' and the Observability of Preferences by Experimental Methods." *Econometrica* 55: 675–685.
Keats, A. S., H. K. Beecher, and F. Mosteller. 1950. "Measurement of Pathological Pain in Distinction to Experimental Pain." *Journal of Applied Physiology* 3: 35–44.
Keeney, R. L., and H. Raiffa. 1976. *Decisions with Multiple Objectives*. New York: Wiley.
Kelly, J. S. 1987. "An Interview with Kenneth J. Arrow." *Social Choice and Welfare* 4: 43–62.
Kennedy, C. 1954. "Concerning Utility." *Economica* 21: 7–20.
Keynes, J. M. 1921. *A Treatise on Probability*. London: Macmillan.
Klein, J. L., and M. S. Morgan, eds. 2001. *The Age of Economic Measurement*. Supplement to *History of Political Economy* 33. Durham: Duke University Press.
Knight, F. H. 1921. *Risk, Uncertainty, and Profit*. Boston: Houghton Mifflin.
Knight, F. H. 1940. "What Is 'Truth' in Economics?" *Journal of Political Economy* 48: 1–32.
Knight, F. H. 1944. "Realism and Relevance in the Theory of Demand." *Journal of Political Economy* 52: 289–318.
Kolmogorov, A. 1933. *Grundbegriffe der Wahrscheinlichkeitsrechnung*. Berlin: Springer.
Koopmans, T. C. 1957. *Three Essays on the State of Economic Science*. New York: McGraw-Hill.
Koopmans, T. C. 1960. "Stationary Ordinal Utility and Impatience." *Econometrica* 28: 287–309.
Krantz, D. H., R. D. Luce, P. Suppes, and A. Tversky. 1971. *Foundations of Measurement*, Vol. 1: *Additive and Polynomial Representations*. San Diego: Academic Press.
Kreps, D. 1988. *Notes on the Theory of Choice*. Boulder, Colo.: Westview.
Kries, J. von. [1882] 1995. "On the Measurement of Intensive Magnitudes and the So-Called Psychophysical Law." In K. K. Niall, "Conventions of Measurement in Psychophysics: Von Kries on the So-Called Psychophysical Law," 282–302. *Spatial Vision* 9 (1995): 275–305.
Kronecker, L. [1887] 1999. "On the Concept of Number." In *From Kant to Hilbert: A Source Book in the Foundations of Mathematics*, Vol. 2, edited by W. Ewald, 947–955. Oxford: Clarendon Press.

Krueger, A. B. 2001. "An Interview with William J. Baumol." *Journal of Economic Perspectives* 15: 211–231.

Krueger, A. B. 2003. "An Interview with Edmond Malinvaud." *Journal of Economic Perspectives* 17: 181–198.

Krzysztofowicz, R., and J. B. Koch. 1989. "Estimation of Cardinal Utility Based on a Nonlinear Theory." *Annals of Operations Research* 19: 181–204.

Lange, O. 1934a. "The Determinateness of the Utility Function." *Review of Economic Studies* 1: 218–225.

Lange, O. 1934b. "Notes on the Determinateness of the Utility Function, III." *Review of Economic Studies* 2: 75–77.

Lange, O. 1942. "The Foundations of Welfare Economics." *Econometrica* 10: 215–228.

Lange, O. 1944. *Price Flexibility and Employment*. Bloomington, Ind.: Principia Press.

Lange, O., F. McIntyre, and T. O. Yntema, eds. 1942. *Studies in Mathematical Economics and Econometrics: In Memory of Henry Schultz*. Chicago: University of Chicago Press.

Lee, W. 1971. *Decision Theory and Human Behavior*. New York: Wiley.

Lehtinen, A. 2013. "Preferences As Total Subjective Comparative Evaluations." *Journal of Economic Methodology* 20: 206–210.

Lenfant, J.-S. 2018. "Probabilizing the Consumer: Georgescu-Roegen, Marschak and Quandt on the Modeling of the Consumer in the 1950s." *European Journal of the History of Economic Thought* 25: 36–72.

Leonard, R. 1995. "From Parlor Games to Social Science: Von Neumann, Morgenstern and the Creation of Game Theory, 1928–1944." *Journal of Economic Literature* 33: 730–761.

Leonard, R. 2004. "'Between Worlds,' or an Imagined Reminiscence by Oskar Morgenstern about Equilibrium and Mathematics in the 1920s." *Journal of the History of Economic Thought* 39: 285–310.

Leonard, R. 2010. *Von Neumann, Morgenstern, and the Creation of Game Theory*. New York: Cambridge University Press.

Lepore, E. 2004. "Interview with Donald Davidson." In D. Davidson, *Problems of Rationality*, 231–266. Oxford: Oxford University Press.

Levallois, C. 2009. "One Analogy Can Hide Another: Physics and Biology in Alchian's 'Economic Natural Selection.'" *History of Political Economy* 41: 163–181.

Levasseur, P. E. [1874] 1987. "Compte-Rendus des séances et travaux de l'Académie des sciences morales et politiques." In A. Walras and L. Walras, *Oeuvres économiques complètes*, Vol. 7: L. Walras, *Mélanges d'économie politique et sociale*, 529–532. Paris: Economica.

Lichtenstein, S., and P. Slovic. 1971. "Reversals of Preference between Bids and Choices in Gambling Decisions." *Journal of Experimental Psychology* 89: 46–55.

Loomes, G., and R. Sugden. 1982. "Regret Theory: An Alternative Approach to Rational Choice under Uncertainty." *Economic Journal* 92: 805–824.

Luce, R. D. 1956. "Semiorders and a Theory of Utility Discrimination." *Econometrica* 24: 178–191.

Luce, R. D. 1957. "A Probabilistic Theory of Utility." In R. D. Luce and H. Raiffa, *Games and Decisions*, 371–384. New York: Wiley.

Luce, R. D. 1958. "A Probabilistic Theory of Utility." *Econometrica* 26: 193–224.

Luce, R. D. 1959. *Individual Choice Behavior*. New York: Wiley.

Luce, R. D. 1989. "R. Duncan Luce." In *Psychology in Autobiography*, Vol. 8, edited by G. Lindzey, 245–289. Stanford: Stanford University Press.

Luce, R. D., and H. Raiffa. 1957. *Games and Decisions*. New York: Wiley.

Luce, R. D., and P. Suppes. 1965. "Preference, Utility, and Subjective Probability." In *Handbook of Mathematical Psychology*, 3 vols., edited by R. D. Luce, R. R. Bush, and E. Galanter, 3: 249–410. New York: Wiley.

Luce, R. D., and J. W. Tukey. 1964. "Simultaneous Conjoint Measurement." *Journal of Mathematical Psychology* 1: 1–27.

Maas, H. 2005. *William Stanley Jevons and the Making of Modern Economics*. Cambridge: Cambridge University Press.

MacCrimmon, K. R. 1965. "An Experimental Study of the Decision Making Behavior of Business Executives." Ph.D. dissertation, University of California, Los Angeles.

MacCrimmon, K. R. 1968. "Descriptive and Normative Implications of the Decision-Theory Postulates." In *Risk and Uncertainty*, edited by K. Borch and J. Mossin, 3–32. London: Macmillan.

MacCrimmon, K. R., and S. Larsson. 1979. "Utility Theory: Axioms versus 'Paradoxes.'" In *Expected Utility Hypotheses and the Allais Paradox*, edited by M. Allais and O. Hagen, 333–409. Dordrecht: Reidel.

MacCrimmon, K. R., and M. Toda. 1969. "The Experimental Determination of Indifference Curves." *Review of Economic Studies* 36: 433–451.

Machina, M. J. 1982. "'Expected Utility' Analysis without the Independence Axiom." *Econometrica* 50: 277–323.

Majumdar, T. 1958. *The Measurement of Utility*. London: Macmillan.

Mäki, U., ed. 2009. *The Methodology of Positive Economics: Reflections on the Milton Friedman Legacy*. Cambridge: Cambridge University Press.

Malinvaud, E. 1952. "Note on Von Neumann–Morgenstern's Strong Independence Axiom." *Econometrica* 20: 679.

Mandler, M. 1999. *Dilemmas in Economic Theory*. New York: Oxford University Press.

Manne, A. S. 1952. "The Strong Independence Assumption—Gasoline Blends and Probability Mixtures." *Econometrica* 20: 665–669.

Manski, C. F. 2001. "Daniel McFadden and the Econometric Analysis of Discrete Choice." *Scandinavian Journal of Economics* 103: 217–229.

Marchionatti, R., ed. 1998. *Karl Marx: Critical Responses*, Vol. 1: *Debate on the First Volume of* Das Kapital, *1867–1895*. London: Routledge.

Marchionatti, R., and E. Gambino. 1997. "Pareto and Political Economy As a Science." *Journal of Political Economy* 105: 1322–1348.

Marschak, J. 1938. "Money and the Theory of Assets." *Econometrica* 6: 311–325.

Marschak, J. 1948a. "Measurable Utility and the Theory of Assets." Cowles Commission for Research in Economics, Economics Discussion Paper 226.

Marschak, J. 1948b. "Measurable Utility and the Theory of Assets," abbreviated and revised. Cowles Commission for Research in Economics, Economics Discussion Paper 226a.

Marschak, J. [1948] 1949. "Measurable Utility and the Theory of Assets" (Abstract). *Econometrica* 17: 63–64.

Marschak, J. 1949. "Prospects, Strategies, Assets." Cowles Commission for Research in Economics, Economics Discussion Paper 265.

Marschak, J. 1950. "Rational Behavior, Uncertain Prospects, and Measurable Utility." *Econometrica* 18: 111–141.

Marschak, J. 1951. "A Simplification of the Axiomatics of 'Measurable Utility.'" Cowles Commission for Research in Economics, Economics Discussion Paper 2012.

Marschak, J. [1951] 1974. "Why 'Should' Statisticians and Businessmen Maximize Moral Expectation?" In J. Marschak, *Economic Information, Decision, and Prediction: Selected Essays*, Vol. 1, 40–58. Dordrecht: Reidel.

Marschak, J. [1952] 1953. "Equipes et organisations en régime d'incertitude." In *Économétrie*, Actes du colloque "Fondements et applications de la théorie du risque en économétrie," 201–211. Paris: Centre National de la Recherche Scientifique.

Marschak, J. [1954] 1974. "Probability in the Social Sciences." In J. Marschak, *Economic Information, Decision, and Prediction: Selected Essays*, Vol. 1, 72–120. Dordrecht: Reidel.

Marschak, J. [1955] 1974. "Norms and Habits of Decision Making under Certainty." In J. Marschak, *Economic Information, Decision, and Prediction: Selected Essays*, Vol. 1, 121–132. Dordrecht: Reidel.

Marschak, J. [1960] 1974. "Binary-Choice Constraints and Random Utility Indicators." In J. Marschak, *Economic Information, Decision, and Prediction: Selected Essays*, Vol. 1, 218–239. Dordrecht: Reidel.

Marschak, J., and D. Waterman. 1952. "On Optimal Communication Rules for Teams." Cowles Commission for Research in Economics, Economics Discussion Paper 2029.

Marshall, A. 1890. *Principles of Economics*. London: Macmillan.

Marshall, A. 1895. *Principles of Economics*, 3rd ed. London: Macmillan.

Marshall, A. [1920] 1961. *Principles of Economics*, 9th (variorum) edition, edited by C. W. Guillebaud. London: Macmillan.

Marx, K. 1867. *Das Kapital: Kritik der politischen Ökonomie*, Vol. 1. Hamburg: Meissner.

Mas-Colell, A., M. D. Whinston, and J. R. Green. 1995. *Microeconomic Theory*. New York: Oxford University Press.

Mata, M. E. 2007. "Cardinal versus Ordinal Utility: António Horta Osório's Contribution." *Journal of the History of Economic Thought* 29: 465–479.

Mathewson, L. C. 1930. *Elementary Theory of Finite Groups*. Boston: Houghton Mifflin.

Maxwell, J. C. 1873. *Treatise on Electricity and Magnetism*. London: Constable.

Mayer, J. 1933. "The Meeting of the Econometric Society in Syracuse, New York, June, 1932." *Econometrica* 1: 94–104.

McCord, M. 1983. "Empirical Demonstration of Utility Dependence on the Fundamental Assessment Parameters." Ph.D. dissertation, Massachusetts Institute of Technology.

McCord, M., and R. de Neufville. 1983. "Experimental Demonstration That Expected Utility Decision Analysis Is Not Operational. In *Foundations of Utility and Risk Theory*, edited by B. Stigum and F. Wenstøp, 181–199. Dordrecht: Reidel.

McCord, M., and R. de Neufville. 1985. "Assessment Response Surface: Investigating Utility Dependence on Probability." *Theory and Decision* 18: 263–285.

McCord, M., and R. de Neufville. 1986. "'Lottery Equivalents': Reduction of the Certainty Effect Problem in Utility Assessment." *Management Science* 32: 56–60.

McFadden, D. 1974. "Conditional Logit Analysis of Qualitative Choice Behavior." In *Frontiers in Econometrics*, edited by P. Zarembka, 105–142. New York: Academic Press.

McFadden, D. 2014. "The New Science of Pleasure." In *Handbook of Choice Modelling*, edited by S. Hess and A. Daly, 7–48. Cheltenham: Elgar.

McGregor, D. 1935. "Scientific Measurement and Psychology." *Psychological Review* 42: 246–266.

McKinsey, J. C. C. 1952. *Introduction to the Theory of Games*. New York: McGraw-Hill.

McKinsey, J. C. C., and P. Suppes. 1953a. "Philosophy and the Axiomatic Foundations of Physics." *Proceedings of the Eleventh International Congress of Philosophy* 6: 49–54.

McKinsey, J. C. C., and P. Suppes. 1953b. "Transformations of Systems of Classical Particle Mechanics." *Journal of Rational Mechanics and Analysis* 3: 273–289.

McKinsey, J. C. C., A. C. Sugar, and P. Suppes. 1953. "Axiomatic Foundations of Classical Particle Mechanics." *Journal of Rational Mechanics and Analysis* 2: 253–272.

Menger, C. [1871] 1981. *Principles of Economics*. New York: New York University Press.

Menger, C. [1909] 2002. "Money." In *Carl Menger and the Evolution of Payments Systems*, edited by M. Latzer and S. Schmitz, 25–108. Cheltenham: Elgar.

Menger, C. 1923. *Grundsätze der Volkswirtschaftslehre*, 2nd ed., edited by K. Menger. Vienna: Hölder, Pichler and Tempsky.

Menger, K. [1934] 1967. "The Role of Uncertainty in Economics." In *Essays in Mathematical Economics in Honor of Oskar Morgenstern*, edited by M. Shubik, 211–231. Princeton: Princeton University Press.

Michell, J. 1999. *Measurement in Psychology. A Critical History of a Methodological Concept.* Cambridge: Cambridge University Press.

Michell, J. 2007. "Representational Theory of Measurement." In *Measurement in Economics: A Handbook,* edited by M. Boumans, 19–39. London: Academic Press.

Mill, J. S. 1848. *Principles of Political Economy.* London: Parker.

Mill, J. S. 1871. *Principles of Political Economy,* 7th ed. London: Longmans, Green.

Miller, G. A. 1975. "Stanley Smith Stevens." *Biographical Memoirs* 47: 425–459.

Mirowski, P., ed. 1994. *Natural Images in Economic Thought.* Cambridge: Cambridge University Press.

Mirowski, P. 2002. *Machine Dreams.* Cambridge: Cambridge University Press.

Mises, L. von. [1912] 1953. *The Theory of Money and Credit.* New Haven: Yale University Press.

Mises, L. von. [1922] 1951. *Socialism.* New Haven: Yale University Press.

Mises, L. von. [1931] 1978. "On the Development of the Subjective Theory of Value." In L. von Mises, *Epistemological Problems of Economics,* 155–176. New York: New York University Press.

Mises, L. von. [1932] 1978. "The Controversy over the Theory of Value." In L. von Mises, *Epistemological Problems of Economics,* 217–230. New York: New York University Press.

Mises, L. von. [1978] 2009. *Memoirs.* Auburn: Ludwig von Mises Institute.

Mishan, E. J. 1960. "A Survey of Welfare Economics, 1939–59." *Economic Journal* 70: 197–265.

Mongin, P. 2000. "Les préférences révélées et la formation de la théorie du consommateur." *Revue Économique* 51: 1125–1152.

Mongin, P. 2009. "Duhemian Themes in Expected Utility Theory." In *French Studies in the Philosophy of Science,* edited by A. Brenner and J. Gayon, 303–357. New York: Springer.

Mongin, P. 2014. "Le paradoxe d'Allais: Comment lui rendre sa signification perdue." *Revue Économique* 65: 743–779.

Montesano, A. 1982. "The Ordinal Utility under Uncertainty." *Rivista Internazionale di Scienze Economiche e Commerciali* 29: 442–446.

Montesano, A. 1985. "The Ordinal Utility under Uncertainty and the Measure of Risk Aversion in Terms of Preferences." *Theory and Decision* 18: 73–85.

Montesano, A. 2006. "The Paretian Theory of Ophelimity in Closed and Open Cycles." *History of Economic Ideas* 14: 77–100.

Morewedge, C. K. 2016. "Utility: Anticipated, Experienced, and Remembered." In *Wiley Blackwell Handbook of Judgment and Decision Making,* edited by G. Keren and G. Wu, 295–330. Malden: Blackwell.

Morgan, M. S. 2001. "Making Measuring Instruments." In *The Age of Economic Measurement,* edited by J. L. Klein and M. S. Morgan, 235–251. Durham: Duke University Press, 2001.

Morgan, M. S. 2006. "Economic Man As Model Man: Ideal Types, Idealization and Caricatures." *Journal of the History of Economic Thought* 28: 1–27.

Morgan, M. S. 2007. "An Analytical History of Measuring Practices: The Case of Velocities of Money." In *Measurement in Economics: A Handbook,* edited by M. Boumans, 105–132. London: Academic Press, 2007.

Morgenstern, O. No date. Papers. David M. Rubenstein Rare Book and Manuscript Library, Duke University.

Morgenstern, O. 1928. *Wirtschaftsprognose: Eine Untersuchung ihrer Voraussetzungen und Möglichkeiten.* Vienna: Springer.

Morgenstern, O. 1931. "Die Drei Grundtypen der Theorie des subjektiven Wertes." In *Probleme der Wertlehre,* Part 1, edited by L. von Mises and A. Spiethoff, 1–42. Munich and Leipzig: Duncker & Humblot.

Morgenstern, O. 1935. "Vollkommene Voraussicht und wirtschaftliches Gleichgewicht." *Zeitschrift für Nationalökonomie* 6: 337–357.

Morgenstern, O. 1941. "Professor Hicks on Value and Capital." *Journal of Political Economy* 49: 361–393.

Morgenstern, O. 1976. "The Collaboration between Oskar Morgenstern and John von Neumann on the *Theory of Games*." *Journal of Economic Literature* 14: 805–816.

Morlat, G. 1956. "De l'usage du calcul des probabilités en matière économique." *Revue d'Économie Politique* 66: 889–907.

Morlat, G. 1957. "Sur la théorie des choix aléatoires." *Revue d'Économie Politique* 67: 378–380.

Morrison, D. G. 1967. "On the Consistency of Preferences in Allais' Paradox." *Behavioral Science* 12: 373–383.

Moscati, I. 2007a. "Early Experiments in Consumer Demand Theory: 1930–1970." *History of Political Economy* 39: 359–401.

Moscati, I. 2007b. "History of Consumer Demand Theory 1871–1971: A Neo-Kantian Rational Reconstruction." *European Journal of the History of Economic Thought* 14: 119–156.

Moscati, I. 2012. "A Review of Daniel M. Hausman's *Preference, Value, Choice, and Welfare*." *Erasmus Journal for Philosophy and Economics* 5: 125–131.

Moscati, I. 2013a. "How Cardinal Utility Entered Economic Analysis: 1909–1944." *European Journal of the History of Economic Thought* 20: 906–939.

Moscati, I. 2013b. "Were Jevons, Menger and Walras Really Cardinalists? On the Notion of Measurement in Utility Theory, Psychology, Mathematics, and Other Disciplines, 1870–1910." *History of Political Economy* 45: 373–414.

Moscati, I. 2015. "Austrian Debates on Utility Measurement, from Menger to Hayek." In *Hayek: A Collaborative Biography*, Part IV: *England, the Ordinal Revolution and the Road to Serfdom, 1931–50*, edited by R. Leeson, 137–179. New York: Palgrave Macmillan.

Moscati, I. 2016a. "How Economists Came to Accept Expected Utility Theory: The Case of Samuelson and Savage." *Journal of Economic Perspectives* 30: 219–236.

Moscati, I. 2016b. Measurement Theory and Utility Analysis in Suppes' Early Work, 1951–1958. *Journal of Economic Methodology* 23: 252–267.

Moscati, I., and P. Tubaro. 2011. "Becker Random Behavior and the As-If Defense of Rational Choice Theory in Demand Analysis." *Journal of Economic Methodology* 18: 107–128.

Moskowitz, H. R., B. Scharf, and J. C. Stevens, eds. 1974. *Sensation and Measurement: Papers in Honor of S. S. Stevens*. Dordrecht: Reidel.

Mosteller, F. 1974. "Robert R. Bush: Early Career." *Journal of Mathematical Psychology* 11: 163–178.

Mosteller, F. 1981. "Tribute to Leonard Jimmie Savage." In American Statistical Association, *The Writings of Leonard Jimmie Savage—A Memorial Selection*, 25–28. Washington, D.C.: American Statistical Association.

Mosteller, F. 2010. *The Pleasures of Statistics*. New York: Springer.

Mosteller, F., and P. Nogee. 1951. "An Experimental Measurement of Utility." *Journal of Political Economy* 59: 371–404.

Munier, B. R. 1991. "Nobel Laureate: The Many Other Allais Paradoxes." *Journal of Economic Perspectives* 5: 179–199.

Musgrave, A. 1981. 'Unreal Assumptions' in Economic Theory: The F-Twist Untwisted." *Kyklos* 34: 377–387.

Mussey, H. R. 1909. "Zur Lehre von den Bedürfnissen by Franz Čuhel." *Political Science Quarterly* 24: 323–325.

Nagel, E. 1931. "Measurement." *Erkenntnis* 2: 313–333.

Nasar, S. 1998. *A Beautiful Mind*. New York: Simon & Schuster.

Nash, J. 1950. "The Bargaining Problem." *Econometrica* 18: 155–162.

Neumann, F. J. 1882. Grundbegriffe der Volkswirtschaftslehre. In *Handbuch der politischen Ökonomie*, Vol. 1, edited by G. Schönberg, 103–160. Tübingen: Laupp'schen Buchhandlung.

Newman, E. B. 1974. "On the Origin of 'Scales of Measurement.'" In *Sensation and Measurement: Papers in Honor of S. S. Stevens*, edited by H. R. Moskowitz, B. Scharf, and J. C. Stevens, 137–145. Dordrecht: Reidel.

Nicholson, J. S. 1893. *Principles of Political Economy*, Vol. 1. London: Black.

Nicholson, J. S. 1894. "The Measurement of Utility by Money." *Economic Journal* 4: 342–347.

Niehans, J. 1990. *A History of Economic Theory*. Baltimore: Johns Hopkins University Press.

Officer, R. R., and A. N. Halter. 1968. "Utility Analysis in a Practical Setting." *American Journal of Agricultural Economics* 50: 257–277.

Olkin, I. 1991. "A Conversation with W. Allen Wallis." *Statistical Science* 6: 121–140.

Osório, A. H. 1913. *Théorie mathématique de l'échange*. Paris: Giard and Brière.

Padoa-Schioppa, C. 2011. "Neurobiology of Economic Choice: A Good-Based Model." *Annual Review of Neuroscience* 34: 333–359.

Pareto, V. [1892–1893] 2007. *Considerations on the Fundamental Principles of Pure Political Economy*, edited by R. Marchionatti and F. Mornati. London: Routledge.

Pareto, V. 1896. *Cours d'économie politique*, Vol. 1. Lausanne: Rouge.

Pareto, V. [1898] 1966. "Comment se pose le problème de l'économie pure." In V. Pareto, *Oeuvres complètes*, Vol. 9: *Marxisme et économie pure*, 102–129. Geneva: Librarie Droz.

Pareto, V. [1900] 2008. "Summary of Some Chapters of a New Treatise on Pure Economics by Professor Pareto." *Giornale degli Economisti* 67: 453–504.

Pareto, V. [1901] 1966. "L'économie pure." In V. Pareto, *Oeuvres complètes*, Vol. 9: *Marxisme et économie pure*, 124–136. Geneva: Librarie Droz.

Pareto, V. [1906/1909] 2014. *Manual of Political Economy: A Critical and Variorum Edition*, edited by A. Montesano, A. Zanni, L. Bruni, J. S. Chipman, and M. McLure. New York: Oxford University Press.

Patten, S. N. 1893a. "Cost and Expense." *Annals of the American Academy of Political and Social Science* 3: 703–735.

Patten, S. N. 1893b. "Cost and Utility." *Annals of the American Academy of Political and Social Science* 3: 409–428.

Peart, S. 1996. *The Economics of W. S. Jevons*. London: Routledge.

Peart, S. 2001. "'Facts Carefully Marshalled' in the Empirical Studies of William Stanley Jevons." *History of Political Economy* 33, supp.: 252–276.

Persky, J. 1995. "The Ethology of *Homo Economicus*." *Journal of Economic Perspectives* 9: 221–231.

Petty, W. 1690. *Political Arithmetick*. London: n.p.

Phelps Brown, E. H. 1934. "Notes on the Determinateness of the Utility Function, I." *Review of Economic Studies* 2: 66–69.

Pigou, A. C. 1903. "Some Remarks on Utility." *Economic Journal* 13: 58–68.

Poincaré, H. 1893. "Le continu mathématique." *Revue de Métaphysique et de Morale* 1: 26–34.

Poincaré, H. [1902] 1905. *Science and Hypothesis*. London and Newcastle-on-Tyne: Scott.

Poinsot, L. 1842. *Eléments de statique*. Paris: Bachelier.

Pooley, J., and M. Solovey. 2010. "Marginal to the Revolution: The Curious Relationship between Economics and the Behavioral Sciences Movement in Mid-Twentieth-Century America." *History of Political Economy* 42, supp.: 199–233.

Porter, T. M. 1994. "Rigor and Practicality: Rival Ideas of Quantification in Nineteenth-Century Economics." In *Natural Images in Economic Thought*, edited by P. Mirowski, 128–170. Cambridge: Cambridge University Press.

Preston, M. G., and P. Baratta. 1948. "An Experimental Study of the Auction-Value of an Uncertain Outcome." *American Journal of Psychology* 61: 183–193.

Quandt, R. E. 1956. "A Probabilistic Theory of Consumer Behavior." *Quarterly Journal of Economics* 70: 507–536.

Quiggin, J. 1982. "A Theory of Anticipated Utility." *Journal of Economic Behavior and Organization* 3: 323–343.

Rabin, M. 2000. "Risk Aversion and Expected-Utility Theory: A Calibration Theorem." *Econometrica* 68: 1281–1292.

Raiffa, H. 1961. "Risk, Ambiguity, and the Savage Axioms: Comment." *Quarterly Journal of Economics* 75: 690–694.

Raiffa, H. 1968. *Decision Analysis*. Reading, Pa.: Addison-Wesley.
Ramsey, F. P. [1926] 1950. "Truth and Probability." In *Foundations of Mathematics and Other Logical Essays*, edited by R. B. Braithwaite, 156–198. New York: Humanities.
Ranchetti, F. 1998. "Choice without Utility?" In *The Active Consumer*, edited by M. Bianchi, 21–45. London and New York: Routledge.
Rapoport, A., and T. S. Wallsten. 1972. "Individual Decision Behavior." *Annual Review of Psychology* 23: 131–175.
Reiss, J. 2013. *Philosophy of Economics*. New York: Routledge.
Rellstab, U. 1992. "New Insights into the Collaboration between John von Neumann and Oskar Morgenstern on the *Theory of Games and Economic Behavior*." *History of Political Economy* 24, supp.: 77–93.
Rescher, N. 2005. *Studies in 20th Century Philosophy*. Heusenstamm: Ontos Verlag.
Ricardo, D. [1821] 1951. *On the Principles of Political Economy and Taxation*. Cambridge: Cambridge University Press.
Richardson, L. F. [1932] 1993. "The Measurability of Sensations of Hue, Brightness and Saturation." In *Collected Papers of Lewis Fry Richardson*, Vol. 2: *Quantitative Psychology and Studies of Conflict*, edited by I. Sutherland, 211–216. Cambridge: Cambridge University Press.
Rima, I. H., ed. 1995. *Measurement, Quantification and Economic Analysis*. London: Routledge.
Robbins, L. 1935. *An Essay on the Scope and Nature of Economic Science*. London: Macmillan.
Robbins, L. 1938. "Interpersonal Comparisons of Utility: A Comment." *Economic Journal* 48: 635–641.
Robbins, L. 1953. "Robertson on Utility and Scope." *Economica* 20: 99–111.
Roberts, H. V. 1963. "Risk, Ambiguity, and the Savage Axioms: Comment." *Quarterly Journal of Economics* 77: 327–336.
Robertson, D. H. 1950. "A Revolutionist's Handbook." *Quarterly Journal of Economics* 64: 1–14.
Robertson, D. H. 1951. "Utility and All That." *Manchester School* 19: 111–142.
Robertson, D. H. 1952. *Utility and All That, and Other Essays*. London: Allen and Unwin.
Robertson, D. H. 1954. "Utility and All What?" *Economic Journal* 64: 665–678.
Rosenstein-Rodan, P. [1927] 1960. "Marginal Utility." *International Economic Papers* 10: 71–106.
Ross, D. 2011. "Estranged Parents and a Schizophrenic Child: Choice in Economics, Psychology and Neuroeconomics." *Journal of Economic Methodology* 18: 217–231.
Roth, A. E. 1993. "The Early History of Experimental Economics." *Journal of the History of Economic Thought* 15: 184–209.
Rothbard, M. N. 1956. "Toward a Reconstruction of Utility and Welfare Economics." In *On Freedom and Free Enterprise*, edited by M. Senholz, 224–262. Princeton: Van Nostrand.
Rothschild, K. W. 2004. "The End of an Era: the *Austrian Zeitschrift für Nationalökonomie* in the Interwar Period." In *Political Events and Economic Ideas*, edited by I. Barens, V. Caspari, and B. Schefold, 247–260. Cheltenham: Elgar.
Rubinstein, A., and Y. Salant. 2008. "Some Thoughts on the Principle of Revealed Preference." In *The Foundations of Positive and Normative Economics*, edited by A. Caplin and A. Schotter, 116–124. New York: Oxford University Press.
Russell, B. 1903. *The Principles of Mathematics*. Cambridge: Cambridge University Press.
Russell, B. 1921. *The Analysis of Mind*. London: Allen and Unwin.
Safra, Z., and U. Segal. 2008. "Calibration Results for Non-Expected Utility Theories." *Econometrica* 76: 1143–1166.
Samuelson, P. A. No date. Papers. David M. Rubenstein Rare Book and Manuscript Library, Duke University.
Samuelson, P. A. 1937. "A Note on Measurement of Utility." *Review of Economic Studies* 4: 155–161.
Samuelson, P. A. 1938a. "The Empirical Implications of Utility Analysis." *Econometrica* 6: 344–356.
Samuelson, P. A. 1938b. "A Note on the Pure Theory of Consumer's Behaviour." *Economica* 5: 61–71, 353–354.

Samuelson, P. A. 1938c. "The Numerical Representation of Ordered Classifications and the Concept of Utility." *Review of Economic Studies* 6: 65–70.

Samuelson, P. A. 1939a. "The End of Marginal Utility: A Note on Dr. Bernardelli's Article." *Economica* 6: 86–87.

Samuelson, P. A. 1939b. "The Gains from International Trade." *Canadian Journal of Economics and Political Science* 5: 195–205.

Samuelson, P. A. 1940. "Foundations of Analytical Economics." Ph.D. dissertation, Harvard University. Samuelson papers, box 91.

Samuelson, P. A. 1942. "Constancy of the Marginal Utility of Income." In *Studies in Mathematical Economics and Econometrics: In Memory of Henry Schultz*, edited by O. Lange, F. McIntyre, and T. O. Yntema, 75–91. Chicago: University of Chicago Press.

Samuelson, P. A. 1947. *Foundations of Economic Analysis*. Cambridge, Mass.: Harvard University Press.

Samuelson, P. A. 1948. *Economics*. New York: McGraw-Hill.

Samuelson, P. A. 1950a. "Measurement of Utility Reformulated." RAND Corporation, Research Memorandum D-0765.

Samuelson, P. A. 1950b. "Probability and the Attempts to Measure Utility." *Economic Review* 1: 167–173.

Samuelson, P. A. 1950c. "Two Queries about Utility and Game Theory." RAND Corporation, Research Memorandum D-0786.

Samuelson, P. A. 1952. "Probability, Utility, and the Independence Axiom." *Econometrica* 20: 670–678.

Samuelson, P. A. [1952] 1966. "Utility, Preference, and Probability." In *The Collected Scientific Papers*, Vol. 1, edited by J. E. Stiglitz, 127–136. Cambridge, Mass.: MIT Press.

Samuelson, P. A. 1977. "St. Petersburg Paradoxes: Defanged, Dissected, and Historically Described." *Journal of Economic Literature* 15: 24–55.

Samuelson, P. A. 1998. "How Foundations Came to Be." *Journal of Economic Literature* 36: 1375–1386.

Sanger, C. P. 1895. "Recent Contributions to Mathematical Economics." *Economic Journal* 5: 113–128.

Savage, L. J. No date. Papers. Manuscripts and Archives Collection, Yale University Library.

Savage, L. J. [1949] 1950. "The Role of Personal Probability in Statistics" (Abstract). *Econometrica* 18: 183–184.

Savage, L. J. [1952] 1953. "Une axiomatisation de comportement raisonnable face à l'incertitude." In *Économétrie*, Actes du colloque "Fondements et applications de la théorie du risque en économétrie," 29–33. Paris: Centre National de la Recherche Scientifique.

Savage, L. J. [1954] 1972. *The Foundations of Statistics*. New York: Dover.

Schlee, E. E. 1992. "Marshall, Jevons, and the Development of the Expected Utility Hypothesis." *History of Political Economy* 24: 729–744.

Schmidt, T., and C. E. Weber. 2008. "On the Origins of Ordinal Utility: Andreas Heinrich Voigt and the Mathematicians." *History of Political Economy* 40: 481–510.

Schmidt, T., and C. E. Weber. 2012. "Andreas Heinrich Voigt and the Hicks–Allen Revolution in Consumer Theory." *Economic Inquiry* 50: 625–640.

Schoemaker, P. J. H. 1980. *Experiments on Decisions under Risk*. Boston: Nijhoff.

Schoemaker, P. J. H. 1982. "The Expected Utility Model: Its Variants, Purposes, Evidence and Limitations." *Journal of Economic Literature* 20: 529–563.

Schröder, E. 1873. *Lehrbuch der Arithmetik und Algebra*. Leipzig: Teubner.

Schultz, H. 1928. *Statistical Laws of Demand and Supply*. Chicago: University of Chicago Press.

Schultz, H. 1931. "The Italian School of Mathematical Economics." *Journal of Political Economy* 39: 76–85.

Schultz, H. 1933. "Frisch on the Measurement of Utility." *Journal of Political Economy* 41: 95–116.

Schultz, H. 1935. "Interrelations of Demand, Price, and Income." *Journal of Political Economy* 43: 433–481.
Schultz, H. 1938. *The Theory and Measurement of Demand*. Chicago: University of Chicago Press.
Schumpeter, J. A. 1908. *Das Wesen und der Hauptinhalt der theoretischen Nationalökonomie*. Berlin: Duncker & Humblot.
Schumpeter, J. A. 1954. *History of Economic Analysis*. New York: Oxford University Press.
Scott, D., and P. Suppes. 1958. "Foundational Aspects of Theories of Measurement." *Journal of Symbolic Logic* 23: 113–128.
Segal, U. 1988. "Does the Preference Reversal Phenomenon Necessarily Contradict the Independence Axiom?" *American Economic Review* 78: 233–236.
Sen, A. 1973. "Behaviour and the Concept of Preference." *Economica* 40: 241–259.
Sen, A. 1997. *Choice, Welfare and Measurement*. Cambridge, Mass.: Harvard University Press.
Shackle, G. L. S. 1949. *Expectation in Economics*. Cambridge: Cambridge University Press.
Shanteau, J., B. A. Mellers, and D. A. Schum, eds. 1999. *Decision Science and Technology: Reflections on the Contributions of Ward Edwards*. Boston: Kluwer.
Shubik, M. 1978. "Oskar Morgenstern: Mentor and Friend." *International Journal of Game Theory* 7: 131–135.
Siegel, S. 1954. "Certain Determinants and Correlates of Authoritarianism." *Genetic Psychology Monographs* 49: 187–254.
Siegel, S. 1956. "A Method for Obtaining an Ordered Metric Scale." *Psychometrika* 21: 207–216.
Slovic, P., and S. Lichtenstein, S. 1968. "The Relative Importance of Probabilities and Payoffs in Risk Taking." *Journal of Experimental Psychology* 78: 1–18.
Slutsky, E. [1915] 1952. "On the Theory of the Budget of the Consumer." In *Readings in Price Theory*, edited by G. J. Stigler and K. E. Boulding, 27–56. Homewood, Ill.: Irwin.
Smith, A. [1776] 1976. *An Inquiry into the Nature and Causes of the Wealth of Nations*. Oxford: Oxford University Press.
Smith, V. L. 1969. "Measuring Nonmonetary Utilities in Uncertain Choices: The Ellsberg Urn." *Quarterly Journal of Economics* 83: 324–329.
Speiser, A. 1937. *Theorie der Gruppen von Endlicher Ordnung*. Berlin: Springer.
Spiegler, R. 2008. "On Two Points of View Regarding Revealed Preference and Behavioral Economics." In *The Foundations of Positive and Normative Economics*, edited by A. Caplin and A. Schotter, 95–115. New York: Oxford University Press.
Starmer, C. 2009. "Expected Utility and Friedman's Risky Methodology." In *The Methodology of Positive Economics: Reflections on the Milton Friedman Legacy*, edited by U. Mäki, 285–302. Cambridge: Cambridge University Press.
Stevens, S. S. 1935a. "The Operational Basis of Psychology." *American Journal of Psychology* 47: 323–330.
Stevens, S. S. 1935b. "The Operational Definition of Psychological Concepts." *Psychological Review* 42: 517–527.
Stevens, S. S. 1936a. "Psychology: The Propaedeutic Science." *Philosophy of Science* 3: 90–103.
Stevens, S. S. 1936b. "A Scale for the Measurement of a Psychological Magnitude: Loudness." *Psychological Review* 43: 405–416.
Stevens, S. S. 1939. "Psychology and the Science of Science." *Psychological Bulletin* 36: 221–263.
Stevens, S. S. 1946. "On the Theory of Scales of Measurement." *Science* 103: 677–680.
Stevens, S. S. 1951. "Mathematics, Measurement and Psychophysics." In *Handbook of Experimental Psychology*, edited by S. S. Stevens, 1–49. New York: Wiley.
Stevens, S. S. 1968. "Measurement, Statistics, and the Schemapiric View." *Science* 161: 849–856.
Stevens, S. S. 1974. "Notes for a Life Story." In *Sensation and Measurement: Papers in Honor of S. S. Stevens*, edited by H. R. Moskowitz, B. Scharf, and J. C. Stevens, 423–446. Dordrecht: Reidel.
Stevens, S. S., and E. H. Galanter. 1957. "Ratio Scales and Category Scales for a Dozen Perceptual Continua." *Journal of Experimental Psychology* 54: 377–411.

Stevens, S. S., and J. Volkmann. 1940. "The Relation of Pitch to Frequency: A Revised Scale." *American Journal of Psychology* 53: 329–353.

Stigler, G. J. 1937. "The Economics of Carl Menger." *Journal of Political Economy* 45: 229–250.

Stigler, G. J. 1950. "The Development of Utility Theory." *Journal of Political Economy* 58: 307–327, 373–396.

Stone, R. 1954. *The Measurement of Consumers' Expenditure and Behaviour in the United Kingdom, 1920–1938*, Vol. 1. Cambridge: Cambridge University Press.

Strøm, S., ed. 1998. *Econometrics and Economic Theory in the 20th Century: The Ragnar Frisch Centennial Symposium*. Cambridge: Cambridge University Press.

Strotz, R. H. 1953. "Cardinal Utility." *American Economic Review, Papers and Proceedings* 43: 384–397.

Suppes, P. 1951. "A Set of Independent Axioms for Extensive Quantities." *Portugaliae Mathematica* 10: 163–172.

Suppes, P. 1954. "Some Remarks on Problems and Methods in the Philosophy of Science." *Philosophy of Science* 21: 242–248.

Suppes, P. 1957. *Introduction to Logic*. New York: Van Nostrand Reinhold.

Suppes, P. 1979. "Self-Profile." In *Patrick Suppes*, edited by R. J. Bogdan, 3–56. Dordrecht: Reidel.

Suppes, P., and K. Walsh. 1959. "A Non-Linear Model for the Experimental Measurement of Utility." *Behavioral Science* 4: 204–211.

Suppes, P., and M. Winet. [1953] 1954. "An Axiomatization of Utility Based on the Notion of Utility Differences" (Abstract). *Bulletin of the American Mathematical Society* 60: 81–82.

Suppes, P., and M. Winet. 1955. "An Axiomatization of Utility Based on the Notion of Utility Differences." *Management Science* 1: 259–270.

Suppes, P., and J. L. Zinnes. 1961. "Stochastic Learning Theories for a Response Continuum with Non-Determinate Reinforcement." *Psychometrika* 26: 373–390.

Suppes, P., and J. L. Zinnes. 1963. "Basic Measurement Theory." In *Handbook of Mathematical Psychology*, 3 vols., edited by R. D. Luce, R. R. Bush, and E. Galanter, 1: 1–76. New York: Wiley.

Swalm, R. O. 1966. "Utility Theory—Insights into Risk Taking." *Harvard Business Review* 44: 123–136.

Tannery, P. 1875. "À propos du logarithme des sensations." *Revue Scientifique* 8: 876–877, 1018–1020.

Tannery, P. 1884. "Critique de la loi de Weber." *Revue Scientifique* 17: 15–35.

Tannery, P. 1888. "Psychologie mathématique et psychophysique." *Revue Scientifique* 25: 189–197.

Tarski, A. 1954–1955. "Contributions to the Theory of Models." *Indagationes Mathematicae (Proceedings)* 57: 572–581, 582–588; 58: 56–64.

Thaler, R. H. 2016. "Behavioral Economics: Past, Present, and Future." *American Economic Review* 106: 1577–1600.

Theil, H. 1965. "The Information Approach to Demand Analysis." *Econometrica* 33: 67–87.

Thurstone, L. L. 1927a. "A Law of Comparative Judgment." *Psychological Review* 34: 273–286.

Thurstone, L. L. 1927b. "A Mental Unit of Measurement." *Psychological Review* 34: 415–423.

Thurstone, L. L. 1931. "The Indifference Function." *Journal of Social Psychology* 2: 139–167

Tintner, G. 1942. "A Contribution to the Non-Static Theory of Choice." *Quarterly Journal of Economics* 56: 274–306.

Titchener, E. B. 1905. *Experimental Psychology: A Manual of Laboratory Practice*, Vol. 2: *Quantitative Experiments*, Part 2: *Instructor's Manual*. New York: Macmillan.

Tversky, A. 1969. "Intransitivity of Preferences." *Psychological Review* 76: 31–48.

Tversky, A. 1992. "Clyde Hamilton Coombs." *Biographical Memoirs* 61: 59–77.

Tversky, A., and D. Kahneman. 1981. "The Framing of Decisions and the Psychology of Choice." *Science* 211: 453–458.

Tversky, A., and D. Kahneman. 1992. "Advances in Prospect Theory: Cumulative Representation of Uncertainty." *Journal of Risk and Uncertainty* 5: 297–323.

Van Fraassen, B. C. 2008. *Scientific Representation: Paradoxes of Perspective*. Oxford: Oxford University Press.

Vickrey, W. 1945. "Measuring Marginal Utility by Reactions to Risk." *Econometrica* 13: 319–333.

Viner, J. 1925. "The Utility Concept in Value Theory and Its Critics." *Journal of Political Economy* 33: 369–387, 638–659.

Voigt, A. 1893. "Zahl und Mass in der Ökonomik." *Zeitschrift für die Gesamte Staatswissenschaft* 49: 577–609.

Voigt, A. [1893] 2008. "Number and Measure in Economics." In T. Schmidt and C. E. Weber, "On the Origins of Ordinal Utility: Andreas Heinrich Voigt and the Mathematicians," 502–504. *History of Political Economy* 40 (2008): 481–510.

Von Neumann, J. [1928] 1959. "On the Theory of Games of Strategy." In *Contributions to the Theory of Games*, Vol. 4, edited by R. D. Luce and A. W. Tucker, 13–42. Princeton: Princeton University Press.

Von Neumann, J. [1932] 1955. *Mathematical Foundations of Quantum Mechanics*. Princeton: Princeton University Press.

Von Neumann, J., and O. Morgenstern. [1944] 1953. *Theory of Games and Economic Behavior*. Princeton: Princeton University Press.

Wakker, P. P. 1994. "Separating Marginal Utility and Probabilistic Risk Aversion." *Theory and Decision* 36: 1–44.

Wakker, P. P., and D. Deneffe. 1996. "Eliciting von Neumann–Morgenstern Utilities When Probabilities Are Distorted or Unknown." *Management Science* 42: 1131–1150.

Wald, A. 1950. *Statistical Decision Functions*. New York: Wiley.

Wallis, W. A. 1980. "The Statistical Research Group, 1942–1945." *Journal of the American Statistical Association* 75: 320–330.

Wallis, W. A. 1981. "Tribute to Leonard Jimmie Savage." In American Statistical Association, *The Writings of Leonard Jimmie Savage—A Memorial Selection*, 11–24. Washington, D.C.: American Statistical Association.

Wallis, W. A., and M. Friedman. 1942. "The Empirical Derivation of Indifference Functions." In *Studies in Mathematical Economics and Econometrics: In Memory of Henry Schultz*, edited by O. Lange, F. McIntyre, and T. O. Yntema, 175–189. Chicago: University of Chicago Press.

Walras, L. [1874] 1954. *Elements of Pure Economics*. London: Allen and Unwin.

Walras, L. [1874] 1987. "Principe d'une théorie mathématique de l'échange." In A. Walras and L. Walras, *Oeuvres économiques complètes*, Vol. 7: L. Walras, *Mélanges d'économie politique et sociale*, 261–281. Paris: Economica.

Walras, L. [1876] 1987. "Une branche nouvelle de la mathématique." In A. Walras and L. Walras, *Oeuvres économiques complètes*, Vol. 7: L. Walras, *Mélanges d'économie politique et sociale*, 290–329. Paris: Economica.

Walras, L. 1886. *Théorie de la monnaie*. Lausanne: Corbaz.

Walras, L. [1909] 1990. "Economics and Mechanics." In *Economics As Discourse*, edited by W. J. Samuels, 206–214. Dordrecht: Kluwer.

Walras, L. 1988. *Éléments d'économie politique pure*. Vol. 8 of A. Walras and L. Walras, *Oeuvres économiques complètes*. Paris: Economica.

Weintraub, E. R. 2002. *How Economics Became a Mathematical Science*. Durham: Duke University Press.

Weintraub, E. R. 2014. "MIT and the Transformation of American Economics." *History of Political Economy* 46, supp: 1–12.

Wells, T. 2001. *Wild Man: The Life and Times of Daniel Ellsberg*. New York: Palgrave.

Weyl, H. 1938. "Symmetry." *Journal of the Washington Academy of Sciences* 28: 253–271.

Weymark, J. A. 2005. "Measurement Theory and the Foundations of Utilitarianism." *Social Choice and Welfare* 25: 527–555.

White, M. V. 1994. "The Moment of Richard Jennings: The Production of Jevons's Marginalist Economic Agent." In *Natural Images in Economic Thought*, edited by P. Mirowski, 197–230. Cambridge: Cambridge University Press.

Wieser, F. von. 1884. *Über den Ursprung und die Hauptgesetze des wirtschaftlichen Werthes*. Vienna: Hölder.

Wieser, F. von. [1889] 1893. *Natural Value*. London: Macmillan.

Wieser, F. von. [1914] 1927. *Social Economics*. New York: Greenberg.

Wold, H., G. L. S. Shackle, and L. J. Savage. 1952. "Ordinal Preferences or Cardinal Utility?" *Econometrica* 20: 661–664.

Wood Winet Gerlach, M. 1957. "Interval Measurement of Subjective Magnitudes with Subliminal Differences." Ph.D. dissertation, Stanford University.

Wundt, W. 1873–1874. *Grundzüge der physiologischen Psychologie*. Leipzig: Engelmann.

Wundt, W. 1880. *Grundzüge der physiologischen Psychologie*, 2nd ed. Leipzig: Engelmann.

Yaari, M. E. 1987. "The Dual Theory of Choice under Risk." *Econometrica* 55: 95–115.

Zappia, C. 2016. "Daniel Ellsberg and the Validation of Normative Propositions." *Oeconomia* 6: 57–79.

Zawadzki, W. E. 1914. *Les mathématiques appliquées à l'économie politique*. Paris: Riviere.

NAME INDEX

The letter "n" after a page number indicates reference to a footnote on that page, the letter "*f*" references a figure, and the letter "*t*" references a table.

SUBJECT INDEX

The letter "n" after a page number indicates reference to a footnote on that page, the letter "*f*" references a figure, and the letter "*t*" references a table.

www.ingramcontent.com/pod-product-compliance
Ingram Content Group UK Ltd.
Pitfield, Milton Keynes, MK11 3LW, UK
UKHW020849150926
475595UK00003B/87

9 780199 372768